The History
of Alta California

Antonio María Osio. Courtesy of the California State Library, Sacramento.

The History
of Alta California

A Memoir
of Mexican California

By Antonio María Osio

Translated, edited, and annotated by
Rose Marie Beebe
and
Robert M. Senkewicz

The University of Wisconsin Press

The University of Wisconsin Press
114 North Murray Street
Madison, Wisconsin 53715

3 Henrietta Street
London WC2E 8LU, England

2   4   6   8   10   9   7   5   3   1

Printed in the United States of America

Library of Congress Cataloging-in-Publication Data
Osio, Antonio María, 1800–1878.
The history of Alta California: a memoir of Mexican California /
by Antonio María Osio; translated, edited, and annotated by
Rose Marie Beebe and Robert M. Senkewicz.
400 pp.   cm.
Translated from Spanish.
Includes bibliographical references and index.
ISBN 0-299-14970-6 (alk. paper).
ISBN 0-299-14974-9 (pbk. : alk. paper).
1. California—History—To 1846.   I. Beebe, Rose Marie.
II. Senkewicz, Robert M., 1947–   .   III. Title.
F864.085   1996
979.4—dc20   95-25695

Contents

Illustrations

Illustrations

Maps

Acknowledgments

Since Julia O'Keefe, the Santa Clara University archivist, suggested a few years ago that the Osio manuscript might prove to be an interesting project, we have accumulated many scholarly debts. The first is to Julie and to her predecessor as archivist, Gerald McKevitt, S.J., who had arranged for the manuscript to be housed at Santa Clara. Julie and Jerry have been unfailingly supportive, sharing their knowledge of Santa Clara and the other missions, answering our many queries, and making the resources of the mission and university archives freely available to us.

Our research was supported by two Santa Clara University Irvine Foundation grants, which enabled us to undertake various research trips that would not have been possible otherwise. We are especially grateful to Francisco Jiménez and the members of the Irvine Foundation committee for that sponsorship.

The staffs of The Bancroft Library in Berkeley, the California State Library in Sacramento, and the Archivo General de la Nación in Mexico City were unfailingly helpful. Their interest in this project sometimes exceeded our own and kept us on track. We would like to thank Linda Arnold for taking time away from her own research to help guide us through the Archivo. The staff at Orradre Library at Santa Clara University, notably Cindy Bradley in interlibrary loan and Alice Whistler in the California collection, demonstrated a patience with our more exotic requests that was exceeded only by their ability somehow to produce the most unlikely materials.

The staffs at the Beinecke Library at Yale, the Peabody Museum at Harvard, the Solano County Historical Society in Vallejo, and the Colton Hall Museum in Monterey were quite helpful in providing some of the illustrations for this volume. Dan Murley of the Fort Ross State Historic Park helped us to understand the sea otter hunts and kindly provided us with photographs of a replica of a nineteenth-century baidarka. Rachel Stoppello of Santa Clara University created the original maps.

W. Michael Mathes, Matt S. Meier, and Ed Lee read earlier versions of the entire manuscript, and each made wonderful suggestions that have immensely improved the final product. Any errors which remain, of course, are ours.

Acknowledgments

We presented an earlier version of the introduction to this volume at the Third Conference of Recovering the U.S. Hispanic Literary Heritage in 1994, and we wish to thank the conference participants for many useful suggestions. Peter O'Malley Pierson, chair of the Department of History at Santa Clara, and Helen E. Moritz, chair of the Department of Modern Languages and Literatures, provided continual support to two of their faculty struggling to carve out time to work on this project in the midst of their teaching responsibilities.

At the University of Wisconsin Press, we appreciate the solicitous assistance of Kris Coppen and the superb editorial work of Rosalie Robertson, Angela Ray, and Raphael Kadushin.

Two different types of families have been enormously supportive. Rose Marie Beebe's husband, Philip Sheehy, and Robert Senkewicz's fellow Jesuits at Santa Clara are, for different reasons, happy that this project has been completed. Philip, along with Rose Marie's parents, Richard and Rose, and sister, Chrisanne, finally get a member of the family back from the beguiling clutches of Antonio María Osio. And Bob's brothers can experience a little less Catholic guilt when they insist that he take his turn doing the dishes.

The History
of Alta California

Very Reverend Father José María Suárez del Real
Santa Clara
April 4, 1851

My dear Reverend Father and esteemed friend:
   Ever since I have had the honor of considering myself to be one
of your good friends, I have always longed to please you. However, what
you now ask of me, that I write about the history of California, is beyond
my capabilities. But in order to satisfy your desires in some way, I shall
describe in this letter what I have experienced and observed since the
year 1825 and what transpired during the tenure of the various governors,
beginning with the year 1815.
   If you can obtain letters from other friends who mention the governors
to whom I do not refer, add this to Reverend Father Piccolo's account
of the distinguished Father Junípero Serra, and then ask for assistance
from another friend who has the proper training and attributes of a good
writer, you will be able to satisfy your desires of composing a history of
Alta California.*

I remain your faithful servant
[Antonio María Osio]

*Francisco María Piccolo (1654–1729) was a major Jesuit missionary in Antigua Cali-
fornia in the late seventeenth and early eighteenth centuries. He wrote a number of historical
and geographic reports, including an influential one in 1702. The biographer of Serra to
whom Osio refers here was a Franciscan, Francisco Palóu, whose work appeared in 1787. See
Crosby, *Antigua California*, 46, 67, 409; Burrus, "Piccolo"; and Palóu, *Life of Serra*. The line,
"The History of Alta California," at the top of the page appears on Osio's letter.

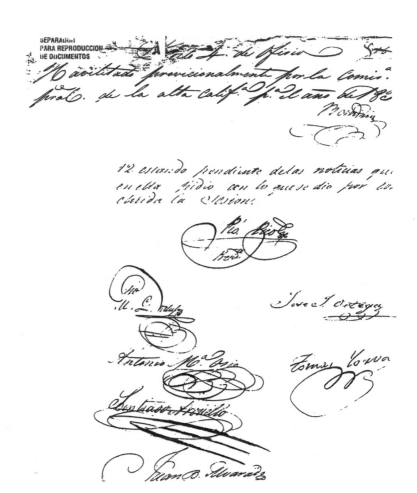

Signatures on the 1832 *diputación* minutes. Antonio María Osio's signature is directly below that of Mariano Guadalupe Vallejo. Courtesy of the Archivo General de la Nación, Mexico City.

Introduction

The signatures are large and pronounced. With the swirls, curves, and bold-ness characteristic of the nineteenth century, they fill the page and almost jump out at the reader. This was clearly what they were meant to do, for by these signatures the group of men told whoever might eventually gaze at that page that they were a substantial company, an important circle, a set of men to be reckoned with.

They were a young group, and not one of them was far removed from humble roots. Pío Pico, whose signature headed the list, was thirty-one years old. His father, José María, was born in Sinaloa, in northern New Spain, and had come to Alta California in 1776 with his own father, a sol-dier; José María Pico, a simple corporal, served in the guard at Mission San Luis Rey. Mariano Guadalupe Vallejo was twenty-three, and his father, a native of Jalisco in New Spain, had been a sergeant at the Monterey pre-sidio. Santiago Argüello was forty. His father, José Darío, was born in Queré-taro in New Spain and entered the Spanish army as a private. Juan Bautista Alvarado was also twenty-three. His father had served as a corporal in the Spanish army in Loreto in Antigua California and was promoted to sergeant when he was reassigned in 1809 to Monterey in Alta California.[1] José Joaquín Ortega was thirty. His grandfather joined the Spanish army in Guanajuato as a private and held the rank of sergeant when he headed north with Junípero Serra in 1769. The father of forty-three-year-old To-más Yorba was a corporal who had also come to Alta California in 1769. An-tonio María Osio was thirty-one. A century before, his great-grandfather, a native of Spain, had been an obscure member of the military stationed at various missions in Antigua California. The Spanish-born father of thirty-one-year-old Juan Bandini, whose signature in the upper right corner of the paper is a bit less prominent, had become a sailor in his twenties and had set up a small trading business in Lima.

These men also had come to know each other well due to a kinship net-work that connected many of them. Antonio María Osio, for instance, had married Santiago Argüello's sister Dolores. Argüello himself married Pilar Ortega, the cousin of José Joaquín Ortega. Ortega, in turn, married Pío Pico's sister María. Pío Pico married María Ignacia Alvarado, a distant relative of Juan Bautista Alvarado. Alvarado's mother was María Josefa Vallejo, the older sister of Mariano Guadalupe Vallejo.

The signatures of these eight men were affixed to the minutes of the 1832 meetings of the *diputación territorial* of Alta California, of which they were the members. In January of that year the *diputación* convened to draw up a case against Manuel Victoria, the Mexican governor whom they had expelled, and to begin what they hoped and expected would be their own rule of the territory. Guided by the twin stars of republican government and economic development, they set about justifying their actions to the central government in Mexico. Their notions of republicanism drew from the theories of the Enlightenment and from the experience of the eighteenth-century revolutions in Europe and North America. So, in their sessions, as good and enlightened political thinkers, they urged an "organic constitution for our territory" and called for "teachers to cement the advantages of the republican system."

Their vision of economic development included a strong belief that the large amount of land controlled by the twenty-one missions should be wrested from the exclusive control of the priests. Then it should be distributed more widely to people like themselves, whose energy and ingenuity would, they were convinced, lead Alta California into an era of growth and prosperity. Therefore, in their sessions and reports they denounced "the detestable system of the missions" which was responsible for the "oppression" of the indigenous peoples who lived within it.[2] They were convinced that they were witnessing the birth of a new and important era.

Within two decades it had all changed. Their land had been conquered by the United States. Soon after the end of the war, the discovery of gold resulted in a massive influx of prospectors and fortune seekers. The *californios* became quite unexpectedly a minority in their own land. The presence of so many newcomers exposed the lands which they had worked so hard to take from the missions to the pressures of squatters, speculators, and gold seekers. In 1851 the U.S. Congress passed the Land Act, which set up a commission to review land claims and required the *californios* to attempt to prove title to their holdings through costly and seemingly endless litigation.[3]

This generation saw its expansive dreams shattered. Instead of being dynamic and influential, they were forced to become petitioners and place their claims for land before a group of foreigners. Antonio María Osio is a convenient symbol: on February 2, 1852, exactly twenty years after he had served as a member of that memorable *diputación*, he filed a claim before the U.S. Land Commission for Angel Island in San Francisco Bay.[4]

Less than a year before, on April 4, 1851, Osio had completed a tightly written 220-page manuscript, which he entitled simply "The History of Alta California." It was written in the form of a letter to Father José María Suárez del Real at Mission Santa Clara. In a cover letter, Osio told Suárez del Real that what the priest had asked him to do, "write about the history of California," was beyond his ability. Instead, Osio said, he would write a letter, or *relación*, of events since 1815, detailing especially "what I have experienced and observed since the year 1825."

Osio was well situated to compose such a *relación*. A native of San José del Cabo in Baja California, he had married Dolores Argüello, the sister not only of Santiago Argüello but also of Luis Argüello, the first Mexican governor of Alta California. Osio worked in the customs service in San Francisco and Monterey in the late 1820s. After serving in the *diputación* in the early 1830s, he became a member of the Los Angeles *ayuntamiento*. As *síndico*, he participated in the movement against Governor Mariano Chico in 1836. During the next year he was a leader in the southern California resistance to Governor Juan Bautista Alvarado. In the late 1830s he became both collector of customs at Monterey and a member of the *tribunal superior*, serving in both positions until the 1840s. Socially and politically, Osio was a very well-connected man in Mexican California.[5] Yet his manuscript has never been published, or even widely studied. In this introduction, besides acquainting the reader with Osio's manuscript, we would like to attempt three tasks. First, we would like to explain why the manuscript was consigned to historiographic oblivion. Second, we would like to introduce the reader to Osio and his family. Third, we would like to prepare the ground for a critical reading of the manuscript by highlighting some of its literary and autobiographical features. We believe that Osio's document offers an important and unique perspective on the history of Mexican California.

The History of the Manuscript

By early 1852 both Osio and Suárez del Real had left Alta California and returned to Mexico. The manuscript's existence remained almost completely unknown in California for a quarter century. Suárez del Real, who

Mission Santa Clara as it appeared when Antonio María Osio composed his manuscript in 1851. Courtesy of the California State Library, Sacramento.

died in the 1850s, never returned to Alta California. Osio, however, did return for brief visits at least twice, in 1864 and in 1875.[6]

By the time of that second visit, Hubert Howe Bancroft's staff, especially Enrique Cerruti and Thomas Savage, were involved in collecting from the old *californios* the reminiscences, dictations, and documents which would serve as the backbone of the Spanish and Mexican sections of Bancroft's seven-volume *History of California*. Osio had apparently heard about this, for he brought the manuscript with him to San Francisco. On April 18, 1875, Cerruti wrote to Bancroft:

> A few days ago Mr. Osio, a resident of California in 1826, arrived in San Francisco, dragging along with him a manuscript history of the early times in California. I believe he originally intended to give it to your library, but certain persons whose acquaintance he happened to make induced him to reconsider his resolution, and made him believe that there was money in it. Actuated by that belief, he has given the manuscript to Mr. Hopkins, keeper of the Archives in San Francisco, with a prayer for enough subscribers to pay for printing it. I believe, with judicious diplomacy and a little coin, you could get some person to purchase the manuscript for your library.[7]

Osio eventually returned to San José del Cabo without giving the manuscript to Bancroft. Instead, before he departed, he left it at Santa Clara with Soledad Ortega, the widow of Luis Argüello. Upon her death, the manuscript passed into the possession of J. R. Arques, the executor of the Argüello estate. He gave it to one of Osio's daughters, Beatrice Osio de Williamson, who was living in San Francisco. During the late 1870s three copies were made of the manuscript. One was made for John Doyle, who was collecting as many old documents as he could as part of his work for the Catholic Church in California on the Pious Fund case.[8] The second was made for James A. Forbes, a translator in the San Francisco Archives. Finally, in 1878 a copy of the Doyle copy was made for Bancroft.[9]

These events had two consequences. First, the fact that Osio did not freely make the manuscript available to Bancroft's staff soured them on him. Cerruti's comments give a flavor of the negative way in which the emerging Anglo history establishment was beginning to deride Osio and his manuscript: Osio was "dragging along with him" the manuscript and was animated solely by the desire to make money.

Actually, Cerruti's letter points to something quite different. Osio was motivated by a desire to have the entire manuscript published on its own and rendered accessible to a wide readership. Osio was in fact a genuine amateur historian. He had at least browsed through the government archives in Monterey, and when he was a member of the *diputación* in the 1830s, he was anxious to create and preserve an accurate historical record.[10] He may well have sensed that to offer the manuscript to Bancroft would have been, in effect, to cede control of the historical record to the very people who had taken over his country and who tended to be scornful of Mexico's past rule in Alta California.[11]

Such a fear would not have been unfounded. One need only contrast the paternalistic and heavy-handed manner in which Mexican reminiscences are sometimes treated in Bancroft's *History of California* volumes with the reverential and awe-filled fashion in which the same author's *Popular Tribunals* handles the reminiscences of the Anglo San Francisco vigilantes of 1851 and 1856 to appreciate how pervasive was the denigration of Mexicans in the former works.[12]

Osio's experience made him very hostile to those who ruled the land where he had spent so many years. The experience was bitter. In 1839 he had been granted Angel Island in San Francisco Bay, and in 1843 he received another grant of land near Point Reyes, on the Pacific coast north of San Francisco. He developed Angel Island quite effectively during the 1840s; by 1846 he had more than five hundred head of cattle grazing there, and he regularly sold beef to San Francisco. As the 1840s progressed, he spent more and more time at Point Reyes, where he intended finally to settle so that he and his second wife could raise their young family in the country. However, in 1846 he had to abandon Point Reyes because of the Bear Flag Revolt. In the same year the U.S. Navy occupied Angel Island and slaughtered his entire herd of cattle. Soon after, North American squatters began to take possession of his land at Point Reyes.[13]

Osio was associated with a group of Mexicans who never made their peace with the U.S. takeover of Alta California. Another of the group, Soledad Ortega, once told Mariano Guadalupe Vallejo, "They [the *norteamericanos*] rule over us in the same manner that the owner of a large farm rules his slaves. Our sweet Castilian tongue has given place to the unpronounceable English jargon—bless the Almighty I have not learned it."[14] Osio's manuscript was written in that same vein. It could be quite sharp on the subject of the North Americans. For instance, in describing Thomas ap Catesby Jones's premature capture of Monterey in 1842, Osio called the United States "an oppressor who displayed arrogance against the weak." And when he described "the brave men" who resisted the U.S. invasion in 1846, he said that they "should serve as an example for other places invaded by forces from the United States."

Osio's manuscript reflects the raw passions and the closely experienced bitterness of watching one's own country taken over by foreigners. He describes himself as "one who has experienced the sufferings of the *californio* landowners, which the political change has caused." He was not, as were so many of the *californios* who later gave their reminiscences to Savage or Cerruti, ambivalent about the U.S. conquest.[15] As early as 1851 he was emphatically and completely hostile to it. This attitude undoubtedly contributed to a negative assessment of his manuscript in what had been Alta California.

A second consequence of the way the manuscript came to be made available in the late 1870s was that Bancroft ended up with an unreliable version, for he had to content himself with a copy of John Doyle's copy. The Doyle copy, dated 1876 and now housed at the Huntington Library, is chronologically the earliest copy. It most closely resembles the original manuscript in content, but it is not 100 percent accurate. Words, clauses, and complete sentences are missing throughout the text. The scribe, Gulielmo B. Chase, may have been editing the manuscript as he went along, but the type of omissions more often suggests carelessness or a lack of attention to detail. Chase made numerous changes in spelling and syntax, indicating such changes by lining out a particular letter of a word and then writing the change in the space above. He also made corrections in subject-verb and noun-adjective agreement. Osio did make a few errors of this type, and while there are indications in the original manuscript of corrections he made, these mistakes indicate that Osio did not always proofread his own work carefully enough. Chase consistently made stylistic and grammatical changes in an attempt either to clarify or to improve the style of Osio's manuscript.[16] Finally, Chase changed the title and dates of the manuscript to "Chronicle of Occurrences in California from 1815 to 1846."[17]

The Bancroft Library copy, dated 1878 and based upon the Doyle copy, differs significantly in content and format both from the original and from the Doyle copy. As Chase had done, the Bancroft scribe changed the title of the manuscript, this time to "History of California, 1815–1848." He also divided the manuscript into chapters; each one begins with a brief summary of the chapter content. On each of the first twenty-six pages of the Bancroft copy, the scribe wrote page numbers in the left margin, perhaps as a guide, since these page numbers correspond directly with the page numbers in the Doyle copy. Unfortunately, the scribe was not as meticulous in his copying after page 26, because words, clauses, complete sentences, and entire paragraphs are omitted. These omissions are in addition to the ones already noted in the Doyle copy, and they compounded the inaccuracies and corrupted the manuscript even more. It appears that the Bancroft scribe made little effort to proofread his work. Instead, he mechanically and imperfectly copied, paying only intermittent attention to the content.

This can be seen in chapter 11 in the Bancroft copy, by far the most corrupt chapter and ironically one of the most important sections of Osio's work. Twenty-one pages of the original manuscript are missing. In this section Osio had been speaking of Nicolás Gutiérrez, who had been appointed governor by outgoing governor Mariano Chico in 1836. Osio remarked that Gutiérrez did not appear to be enjoying his new post: "Now that Gutiérrez was free from the man who annoyed everyone, including himself, he could have been happy. However, people began to notice that he was very sad, as if his festive mood were fighting against a strong, invisible force which prevented him from dealing with his friends in his customary straightforward manner. That was the way in which Captain Zamorano, Lieutenant Navarrete, and others whom he respected described Gutiérrez' behavior to him." The Bancroft manuscript renders that last sentence "That was the way he appeared to them." Then the Bancroft copy continues, "and he could not do or resolve anything until his commissioners returned. Even though a strong storm was obviously approaching, Sepúlveda did not even have the decency to ask them to spend the night at his camp; they were forced to ask him if they could." This describes a conversation between José Sepúlveda and the brothers Carlos and Anastasio Carrillo, an event which occurred the next year, as factions in southern Alta California resisted the rule of Governor Juan Bautista Alvarado. The result of combining these two distinct events in a single paragraph and of omitting twenty-one pages of the original manuscript is that a large section of the Bancroft copy is completely bereft of meaning and coherence.

At some point the scribe realized that the material he was copying did not make any sense, and he expressed his observation in a parenthetical note at the bottom of the page. He stated that he noticed a certain vagueness in this chapter, and it seemed to him that either the author was in a hurry or some other circumstance prevented him from describing the facts clearly. Perhaps, he joked, the individual who copied from the original left something in the inkwell. Other examples of the corruption of the Bancroft copy occur in its chapter 12, where six pages of the original are missing, and chapter 13, where the last six and a half lines are misplaced on the previous page. This carelessness resulted in a confusing and unintelligible copy. This is doubtless another reason why investigators have not consulted the Osio manuscript more frequently.[18]

Bancroft did more than just criticize the Osio manuscript, however; he subsumed it into his own work. Had Osio been alive when the *History of California* was published, he surely would have been outraged to learn that Bancroft had appropriated his manuscript into the corpus of dictations and reminiscences which Bancroft and his staff had collected. At the beginning of the first volume of the series, Bancroft wrote: "The memory of men yet living when I began my researches, as aided by that of their fathers, covers in a sense the whole history of California since its settlement. I have therefore taken dictations of personal reminiscences from 160 old residents. Half of them were native, or of Spanish blood; the other half foreign pioneers who came to the country before 1848. Of the former class, twenty-four were men who occupied prominent public positions, equally divided between the north and the south."[19] At the bottom of that page, in a footnote right between "Ord" (who was actually Angustias de la Guerra y Noriega, the daughter of José de la Guerra y Noriega, longtime commander of Santa Bárbara) and "Palomares," we read "Osio."[20] In other words, Bancroft presented himself as the one who had called Osio's manuscript into being in the 1870s! In the pages of the *History of California*, Bancroft and his staff stripped Osio of his own authorship.

Introduction

Antonio María Osio

Antonio María Osio was well qualified to do what Father Suárez del Real asked, for his roots in California extended back into the early decades of the eighteenth century. His great-grandfather, Manuel de Ocio, was born around the year 1700, most likely in Andalucía in Spain. He joined the army at an early age, and by 1730 he was serving as a soldier in Loreto in Antigua California. In 1741 a freak storm threw up a great number of pearl oysters on the coast east of Mission San Ignacio, where Ocio was stationed. Previously, this area had not been regarded as rich in pearls. Manuel de Ocio was able to take advantage of the situation, and he rapidly became a prosperous trader in pearls between Antigua California and Guadalajara. He resigned from the military and went to Guadalajara, where he was aided by an emerging elite anxious to establish commercial enterprises independent of the dominance of Mexico City. Helped by Guadalajara investments, Ocio discovered silver near Real de Santa Ana, which became the first civil settlement in California. He also invested in land and cattle. Toward the end of his life he gambled away some of his riches, but he was still prosperous when he was murdered in 1771.[21]

In 1736 Manuel de Ocio married Rosalía Rodríguez, one of the daughters of Bernardo Rodríguez, an officer at Loreto. About 1748 Rosalía gave birth to a son named Antonio. In 1767 Antonio married Manuela de Mena. She was the daughter of Antonio Ignacio de Mena, a *teniente coronel* in the militia and a member of a wealthy Guadalajara family, and Josefa Sánchez Calderón.[22] After Manuela died, Antonio remarried. He and his second wife, María Jesús de Castro, had two children. One of them, Juan de la Cruz Ocio, later married Juana Higuera, and the couple had three children: Antonio María, María Beatriz, and José María. Antonio María was born in 1800.[23]

Little is known of Antonio María's early life. On November 28, 1822, he married Dolores Argüello, the youngest daughter of José Darío Argüello, who had just resigned as governor of Baja California. In the spring of that year Argüello's house in Loreto, the capital of Baja California, had been sacked by insurgents from Thomas Cochrane's Chilean squadron, and Argüello, wracked by ill health, had retired to Guadalajara.[24]

Antonio and Dolores lived in Baja California for several years, and they had one child there, Salvador, born in 1824. According to his manuscript, Osio and his family moved to Alta California in 1825. Through his marriage, Osio now had connections there. Dolores Argüello herself had been born in San Francisco, and her brother Luis had been chosen as governor of Alta California in 1822. The story of Osio's public life in Alta California constitutes the major part of the manuscript itself, so there is little reason to detail it in this introduction.

Since Osio mentions very little about his personal life, however, a brief sketch might render him more familiar to the reader. He and Dolores settled in the capital of Monterey, where she gave birth to twin girls in 1826. One child died immediately after birth, and the other survived only two weeks. Another daughter, María de la Paz Maximiana, was born on May 29, 1827, but both she and her mother died in November of that same year.[25] Osio did not marry again for ten years, and the intervening decade was the time of his greatest involvement in the politics of Alta California. When Governor Alvarado appointed Osio to the Customs House at the end of 1837 or the beginning of 1838, Osio ended a residence of some seven years in the Los Angeles area and returned north. He also changed his life in another important respect, for he married Narcisa Florencia Soto at Mission Santa Clara on February 15, 1838. Narcisa was descended from two old military families in Alta California. Her paternal grandfather, Francisco José Dolores Soto, and her maternal grandmother, Juana María Lorenza Sánchez, were the first two children baptized at Mission San Francisco in 1776.[26] By 1845 she had borne five children: José Antonio (1839), Juan de la Cruz (1840), Antonio (1842), Beatriz (1843), and José Manuel (1845).[27]

Osio benefited from Alvarado's generous land grant policy. He received Angel Island on June 11, 1839, and on January 4, 1842, Alvarado granted him Rancho Punta de los Reyes on the Pacific coast north of San Francisco. Governor Manuel Micheltorena confirmed that grant on October 28, 1843. In 1844 Micheltorena granted Osio Rancho Aguas Frías, about 150 miles north of San Francisco. Osio's son Salvador would settle there upon his return to California after some time in "the United States of the North," where his father had sent him to study carpentry.[28] After Osio resigned his position at the Customs House on September 22, 1842, he began to spend more and more time at his *rancho* at Point Reyes. He probably intended to raise his family there, although he continued to remain involved in public affairs in Monterey. Until 1845 he served on the *tribunal superior*, to which Alvarado had appointed him. In the previous year Micheltorena appointed him to head the Monterey squadron of the new auxiliary militia, which was formed to defend the country from the United States.[29]

In April 1846 U.S. consul Thomas O. Larkin called Osio a "merchant." In a long report on the character of the principal men of Alta California, Larkin grouped Osio with Juan Malarín, Rafael González, and Pedro Navárez and portrayed them as "four men with landed property and cattle." Larkin described the four as "married, and have lived over ten years in Monterey. Of some note and influence, quiet and unobtrusive in their inclinations. Inclined to politics or Government affairs only in canvassing its merits."[30]

In June 1846 Osio was apparently at Point Reyes when the Bear Flag Revolt broke out. Warned by the U.S. vice-consul in San Francisco that he might well be arrested if he remained there, he headed first for San Francisco and then to points south. When war formally broke out between the United States and Mexico, the U.S. Navy took possession of Angel Island. As Osio later told the Land Commission, "They commenced killing the cattle for military and naval uses and continued to do so until there were none left."[31]

Osio then took his family to Honolulu, where another daughter, María Lucrecia, was born. Osio and his family remained in Hawaii for an undetermined time. They were back in California by 1849, though, and Osio purchased a lot in Santa Clara from Father José María Suárez del Real in December 1849. Osio and his family lived at Santa Clara for a time, and Osio became involved in a dispute over the mission orchard. He claimed title to it stemming from an 1846 agreement with José Castro. Two other men (one of whom, interestingly, was Thomas Larkin) claimed title based on grants by Pío Pico, and yet another person claimed title based on squatter's rights. In the midst of this complicated situation, Osio returned to Monterey, where he lived in 1850. He seems to have returned to Santa Clara in 1851 and presented his claim for Angel Island to the Land Commission in 1852.[32]

Characteristics of the Manuscript

The manuscript which Osio penned in 1851 is significant for a number of reasons. The most important is the date, for it is the earliest extant narrative account of the period 1821–46. The most utilized primary sources for the history of Mexican California have been documents concerning governmental and ecclesiastical affairs. Most of these sources have an ad hoc quality about them; they were written to compile a required annual report, to deal with a current problem, or to answer a specific question. These sources have the closeness and the texture of day-to-day life that often gives them much of their value. Historians and literary scholars know, however, that to understand a culture and a people, one needs to know not only what they did in the lived ordinariness of their lives but also how they perceived what they were doing. Explicitly self-reflective work—fiction, autobiography, memoirs—can be of great assistance as we seek to understand the past. Imagine, for instance, how incomplete would be our understanding of the Pilgrims if we did not have William Bradford's *Of Plimouth Plantation* and Mary Rowlandson's *Narrative of Captivity*, or of colonial and revolutionary America if we did not have *The Autobiography of Benjamin Franklin*, or of the Jewish immigrant experience if we did not have Abraham Cahan's *The Rise of David Levinsky*. Analysis of these works, of course, is far from simple, but the documents often provide a unique entry into a culture. Osio's manuscript does the same.

This leads to a second reason for its importance. The manuscript is clearly based on two types of sources: Osio's own experience and what he was told by others. When the sources are not personal, they are derived from an oral tradition. This oral character of the sources is indicated by a number of factors. The most obvious is the fashion in which Osio presents non-Spanish names. He often spells them phonetically, which demonstrates that he had heard the name but had never read it. Bouchard, for instance, is rendered "Buchar," and Riley becomes "Rayle." The lieutenant on board the U.S.S. *Portsmouth* in 1846 was named John S. Misroon. When Osio heard the man's surname, he assumed that the first syllable was a shortened form of "Mister," so he called him "Mr. Rum"!

In addition, the manuscript bears the marks of being the product of a culture that was primarily oral. The entire tone of the work is conversational rather than analytic. In the process of telling one story, Osio is reminded of another, which he then proceeds to relate before finishing the first story, much as one might normally do in conversation. For instance, Osio describes a scene at Mission La Purísima during the 1824 Chumash Uprising. An indigenous rebel entered the church, took a small crucifix down from the wall, and hung it around his neck as a protective charm against the guns of the soldiers. As Osio begins that story, he remarks that native Californians had never adopted a true Christianity "simply because they had been sprinkled with baptismal water." Rather, he says, they tended to join missions out of "fear, deceit, or self-interest." That observation reminds him of a story about an Indian at Mission San José who once threw his shirt at the feet of Father Narciso Durán and told him, "Take your Christianity. I don't want it anymore." Only after telling that story does Osio return to finish the 1824 story. This type of conversational stream of consciousness can make parts of the work a bit difficult to read, but it is entirely understandable in light of the oral and conversational roots of the stories Osio recounts. For, as Walter Ong and others have shown, orally based thought tends to be "aggregative" rather than analytic.[33]

Osio was quite aware that he was attempting to transmit an entire tradition. His decision to begin his account in 1815, with the appointment of Pablo Vicente de Solá as governor, rather than with his own arrival in 1825, is significant in this regard. This strategy allowed him to include many aspects of the Argüello family tradition which otherwise would not have easily fit into his work. The preservation of that family tradition, which had become his own tradition through marriage, was obviously important to Osio. Likewise, at times he specifically credits others with providing him with stories. One anecdote about José de la Guerra y Noriega, for example, is attributed to "the accounts of one of his brothers-in-law." This is a method of enlarging the circle of authorship and making it clear that Osio was attempting to preserve not only his own story but also the stories of an entire people.

At times Osio can be seen reacting to the received oral tradition and trying to modify and reshape it. One such instance is evident in his description of the battle of Cahuenga in 1831. Osio says that even though two of the rebel commanders "have bragged tremendously since the insurrection," their boasts were unwarranted. In his opinion, "They never had the decency to say later why they had not somehow aided Avila and Talamantes [two insurgents in the battle], the only two men, out of more than two hundred in the force, who joined the battle and distinguished themselves courageously." Through the master narrative he was trying to compose, Osio hoped to alter the tradition as well as preserve it.

Also, Osio's presentation of events is about as close as we are ever going to get to the oral culture as it existed before the U.S. invasion. The Osio manuscript differs markedly from other reminiscences by his contemporaries, notably the multivolume works of Mariano Guadalupe Vallejo and Juan Bautista Alvarado, which were composed in the 1870s, more than a quarter century after the conquest and in some cases more than fifty years after the events they describe. With the passage of time a person's recollections do not always remain unchanged; memories tend to fade or become confused, and facts may be exaggerated or forgotten. People continually revise the memories of their lives to harmonize with events that have happened or are happening at the present time.[34]

The Osio manuscript, on the other hand, was written a mere five years after the U.S. conquest of Alta California. The accounts of various events often tend to be more sober, less exaggerated, and less given to the grandiloquent pathos which one can find in some of the other reminiscences. In general, Osio's more matter-of-fact accounts are probably closer to the way these events were remembered by the *californios*. For instance, in his discussion of the Bouchard raid, Alvarado has a long story about how Hipólito Bouchard, disguised as an English captain on a scientific expedition, visited Monterey in 1817 to scout Monterey's defenses. Speaking of the same episode, Vallejo says that Bouchard was frightened away from attempting to land at San Francisco when Commander Luis Argüello posted all of his soldiers in plain view of the privateer and fired a cannon at him.[35] Neither account reflected what actually occurred, and both are doubtless the results of the passage of time and perhaps of the designs of Alvarado and Vallejo as they were talking to the Bancroft staff almost sixty years after the events they had witnessed. Osio, whose oral sources included Luis Argüello, includes neither story in his account of the Bouchard affair.

Osio's work also differs from the Vallejo and Alvarado works in two other important respects. First, unlike Vallejo and Alvarado (and also unlike Juan Bandini, who began his own history in the 1850s but was not able to complete it before his death), Osio lived in both northern and southern Alta California. Vallejo and Alvarado resided only in the north, and Bandini lived only in the south. Of all the Mexican Alta California authors, only Osio offered a perspective on events from the points of view of both north and south. His work treats the 1837 insurrection against Alvarado from the perspective of a resident of Los Angeles; yet it also treats the Customs House from the perspective of a dedicated civil servant laboring for the good of the government in Monterey. Osio's ability to identify with both the north and the south gives his work a territory-wide perspective that is at times lacking in the other accounts. This perspective might also account for the strong California and Mexican nationalism so pronounced in the later sections of the work.

Second, unlike Vallejo or Alvarado, Osio was not a major political or social figure in Alta California. Although he was elected to the *diputación* and to the Los Angeles *ayuntamiento,* he served only one term on each body. For most of his life in Alta California he was a civil servant and a bureaucrat in the customs service. Although he was acquainted with the upper strata of the *californio* elite—the Picos, Vallejos, Alvarados, and the like—they did not contribute very much to his manuscript. The circle in which Osio moved, the group whose experiences his manuscript generally reflects, was a second-level coterie, composed of those who were eminent, but hardly preeminent, in Alta California. The circle included families such as the Argüellos, Carrillos, and Estradas, all of whom, like Osio, could trace their California ancestry to eighteenth-century Antigua California. It also included people such as the Tapias and the Sepúlvedas. These people were not the elite who gave the territory its direction, but rather those immediately below them on the social scale, those who provided the initiative, the commitment, and the capability that allowed the territory to develop.

Osio's work reflects the down-to-earth concerns of these people: the manner of rounding up the presidio cattle, the distance the military was willing to travel in pursuit of horse thieves, the direction and force of the currents in San Francisco Bay, the shape of the boats used by the Kodiak Aleuts to hunt sea otters, the location of the passable crossings over the San Gabriel River, and similar items. These details, which were an integral part of everyday life for this second-level group, give Osio's manuscript an immediacy and an engagement with its own time which one fails to encounter consistently in the later Bancroft dictations.

Finally, Osio offers a definite interpretation of the period he covers. He clearly regarded his role as more than simply collecting and preserving a bundle of stories. He was deeply aware of what we today would term his authorship: he was the one who decided which stories to include and how to group them. This may be another reason he decided to begin his account in 1815, even though he did not arrive in Alta California until 1825. For then there could be no doubt that he was the one responsible for the order which existed in the manuscript. In fact, as we shall see, he uses the pre-1825 section of his work to introduce all the themes he wants to cover in the body of the work.

The manuscript begins with a description of the sadness and loss felt by the inhabitants of Alta California when their governor died, and it ends with Osio stating that he himself has experienced the sufferings of the *californio* landowners which the recent political change has caused. These themes of sadness and loss frame the entire manuscript. The work is Osio's lament on his and Alta California's lost possibilities and on the disorder and chaos that affected both of them after the U.S invasion. Osio's history of California is not simply a record of scattered recollections but rather a carefully crafted response to the changes that were occurring around him. Osio is attempting to come to terms with what it meant to be a *californio* in 1851. At one point, for instance, when he is discussing "the veil of schemes which was drawn to hide the uprising by foreigners in 1840, an up-rising which finally took place in 1846," Osio remarks, "That is why today those people with their *considerandos* need to be reminded of a familiar story about two people who inherited vast expanses of adjoining lands." The mention of *considerandos* is a reference to the 1851 California legisla-ture, which was meeting in San José, immediately adjacent to the city of Santa Clara, while Osio was composing the manuscript. Some *californios* sat on this body, and Osio may have been making direct reference to them.

Osio differs from the other *californio* authors in that he maintained com-plete authorial control over his narrative, and it is his voice that resonates throughout. Osio alone decided on the material that would be included and on the manner in which it would be presented, and the manuscript was written in his own hand. The other *californio* authors were not able to maintain this degree of control over their work because the material for their narratives was obtained through oral interviews conducted by Ban-croft's staff.[36] The topics and the order in which they were to be discussed were partially controlled by the interviewers, who took notes as the per-son spoke. Later the information was transcribed. During the transcription process, it was not uncommon for the material to be edited or "filtered" through the scribe's pen.[37] Informants' responses and opinions were often influenced by the manner in which the interviewer asked the questions, which could be considered a form of manipulation. Osio, on the other hand, did not answer a set of predetermined questions, nor did he allow anyone but himself to edit the manuscript.[38] The form of the work was his and his alone.

Osio was familiar with many different literary forms, and throughout the manuscript he drew on a number of them.[39] For example, he could em-ploy classical mythology. In one highly symbolic episode, Mariano Chico (whom Osio calls "Argos the observer") catches his mistress ("the beauti-ful Napea") flirting with a handsome young American ("Narcissus") she has met aboard ship.[40] Osio's obvious knowledge of and appreciation for a wide variety of literary genres may have influenced the stylistic framework he chose for his manuscript. Characteristics of three literary genres—epistle, memoir, and autobiography—appear in his work. The manuscript begins with the letter to Father Suárez del Real and ends with closing lines addressed to the same man. In this manner, the letter, which on the surface simply appears to be Osio's reply to the priest's request that he write a history of California, becomes the exterior framework for the work as a whole.

The conversational or dialogic tone that we have already seen also characterizes epistolary literature: the author writes the way that he speaks. Underlying the epistolary discourse is the important relationship between the reader and the author which will dictate the manner in which the information in the manuscript is conveyed.[41] The reader, Suárez del Real, plays a generative role in the creation of the work, for the common memories, experiences, and trust shared by the two men give Osio the freedom to compose. If one were to read the letter, or for that matter the entire manuscript, aloud, it would be easy to imagine Osio engaged in a long evening of conversation as he reminisced with his friend.[42] The oral motif is maintained throughout the manuscript. In numerous instances Osio adopts an explicitly conversational relationship with the reader, as he says "Take note," "Look," "Notice," or "Imagine."[43]

Osio concludes the introductory letter by suggesting that Suárez del Real obtain letters from other friends who can provide him with information that Osio does not include. Although Osio appears to have taken his role as author very seriously, he never claims to be the supreme authority on California history. In fact, he openly submits his work to the scrutiny of others when he suggests that Suárez del Real ask for assistance from another friend who has the proper training and attributes of a good writer and who can help him compile a comprehensive history of California.[44] The closing lines of the introductory letter parallel the closing lines of the manuscript, in which Osio states, "As one who has experienced the sufferings of the *californio* landowners, which the political change has caused, I would ask that you please allow me to conclude the present letter here. Another friend of yours, with a very small pen, might continue the story. Please accept this brief work which your dear, devoted servant dedicates to you as a token of our friendship."

Here, as in the introductory letter, the ritual of closing allows Osio to reiterate the mood of the entire work, the tone of sadness and loss. He also implies that his work is incomplete and that it will take on a larger significance when different perspectives and interpretations are added to it. Epistolary texts are never closed; they are merely a selection from a larger body of information, or just one side of an exchange.[45] The epistolary text is not merely a historical object or an antique curiosity but rather a living thing that can be framed and reframed as part of an ongoing process of creation, transmission, and interpretation.[46]

While Osio is the narrator of the manuscript, it is important to note that his own presence does not stand out. Osio does not assume the role of narrator-protagonist and never overshadows or dominates the work. He chooses, instead, to appear slowly and subtly on the social and political scene, presenting different sides of himself in different contexts. He thus engages in an exercise of self-creation in which the reader is a witness and an indirect participant. This technique of subtle, progressive self-disclosure allows Osio, as narrator-observer, to position himself both inside and outside of his "history."

Osio refers to himself by name only twice in the manuscript, and then he calls himself "someone named Osio" and "this fellow Osio." As he becomes more involved in the political and social arenas, he appears in the text more frequently, but he always describes himself in cryptic, indirect, or self-deprecating ways. He refers to himself as "the lowly Customs employee" or disguises himself as the "friend of Sepúlveda," "Gutiérrez' friend," or "the clumsy, foolish narrator." The restraint he employed in "creating" his public persona and in positioning himself in the manuscript in relation to other people indicates that he did not view himself as a person who operated and developed in isolation, but rather as someone who had been shaped by a collective experience.

Those two aspects of Osio—being described in a deprecatory fashion and being formed by a collective experience—also define the life of the other main character in the manuscript. That character is nothing else than Alta California itself. "Alta California" are the fifth and sixth words Osio placed in his manuscript, and it is never far from the center of attention. Throughout the work, Osio often, indeed repetitively, adopts the point of view of the *californios* and criticizes Mexico for neglecting the welfare of the territory.[47] For instance, he breaks off an account of an artillery battle between the defenders of Monterey and one of Bouchard's ships to state, "No *hijo del país* was recognized by the Mexican government during its different periods." Or again: "The Mexican government declared itself California's stepfather and denied it protection as if it were a bastard child." Or yet again: "The government [of Mexico] never considered the advantages to be gained by stimulating development in different parts of this territory, which was so ready for it." The modest way in which Osio speaks of himself is matched in the manuscript by the minimal fashion in which the central government treats its faraway territory.

Osio emerges fully only at the end of the manuscript, as he writes about his own part in the history of the Bear Flag Revolt and the U.S. invasion. In this section, he consistently refers to himself as a *californio*. But in his mind this identity is inextricably intertwined with another identity. As he describes the help given to Robert F. Stockton in San Diego by "some corrupt *californios* and some Mexican traitors," he fumes, "Because I am a *californio* who loves his country and a Mexican on all four sides and in my heart, as a point of honor, I should keep quiet about the following event or let it go unnoticed or be forgotten, but this would not be in keeping with the purpose of my narrative." This is the only time in the narrative section of the work that he refers to himself in the first person and explicitly mentions a design in the manuscript. For Osio, to be a *californio* is always to be Mexican. Moreover, the "purpose" of this whole manuscript is to make that point against those who in 1851 thought they could successfully negotiate the transition to U.S. rule. The quarrels with Mexico, really quarrels within an extended family, had blinded too many people, Osio thought, to their own identity.[48]

At the end of his work, Osio describes the negotiations between Andrés Pico and John C. Frémont after the battle of San Pascual. He writes that even though the *californios* might well become "excellent citizens of the United States," they would always be "viewed as foreigners in their own country."

Part I

Introduction to Part I

We have divided Osio's manuscript into chapters. Our division attempts to reflect the fashion in which we think that Osio arranged his material. For instance, Osio clearly arranges his narrative of the decade before his arrival in Alta California into three episodes: the attempts by Luis Argüello to improve the San Francisco presidio in the 1810s, the 1818 Bouchard raid on Alta California, and the 1824 Chumash Uprising. Accordingly, we have divided that section of the work into three chapters.

In the introductory pages of his work, Osio does not attempt to write a general history of Alta California. Rather, he uses these three episodes to introduce three themes which will be very important throughout his work: the *californios* did try to develop the resources of Alta California; Spain, and later Mexico, never gave Alta California the support it needed if development were to succeed; and the mission system was never as effective in converting and/or hispanicizing the indigenous peoples as its proponents claimed. Indeed, the first incident that Osio recounts in his work sets the tone. Osio describes the scene when Father Vicente de Sarría, the head of the missions, finished his first meeting with Governor Pablo de Solá: "When the Superior returned to the room in which he had left the other Fathers, he found them with some officers. One of the Fathers gestured with his head, as if to ask him if he had succeeded. The Superior understood and, in response, placed his right arm all the way up his large left sleeve to indicate that he already had him in his pocket." This vivid picture of clerical manipulation and power is gradually undone in the course of the manuscript. In fact, the last scene in the manuscript describes the Fathers' inability to find gold in California and symbolizes what Osio takes to be the futility of much of their time there.

In the first chapter, which is framed by two mentions of Solá's predecessor, José Joaquín de Arrillaga, it is significant that the first glance the reader obtains of Argüello is one of the captain attempting to improve the condition of his men, whom Osio calls his family. Argüello's care for his men and interest in developing the potential of Alta California are deliberately contrasted with Solá's initial obstruction. The two men represent struggling California and an uncaring central government. In addition, foreigners, especially from the United States, were never too far in the background during the Mexican period, and they are introduced by Osio in this first chapter as well. The first view of a U.S. citizen is intrusive: William Heath Davis is bluntly described as a smuggler. This chapter ends when the central government (Solá) realizes the wisdom and vision of California (Argüello).

In the second chapter, which begins with Bouchard's appearance at Monterey and ends with the departure of Solá and Canónigo Agustín Fernández from the same port, Osio jumps to 1818 and the Bouchard raid. Osio writes this section of the manuscript with great attention to a series of tensions, contrasts, and contradictions. The most compelling scene in the chapter describes José de Jesús Vallejo manning his cannon on the beach and caught between contradictory orders. Osio explicitly views Vallejo's dilemma as a reflection of that of Alta California, not allowed to perform the deeds of which it was capable. But there are other contrasts in the chapter. Sergeant Gómez "quickly experienced the great difference that exists between the joy of the victor and the sorrow of the vanquished," when Bouchard's men appeared on land. In Santa Bárbara, troops "had traveled at a gallop to try to prevent the landing," but they were unsuccessful, for "from a distance they experienced the sorrow of seeing the smoke rising from the homes." In these and other ways, Osio structures the Bouchard section around the general theme of contradiction and loss, and he regards the privateer's success in Alta California as exposing to view the contradictions which plagued the territory.

The third chapter also represents a jump ahead, to 1824. This chapter is ironically framed with descriptions of peace and harmony. In it, Osio treats the Chumash Uprising as an example of another weakness in Alta California: the inability of the mission system to do what it claimed it was doing, that is, to convert the Indians to Christianity. In the course of the manuscript Osio's criticism of the missions revolves around two items: the spiritual state and the physical care of the native peoples. In chapter 3 he dismisses claims that the Indians were genuinely converted. Later in the manuscript (chapter 7), he will attack the mission claims that the system provided for the physical welfare of its charges.

In Osio's account of the uprising, little is as it should be. One of the priests talks and acts like a soldier. Women go to confession in the presence of their husbands. The native peoples prove themselves more adept and sophisticated in planning their revolt than anyone had ever expected. José de la Guerra is misnamed. And much else. If the Bouchard raid exposed the contradictions of the territory in its relations with the central government, the Chumash revolt exposed the contradictions of the mission system.

· 1 ·

The inhabitants of Alta California were generally saddened by the loss of such a fine governor as Don José Joaquín de Arrillaga. The Reverend Fathers at the missions, in particular, wanted to know who would be selected by the Viceroy to govern the territory and what type of man he would be.[1] They impatiently awaited the customary notice from the Colegio de San Fernando,[2] which would inform them of even the most intimate characteristics of the person entrusted with such an honorable appointment, such as his background, temperament, and habits.

Finally, the brigantine *Altivo* of the Royal Spanish fleet brought the desired report when it arrived from San Blas with the wages of the soldiers stationed at the presidios. Colonel Don Pablo Vicente de Solá, from the Basque provinces, was the man appointed to be governor of Alta California. The report on Solá was favorable, but it concluded that he did not possess Arrillaga's prudence and knowledge; he was a very proud man, and none of the subordinates in his regiment were pleased with him. When this leader arrived to take over his command in 1815, he was not reluctant to demonstrate his displeasure with his officers, so the Reverend Fathers were quite nervous at having to pay him, as a representative of Fernando VII, the requisite courtesy visit.[3] They discussed the matter among themselves and with clerical shrewdness decided that the Reverend Father Prefect,[4] who was the Superior and also a Vizcayan,[5] would make the obligatory visit, accompanied by two other Fathers of his choosing.

Being a good clergyman, the Superior was reputed to be very well informed and clever. Yet he had a bit of vanity in him as well, as can be seen in the outcome of the visit. When the appointed day arrived, the three Fathers presented themselves at the government house. There, the Superior explained to the others that he had given the matter more thought and felt

N

0 20 40 60 80 100
Miles

San Francisco Solano
San Rafael
San Francisco de Asís
Santa Clara
San José
San José
Santa Cruz
Branciforte
San Juan Bautista
San Carlos de Monterey
Soledad
San Antonio
San Miguel
San Luis Obispo
La Purísima
Santa Ynez
Santa Bárbara
San Buenaventura
San Fernando Rey
San Gabriel
Los Ángeles
San Juan Capistrano
San Luis Rey
San Diego

✝ Missions
▣ Forts
● Towns
- - - - Royal Road

Missions, forts, and towns during the Spanish period, 1769–1822. Redrawn from *Historical Atlas of California*, Warren A. Beck and Ynez D. Haase. Copyright ©1974 by the University of Oklahoma Press.

that since the governor was alone, it would be best for him to speak with him privately. So he entered the parlor by himself, and he was received with the decorum due his position. After an exchange of greetings, he and the governor had a long and serious conversation. Then they began to speak in a combination of Spanish and Basque, and soon both of them had forgotten the seriousness with which they had begun. When they bade farewell to one another, they parted on such good terms that it seemed as if they had been friends for a long time.

When the Superior returned to the room in which he had left the other Fathers, he found them with some officers. One of the Fathers gestured with his head, as if to ask him if he had succeeded. The Superior understood and, in response, placed his right arm all the way up his large left sleeve to indicate that he already had him in his pocket.

The governor's officers included an Andalusian and an Asturian, and he treated both of them harshly and scornfully. He even went so far as to beat the first man with his cane, and the second one had to run away to escape the same punishment. This type of conduct, taking advantage of the respect due him, accounted for his close friendship with Don Luis Argüello, Captain of the San Francisco presidio company.[6] As an aside, and because of his significance, I will explain how this came about.

When the pace of their military service permitted it, Captain Argüello liked to keep his soldiers either well entertained with honest diversions or involved in hard work, which he would direct. Once, when he and his men were returning to the presidio at sunset after a day on horseback, he stopped on the crest of the low ridges that overlook the military square.[7] From that vantage point, he pointed out to them that all of the homes were in poor condition. He suggested that, if they agreed and were willing, the homes could be quickly and completely destroyed and then tastefully rebuilt around a larger square, which would provide each house a larger lot and a better appearance.

One of the sergeants, with whom he would discuss nonmilitary matters or converse informally as if he were his own nephew, answered that his sergeants, corporals, and soldiers had never demonstrated any other desire than to do the captain's bidding. Therefore, he would soon see them all working on the project he wished to complete. Since everyone was in such a good mood, the new presidio square was sketched out by dawn the next morning. Sergeants, corporals, and soldiers were appointed to begin to break ground and lay the foundation as soon as they could obtain the assistance of the Indians. Other men were appointed to go to the spot named Corte de Madera de San Rafael to prepare the different types of timber.[8] The captain appointed himself director of this project. But there was no barge, which was essential for transporting the timber across the mouth of the port. Everything works out in the end for the one who does not delay for fear of difficulties. However, at that time, this problem appeared to be insurmountable.

Work on the foundation and on the adobes was already well under way when, by accident, Don Luis Argüello found an English carpenter. Despite not having the proper tools, this man managed to construct a suitable barge.[9] When it was completed, he asked the carpenter to teach him the art of navigation and how to handle a rudder, and for several days he received instruction. After having learned a little, he set out for Corte de Madera with a crew of soldiers he dubbed sailors. He was not acquainted with the risks of the crossing, and so he managed to leave at the worst possible time— when the prevalent northeast wind picks up, the offshore current gains strength, and the sea becomes more turbulent. As gusts of wind pound the vessel repeatedly with ever greater force, waves continually wash over the vessel. Once the vessel has been hit four times, it is in danger of capsizing. Even the most experienced swimmer would be helpless in the middle of such strong crosscurrents. When Señor Argüello was between Alcatraz and Angel Island, the gusts of wind hit so hard that twice the barge filled halfway with water and he found himself in great danger of sinking. But his presence of mind saved him. His improvised crew, stricken by seasickness and afraid of sinking, had given up, but Señor Argüello did not appear at all alarmed and kept bailing out the water. When his men saw his example, they took courage and began to pitch in and do their duty.[10]

When they safely arrived at Corte de Madera, he was satisfied with how far along the work had progressed. Those who had been sent ahead on a raft had to make a wide detour to go through the Carquínez Strait. As a result, they traveled more than sixty leagues, while a direct line from the presidio totals no more than five leagues altogether.[11] Since there was already enough timber at the dock, the so-called sailors were able to design and tie together a large raft from the timber left over from the crosspieces and andirons. The first crossings went very well since Señor Argüello had learned which tides were favorable from an old Indian named Marín, who was accustomed to crossing in a tule craft whenever he wished or when he was sent with official or private communications from the Fathers.[12]

The first time that Señor Argüello entrusted the command of the barge to the corporal in his company, who he thought had acquired the necessary skills, he had the pleasure of seeing the barge sail past Angel Island before losing sight of it. It arrived soon after at its destination. As he was towing the large raft on the return trip, the corporal congratulated himself on how quickly he had learned to navigate the vessel. As he was boasting to himself about his skill, he found himself even with Alcatraz near the Sausalito side. But he was unaware that the current was at its strongest. When he realized his error in having taken that route, he rowed as hard as he could toward the pier, but he could not get the raft across the strong current. Under these difficult circumstances night fell upon them. The nights in the bay are usually quite dark because of the fog. When dawn broke they discovered that they had been carried outside the bay to the Farallon Islands, about eight leagues from the presidio. There they discussed whether they should abandon the raft and try to make it to Point Reyes, but when the regular southeast wind began to blow, they decided not to leave the raft behind. Instead they headed for the mouth of San Francisco Bay. Because the raft was very large and heavy, they made little progress, and by nightfall they had only reached Point Bonetes.[13] Since the previous trips had lasted only about five to eight hours, they had not bothered to bring food or water along, and they were beginning to get hungry and thirsty. Fortunately, at dawn they found themselves in shoal water. The wind was favorable, and so they were able to arrive with their cargo at about two in the afternoon.

This accident taught them a good, if harsh, lesson. On subsequent trips they would need to take care not to endanger their lives again by testing their strength on the oars against the greater force of the current. Rather, they would need to wait and take advantage of its natural ebb and flow. Finally, they would need to provide themselves with sufficient food and water for three days.

The work on the presidio was proceeding well. The captain was indistinguishable from the other workers except for the respect which they showed him. Since each member of the company was bent on protecting his own and his parents' honor and on never giving his captain and other superiors a reason for even the slightest reprimand, everything moved rapidly, nothing fell behind due to carelessness, and all of the projects were progressing. The planks for doors, floors, and the other parts of the homes were obtained from redwood trees or larch trees which had straighter filament. Mallets and wedges were used instead of saws to split the wood to the desired thickness, and it was smoothed down afterward with a hatchet or adze. The work went on steadily, and they were almost finished with the officers' homes when jealousy or flattery managed to interfere with the project. Eventually it caused the loss of most of what had been started.

Señor Solá was informed that various vessels were sighted holding their position between Point Año Nuevo and Point Reyes and that there was

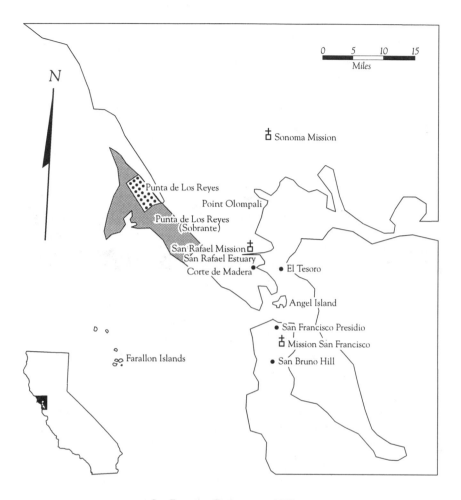

San Francisco Bay area, ca. 1840

no doubt that they were smugglers.[14] Actually, they were four American frigates, and one of them belonged to Don Guillermo Davis,[15] who was engaged in smuggling and in seeking the otters and sea lions which the Kodiak Indians captured in the hide canoes they used for hunting.[16] Their favorite anchorage was at Point Reyes in the bay named after Francisco Drake.[17] Knowing that there were many otters there, Davis wrote to Don Luis Argüello and offered to give him three thousand pesos if the Kodiak canoes were allowed to enter the port. Davis served notice that if Argüello granted permission, his Indians would go in and fish. However, if he refused it, they would still enter the bay and kill as many otters and sea lions

San Francisco Bay, 1837. From *Sunset Magazine*, Sept. 1915, 522. Courtesy of the California State Library, Sacramento.

as they could find. Don Luis Argüello retorted that he could never grant him such a permission and that, if the canoes did go in to fish, he was capable of destroying some and forcing the others away. He concluded his reply by observing that the canoes would never be able to get close to the port, since he had already taken preventive measures. He then proceeded to outfit his barge with a small cannon. However, once it was set up, as he waited for the Kodiaks, he began to fear that everything that he had prepared to use against them might be destroyed. In that event, he would not be able to transport any more timber for the construction project.

At that time, an unknown Englishman, accompanied by three other people from different nations, arrived and introduced himself to Argüello. The Englishman handed him a very disagreeable official letter from Señor Solá. It stated that the governor had found out that Argüello had built a barge and had launched it without requesting permission from his superior. The governor accused him of insubordination, since the barge might come into contact with the smugglers' ships that were sailing outside the bay. He therefore ordered Argüello to turn over the barge, immediately and without any argument, to the Englishman, who was commissioned to take it to Monterey.[18]

When Señor Argüello handed over the barge, he also sent a message explaining that he had built it himself so as not to put any burden on the royal treasury. He said that contact with smugglers was impossible because they only dealt with traders who had money. He himself, he added, did not have one peso, not even the long overdue wages he had never received. The proud governor was greatly offended by this message and ordered Argüello to appear personally before him in Monterey.

Señor Argüello had been certain that his letter would elicit that precise reaction from the governor. In fact, he wanted to meet his new leader. So, on the day after receiving the order, he left San Francisco for Monterey. He spent the night at Mission Santa Clara at the insistence of the Reverend Fathers Magín and Viader.[19] The following day he arrived at Mission San Juan Bautista. The Fathers there wanted him to spend the night and entertained him until very late. He refused their repeated requests to spend the night, so they gave him good horses so that he could travel. Everyone knows that the *californios*, if they took only what would fit under their saddle, would generally cover about four or five leagues per hour. Señor Argüello was traveling in that manner so he could cover the twelve leagues between San Juan and Monterey quickly. About one league from his destination, his horse tripped and fell, and Argüello's foot was caught underneath it and against the stirrup. It was dislocated in two places. When he dismounted at his sister's home, he could not take a step without assistance.

The following day his sister had everything prepared to treat him and set his foot, but he refused treatment since he wanted to see the governor as soon as possible. He promised that he would submit to the treatment when he returned from the visit. Suffering tremendous pain, he was able to get out of bed with great effort by supporting himself with a cane. When the time came for him to go see Solá, he asked for his saber, since he thought that it would serve as a more appropriate support than the cane. Using the saber as a cane, he was able to walk, but only with great difficulty. When he introduced himself to the governor, Solá addressed him in his customary hostile manner and accused him of having constructed the barge and erected buildings without obtaining permission from his superior. Captain Argüello replied calmly that he had not asked for permission because he, his officers, and his men were all living in ramshackle homes, which were threatening to fall down. Before that calamity could occur, everyone agreed to work like *peones* for their own benefit, so as not to place any burden whatsoever on the royal treasury. This reply enraged Solá. He turned around and hurried to the sofa to get the cane he had left there in case he might need it. Cane in hand, he headed toward Captain Argüello. Argüello was standing firmly, supported by the point of the saber, which was placed next to his injured right foot. He changed the position of the saber slightly, tilting it somewhat toward his left foot. This sudden movement startled Señor Solá. He jumped backward and asked why the saber had moved. The captain replied that the first reason was that his foot was injured and standing erect was causing him pain. The second reason was that, since he was an officer of decency and honor, he wanted to have the saber nearby, ready to draw and strike him with its cutting edge if the governor tried to beat him with the cane, as he knew that he had done with two of his own officers who were present there. The governor was quite surprised at this answer. He looked steadily at him, and later, after a period of silence in which he felt almost wounded by Señor Argüello's penetrating stare, he tossed the cane aside and extended his hand to him with the words "This is fitting behavior for an honorable military man. I ask you for your friendship, and I will leave the cane for the fainthearted who deserve it." Solá had Argüello sit down, and they became friends. They remained genuine comrades and confirmed their friendship many times throughout the governor's tenure.

About three months later Señor Solá left for the San Francisco presidio to visit and become familiar with that area. Since the Reverend Fathers assigned to each mission asked him to do so, he stopped for two or three days at each one along the way. When he arrived and saw that beautiful port, the best in the entire Mexican viceroyalty, with the presidio building left unfinished, he had to admit that he had caused damage by listening to erroneous reports and confiscating the barge. He also had not realized the difficulty in getting the barge back when it might be wanted, for the man who took it to Monterey never did return it.

Señor Argüello indicated to him that the lack of a barge was a greater problem than the unfinished construction project. The Kodiaks had entered the bay to hunt otters. Since there was no way to pursue them, they had gotten away with more than eight hundred pelts. We shall give an account of this episode. When Don Guillermo Davis was denied the permission he requested, he nevertheless sent out all of his canoes to hunt within the bay. They entered along the shore opposite the fort. The soldiers fired a few cannon shots to see if they could scare them off, but to no avail. Since the soldiers knew that the canoes were fashioned of sealskin and had to be occasionally taken out of the water to be dried and oiled, they always kept

N

0 20 40 60 80 100
Miles

o Ross

San Francisco □
San Jose •
Santa Clara •

Monterey

• San Luis Obispo

• Santa Barbara

Los Angeles

Old Spanish Trail

• San Pedro

• Hide and Tallow Ports

□ Whaling Stations

o Russian-American Company Outpost

Major Sea Otter Fields

• San Juan Capistrano
• San Luis Rey

• San Diego (hide depot)

Trade during the Spanish-Mexican period. Redrawn from *Historical Atlas of California*, Warren A. Beck and Ynez D. Haase. Copyright © 1974 by the University of Oklahoma Press.

a man on guard to keep an eye out for this. After a few days a sentry arrived with a report that at dusk the fishermen had gone ashore and beached some canoes in one of the most protected coves below the hill of San Bruno.[20]

When he received that news, Lieutenant Don José Sánchez immediately set out with twenty men. When they reached the vicinity of the Kodiak camp, they dismounted and crept along the top of the rock wall of the cove. In spite of the Indians' vigilance, they went unnoticed. Even though it was a very dark night, when they got within musket firing range, they fired at whatever they could see. In the volley, two Kodiaks were killed. They never found out how many were wounded, since the Indians immediately jumped in their canoes and retreated from the shore. Two canoes remained on land, since one man alone could not launch them because of the load of pelts that they contained. So Lieutenant Sánchez managed to seize both of them. Two men were assigned to bury the two dead men and to frighten away the other Indians, who quickly headed for Point Reyes, where the frigate was anchored.

The Kodiak canoes are made with strong, flexible branches. When they are tied together well, they create the approximate shape of a *chalupa*.[21] Next, they line this frame with sealskins, well prepared with the oil of the same animal. The skins are sewn together with sinews fashioned into cord for this purpose. Depending on its size, each vessel has two or three openings on top of the covering. The Kodiak inserts almost half his body through the hole and sits with his legs stretched out forward. Because they are accustomed to it, they are the only ones who can tolerate up to ten or twelve continuous hours in that uncomfortable position. Each person usually wears a shirt made from seal gut. When he sits in the manner that has been described, he ties the flaps of the shirt to a type of rim on the canoe openings. So, even though water might wash over them, not one drop makes its way into the canoe. They also carry a musket to defend themselves and to hunt, and they feel no repugnance eating the animals that they kill. If the animal is large, they use the guts to store their drinking water, no matter how bad-tasting it might become. Because their palates are already accustomed to decay, only one who suffers from a cold can bear being close to them, since the stench that they give off is intolerable even at a considerable distance.

Their skill in catching otters seems incredible. They have a type of arrow which they hurl accurately, without a bow, from a distance of up to eighty yards. They insert about half of the arrow, or slightly less, into a shaft, two yards long, which is grooved along the top. When they hurl the arrow, it runs backward along the groove until it hits the back part. Then it recoils and shoots out with great force, leaving the shaft behind in the individual's hand. The arrow carries a bladder hanging from a cord of sinews. When the otter is struck, the bladder detaches from the arrow. The tip of the arrow, which usually is made from bone and shaped like a harpoon, remains buried in the animal. Due to the force that the animal exerts when it

Kodiak Aleut dressed for the sea otter hunt, 1778. Sepia and watercolor drawing by John Webber. Photo by Hillel Burger. Courtesy of the Peabody Museum, Harvard University.

Sea otter hunt off Unalaska, 1827. Lithograph from a drawing by Friedrich H. von Kittlitz, in the atlas to *Lütke's Voyage, 1835.* Courtesy of the Yale Collection of Western Americana, Beinecke Rare Book and Manuscript Library.

swims, the arrowhead remains lodged in it. The bladder hinders the animal's ability to dive, because the pain that it feels does not allow it to garner enough strength to submerge the bladder. Meanwhile, in their swift vessels, the Kodiaks approach the animals and club them to death. Whenever two of them jointly pursue an otter, it will not escape, because they quickly tire the animals, get near them, and strike them as has been described. When a storm catches the Indians off guard and they cannot land, they protect themselves by joining together three or four canoes. They tie one to the other in the middle and on the ends, and thus form a raft so safe that it cannot capsize.

Besides the frigate which Don Guillermo Davis was using as his headquarters at Point Reyes, which was then under the command of Captain Don Santiago Smith (who later, as an old man, would become well known because of his love for Alta California and die in Sonoma),[22] he owned another frigate named the *Mercurio.* This vessel sailed along the coast down to Cabo San Lucas or San José, all the while engaged in smuggling under the authority of George Washington. On one of the many calls that the frigate made at the Bay of Santa Bárbara, a Spanish frigate of greater size, the *La Flora*, arrived and seized it. This news later reached the owner at Point Reyes, where two American ships, the frigate *Sultana* and the corvette *Urbana*, happened to be anchored.[23] Their captains, Isaac and Raynaldo, immediately suggested to Don Guillermo Davis that they all go together to recapture his frigate and seize the Spanish one. Davis explained that he appreciated their concern but that it was more important to him to remain where he was. He had calculated that the value of his seized frigate would not amount to one-tenth of what he would take away from Point Reyes. And he was correct, for he bagged eighty-five thousand otter and seal skins, which sold well in Canton and allowed him to amass an immense fortune.[24]

Returning to Señor Solá's doings in San Francisco, it is reported that after having visited the small fort, he wanted to take advantage of one of the beautiful afternoons which, because of the weather, were infrequent in that port during the months of June and July. He commanded Captain Argüello to order his troops to outfit themselves with their weapons. He wanted to lead some infantry maneuvers and see how they would handle themselves. After an hour and a half of maneuvers, punctuated by breaks, he spent another half an hour haranguing them. He urged them, in great detail, to continue to be highly regarded by their superiors. He also said that he would want to continue to be accurately informed about how things were proceeding. Finally, it would please him if the soldiers of the San Francisco presidio company maintained their integrity and good conduct and never gave their officers the slightest reason to reprimand them.

On his return journey to Monterey, he spent more time in the company of the mission Fathers. Each of them wished to impress him with gifts and kind words so as to gain the best friendship possible with him as a representative of Fernando VII. On his return to the capital he did not have to settle anything, since he found everything in the same good order as his predecessor Señor Arrillaga had left it. So he governed without making reforms and lived quietly.

· 2 ·

Around the middle of October 1818, two privateering frigates of the Frenchman Bouchard were sighted in the port of Monterey.[1] One of them stayed in the middle of the bay, out of cannon range, while the other one anchored so close to the *castillo* that the fire from the fort could not hit it except on the highest part of its masts.[2]

At that time the presidio companies were quite well organized. However, fewer than half the troops were on hand because the rest had to protect the missions within their jurisdiction, the Ranchos del Rey and the soldiers' horses.[3] Therefore, when Señor Solá inspected the troops after the two frigates appeared, he found himself with a force of two officers, nineteen cavalry soldiers, and one artillery lieutenant commander who did not have enough men to manage the large-caliber guns. In spite of this small force, he thought it best to order that they defend themselves and fight, if necessary. The identity of the ships was not known, and the captain of the anchored ship refused to reveal it even though he could communicate very well from aboard ship with those who were on land. Claiming that it was already getting dark, he offered to disclose that information early the next morning.[4]

A cannon had been positioned on the lower part of the beach next to the sea, commonly called El Mentidero, or "the gossiping place."[5] It was entrusted to Don José de Jesús Vallejo and four young militiamen. Although Vallejo and those with him were young, they demonstrated courage and skill. They operated with incredible and praiseworthy energy, but because they were *californios*, they did not even receive the thanks that they deserved, for no *hijo del país* was recognized by the Mexican government during its different periods.[6]

As soon as the next day's light allowed the captain of the anchored frigate to make out the objects at which he wanted to aim, he opened fire on the principal homes of the presidio.[7] But at the same time, he began to receive hits on his waterline from El Mentidero. After each hit, so much water would pour into his vessel that within a few minutes the pumps could not empty even half of the water that was entering. Señor Vallejo's cannon, positioned at a distance of less than a rifle shot away from the frigate, was protected only by a barricade of loose earth and branches, which absorbed or deflected the enemy shots. Fortunately, no shots penetrated the embrasure, so Vallejo's cannon could fire without being hit or wasting one cannonball in its constant and accurate volley. The crew of the frigate did not have time to patch the holes that were being made so quickly, and they began to cry out that they were in danger. They loudly proclaimed their surrender and begged that the shore battery cease fire for the sake of God and his heavenly court.[8] When Don Manuel Gómez, the artillery commander of the fort, heard their pleas, he was deeply moved and ordered a cease-fire.[9] But as soon as Señor Solá, who was watching from the presidio, noticed that Señor Vallejo's cannon had ceased firing, he demanded to know the reason why. He ordered that the firing be resumed if nothing had happened to the shore battery. When Vallejo received the order, he immediately resumed firing, with even more zeal because of the short break which he and his men had taken.

The cries from the frigate began anew, and they caused the artillery commander to become greatly enraged. Believing that Señor Vallejo was mocking the cease-fire command he had received from a superior officer, he sent a second order, accompanied by great threats, to stop the firing. Vallejo received this order at about the same time that another order arrived from the governor, who was still observing everything closely, to continue firing until he had sunk the frigate. Here one sees how the contradiction between two leaders results in disastrous consequences for a lower-ranking officer, who is always the one to suffer. Don Jesús Vallejo, like all young men filled with martial zeal who aspire to the glory of performing difficult feats, wished to finish what he had begun so successfully. He also preferred to obey the governor's orders. But everything turned against him because of the artillery commander's proud, dim-witted disposition and lack of military expertise. Filled with rage because he believed that Don Jesús Vallejo did not want to respect his orders, Gómez gave the brutal order that a heavy cannon be brought toward him so he could fire it at Don Jesús Vallejo. Jesús' father, Don Ignacio Vallejo, a distinguished

Monterey Bay. From the *Illustrated London News*, Feb. 10, 1849, 84. Courtesy of the California State Library, Sacramento.

cavalry sergeant who was also at the fort, saw what was happening. He begged the commander to permit him to go and carry the new cease-fire order to his son. Because he was highly regarded, he received permission, and he hastily went down and strongly addressed his son: "Young man, I have been tremendously satisfied to see how much you have done, but now the commander and I strongly order you to abandon that cannon immediately." Young Vallejo first stared at the frigate and then directed a look of anger and contempt at the fort. Then he ripped from his body the straps that supported the equipment for the cannon and angrily threw them to the ground. The four young men with him did the same, and they all withdrew together to a house outside the presidio.

Those on the frigate simply wanted to escape from the hardships in which they found themselves, and they were ready to take advantage of the opportunity that presented itself. After the firing had ceased, they moved all the artillery to one side of the vessel so that the damaged side could raise itself up. Then they fully loaded all of their small boats with muskets and ammunition and launched them. Instead of kneeling in homage before the conceited commander of the fort, as he expected, they set sail toward the other frigate, which then went toward Point Almejas. There they put ashore four hundred men and two well-mounted cannons in one of its fine coves.[10] Taking a small detour so as to pass behind the fort, they set out to take the presidio.[11]

With these sad consequences of his imprudent compassion, Commander

Part I

Gómez quickly experienced the great difference that exists between the joy of the victor and the sorrow of the vanquished. For now he had to escape, since his artillery was positioned so that he could neither prevent the landing nor hamper the enemy on its march. Therefore, he abandoned his stronghold and headed for the presidio to meet with the governor. The governor greeted him by condemning his conduct. He also berated him in the most degrading terms that his tremendous anger suggested to him, stressing how shameful it was that Gómez found himself forced to flee, when a scarce two or three hours earlier his triumph had been inevitable. Since it was not prudent to delay any longer, Solá gathered together the few troops that he had and left to set up camp at the Rancho del Rey, located five leagues away on a beautiful plain along the banks of the river.

The officers and the soldiers would have preferred to take their families away instead of accompanying the governor in his hasty escape. However, their military duty obliged them to leave their families to the mercy of Providence and to escape as best they could. By a careful calculation, one can affirm that each *californio* married couple brings ten children into the world.[12] Any traveler who might say that he saw various childless couples also should have known that an equal or greater number of these couples had more than twenty and even twenty-five children. Now then, consider what anguish the parents, principally the mothers, experienced. Carrying the youngest ones, and practically dragging their older ones by the hand, they could take nothing from their homes but their children. Strengthened by fear, they walked quickly and arrived dead tired at the encampment where the troops were situated.[13]

Bouchard's troops marched unchallenged into the presidio, which they found completely abandoned. After they had taken everything out of the homes that they could use or carry, they set fire to all of them. For the next few days they stayed mainly at the fort and repaired the frigate as well as they could. To break up the cannons more easily, they loaded and buried them, muzzle down, more than halfway into the ground. Thus, by firing them they were able to break them apart and pound out any remains which were partially usable.

Soon after Señor Solá had arrived at the Rancho del Rey, he sent communiqués to the presidios at Santa Bárbara and San Francisco, ordering the immediate dispatch of any available soldiers. He also ordered the company captains not to move from their positions and to keep him informed of events. Because of the discipline that he maintained, the captain of the

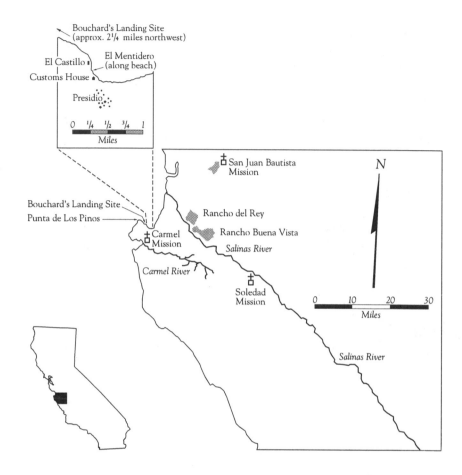

Bouchard's Landing Site
(approx. 2¹/₄ miles northwest)

El Mentidero
(along beach)

El Castillo ▪

Customs House ▪

Presidio

0   ¹/₄   ¹/₂   ³/₄   1
Miles

San Juan Bautista
Mission

N

Bouchard's Landing Site
Punta de Los Pinos

Rancho del Rey

Rancho Buena Vista

Salinas River

Carmel
Mission

Carmel River

Soledad
Mission

0   10   20   30
Miles

Salinas River

Monterey Bay area, ca. 1840, with an insert showing Old Monterey

San Francisco company was not caught unprepared. He did not have to make any preparations, and he was able to set out very quickly. He and his men marched double-time until they reached the governor. When he first saw the governor, he begged him to overlook the fact that he personally had escorted his soldiers. His reason for this was so they would arrive without delay and, also, so he could request, as energetically as possible, permission to share in any hardships his men might experience. The governor was greatly pleased by this and expressed his approval. He congratulated him on his safe arrival and appointed him second in command.[14]

They spent the next several days doing very little. Since they already had gathered together more than two hundred men, he suggested to the governor that they go to the presidio to harass Bouchard from the edge of the pine grove or to see if they could take prisoners, since it was known that some men would go out to hunt in the nearby forests. The governor, alleging that he wanted to keep his forces united in case the enemy tried to attack him, did not permit this. Therefore, they spent a few more days in their camp. This gave Bouchard enough time to repair his frigate. Since he was more inclined to wreak havoc than to be peaceful, he left Monterey with the intention of visiting some points along the coast. The first stop was the Ortega family's Rancho del Refugio, nine leagues away from the Santa Bárbara presidio.[15]

The residents of that ranch, as well as the rest of those living along the coast, had been informed of the incident in Monterey. As soon as they saw the two frigates, they sent word to the presidio and prepared to flee. When the ships approached the land, they put their boats in the water, and about fifty armed men came ashore. They went to the ranch, which was a little less than a league away from the seashore. Finding the homes unoccupied, they took what they wanted from them and then burned them all. As they were returning to the beach, about halfway down the road they encountered thirty men from the Santa Bárbara presidio. These men had left as soon as they received the news of the ship's arrival, and they had traveled at a gallop to try to prevent the landing. But from a distance they experienced the sorrow of seeing the smoke rising from the homes and realized that the damage already had been done. Nevertheless, they kept on until they met up with the arsonists. Then each commander quickly prepared his men for action, and they began to exchange fire. Bouchard's men quickly realized that, despite their numerical superiority, they were at a disadvantage, so they retreated as they fired. Fleeing as rapidly as they could, they quickly arrived at the beach and immediately embarked. A number of those who fled were injured, and in the rush two prisoners were left behind. When the men from Santa Bárbara took stock of their own situation, they discovered that only four horses had been injured.[16]

As soon as the band boarded the frigates and stowed the small boats, the vessels sailed down to the Bay of San Juan Capistrano, where they made their last landing. The Reverend Father and the Indians had fled the mission. When Bouchard's men entered the mission grounds, they set fire to different parts of the main building. However, they respected the church at the request of a few among them who said they were Roman Catholics. After setting this last fire, they took off for the southern ocean.[17]

Hipólito Bouchard. Courtesy of the Colton Hall Museum, City of Monterey Collection.

It was later learned from reliable sources that this Frenchman had out-fitted a frigate and had acquired from the rebels of Buenos Aires a letter of marque against the King of Spain. Bouchard had experienced a period of success and, with his two frigates, considered himself to be quite rich. But luck is not constant, and in the end things turned out quite adversely for him. All his undertakings resulted in the opposite of what he expected. As proof, I will cite one of many examples.

When Bouchard found out that the Spanish frigate *María*, owned by Don Alonso Morgao, was in the port of San Blas and about to transport silver to Manila, he went to wait for it near those Islands.[18] There, he lay in wait for a few days. But the Luzón merchants discovered his plans and requested that the governor dispatch one or more government vessels to protect the *María*. So the corvette *Fidelidad* set sail to pursue Bouchard. However, he had been warned. He wanted to avoid the *Fidelidad* without abandoning his position along the route he was expecting the *María* to take. Unfortunately for him, he was not familiar with either of the two vessels. When the *María* appeared unexpectedly, Bouchard held his position and waited hesitantly for it to approach him. No one on the *María* knew the identity of this other ship they had encountered. Don Domingo Yndart, the first pilot of the *María*, suggested to the captain and owner that they attempt to speak with the other captain, to determine the identity of the frigate and to obtain some news from Manila, if indeed the other ship had come from there. This suggestion was not received favorably, perhaps because of their genuine friendship or because Yndart was in command. But Yndart paid no attention to the doubts of others, because he wanted to satisfy his own curiosity. So he gave orders to set the course in Bouchard's direction. This maneuver was executed with such speed and skill that, when Bouchard observed it, he immediately ordered more sails unfurled and headed in another direction, saying that the frigate was not the one that he wanted to ambush, but rather was the one pursuing him. Fortunately, those who should have been taken prisoner, while their vessel was being sacked, passed right by.

The following day Bouchard encountered the *Fidelidad*. Its commander, Don José Martija, realized that the other vessel was swifter and that a chase would be useless. He decided to try trickery, so he closed his portholes and maneuvered very slowly, always making sure that his bow was pointed at Bouchard. Fortunately, the Frenchman was certain that this was the frigate *María*. He came upon it with the intent of boarding and seizing it. This was exactly what the experienced Spaniard expected. Martija intended to seize Bouchard's ship, so he hid his armed men and allowed only the crewmen who were absolutely necessary for the operation of the sails to be visible as the other ship approached. As soon as the two vessels were side by side, the Spaniard immediately opened his portholes and fired all of his artillery from that side. Bouchard received so much damage that he did not try to do anything except escape. His life was in as much real danger from this battle between unequal forces as if he were about to be hanged from a yardarm. But luck did not abandon him entirely, because he was able to take advantage of a light breeze that carried him out of danger. Although the major part of his rigging was broken, his upper works were gone, and he had lost a substantial number of men, the speed of his frigate saved him. This loss, compared with the benefit that would have resulted from his seizure of the more than one million Mexican pesos aboard the frigate *María*, was a prelude to his subsequent ruin. About five years later he died in Lima in such abject poverty that he even received food as charity.[19]

Although from his camp Governor Solá did not openly express his fears that Bouchard would head to the anchorage of Mission Santa Cruz after leaving Monterey, he did forward some orders to the authorities there. An official note dated from the time that Don Joaquín Buelna was the judge of the Villa de Branciforte was later found in the government archives.[20] The note said: "In response to the earlier order from Your Lordship, I am informing you that two large ships were near here yesterday, and one frigate with three masts came close to shore, and we believed that they were going to land. It seems that Your Lordship read my mind, because we already had prepared the pots of food with one hundred or so ingredients so that they could eat, if they came ashore, but they left, and they have not returned again."[21]

Sometimes Solá exhibited characteristics of generosity typical of the Vizcayan personality. At other times he would behave like a true descendant, or at least a disciple, of the Borgias, as shown by the aforementioned communiqué.[22] But during that period when everyone was petrified of the mortal sin of speaking or saying something about the faults of a priest or a superior, the *californios* knew how to restrain themselves and their families. The territorial governor was not open to public criticism. He could, of course, be admired as much as one wanted, but the admiration for him was tempered with appropriate circumspection and with your cap placed firmly on your head.[23]

When the watchmen reported that Bouchard's frigates had set sail from Monterey Bay and disappeared, the governor broke camp and sent the troops back to their respective presidios. He went to Mission Soledad, where he gave orders for the reconstruction of the presidio. All of the nearby missions cooperated by providing laborers, the necessary provisions and tools, and oxen and wagons. Because of his skill and great energy, Sergeant Don Ignacio Vallejo was appointed to direct the project and to oversee all the jobs. This honorable man immediately parceled out all the tasks. He was present to supervise the workmen at every job site, even when it meant tiring his horses and himself by riding hard from one point to another. With a fine group of workmen and with the able direction of Señor Vallejo, the buildings were completed very quickly and proved to be better than the previous ones. While he was building the homes, Señor Vallejo was told to build a fine home for himself and his family as a form of compensation. But because of his great sense of moderation, it seemed to him to be an abuse of trust to build the home outside the presidio, so he built it in a corner of the square. During his lifetime the home was his alone. Afterward his family experienced the sorrow of having to leave it, since it was a military building.

When the governor was informed that the presidio homes were finished, he left Mission Soledad, where he was already very disgruntled. Upon his arrival in Monterey he was delighted to see the homes, superior in every way to the ones that he left when he had fled.[24]

As a result of the report that the governor sent to the viceroy about Bouchard's actions, the captain general ordered that the number of troops in Alta California be increased. An infantry company from Tepic and seventy-five men from the Mazatlán squadron were dispatched. They arrived toward the end of the year 1819. From the moment that the troops from Tepic set foot on the beach of Monterey, robberies, excesses peculiar to coarse men, and depraved practices entirely unfamiliar to the *californios* began to be experienced. One can truthfully say that during that year robberies, stabbings, assassinations, and other actions by despicable people occurred. And without the slightest fear of being untruthful, I will say even more. In their public and private conduct, none of the officials sent from Mexico during this time behaved with honor. Indeed, they were less honorable than the corporals and sergeants of the presidio companies, if the meaning of *honor* includes the concept of honesty.[25]

As a Spaniard devoted to Fernando VII and fearful that the events of 1810 would repeat themselves, the governor experienced his greatest disappointment in 1821. In 1822 the war brigantine *San Carlos* arrived under the command of Don José Narváez. Aboard ship was Canon Don Agustín Fernández, commissioned by Emperor Agustín I, who had given him broad authority to act as he deemed most just and proper in political, military, and ecclesiastical spheres.[26] As soon as he arrived in Monterey, he began a thorough investigation about why the Russian-American Company was occupying lands within territorial limits, such as the fortification at Point Ross, and the establishment at Bodega Point.[27] When he had satisfied himself on that point, he addressed other issues, especially the matter of Governor Solá's replacement. He appointed Don Luis Argüello to the position, even though there was another company captain with more seniority. Later Fernández sent him an order to come down to the capital to assume the political and military command. Señor Argüello showed that order to his troops. Although it saddened him to have to leave them for a few months, he assured them that his absence would not be long because he could not live happily apart from them. A number of them attempted to speak, but their voices failed them, and tears replaced their words. Finally, the soldiers whose enlistments had expired broke the silence and begged to be discharged, even waiving their right to veterans' benefits. They knew that they could not get along well with their lieutenant, Don Ignacio Martínez, who would become commander. Their wishes were granted. The day that Argüello departed from San Francisco was one of the saddest days those soldiers ever experienced. Each one wanted to be appointed an assistant or a member of the escort that was to accompany the captain.

Canon Fernández was waiting for Argüello to arrive in order to install him as governor. After officially doing this, he and Señor Solá sailed from the port of Monterey, stopping to visit the presidios of Santa Bárbara and San Diego along the way.[28]

· 3 ·

During his tenure as governor, Don Luis Argüello took pleasure from the tranquility and genuine harmony maintained by the *californios*. That is how the year 1822 ended. During part of 1823 the Indians from the missions in the middle of the mission chain plotted an uprising with unexpected discretion.[1] The ultimate goal was to kill the *gente de razón*, those who did not belong to the Indian race.[2]

It had been observed that since the conquest of the territory, fortunately, the Indians did not band many tribes together for mutual defense. Although the distance from one *ranchería* to another was short, rivalries were common. Bloody wars often arose over boundary disputes, especially during the time of the wild fruit harvests. Violating recognized boundaries to gather fruit, without previous permission from the owner or leaders, was considered thievery or a declaration of war, and fighting would begin.[3]

According to the annual statistics provided to the governor by the Reverend Fathers who administered the missions, the number of those "reduced" to the missions in the year 1823 was quite large. These numbers gave the Indians confidence that their plot would succeed. Missions San Luis Obispo, La Purísima Concepción, Santa Ynés, Santa Bárbara, San Buenaventura, and San Fernando indeed were ripe for revolt. They all agreed to attack at the same time, at the hour of Sunday mass, so they could catch the mission soldiers and the Fathers off guard and unarmed.[4]

Messages traveled from one mission to another with such an incredible speed that people who never saw how news was received in Alta California find it difficult to believe. The horses, running faster than a gallop, had such stamina that they could cover twenty leagues in three hours. Also, the Indians were accustomed to riding without a saddle, which could add as much as two-thirds to a rider's weight. Thus they put no more than their

N

0 20 40 60 80 100
Miles

Native groups, 1770. Redrawn from *Historical Atlas of California*, Warren A. Beck and Ynez D. Haase. Copyright © 1974 by the University of Oklahoma Press.

backsides on the horse's hindquarters, and the lesser weight gave them an advantage over others when they ran the horses. The horse's hindquarters would come through a long ride in good condition, while every limb of the rider's body that would scrape against them would be severely injured, even bloodied. Yet the messages were delivered with great speed and discretion.

Finally, through an Indian woman devoted to his family, Captain Don

Mission Santa Ynés in the late nineteenth century. Courtesy of the California State Library, Sacramento.

José de la Guerra y Noriega found out that the Indians from the missions within his jurisdiction were plotting an uprising that would erupt at the end of the week. He subsequently took precautions by giving the orders he thought most fitting. However, he did not give much credence to the Indians' determination.

Sunday was the day chosen for the war cry, but at Mission Santa Ynés it was given prematurely, on Saturday at about two in the afternoon, when Father Francisco Xavier Uría was taking his afternoon nap, even though he had discovered the intentions of his neophytes.[5] They would have killed him in his sleep, but a young Indian servant who loved him very much went running to awaken him and warn him that they were ready to kill him and that he must get up quickly. When the Father heard this shocking information, he jumped from his bed and looked out the window. He saw a throng of Indians, painted and equipped with arrows, heading toward the door of his house. This Reverend Father was an eminently religious man, but he made a habit of using vulgar words so that the Indians would not take advantage of his kindness. He was a Vizcayan to the depths of his soul, so much so that he even owned a musket with the horseshoe brand from Eibar.[6] At that critical moment he made a decision. By chance, a lay person was with him, and he quickly armed him with a musket. To give his companion a good example to imitate, he shot and killed the first Indian who dared to set foot on his threshold. When those who were following the victim saw how effective the force of the Vizcayan musket was, they held back a bit. The Father did not waste any time. He readied a second shot and aimed it directly at one of the better painted Indians who had shot an arrow at him. The Indian dropped dead the instant he was hit by the bullet. By this time the lay person already had three arrows in him and was spewing blood from his mouth. The Father's keen eye saw everything, and he quickly went over to help him. He pulled two of the arrows that were torturing him out of his chest. Then he draped some pieces of deer skin around his neck. These cloths kept him from being killed by the many arrows that struck him. Meanwhile, the Father's shots were becoming accurate and deadly. His arms, quickly loading and firing, moved even more skillfully than they did when he was collecting alms. Fortunately, the Indians retreated, and so he went out to the hall. There he noticed that one of the Indians, also armed with a musket, was stalking him from behind a pillar. The Father then scurried behind another pillar to protect himself. Each was setting a trap for the other, but in the end, the Indian was less careful. While still behind the pillar, he exposed his left elbow or arm. In that very spot he received a gunshot wound which shattered his bone up to the shoulder.

The soldiers living on the mission grounds were also active. They were well protected, for not one arrow penetrated their *cueras* (a type of jacket fashioned from six or seven layers of leather sewn together) to reach their skin.[7] When the Indians realized that they did not have any advantage over the barricaded Father, lay person, and soldiers, they decided that fire might give them an advantage. They set various parts of the homes ablaze in an attempt to reduce everything to ash so they could seize the Father, the lay person, and the soldiers when they would be forced out into the open. Just as the flames were reaching their greatest intensity, Sergeant Don Anastasio Carrillo arrived with a squad of soldiers. He had been sent to reinforce the garrison in anticipation of the outbreak of the revolt. Fortunately, he always arrived just in time to bring relief or prevent a greater calamity. Since the rebels were not expecting him, they fled in surprise. Later, those who had not taken part in the uprising appeared and asked for some tools to put out the fire. They managed to do so, but only after two-thirds of the main buildings had been destroyed.

Since the distance between Mission Santa Ynés and Mission La Purísima is the shortest according to the order in which the coastal missions had

Typical mission corridor in the late nineteenth century. Courtesy of the California State Library, Sacramento.

been founded, the Indians from Mission La Purísima found out very quickly that their neighbors had already begun the war. Therefore, they also began to paint themselves in order to attack the soldiers right away. These Indians were very fond of the two mission Fathers and the corporal of the garrison because of his great honesty and generosity.[8] So they promised him that, if he turned over his weapons, they would treat him with as much respect as they had intended to show the Fathers. However, his friends the four soldiers, as well as their families, would have to die, because they, like the other *gente de razón* at the mission, wanted to kill all of the Indians. They said it would be impossible for five men, surrounded by a throng of angry warriors, to defend themselves. They warned the corporal that, if he did not grant their request, they would kill him as well, even though it would pain them to see him dead and they would later grieve for him. The brave Corporal Don Tiburcio Tapia was undaunted by the large number of warriors and their terrible, angry threats. He calmly replied that the soldiers would never surrender out of fear. As long as they lived, they would never hand over to the Indians the very weapons they had received to defend themselves. He told them that he was already prepared, and they could very well begin an attack whenever they wanted. Almost in unison, the Indians let out a shriek or war cry, and the battle began instantly. The five determined men courageously resisted the attack. Their adversaries realized that, despite their greater numbers, they could not harm the five combatants. Instead, they seized and set fire to the homes. They expected that the soldiers, who were so few in number, would all rush over to protect their families from being burned and prevent the Indians from setting a larger fire. The Indians did not anticipate what happened. The intense flames quickly consumed the timbers, and the tile roofs collapsed. There was soon only one house left untouched by fire and able to shelter the families. However, it soon caught on fire as well, and the people were forced to abandon it.

As they were about to leave the house, the experienced corporal encouraged them not to fear being killed. They could save themselves by walking quickly toward the first homes that had burned. This they could easily do, even though they would have to walk over live embers and might suffer some burns on their feet. They decided to do this. They covered the women and children with blankets as well as they could, even adding some leather from chairs to protect them from the arrows. After double-checking the exit, the soldiers fired a lively round, which forced the Indians to retreat a bit. The women and children then ran through a shower of arrows. They were so frightened that they did not feel the burns on their feet as they hurried out. Only one woman was injured. To protect her child better, she covered him with some of her blankets, and she was struck by an arrow which penetrated about three inches into her belly. As it turned out, even though she was injured in her noble part, she recovered rapidly.

The Indians, unable to clear out the soldiers, desperately decided to try to strike a massive and decisive blow. But their bravery was not steadfast, for when they saw the first or bravest fall dead, those who were following behind fell back. One of the chiefs was designated their leader. He shouted a request to Corporal Tapia to cease fire so that he could present new proposals. That was exactly what the soldiers wanted most, since they had run out of ammunition and were defenseless. The Indians proposed to let them and their families go unharmed if they handed over their weapons and headed for the safety of Mission Santa Ynés, where, the Indians knew, Sergeant Don Anastasio Carrillo had arrived with more soldiers. The corporal replied again that he preferred to die fighting rather than earn the reprimand of his superiors by agreeing to their demands. When the Indians heard this, they went to see the young priest, Father Blas Ordaz. They asked him to go and convince Corporal Tapia that they loved him very much and did not want to kill him. If he handed over his weapons, they would set him, the other soldiers, and their families free. They promised the Father that, if he convinced the corporal, they would not go back on their word. The Father consented to try to carry out this task. Either because of his great power of persuasion or because of the lack of ammunition, the corporal agreed to the terms. However, he set the condition that the Father not leave their side from the moment that they handed over their weapons and especially that he accompany them to Santa Ynés. With these understandings, everyone went to the Father's house and handed over his weapons. When the Indians had them in their possession, they refused to comply with their promises. The leader claimed that, while he had acted in good faith when he made his offers, his people now wanted to kill them all instead of obeying him. With this in mind, the Indians rushed toward the door. Fortunately, the Father had time to close it. When he turned around to look at his defenders, he found himself surrounded by women kneeling and begging for confession, so he told them to confess their sins. All of them, terrified or confused during these dire moments, began to speak out loud at once, as if each were alone with the Father. Those poor souls, imprudent because of their fear, began to disclose things which their husbands, who were present, should not know. The Father quickly ordered them to be quiet and simply to recite the act of contrition instead of confessing, so that he could grant them absolution.[9]

With that very serious obligation fulfilled, the Father turned his attention to the Indians. He called to the leader, in whom he had more confidence, and spoke kindly to him. Because the Father was aware of the *alcalde's* standing at the mission, or perhaps out of respect for the Indian's words, he opened the door. But then the Father began to speak with superiority and reprimanded the Indians for compromising their word and good faith. The Indian then addressed himself to the others and took them to task for the last decision they had made. After conferring with them for a while, he turned and said, "Father, I have just assured them that you will fulfill your word. Now leave quickly with your people for Santa Ynés. I will accompany you until you are almost there. Let's go then, before the Indians change their minds again." The Father knew his neophytes very well and did not want to waste that favorable opportunity, so he set out immediately with his group. They walked, despite the fact that some of those poor women had no skin left on the soles of their feet. They walked briskly in that condition until they arrived safely at their destination.[10]

That same day the Indians killed two *hombres de razón* who worked at the mission. They also killed a member of the Sepúlveda family of Los Angeles, who unfortunately was returning from Monterey on foot.[11] This incident was regarded as a major crime. Determined to defend themselves and not be subjected to a punishment equal to the crime, they barricaded themselves with whatever they could find nearby.

The Fathers had purchased two cannons of about eight-pound caliber. They always had enough gunpowder to fire one as a celebratory salute to the patron saint and on other solemn occasions. A native artisan named Pacomio mounted these cannons on very fine carriages and then placed them in a redoubt constructed by an Indian stonemason named Mariano.[12] This was constructed as perfectly as if it had been done by an engineer. But he could not have positioned the carriages in a worse spot, as will be explained later. Those who had been able to obtain firearms formed a company of marksmen. They formed their parapet with the roof planks of the main house, creating embrasures as necessary and always keeping themselves protected by the tiles of the roof. They believed themselves to be as safe there, offensively and defensively, as if they were in a great fort.

Mission Santa Bárbara, 1879. Courtesy of the California State Library, Sacramento.

The Indians from Santa Bárbara began the attack on the very day and hour upon which they had agreed, although they were aware that everyone already knew of their intent and planned to do battle against them.[13] The presidio was very close, only a gunshot away, so the soldiers posted there were easily joined by those from the garrison. Their families remained in place without experiencing the scare suffered by the families at Santa Ynés and La Purísima.

It was the general opinion that Captain Don José de la Guerra y Noriega possessed, professionally, no more than his second last name. The following item is taken from the accounts of one of his brothers-in-law.[14] When this captain left the presidio to fight the Indians of the nearby mission, the battle began with little zeal on either side. There was simply a leisurely exchange of long-range gunfire, without any consequence or bloodshed.[15] After a few minutes the noonday bell tolled, and a voice called out, "Cease fire." After the captain's order had been obeyed, he took off his hat and began to recite the "Angelus." Apparently the meal hour had arrived, and they had to fulfill that obligation first so that they might return to firing later with more vehemence. In fact, they returned to fight "English style," that is to say, with full stomachs. The method must be very effective, because, noting that the soldiers were firing with much more energy than they had been before eating, the Indians fled.[16]

Most of the fugitives did not stop until they reached the tules.[17] Others, who considered themselves very brave, went to the general barracks of Mission La Purísima, where they enthusiastically waited for the attack. They spent a number of days in this manner. Reports sent to the governor informed him of everything that had happened at the rebellious missions. He ordered the cavalry and infantry companies from Monterey to go down, and he sent along enough artillerymen to handle a large cannon. All the troops were to be commanded by Don Mariano Estrada. Once on their way, they proceeded without any interruption to Mission La Purísima, where they took up positions on the most dominant point, a gunshot away from the homes.[18]

The mission was situated between two low ridges which create a narrow ravine. Fortunately, since the Indian rebels had constructed their redoubt there, it was impossible for them to defend themselves from cannon fire aimed at them from the ridges. They realized the problem as soon as the soldiers fired the first shots, so they quickly abandoned their position and sought refuge at the main house. There the Indian marksmen who stationed themselves on the top floor tormented the troops the most. The commander, out of consideration for the venerable Father, whose bed was directly below the feet of the Indian marksmen, did not want to allow Flores, his best artilleryman, to dislodge the Indians with the cannon. For the Father was too old and sick to be able to get up from his bed. However, when Estrada saw one of his soldiers die from a shot that passed clear through his chest to his back, he decided that he must order that the cannon be fired. The shot hit about halfway up the slope of the roof, directly above where the Indians were firing. Because of the way the homes were constructed, a huge portion of the main wall was blown apart. The severity of the blow caused the building to shake and the Indians to tremble. Thoroughly frightened, they did not know what recourse to take. Their favorite one is to flee, but this was impractical for them because they were completely surrounded. Two more cannon shots were directed at the pillars of the corridor in an attempt not to destroy the building or have any of the debris fall on the Father. With this, all of the Indians lost their nerve, with the exception of one person, whose conduct deserves mention, even though some will doubt the incident. Others will ridicule the beliefs, perhaps seeing fit to add gratuitous criticism. Others, raising their thoughts higher, will solemnly ponder a very remarkable event.

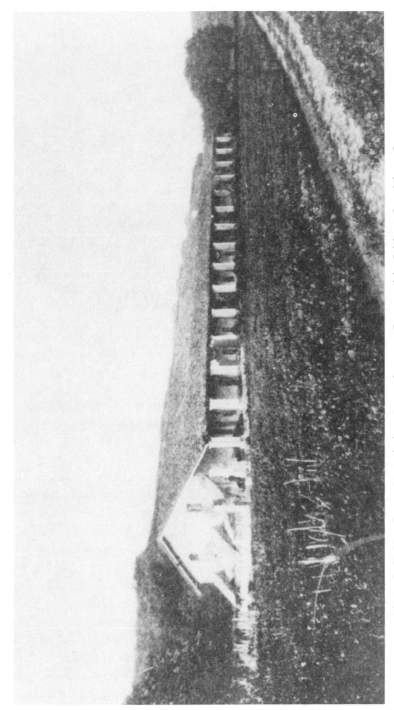

Mission La Purísima Concepción in the late nineteenth century. Courtesy of the California State Library, Sacramento.

Typical tile roof framework, at Mission San Fernando in the late nineteenth century. Courtesy of the California State Library, Sacramento.

It is known and well proved that the Indians of Alta California, especially the adults, who were called Christians simply because they had been sprinkled with baptismal water, were never true Catholics. They would leave their *ranchería* or their errant lifestyle and, out of fear, deceit, or self-interest, head for the mission that was beckoning them.[19] They listened to the Fathers preaching the gospel, but they did not understand what was being said. The interpreters should have concerned themselves with translating the concepts which corresponded to the oratory, but they were in the same position as the other Indians. The words were foreign to them, and they could only translate them poorly. And they really did not believe in the meaning of the words that they did understand, especially those regarding faith. For their strongest conviction was "What is visible is real." Years of experience demonstrated that the catechists who more or less fulfilled their obligation never gained the attention or earned the reputation of the better-known *hechiceros*.[20] The Indians eagerly sought out these *hechiceros* to hear them describe the favors which the devil bestowed on those who served him well. One could see in the missions' baptismal registries that Catholicism was making great progress with this type of Christian. In

Father Narciso Durán and an indigenous child. From Duflot de Mofras, *Exploration du territoire de l'Orégon, des Californies et de la mer vermeille*, 200. Courtesy of the California State Library, Sacramento.

order to give a further indication of their tenuous commitment, I shall offer another example before the one I just mentioned.

At Mission San José, administered by Reverend Father Narciso Durán, a number of Indians from the Cosumes tribe appeared and claimed that they wanted to become Christians. A few days later they received the baptismal water and the usual blanket and shirt. A custom had been established that a neophyte who had not appeared for work or who had committed some minor crime during the week would receive a dozen or more lashes at the church door after Sunday mass. Then, as a sign of submission, he would go and kiss the Father's hand. Among those to whom this happened was one of the Cosumes, but he would not conform to the formalities of the custom. When he approached the Father, he took off his shirt and wrapped it up in the blanket. Then he threw them both at the reverend feet and said, "Father, take your Christianity. I don't want it anymore because I am returning to my land as a gentile." The Catholicism of those poor souls was more or less of this sort. I shall now return to the story about the Indian from Mission La Purísima, whose actions will explain this more clearly.

When everyone, confused by fear of the soldiers and the havoc wrought by the cannon, was running from one end of the mission compound to another looking for a place to hide, this Indian entered the church. He remained there with his gaze fixed on a Christ figure about a foot in length. When he finished contemplating that image of the crucified Christ, he said, as if addressing him directly, "Now I will know if you are God almighty, as the Father says. Carrying you completely hidden so that no one will see you, I am going alone to fight against all of the soldiers. If they don't kill me or shoot me, I will serve you well until I die." He immediately took down the figure, hung it around his neck, and covered it with his blanket so that it would not get in his way. He approached to within arrow shot range and stood fast against the soldiers. He continued fighting until he had shot the last arrow in his quiver. Then he immediately turned around and walked at a normal pace toward the church. Many shots were fired at him, but not one hit him. He fulfilled his promise and served as a sacristan, living an exemplary life as a true Catholic until he died.

The other Indians were panicked by the power of the cannonballs and did not know what to do. Finally they resolved to beg the Father to go and intercede for them, but when he showed them that he could not even stand up, they decided to carry him out in his own bed.[21] In this manner, they brought him to Captain Don José de la Guerra y Noriega, who had just arrived and taken command. After listening and agreeing to a number of the Father's requests, he assembled all of the now disarmed Indians to try to discover the identities of the principal instigators of the revolt. When he found out who they were, he ordered them shot on the spot.[22] Others were exiled in perpetuity to various presidios, where they were sentenced to a period of forced labor. Pacomio and Mariano were assigned to the Monterey presidio, where, on account of their good behavior, they found steady employment.[23]

The governor was sent a communiqué detailing everything that had occurred. He had the pleasure of learning that the rebellious Indians at the missions had been brought under control. However, the fugitives in the tules were yet to be caught.[24] There was no alternative but to go after them. The company from the Santa Bárbara presidio was ordered to join the operation. Captain Don José Noriega was put in charge, accompanied by a chaplain.[25] The departure took place as soon as the necessary provisions had been prepared. When the expedition arrived at the tules, the commander first decided on gentle measures to attract the Indians.[26] But they had decided not to return to the missions and expressed the low regard in which they generally held the inhabitants of California.[27] Yet at the same time they revered Reverend Father Vicente Sarría for his many virtues. Only he had the necessary power of persuasion to calm the Indian's fears. The commander made several promises, assuring them of their safety and promising to forget the events of the past. The Indians were persuaded to return to the missions, and everything ended peacefully.[28]

During that time, the rearing of large livestock had increased so much that owners earned little profit from cattle and none whatsoever from horses and were even forced to kill a great number of mares and foals. In addition, many mares would flee and join the countless other horses which were already crowding the fields. Since they did not belong to anyone, these horses multipled at such a rate that travelers in the habit of riding at a gallop at great distances with six or more horses were endangered. For when these horses would see others, they would charge ahead and try to join them. If they succeeded, they would be lost, since it was impossible to separate them out. All that a poor man living in the countryside had to do if he wished to obtain fine horses was to tame them. He could ask permission of the owners or simply take them from among the strays. These horses generally proved to be excellent animals. The best horses did not sell for more than five pesos, and good workhorses, considered only average, could be obtained for six reales or one peso each.[29]

None of the cattle breeders ventured into the dairy business because there was no use or market for their products. Therefore, it was very common at many *haciendas* for the owners to say that while they had six or seven thousand head of cattle, they could not offer a traveler a glass of milk if he requested it. They gladly would offer him a calf, but they only used the meat they could eat at one sitting. They would dump the rest out in the same fields where they would sleep or nap while their animals grazed and rested.

With respect to commerce, when ships from Peru or San Blas came to purchase some tallow, they would offer to pay one peso per *arroba*, which was practically nothing, if the tallow could be delivered quickly. The cattle owners, not wanting to waste any time in striking a deal, would rush out with their *vaqueros* and helpers to round up the animals. They would kill the cattle on the spot, cut open the bellies to take out the fat, and leave the rest behind as food for other animals. It was not worth the effort to carve up the animal, stretch the hide, and take out the rest of the fat.

American ships that called on the coast would sell their wares only in exchange for silver or for otter pelts. There was no regular trade until the end of that year when Don Guillermo Hartnell, an agent of the British Company of Lima, headed by Don Juan Begg, arrived in Monterey to establish it.[30] Señor Hartnell immediately negotiated a trade agreement with the Fathers of the twenty-one missions for all the hides and tallow they could provide, at a rate of one peso per hide and one peso per *arroba* of tallow. During the two years it was in effect, this agreement was quite profitable for the Company.

The Russian-American Company already had begun its trade, which benefited those engaged in agriculture. Each December two or three ships would come down from the settlements which they had on both sides of the Bering Strait and load up with wheat. Don Kiril Khlebnikov, the agent in charge of this operation, gained the respect of every inhabitant of California by his gentlemanly behavior. In conducting his business, he never experienced any problems or had any disagreements with anyone, since he always acted clearly and honorably. To assure himself of a regular supply of wheat, he offered to pay three pesos silver per *fanega* every year, even though he knew from various people in the country that, depending on the harvest, the wheat was not worth more than one peso or twelve reales per *fanega*. He also would bring very fine goods from Europe and Asia, including fabrics of superior quality and beauty which were ordered by the Reverend Fathers of the missions for vestments and church ornaments.

In the year 1824 the agent for the Sturgis Company of Boston, the American Don Guillermo A. Gale, established trading relations by offering to pay twelve reales per cattle hide.[31] His frigates would leave Boston with express orders not to smuggle in so much as one ball of thread and to report all profits, whether large or small, to the customs employees. The conduct of Señor Gale, so different from that which normally is attributed to his national character, naturally earned the trust of all who came into contact with him. He alone would keep an account of the goods he dispensed and the harvests he obtained during the approximately two years which it took to obtain a full load, and not a single person ever complained of bad faith or abuse of trust. About six or seven years later, he was made a partner in the company and was succeeded as head of operations in California by Don Alfredo Robinson, whom he had instructed in the business from a very young age. Robinson took after Gale in integrity and honor and also won the widespread friendship of the inhabitants of the territory.[32]

Part II

Introduction to Part II

This section of the manuscript treats events in Alta California after Osio's arrival in 1825. Osio's work from this point on should be regarded as a collective autobiography. While Osio generally offers a chronological account, he does not do so consistently. We offer a brief time line to aid the reader in contextualizing the events of which Osio speaks. Since Osio organizes most of his material according to the administrations of the various governors, we will do the same here.

1825–1831: Governorship of José María de Echeandía

    1825: Arrival of the *Asia* at Monterey
    1827–30: Intrigues of Solís and Herrera
    1829: Revolt of Estanislao
    1831 (January): Echeandía's secularization decree

1831–1832: Governorship of Manuel Victoria

    1831: Movement against Victoria
    1831 (December): Battle of Cahuenga
    1832 (January): Departure of Victoria

1832–1833: Governorship of Pío Pico (1832, Acting), José María de Echeandía (in the South), Agustín Vicente Zamorano (in the North)

1833–1835: Governorship of José Figueroa

    1833: Arrival of friars from Zacatecas
    1833: Secularization of the missions
    1834: Arrival of Híjar-Padrés colony

1835–1836: Governorship of José Castro (Acting)

1836 (January 2–May 3): Governorship of Nicolás Gutiérrez (Acting)

1836 (May 3–July 31): Governorship of Mariano Chico

1836 (August 1–November 5): Governorship of Nicolás Gutiérrez (Acting)

    1836 (November): Alvarado revolt against Gutiérrez

1836–1842: Governorship of Juan Bautista Alvarado

    1837 (January): Opposition to Alvarado in Los Angeles
    1837 (May): Opposition to Alvarado in San Diego
    1837 (May): Arrival of Andrés Castillero
    1837 (June): Appointment of Carlos Carrillo as governor
    1838 (March): Battle of San Buenaventura
    1838 (August): Departure of Castillero for Mexico City
    1838 (November): Return of Castillero from Mexico City
    1838 (December): Osio takes position at Customs House
    1840: Isaac Graham revolt
    1841: Tensions between Alvarado and Mariano Guadalupe Vallejo
    1842: Víctor Prudón and Manuel Castañares mission to Mexico City

1842–1845: Governorship of Manuel Micheltorena

    1842 (October): Thomas ap Catesby Jones seizes Monterey
    1845 (February): Battle of Cahuenga; departure of Micheltorena

1845–1846: Governorship of Pío Pico (in the South) and José Castro (in the North)

    1846 (March): John C. Frémont outside of Monterey
    1846 (April): Arrival of Archibald Gillespie
    1846 (June): Bear Flag Revolt
    1846 (September): Gillespie abandons Los Angeles
    1846 (October): William Mervine driven away from Los Angeles
    1846 (December): Battle of San Pascual
    1847 (January): Battle of San Gabriel; Treaty of Cahuenga

· 4 ·

As the year 1825 began, the governor was pleased to see that every-thing was progressing in an orderly and peaceful manner. This continued until an unsettling afternoon in the middle of April. The watchman, who usually stationed himself at a dominant position on the Point of Pines, came down to report that there was a large ship outside the bay, headed for the entrance.[1] A short while later the ship appeared. Since it was the first *navío* to ply the waters of the bay, it created an impressive sight. However, it also created apprehensions due to the very understand-able fear that, even though it was sailing under the American flag, it might be a Spanish ship from the South Sea squadron. The ship anchored at around five o'clock in the afternoon. Even though they were a bit fearful, the people of Monterey refused to give up the custom of going to El Men-tidero, so a number of curious men and women waited on the rocks for the crew to come ashore and dispel their doubts. One of them was a Spaniard, a lieutenant in the Royal Regiment which had surrendered in Mexico in 1821. Since he understood a bit of English, he hoped to catch a word or two from above the din. But when he definitely recognized a very vulgar, commonly known word in Spanish that ends in ——*ajo,* he said that he clearly remembered that his grandfather would use that expression.[2] So he ordered that horses be readied to leave for the interior. He said that, even though the vessel had arrived masquerading in a foreign disguise, he defi-nitely recognized it as the *Asia* when it showed its face and three rows of teeth.[3] He immediately rode as fast as he could and did not stop until he reached Mission Soledad, fourteen leagues away from Monterey.

About two and a half hours later the sun began to set, and the ship still maintained its position without putting a single boat in the water. The fact that it did not even ready a boat for the health, harbor, and customs inspections increased the fear and uncertainty, since the people had memories of Bouchard. Fortunately, Don Luis Argüello alone remained undaunted, even in the face of pleas to order a withdrawal from the presidio, on the grounds that it would be impossible to resist a hostile ship bearing such a superior force. Lieutenant Don José Ramírez, commander of the artillery, was especially insistent on withdrawal. The major reason he did not want to risk his life was that, just a few months earlier, at the age of sixty plus, he had married a very beautiful young woman who was keeping six or eight thousand pesos for him. Nevertheless, he could not intimidate the governor, who replied, as if in agreement, that he was certain that the ship was Spanish. However, he continued, he was taking the risk of remaining for that very reason. He would put his faith in the national character and on the assumption that the ship's commander would not act arrogantly against the weak.

As it began to get dark a boat moored alongside the pier. The commander, who believed that he had tricked the *californios* with the American flag, spoke to the sailors in English, knowing that they did not understand him. Once ashore, he headed toward Don José Tiburcio Castro and asked him the name of the governor. Upon hearing Don Luis Argüello's name, he told his companions in excellent Spanish that, just as everything up to then had been as he had wished, he expected everything in the future to turn out well also. He immediately set out for the governor's house with one of his officers. When he presented himself at the parlor door, he unceremoniously called the governor by his first name. The governor at first did not recognize who was addressing him, but when he told him that his name was Don José Martínez, both leaders hugged one another as they recalled their close and long-standing friendship.

That moment, one of intense joy, passed. Although they would have preferred to tell one another about their lives during the time they had been apart, duty obliged them to discuss some fairly serious matters. The ship commander asked the presidio commander to designate two of his most trusted officers so that he could inform them in private of the purpose of his arrival. When they all had taken their seats in the government office, Señor Martínez briefly explained that the Spanish naval squadron sent to the South Pacific had operated against the republican squadron along the coast of Peru under the command of Captain Gáes. The Spanish squadron's complete superiority was clearly evident from the moment the fighting began. However, the commander of the *Asia*, who was also the leader of the squadron, had no strategic plan other than to defend himself. He would take the offensive just long enough to insure that his own ship was not seized. The effect of this strategy became evident when two enemy ships were cut off from their own line. Finding themselves defenseless, the soldiers lowered their flags in surrender. At that moment the *Asia* was battling with the frigate *Prueba*, which was unable to resist. Heavily damaged, the *Prueba* retreated, and it was followed by all of the other ships of the squadron. But the *Asia* became inactive. It did not give chase, even though it had received no damage other than being hit by two twenty-four-pound cannonballs. One struck the middle of the main mast, while the other hit between decks and resulted in a single fatality.

The Spanish squadron thus was left by itself and soon was ordered to leave the Pacific Ocean and head for the Asian Ocean. The squadron headed in that direction, but the crew was highly dissatisfied with its commander in chief. When they arrived at the Mariana Islands and anchored at Guam, the disgruntled crew immediately revolted. They placed the commander and the other officers on land. Then they took the commander of the brigantine *Constante* from his ship to the *Asia* as their prisoner. There the principal instigators of the revolt announced to him that they had unanimously selected him to be commander in chief because they had great confidence in him. They begged him to put aside all personal anger, accept their offer, and guide them with his good counsel. They wanted to take the ships back and negotiate an advantageous surrender agreement with one of the new republics. As he pondered their request, he remembered his good friends in Alta California. Naturally, he thought that he would find a member of the Argüello family as governor there. With that in mind, he promptly suggested setting course for the port of Monterey, an idea which everyone approved. Three ships ultimately joined together to set sail on convoy: the *Asia*, the brigantine *Aquiles* under the command of Don Pedro Angulo, and the brigantine *Constante* under Don Antonio Roteta. They had become separated in a violent storm, and Angulo feared that the less sturdy *Constante* might not have had the necessary strength to withstand the furor of the storm.[4]

Martínez and Argüello met again on the following day to formulate an agreement on the formal surrender. When the negotiation was concluded and the agreement was signed by both commanders and other officers from both sides (according to the attached copy), the surrender was celebrated aboard the ship with a twenty-one-gun salute. The largest cannons were fired as the flag of the "three guarantees" was being unfurled on the flag-pole where the flag of "castles and lions" had waved previously.[5] The salute was answered immediately with another twenty-one rounds from the fort, which created a cloud of smoke so dense that nothing could be seen. Cheers could be heard hailing the advancement of the Mexican nation and its worthy president, but no mention of Fernando VII, either pro or con, was uttered.

About eight days later the brigantine *Aquiles* landed in the Santa Bár-bara harbor. Commander Angulo was a Chilean of the lower classes. He did not even know how to sign his name, and the only reason he could call himself commander was that he had been one of the instigators of the up-rising. He leaped ashore dressed in a grand uniform to enhance his image, but one glance at him and his manners revealed his true nature. Feeling pompous because of the stripes on his uniform, he presented himself at the home of the presidio commander, Don José de la Guerra, at the very time, as luck would have it, that his eldest daughter had just married Don Guillermo Hartnell.[6] When the warship commander saw the splendor of the celebration and the refinement of those guests, he was very embarrassed because he could not express himself in his native Spanish with an ele-gance equal to his epaulets. Trying to get out of that predicament, he said in poor Spanish that he was a Frenchman who did not understand Span-ish. But his troubles were compounded, for he happened to be speaking to Señor Hartnell, who was well educated and spoke five languages, including French, perfectly. Hartnell spoke to him in French, and the "Frenchman," or peacock, was dumbfounded, since he could neither understand what was being said to him nor reply.

When his embarrassment subsided enough so that he could speak, he had to do so in Spanish in order to find out if the *Asia* and the brigantine *Constante* had arrived in Monterey. When he was informed that only the *Asia* had arrived, he rushed back to his ship, despite repeated requests that he at least stay for soup. Once on board, he ordered that the anchors be raised. When he had set sail, he showed the inhabitants of the presidio that, even if he did not know how to speak French, he certainly did know how to fire cannons in any language. He fired a cannonball at them, but fortunately it did not harm anyone, even though it fell in the populated area. He then sailed to Valparaíso, where he surrendered the brigantine.

The *Constante*, saved by Providence when it had almost sunk, arrived in Monterey around the same time. The ship had been so filled with water that it could no longer support any sails except the foresail, which was its only hope to avoid capsizing. When a vicious gale thrashed them, they experienced the sorrow of seeing that sail rip to shreds in an instant, with only the bolt ropes left intact. But God does not abandon those who ask for his help under the gravest of circumstances, especially when the Holy Virgin Mary acts as intermediary. The following incident was not fabricated; it actually occurred. When they invoked the protection of such a great woman, they offered to have a mass celebrated in her honor and to give as alms the value of the spare foresail, which, even though it had been considerably weakened by use, they were preparing to hoist. They promised that if the sail withstood the winds, they would walk barefoot, with their shoes in their hands, as they carried the sail from the beach to the church for mass.

As they made that vow and hoisted the foresail, which was not even half as strong as the one they had lost, the ship began to respond and defend itself against the horrible waves which were sweeping over it. The way in which the old foresail withstood the constant furious wind seemed incredible to everyone. If one agrees that a hand which cannot be moved by even the strongest of hurricanes must be a powerful hand, then one can say that those almost shipwrecked sailors were being protected by such a hand that was supporting the wretched old sail, a sail that could have withstood all of the typhoons of Asia as well. When the storm was finally over, they experienced a period of fair weather, and they took advantage of it and headed toward Monterey. After lowering their anchors there, they immediately fulfilled their vow. One morning they were seen leaping ashore with the foresail rolled up lengthwise, secured with twisted cables which each man held on to with one hand. Carrying their shoes in the other hand, they walked two by two to the presidio church, where Reverend Father Ramón Abella was waiting to begin the mass. When it was time for the sermon, the ship's chaplain, Father Gaspar Fernández, ascended the pulpit. He preached eloquently in praise of the Virgin Mary, using as his text the Teacher's words to his beloved disciple, "This is your Mother."[7]

For shore leave, three or four hundred men would come ashore daily, many of them completely intoxicated. Because of this the land and sea commanders agreed to commission joint patrols to prevent disorder. The patrols comprised men from both of their units, and they were commanded by the most trustworthy sergeants. With the patrols' vigilance and the continual warnings each commander gave his subordinates, they managed to prevent the men from engaging in the disorderly conduct which they feared. It was known that the California detachment conducted itself well because it observed Spanish discipline. The men from the ship did not want to appear to lag behind in this matter. That served as an incentive to dampen disputes between them and the soldiers, disputes which they feared but which turned out to be the least of their worries.

Since the older presidio soldiers still enjoyed sharing with one another memories of their faithful service to His Catholic Majesty, they retained the custom of not pronouncing the meaning of the three initials without first stopping and removing their hats out of proper respect.[8] They were not at all pleased that native-born Spaniards had surrendered two warships to an enemy. This surrender sparked discussions about rebuking those who had surrendered and accusing them of treason. However, the commanders avoided the disastrous results this would have produced by taking precautionary measures. Despite their efforts, there always was some trouble with the soldiers. For example, when one of the ship's artillerymen returned from the field where he had gone to hunt, he had a disagreement with one of the locals. Since he had a shotgun in his hands, he shot the man with buckshot, which blew his face to pieces and killed him. When the cause was quickly discovered, it turned out to be the usual one: A Woman.[9]

It might appear strange that those old men remained so steadfastly loyal to the Kings of Spain. However, for soldiers in general, no better government exists than one which pays, protects, and punishes. They all had been satisfied with these three elements. For example, if they prepared an invoice with the total wages they had earned and sent it to the paymaster general in Mexico, he would send them the full amount requested. They knew that their pay would arrive every year on the warship from San Blas which carried the sealed orders from the royal officials.[10]

There were other reasons that they always wanted to express their gratitude to the benefactors of both Californias. They knew very well that the Spanish kings had been keenly bent on the conquest of Baja California ever since they became aware of its existence. They ordered it done, without bothering to calculate its cost, and they simply wanted the order to be carried out. However, from then on the Mexican government declared itself California's stepfather and denied it protection as if it were a bastard child. This attitude was demonstrated by the way it created insurmountable obstacles to carrying out the royal orders which the Mexican government would receive.

Look at the expenses incurred by Admiral Atondo and others who undertook the conquest for speculative purposes.[11] I believe I am not mistaken in saying that these men, with no incentive other than money, spent more copper reales than there are grains of corn in order to make an impression on the distinguished and fearless Father Juan María Salvatierra, yet they actually did nothing. Note the passionate complaints this noble man had to voice to try to get the royal decrees ordering the development of California carried out. To elicit some response, Salvatierra had to undertake a difficult trip to the capital. Once there, he received nothing but negative responses from the Viceroy and was forced to appeal to Madrid, which finally issued various decrees in his favor. These royal orders were not carried out fully, because the usual obstacles continued to be raised in Mexico.[12] Also, take note of how Alta California was presented with similar difficulties. There, the venerable Father Junípero Serra, the commander, and the officers suffered many hardships for the same reason. Finally, take note of the most essential issue for the soldiers at the presidios: their repeated demands that they not be deprived of their monthly pay of eighteen pesos. Also, they constantly had to request that supplies sent to them from Mexico not have transport fees added to the basic cost.

The old *californios* struggled with these and other issues. It is certain that when the government changed in 1821, if the *californios* had been offered the opportunity to serve the republic or to serve the King in the labors of the conquest, in spite of their advanced age there is no doubt that they would have chosen the King. This would have been the case even if the republic had given assurances that, even though it was not formally responsible for them, it would fulfill its obligations to them, rejuvenate the California military, and pay them a good salary. Such loyalty was substantiated in many cases. As proof, I shall relate a story which was told as late as 1842 by a ninety-six-year-old retired gentleman. In spite of his advanced age and blindness, he had the strength to walk and retained his good sense and memory.

When he was either *alcalde* or judge of Monterey, Don Florencio Serrano received a memorandum asking him to question the retired Don José Antonio Rodríguez about the ownership of a piece of land with a watering hole, since Rodríguez had served as a witness.[13] Rodríguez did not keep the appointment. Instead, he answered that he did not know if a servant of the Catholic Kings should testify before an *alcalde*, and he would have to consult with his commander, Don Mariano Estrada.

A Spanish Californian, *Don* García. Sketch by I. G. Voznesenskii. From Alekseev, *The Odyssey of a Russian Scientist,* 19. Courtesy of Limestone Press, Ontario, Canada.

Part II

Let me return to the story about the now nationalized Spanish warships. After the crew members who had surrendered had spent enough days wandering around and resting, preparations were made to send them to the port of Acapulco. They would be accompanied by a person commissioned to deliver sealed documents from the territorial government to the general of the republic. Don Juan Malarín was deemed capable of carrying out the assignment and was entrusted with this task. In addition, he could act as a substitute pilot, since the ship would not have a pilot with knowledge of the coastline. They left Monterey and anchored in Acapulco eleven days later. The government approved the surrender, but the ships proved of no use except as a settlement of some very large debts and as a source of needed replacement parts. As recompense for the service which Don Luis Argüello and Don Juan Malarín had rendered, the latter was promoted to lieutenant of the national navy and the former to lieutenant colonel. Unfortunately for Argüello, a person driven by petty revenge kept the appointment from him, and he did not have the pleasure of receiving it.[14]

· 5 ·

There usually have been many aspirants for jobs in the different branches of the Mexican government. These people easily obtain positions for themselves, at the expense of others whose skills are ignored because they live far away from the capital. That is how Don José María de Echeandía, lieutenant colonel of engineers, obtained the political and military command of both Californias.[1] He was dispatched at the beginning of 1825. In July he arrived at the port of Loreto, where he assumed the political and military commands. He did this for himself and in his own presence, since he did not care about the customary formality of taking the oath in the presence of the retiring official. When he found that a duplicate set of sealed documents concerning the surrender of the *Asia* and the *Constante* had been accidentally left behind, he took the liberty of opening them. When he became aware of the contents, he refused to believe that the two ships had surrendered in good faith. Echeandía then sent an urgent dispatch to Don Luis Argüello, in which he stated that, since he had been appointed political and military leader of both Californias, he had assumed authority over both ships when he arrived in Baja California. He ordered Argüello immediately to strip them both of their sails and rudders, if they were still at Monterey. If they resisted, he should declare them enemies and retreat to set up camp a reasonable distance away from the shore. From there Argüello could harass them with the knowledge that very soon sufficient forces would appear by sea and land to enable him to compel the enemy to obey him.

This new governor saw the ocean for the first time in his life when he arrived at the port of San Blas. While there, he spent his free time like a good mathematician. He obtained a map of the coastline and began to measure the waters of the small Gulf of Cortés, comparing it with the great Sea of

Texcoco.[2] He also saw ships for the first time. Since he was quite afraid of sailing, he consulted with the commander of the warship *San Carlos*, Don Flaminio Agacini, about the voyage.[3] Agacini was ready to take him to Monterey and assured him that, of the ships anchored in that bay, there were none larger or more powerful than the *San Carlos*. However, when Echeandía learned that the voyage would take at least thirty days, he decided to put most of his officers on the *San Carlos*. He kept four officers whom he trusted behind with him. They would set sail for Loreto on the schooner *Constanza*, because this was a voyage of only eight days.[4] However, Echeandía always believed that the brigantine *San Carlos* was the most powerful ship of all, perhaps because of what he was told, or perhaps because he had never seen a larger ship with so many cannons. That is why he had no doubt that when the *San Carlos* appeared in Monterey, it could destroy the *Asia* in an instant if Captain Don Luis Argüello were to order it done.

At the end of that same month, July, the *San Carlos* arrived in Monterey. After giving the customary salute of a warship, Señor Agacini went ashore to pay his respects to the commander of the presidio. He was informed that the two Spanish ships had surrendered and had been sent to Acapulco. In turn, he informed Captain Argüello in detail about the disposition, qualities, and education of the governor of both Californias who was to arrive shortly. When Agacini concluded his tribute, Captain Argüello told him, a bit sarcastically, that he believed that all of it was true, at least judging from the contents of an order that had been sent to him from Loreto. Argüello begged Agacini to allow him to place the order in his hands so he could read it aloud. As Agacini was reading it, he passed quickly over the section that related to the takeover. When he finished the part about the brigantine *San Carlos* and it forcing the *Asia* and the *Constante* to surrender their sails and rudders, he threw the communiqué on the table and said that it was his turn to implore. He begged that they pardon him for his misguided description of Señor Echeandía's wisdom. Now that he had seen the order, he declared that Echeandía was a beast and incapable of governing.

A number of subordinate military officers arrived with Señor Agacini. In addition, there were also exiles, some convicts, and a *comisario* who was the first treasury employee assigned to the territory.[5] Before his arrival, the paymasters of the presidio companies had carried out these functions themselves without receiving extra pay beyond what they drew as officers.

When Señor Echeandía dispatched the already mentioned order to Don Luis Argüello, he also sent the general government an account of his plans

concerning the *Asia* and *Constante*. He repeated that he believed their surrender had been in bad faith and that they had arrived in Alta California
with hostile intent. When this communiqué arrived in Mexico, the government already had decided what to do with the surrendered ships. When
the minister of war was informed of the communiqué, he could not refrain
from remarking that he had believed that the governor who had been sent
to Alta California had better sense and education. He warned Echeandía
quite harshly to abstain from giving reports based solely on suppositions in
the future, and to seek information and ask questions about matters that he
did not understand. When the governor received this reprimand instead
of the commendation he was expecting, and when he further discovered
that Don Luis Argüello had been commended, he began to harass Argüello
with all the rancor he could muster. This behavior continued for five years
and caused the illness of which Argüello died.[6]

When it became known that the new leader had arrived in San Diego,
orders were circulated so that he would be recognized throughout the territory as the *jefe superior*. He started to issue his own edicts and began by
weakening the presidio companies. He wanted to organize them as he
pleased and to assign the posts there to the officers who had accompanied
him. Next he committed himself to the large task of instilling republican
ideas in the Indians' minds; but he did not provide them with the basic and
necessary instruction they needed to grasp these ideas, offering instead just
pompous words that the Indians did not understand. Those who were more
intelligent and had been pages for the Fathers managed to comprehend
what was being said to them about the Indians' being equal to people of
other classes. So, according to the fictitious social status that was being
granted them, they deemed themselves important persons and took to calling each other "sovereign," since they wanted to give themselves the full
treatment to which citizens were entitled.[7]

With this slight improvement in their status, the practices adopted by
the Fathers to supervise the Indians' conduct and punish them appropri-
ately when they deserved it gradually fell into disuse. Consequently, a person who committed either a trivial or an atrocious crime and wanted to
avoid punishment could simply flee quickly to the tule grove or *ranchería*
of his birth without having to worry about being pursued there. For it required great effort to pursue them promptly, since the original organization
of the presidio companies was no longer in effect. The majority of the older
soldiers, genuinely distinguished by their honesty, had disappeared from

the ranks. In their place one could see lost men, full of vice, who, unlike the previous soldiers, were not permitted to have their own horses or saddles. Rather, for review they were issued supplies from a stock which consisted of eight horses and the necessary gear. This left more than twenty-five horses which still could be issued.[8]

The large livestock ranches belonging to the presidio companies were put under the care of these soldiers. The ranches were very well-cared-for by a lieutenant who functioned as foreman and by four soldiers who acted as cowboys. Each year, during a specific month, the off-duty soldiers would gather to do the branding. The commander generally would supervise, and the job would end with a dance. On the meadow of the river where the Monterey Ranch was situated, these soldiers, who conducted themselves with good discipline and comradeship, were also able to harvest large amounts of corn, beans, and wheat.

During the last era the ranches were given the name *ranchos nacionales*, and Comisario Don José María Herrera wanted them to be known solely by this name. He was especially concerned about the *rancho* in Monterey, which had a great number of cattle and which he wished to manage as he pleased. Despite being well informed that the proceeds were private property, he claimed, for his own benefit, that they were national property. This policy resulted in a quarrel between the *comisario* and the commander of the presidio company which the *jefe político* had to resolve. He decided that the owners should be stripped of their interests. The *comisario* obtained this unjust ruling mainly because the *jefe político* wanted to indulge him.[9] Herrera then mustered the courage to engage in more complex business dealings which could enable him to amass rapidly the fortune that he desired. His ambition to acquire wealth even led him to speculate with customs duties which had not yet been generated. His audacity reached the point that he picked another quarrel with Señor Echeandía by stating that cleaning up his poor management of the public treasury fell outside of the governor's responsibilities. The *jefe* finally had to dismiss him from his post and appoint someone else. Echeandía immediately reported his reasons for this action to the general government.[10]

The *comisario* was angered when he saw his grand projects instantly destroyed. In the year 1827 he occupied himself in plotting a revolution, but he did not appear in it. Using the troops' lack of pay as a pretext, he managed to seduce the Monterey troop, except for the older sergeants and lieutenants, into not serving. One of the new lieutenants was placed in command of forty soldiers. They left the presidio armed, intending not to with-draw any farther than five leagues into the meadow by the river. However, when they found out that Lieutenant Don Romualdo Pacheco was prepar-ing to pursue them with soldiers from their own company and from another detachment, they retreated twelve leagues instead, to the Codornices mountain range, where they set up camp.[11] Lieutenant Pacheco, obeying Commander Don Mariano Estrada's orders, followed them to the point called El Toro.[12] He fully realized that persuasion would work better than force, which is what in effect happened.

Pacheco sent one of the sergeants to give the dissidents paternal advice. He offered to use his influence, as a commander, with the general to obtain a pardon for their rebellion. When they went to consult with the Fathers about their insubordination, the Fathers offered them the same counsel, as if they had come to an agreement beforehand. When they admitted their error, they were pardoned and returned to duty according to the terms of the offer that had been made to them.[13] Comisario Herrera did not lose a minute in currying favor with that most immoral group of soldiers. He sug-gested subversive ideas to them and promised that their wages would be paid only when he returned to take control of the *comisaría*.

Since a secret cannot be kept among many people, Herrera's machinations were soon made public. All that he needed was a *corifeo* to spread the plan for revolt.[14] Finally, after much searching he designated Joaquín Solís, an exile who had arrived with him on the brigantine *San Carlos*, as his spokesman. Solís belonged to the gang headed by Vicente Gómez, known as El Capador (The Castrator); he had offered his services as a lieutenant in that gang.

That first difficulty was accordingly smoothed out, but others soon presented themselves. The lack of money proved to be an insurmountable problem. They agreed that they had to leave matters as they were until an opportunity to acquire the money they needed presented itself.

Since Señor Echeandía could not tolerate the cold of Alta California, he had established his residence in the milder climate of San Diego. There he received detailed reports of Herrera's preparations, but they did not cause him any anxiety. He only wished that something of more substance would materialize so that he could proceed against Herrera. That is how the year 1828 ended.

In 1829, because of the governor's poor administrative practice of pro-hibiting the usual punishments against the Indians, it began to be noticed at various missions that the *alcaldes* were behaving insolently and were entertaining subversive threats. The territorial leader was informed of all this activity. However, his habitual apathy prevented his giving credence to reports about the Indians' ultimate capabilities if the abuses which they were fearlessly committing continued to be tolerated.

This situation produced the following consequences at Mission San José. The *alcalde*, Estanislao, left the mission with all of the members of his tribe.[15] They headed for their *ranchería* (which was eventually named after Estanislao) in order to fortify it.[16] He was already somewhat obstinate, and he could not tolerate anyone giving him orders. Reverend Father Narciso Durán notified the commander of the San Francisco presidio of the occurrence and begged him to send enough soldiers to bring back the fugitives. Sergeant Don Antonio Soto and fifteen men who could be outfitted quickly were appointed for this purpose. Since this sergeant was one of the old guard, he deserved the confidence of his superiors. He also had the advantage of knowing the language of those Indians; but he was too daring, and this fault worked to his disadvantage, resulting in disastrous consequences.

When Soto began his march from San Francisco, he deliberately stopped at Mission San José, where the Father had prepared the necessary provisions for the expedition. From that point on, nothing slowed down their march toward their final destination. The *ranchería* was situated in the middle of a large grove of willow trees, intertwined together by a great number of shoots from climbing vines and other foliage. As a result, neither the rays of the sun nor soldiers could easily penetrate the *ranchería*. As the troop approached, the war cry echoed throughout the grove, and a few Indians appeared at its edge, calling out to the soldiers with the most obscene words possible. They specifically targeted the sergeant, since they knew that he could understand everything addressed to him in their language. He paid no attention to the insults at first, since he wanted to try to arrange a meeting with Estanislao. Estanislao absolutely refused to speak with him; instead, he urged his people to yell as many obscenities as they could to enrage the sergeant and thus induce him to enter the grove. When he heard them calling him by his first name, calling him a coward, and goading him to enter if he were a man, he could control himself no longer. He gathered together six soldiers in whom he had the greatest confidence. As he dismounted, he ordered a corporal to take the rest of the soldiers and go around the edge of the grove until they arrived at a tall tree which he pointed out on the opposite side of the grove. He said that he would go through the middle of the grove and meet them there. He had the good for-

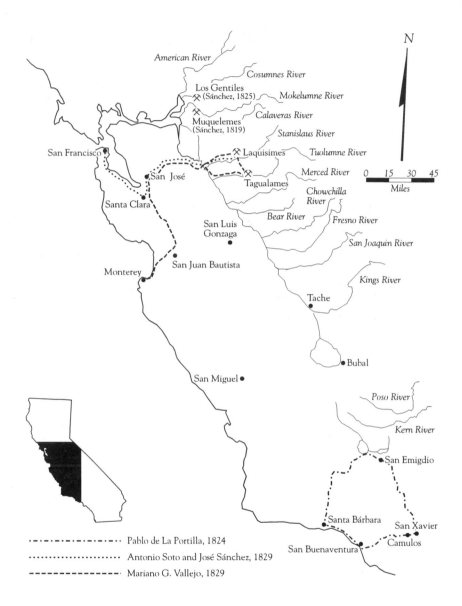

American River
Cosumnes River
Los Gentiles
(Sánchez, 1825)
Mokelumne River
Calaveras River
Muquelemes
(Sánchez, 1819)
Stanislaus River
Laquisimes
Tuolumne River
San Francisco
Merced River
San José
Tagualames
Santa Clara
Chowchilla
River
San Luis
Gonzaga
Bear River
Fresno River
San Joaquin River
Monterey
San Juan Bautista
Kings River
Tache
Bubal
San Miguel
Poso River
Kern River
San Emigdio
Santa Bárbara
San Xavier
San Buenaventura
Camulos

N

0   15   30   45
Miles

·············-·-·   Pablo de La Portilla, 1824
·····················   Antonio Soto and José Sánchez, 1829
----------------   Mariano G. Vallejo, 1829

Mexican expeditions to the interior, 1820–1830. Redrawn from *Historical Atlas of California,* Warren A. Beck and Ynez D. Haase. Copyright © 1974 by the University of Oklahoma Press.

tune of making the crossing safely and arrived at the designated tree. But the soldiers who went around the edge were hindered by the obstacles they encountered and had to return quickly to the point where the sergeant had entered the grove. He returned at the same time as well, but with two fewer men. The four survivors had been wounded by five or six arrows in their faces and heads, and the sergeant himself had been struck by an arrow under his right eye. So that they could continue defending themselves, they had been forced to jerk the arrows out rapidly, and as a result, the flint arrowheads remained embedded in them. The Indians were well aware that their arrows would have no effect if they aimed them at the soldiers' bodies, since the arrows could not penetrate the leather vests the soldiers wore as protection. Therefore, aided by the advantage of the dense foliage, their knowledge of the terrain, and their invisibility at even a distance of six yards, the Indians took very careful aim. Even though many of them died, they left the soldiers too disabled to continue to fight. Because the wounded needed prompt medical treatment, the soldiers retreated immediately. The sharp pain the wounded were experiencing made the walk to the *pueblo* of San José a very difficult one. A few days later the sergeant died. The soldiers, however, recovered.

This encounter was the Indians' first victory over the soldiers, and they celebrated it with great festivities and dancing. The bodies of the soldiers were put on display so that the neighboring tribes, who were invited to the festivities, would admire the natives' great valor and prowess.

The commander of the San Francisco presidio wanted to punish the hostile Indians severely, so he was bent on dispatching a second expedition. It was difficult for him to outfit a number of his soldiers, since they had neither horses nor even saddles, so the departure of a forty-man expedition under the command of Lieutenant Don José Sánchez was delayed. Sánchez, who spent many years as a frontier soldier, was both prudent and valiant. It was therefore expected that his expedition would be successful. As he was making preparations for the march, it occurred to him that modifications could be made to the protective leather vests the soldiers used during campaigns. None of the vests ever had collars on them. At this time, after so many years of using the same style vest, Sánchez had a collar attached to his vest. This modification proved to be very beneficial, as the following description will show.

When he reached Estanislao, he sensed a profound silence throughout the grove, as if no one lived there. As a precaution he began to set fire to different parts of the grove. However, he found it impossible to fuel the flames, because he could not find dry branches to use as kindling. His effort did have the effect of forcing the Indians to make themselves visible, since they wanted to see what the soldiers were doing. They were especially concerned that the flames would spread and destroy the barricade which they wished to keep hidden.

Since he did not want to risk having even one man wounded or killed, the lieutenant hesitated to enter the grove to make a preliminary inspection. When he finally did enter it, he was confronted with a stockade made of thick, strong poles, from where the Indians could resist attacks without being harmed. They resisted well, and the lieutenant considered it prudent to retreat. Firing in all directions, he managed to leave the grove safely. The only harm he suffered was from an arrow which was aimed at his neck and which would have been deadly if it had not struck the collar on the leather vest. Sánchez immediately ordered a march back to Mission San José. When he arrived there, he sent his commander a communiqué in which he informed him of everything that he had experineced and seen. He added that he had complied with his orders by returning without engaging in an action which would have cost the lives of eight or ten men, even if he had won the battle.

Consequently, the commanders of the San Francisco and Monterey presidios agreed to send out a joint expedition. About one hundred men from the cavalry, infantry, and artillery left Monterey. They joined up with the soldiers from San Francisco at Mission San José. They were joined by some inhabitants of the *pueblo* of San José and some allied Indians who were long-standing enemies of Estanislao's *ranchería*. Headed by Lieutenant Don Guadalupe Vallejo, they formed an imposing and confident corps. When Vallejo arrived at his destination, the Indians, who had been warned that they were going to be attacked, were already well prepared. They were also anxious to prove their mettle against a greater number of troops than they had previously encountered. They were confident that their type of fortification would withstand the test of the soldiers. The barricade consisted of a fairly well-constructed series of three stockades, designed to protect them from the soldiers' carbines. The troop would not be able to dislodge the defenders in the first stockade without a continuous assault and serious losses. Even if they did manage to dislodge the other two lines, they would arrive at a labyrinth of large, deep, interconnecting holes where, as a last resort, the Indians intended to die fighting.

When the troops had been placed in formation according to the plan of attack, they entered the grove to within musket range of the stockade. The "proprietors" were waiting behind the barricade. They began the battle with a volley of arrows that was answered by a cannon shot, fired in order to open a breach. A number of thick splinters snapped off and killed a few Indians. A second blast had the same effect. The Indians were quickly disillusioned, as the stockade was not proving to be an adequate defense against the artillery. For even if the cannonballs did not harm them, the splinters from the logs would kill them as they snapped off with great force. Losing confidence in the second and third lines of defense, the Indians subsequently abandoned the barricades and went to wait in the holes. After the troops passed through the stockades, they arrived at the labyrinth, unaware of what they should guard against. A poor old man who was part of the auxiliary troop from San José happened to be the first person to approach the mouth of a hole, which was covered with blackberry brambles. An arrow shot out from the hole and passed through him from one side of his body to the other. He fell and later died.

The death of that old man affected everyone and sparked a desire to punish the aggressors more severely, so an order was issued to show them no mercy. Among the *californios* one frequently heard the proverb "No hay cuña como la del propio palo," and it was well proved during this expedition.[17] The allied Indian troop was anxious to avenge long-standing grievances, and they had been awaiting the right moment to attack Estanislao and his people. The opportunity presented itself to them when they heard the order to kill and destroy. The Indians set out like hungry greyhounds and immediately engaged in a savage massacre. The grove blazed, they dragged the naked Indians out of their holes, and, in the end, they destroyed everything. However, Estanislao escaped. In his place they took another Indian and bound his hands tightly. Accusing him of countless murders and robberies, they presented him to Señor Vallejo and requested permission to execute him. When it was granted, one of the Indians untied a strip of dirty rag which he used as a belt and blindfolded him. When he finished, he very quickly jumped backward two steps and shot him with an arrow, which struck with such force that it passed through his skull. The poor soul died from the blow, with the arrow's feather visible on his forehead.

The holes which they had excavated for fighting served as their graves. Some Indians who were considered very evil were hanged from the tallest trees with vine ropes around their necks, as a warning to the other Indians, especially those who had escaped from the *ranchería*.

Deeming the expedition successful, Señor Vallejo ordered a return march to Mission San José. After he arrived, he learned that the priest had Estanislao hidden in one of the rooms in his dwelling. Vallejo then submitted a complete report and set out for Monterey. Estanislao was pardoned by Señor Echeandía at the request of Reverend Father Narciso Durán. When Father Durán made this request, he also sent the governor a type of dossier, which he gratuitously directed against Señor Vallejo.[18] It was not a charitable document. He desired that the deaths of the Indians at the *ranchería* of Estanislao be viewed as horrible assassinations and that suitable punishment be given to the perpetrator of the crime. The reading of the dossier merited only an oral judgment, and it ended up where documents of that nature usually go, in the wastebasket on the floor.

Outwardly everything was as peaceful as in previous times, but in Monterey Comisario Herrera continued plotting. He was increasingly enthusiastic about his scheme, and he was waiting for the right moment to execute it. The infantry company found itself practically dissolved for lack of pay, and the cavalry and artillery were given nothing more than their meals. By playing on these grievances Herrera was able to get all the disgruntled soldiers under his control. He intended to order them to disobey the commanding general. It also happened that the cavalry soldiers' long-standing commander, whom they respected and loved, retired.[19] His replacement as commander of the presidio was Second Lieutenant Don Juan Rocha. Various communiqués had already made him aware of Herrera's machinations, and he kept Señor Echeandía apprised of everything that he saw and knew about the plot. However, Echeandía did not order any preventive measures to be taken. Reports which the artillery and cavalry commanders, Don José Fernández and Don Guadalupe Vallejo, sent him had the same outcome. They thus waited for the inevitable to happen, until the beginning of November, a month of perilous crisis for the territory.

During those days the English brigantine *Danube*, which was consigned to Don Guillermo Hartnell, anchored in Monterey and generated about nine thousand pesos in duties.[20] With that customs' revenue, Herrera naturally believed that all of his difficulties were over and quickly decided to begin the revolt. When everything was ready and they were favored with a very dark night, two corporals, one from the artillery and the other from the cavalry, were appointed as ringleaders of their respective barracks. Don

First jail constructed in California, at Monterey. Courtesy of the California State Library, Sacramento.

Joaquín Solís volunteered himself as the principal military commander. Their first step was to summon Commander Don Juan Rocha to the artillery barracks, under the pretext of discussing an "interesting matter." Despite the fact that he was almost certain of the reason he was being summoned, he refused to avoid the situation, and as soon as he arrived they put him in jail.

Next, the rebels tricked the cavalry and artillery commanders into following Commander Rocha by saying that Rocha wanted to see them. They arrived in succession to see what the commander wanted. When he saw them through the bars in the door, he almost choked with anger as he ordered them to enter his humble abode. The last one to enter was Comisario Don Manuel Jimeno. Having been accused of a crime against the state, they spent the entire night standing. In that place an act of courtesy such as offering them a place to sit down was unheard-of.

The following day, perhaps because the artillery corporal felt distressed about his own crime or perhaps because he wanted to sound out Commander Rocha's state of mind, he leaned against the bars of the jail and asked Rocha to come close because he wanted to ask him for some advice. Rocha was so angered that his response, before giving any advice, was to tell him to go to hell. And as soon as the corporal arrived there, he was to tell the captain general of the devils to send Rocha twenty-five armed men

immediately. With these men he could shoot all the people who were un-
worthy of being called soldiers because they had placed their immediate
commanders in jail. With such a response, the corporal had no other recourse than to try to seize some money from wherever he might find it.
Herrera, the leader, was finally able to persuade them to wait a while, saying that they could obtain the money legally by freeing the *comisario*, who
had access to the duties from the *Danube*. However, the *comisario* explained that there was a problem in seizing money, since the *jefe* had declared that all merchant ships should pay duties in kind instead of cash.
Herrera then found out that the municipal government had a surplus of
one thousand pesos in cash in a box and demanded it. The *alcalde*, Don
José Tiburcio Castro, gave them the money in the form of a loan, so that
technically they would not be committing a crime.

When they had received that money, the soldiers wanted to be given
what they needed to make some clothes for themselves. But they did not
want the interference of Comisario Don Manuel Jimeno. Herrera resolved
this problem by making them understand that someone named Osio, appointed *contador* for the Customs House and *comisaría*, was due to arrive
from San Francisco that very day and would immediately begin work as the
comisario's assistant. They agreed to wait for this man, whom they already
knew and even respected. At four in the afternoon he arrived on the *Danube*, which was returning from San Francisco. When he went ashore, he met
someone who had been commissioned to inform him ahead of time of the
troop's wishes that he not refuse the position because of recent events and
that he assume his customs and revenue posts the following day. He
promised to do so, provided that a few conditions, above all respectability,
be met. In the evening Don Joaquín Solís arrived and was recognized by
the soldiers as the principal military commander. This fellow Osio, wishing
to see his friends, the *comisario*, and the imprisoned officers, went to Solís to
request the necessary permission. Solís responded negatively, claiming that
the jail in which they were being held was not a decent place. He offered
instead to have them sent to rooms in the warehouse within fifteen minutes and to let him visit them whenever he wished. As a result, they had
the pleasure of conversing until eight o'clock that night, when the doors
were closed.

The following day the new employee was officially appointed *comisario*
and customs administrator by Commander Don Joaquín Solís. He received
a similar appointment from the president of the *ayuntamiento*, who also

wanted to be involved in the matter as the only constituted authority. That employee was fortunate to begin work with the security of three appointments, including the one that he had already received from Señor Echeandía. He immediately distributed a little more than three thousand pesos' worth of supplies to the soldiers. Next, with various respected people from the community, he went to beg Solís to release the officers and the *comisario*. Since Herrera's approval was anticipated, they were released later, under the express condition that they leave Monterey as soon as possible and head south. A few days later they started for San Diego.[21]

Solís spent considerable time preparing to go south and forcefully take over the government and seize the weapons from Señor Echeandía. When everything was ready, he claimed that he first needed to travel to San Francisco, so he could be acknowledged there as *jefe principal*. He encountered no opposition to his plan, either from the bad soldiers or from Lieutenant Don Ignacio Martínez.[22] On his return to Monterey, he encountered his former captain and fellow exile, Antonio Ávila, who reproached him for having allowed himself to be seduced by Herrera. At the end of the conversation Ávila promised that, if Solís did not give up being the old *comisario*'s puppet, he could be certain that Ávila would join the ranks of those who would definitely pursue, fight, and defeat him.

On his return to Monterey, Solís spent time and money on new plans to relinquish his command. However, he was forced to march south as soon as he learned that the troop from San Diego had advanced as far as Santa Bárbara. During the journey an artillery detachment headed by a sergeant joined him with the intention of betraying him.[23] En route the sergeant had time to reveal his plan to the other artillerymen, except the corporals, who were the initial ringleaders of the revolt. Señor Echeandía was kept informed by messages from the Fathers at each mission where Solís stopped. When the Father at Mission Santa Ynés reported that Solís had been there, the troop from Santa Bárbara left to wait for him at a place called La Cieneguita.[24] When the two forces approached within cannon range, Solís was the first to open fire, but he fled in disgrace after the first shot from the other side. He left behind his entire campaign convoy, which his new artillery detachment rounded up and handed over as they had promised.

A portion of the troop under the command of Captain Romualdo Pacheco was quickly mobilized to pursue those who were fleeing.[25] When the inhabitants of Monterey learned of Solís' defeat, they immediately armed themselves, rallied together in considerable numbers, and took possession of the barracks. As he had promised, Don Antonio Ávila left in search of Solís and managed to apprehend him and his entire group without firing a single shot.

When Captain Pacheco's troops arrived in Monterey, they arrested Herrera and placed him in solitary confinement. They took the other prisoners into custody and immediately began an investigation. Señor Echeandía arrived about ten or twelve days later with the rest of the soldiers. Don Agustín Zamorano, the governor's secretary, expedited the trial against the revolutionaries. At its conclusion they were sent in an American ship chartered by the general government to San Blas, where the captain handed them over.[26] The accusations against them were considered rather minor, since they had only engaged in a small-scale revolt in a remote area. On the other hand, in the capital people could revolt on a large scale to secure jobs. Consequently, Solís and the other prisoners were released, and Herrera was given a position in the Treasury Department.

After the commander general was rid of the rebels, he ordered the troops who had come up with him from San Diego and Santa Bárbara to return to their respective companies. He discharged the infantry and reorganized the Monterey cavalry, appointing Don Guadalupe Vallejo commander, Don José Fernández commander of the artillery, and Don Manuel Jimeno customs administrator and *comisario*. At last everything appeared to be stable.

Since contributions or taxes of any kind were unknown, the customs revenue provided the only income, and this did not suffice to cover even half of the military expenses, which are totaled below:

Cavalry Company of San Francisco	12600
Idem of Monterey	13428
Idem of Santa Bárbara	12300
Idem of San Diego	11800
Artillery	6300
Infantry	11904
Squadron from Mazatlán	11828
Veterans	3200
Jefe and *plana mayor*[27]	5000
Commissariat and Customs	1500
	89860

Comparing this total with the fifteen to thirty thousand pesos which were collected annually, one can understand the soldiers' hardships. The

Monterey Customs House from the beach. Courtesy of the California State Library, Sacramento.

jefe could very well have lessened them. For instance, the infantrymen could have been permitted to work as agricultural laborers, or they could have been allowed to hold other jobs, as they wished to do, and earn four to six reales a day. Instead, they had to confine themselves exclusively to military service. The missions assisted as much as possible by sending all types of provisions, such as soap, shoes, and *sarapes,* to the presidios, which provided them with escort soldiers. Over an entire year this would amount to a considerable sum, as much for the *jefe* as for the Fathers, who would give all of these items without placing a burden on the missions. Even though the missions were wealthy, an exact account was kept of the goods distributed for future recompense.

Since the *jefe principal* was also the head of the treasury, he condoned the customs abuse by which the merchant ships were allowed to pay duties in kind, since the supercargoes claimed that they were not carrying enough money. They also argued that since they conducted business in exchange for goods from the country, they could pay with cotton cloth and printed calico valued at four reales a yard. Other items were similarly priced.

Due to a slight difficulty which Don Manuel Jimeno experienced, he wished to resign from his job.[28] The *jefe* named as his replacement the individual who was serving as *contador* and allocated eight hundred pesos as his annual salary. That lowly employee, unaware of the additional work which awaited him, was very pleased, because he had never worked for such a large salary. By himself, he had to fulfill the duties of customs ad-

ministrator, guard, scribe, *comisario,* and provider. Because the *jefe* econo-
mized so drastically, the *comisario* had to spend at least two hours very early
each morning in the warehouse, distributing the daily provisions to the different branches of the troops. Throughout the remainder of the day he continually had to set his office work aside and go to the warehouse when soldiers brought him papers from their commanders requesting provisions. In
addition to that labyrinth of minutiae, he had to spend at least three hours
a day keeping the office books while everyone else was taking a siesta. The
first and last days of each month, he would stay awake the entire night,
drafting statements of income, expenditures, and cash shortages.

During one of those nights, the commander general was not sleeping in
his own bed and thus had to get up before dawn, which was not his habit.
He was curious when he saw a light on in the Customs Office, so he went
over, peered through the window, and then carefully tapped on the glass.
The employee saw him and immediately got up and let him in. When the
commander general became aware of the workload for that night and the
night before, he talked with the employee about the great amount of work
that had to be done by only one person. He said that, since limited resources
made the volume of work unavoidable, it was essential that the employee
be compensated for all the services he was rendering. The commander suggested that, after the employee calculated the exact price of all grains and
other provisions provided by the missions, he should arbitrarily increase,
by two reales, each *fanega* measured and each *arroba* weighed. With regard
to the goods, since the fractions that appeared on the measuring rods were
specified in grains, he should round off half a real to a whole one although
it might actually be one to five grains short. With luck, these strategies
would gain him about four thousand pesos by the end of the year. However,
the employee never received one real, as shall be explained later.[29]

During that time Lieutenant Colonel Don José María Padrés arrived in
Monterey in the capacity of *ayudante inspector.* He naturally was determined to encourage Señor Echeandía to issue the decree secularizing the
missions, but he was careful to conceal his ulterior motives and numerous
interests. After his plans had progressed sufficiently, he decided to take advantage of Señor Echeandía's eagerness to improve the well-being of the
mission Indians. Without advance notice, he presented the *jefe* with a program. For so many years the yoke of semislavery had been imposed upon
them. They always had been forced to work together and never had been
allowed to own anything or to say, "This is mine." With so many Indians,

some should have possessed sufficient virtue and honesty to have earned the Fathers' trust without abusing it. In fact, there had been a few such Indians, and they had been placed in charge of the keys for the money, clothing, and liquor. However, even these exceptionally virtuous Indians, who would have been good role models for others, were not deemed worthy of owning property, even a cow, a horse, or sheep. Often, friendships developed between soldiers and Indians. As friends do, the soldiers would give their protégés animals to raise, but the Fathers strongly opposed this, declaring that no Indian should ever be permitted to own even the most insignificant possessions.

Señor Echeandía had received very detailed reports of these matters. Since he saw his own good intentions furthered in Padrés' program, he naturally focused on the provisions that he approved. These especially concerned the Indian artisans and stated that the missions should provide them with the necessary tools of their trade so that they could support themselves on their own. The missions would be able to hire them, and the Fathers would always retain authority to supervise them but would have to pay them for their work.[30]

The decree of secularization was issued in 1830, despite the general disapproval of the Reverend Fathers of the missions. Since their superiors were unable to protest, they voiced their various objections to the *jefe* instead. Their objections were not heeded at all. Instead, commissioners were quickly appointed and ordered to go to the missions and enforce the decree.[31]

Señor Echeandía next wanted to open the port of San Francisco to foreign commerce. Don Joaquín Gómez arrived with letters of recommendation, and the governor appointed him *contador*. Since there were already two people working in the Customs House, he decided to transfer the administrator to San Francisco to establish a receiving port there. The administrator would nominate the other person as receiver, and then the administrator would return to occupy his post. Neither man had any idea what was about to happen.[32]

· 6 ·

W hen he served as political and military leader of Baja California, Lieutenant Colonel Don Manuel Victoria had not earned
the trust or respect of its inhabitants. Nevertheless, through
sheer determination he secured the same position in Alta California.[1] As
soon as he received the appointment, he set out overland, even though the
route was as treacherous as it was vast. He had the good luck never to be
without animals during his trip, so he traveled without delay all the way up
to Mission San Luis Rey. Once there, he introduced himself and his new
title.[2] He received the most hearty congratulations and as many gifts as a
Father could make to a newly arrived government official. The following
day he deemed it appropriate to assist Father Antonio Peyri at mass. When
the celebration of the venerable mysteries was concluded, they left the
church together. The Father was walking in a serious but satisfied manner,
but to his dismay, the scene was not complete. He needed to have another
Father by his side to whom he could say, "Now I have him in my left sleeve,
and I can take him out with my right hand anytime I need to."[3]

The previous night they had held a long conversation about the secularization of the missions. They decided that morning that Señor Echeandía's orders would not go into effect. However, for this to happen, Victoria first had to grasp the reins of government. With 150 leagues left to
travel, he set out that same day for Monterey and traveled as fast as an urgent dispatch.[4] After Mission San Luis Obispo, he began to encounter the
commissioners sent out to enforce the decree of secularization. As he
passed them, he informed them briefly that their jobs would be abolished,
since he was going to countermand Echeandía's orders.[5] When Victoria arrived unexpectedly in Monterey at dusk, he dismounted at the governor's
house. As he was dismounting, he ordered that the saddles not be removed

until he told them to do so. Señor Echeandía, unaware of who Victoria was, went out to receive him and escorted him into the parlor. As soon as the visitor sat down, he displayed his dispatches and the superior order instructing Echeandía to surrender the command of the territory. After Señor Echeandía finished reading these documents, Victoria demanded that he comply with them and surrender his command without delay.

The *jefe* was surprised by such strange rashness and by the very offensive language with which he was being addressed. He later realized that he was dealing with a man whose various promotions had improved neither his manners nor his rough speech.[6] Señor Echeandía's pride was a bit wounded, since this incident involved a questioning of his own dignity. As a result, he responded that now was not a convenient time but that he would be ready to transfer the command at nine o'clock the next morning. When the new *jefe* heard this reply, he immediately took his leave in as sophisticated a manner as a corporal can display to members of his squadron. He spent the night with the Reverend Fathers at Mission San Carlos, about a league and a quarter from the presidio.[7]

The following day Victoria returned at the appointed hour. He found everything arranged with the appropriate formality, and he took the customary oath of office in Señor Echeandía's presence. Then, since Echeandía wished to distance himself as quickly as he could from that man, he went to occupy a small house which had been loaned to him outside of the presidio or military quad.

The moment that Señor Victoria assumed the governorship, he ordered Secretary Don Agustín Zamorano to dispatch a circular directing that the secularization of the missions be suspended. The circular was sent out as soon as it was drafted. Next he requested a report on pending court cases on which he might take action which would serve as an example to the public. He was informed that a case of two infanticides, apparently perpetrated by a soldier from the San Francisco presidio company, had been pending for more than two years. He was also told about another case against an Indian for having stolen some ordinary metal buttons and a few yards of cotton cloth and calico from the *comisaría* warehouse. He was scandalized that his predecessor allowed such atrocious crimes to go unpunished. He immediately commanded Don José María Padrés to march to San Francisco the following day. As soon as he arrived, he was to arrest the soldier, Francisco Rubio, and to prosecute him for the infanticides.[8] Victoria then ordered that the young Indian who stole from the warehouse be arrested and his case prosecuted. The case had been abbreviated since the lawyer Don Rafael Gómez, was serving as *asesor*. When Gómez received the case for review, he reversed his previous position in order to please his new boss. He handed down an opinion that the young Indian deserved the death penalty since he had stolen from the public treasury. He was placed in custody and shot three days later. The most striking element of the case was that the *asesor* knew the hour when the Indian was to be executed. Yet a scant hour after he died, Gómez sent a dispatch to stay the execution because he had found in his research that the laws protected the Indian, since he was underage.[9]

A few days later the *asesor* was robbed by a convict who worked for him as a servant. The theft consisted of a few yards of cotton cloth and some other trifles which were not worth more than thirty pesos, but in his opinion the case merited the death penalty. The *jefe* ordered that the sentence be imposed, and the thief was promptly shot.[10]

The case in San Francisco against the soldier Francisco Rubio was referred to Señor Victoria for a ruling. The testimony of three witnesses was included. When they were summoned to substantiate their declarations, they denied not only having given them but also ever having appeared to testify. Therefore, they said, the declarations were invalid. They attributed them to the desire of the prosecutor, Lieutenant Don Ignacio Martínez, to take Francisco Rubio prisoner. The proceedings were sent to the *asesor* for review. He alleged that in order to save Rubio, Lieutenant Colonel Padrés had convinced the witnesses to deny what they had previously declared. Gómez and Señor Victoria agreed to countermand Padrés' opinion. Gómez recommended the death sentence, and Victoria ordered that it be carried out. Blindfolded and shackled, with a small crucifix placed in his bound hands by Reverend Father Tomás Esténaga, who was comforting him, Rubio left the *capilla* for the gallows. Lieutenant Martínez commanded the soldiers who were guarding him. When Rubio arrived at the execution site, Martínez ordered him to kneel while he read him the sentence. When he finished, he placed it on Rubio's lips for him to kiss it. With that ritual concluded, Rubio requested permission to speak, and in a fairly strong voice, he said, "Lieutenant, Sir, you have finally received the satisfaction of taking me prisoner and leading me to the slaughter. But as far as I am concerned, you are forgiven. I further promise you that my pleas to the Supreme Being will be that He, too, forgive you." Turning around so that the other onlookers could hear him, he continued, "I shall presently account for my actions to this Divine Redeemer I hold in my hands. I tell you—He is my witness—that it was not I who killed Ignacio Olivas' children. Someday you will realize this. But I have committed other offenses, and I should resign myself to the decrees of Providence."

When he finished speaking, they sat him down on the death bench. Intending to recite the Creed, the Father approached him, but Rubio's dismay was such that his tears blinded him. Choking from anguish, he could articulate only the first words of the Creed up to the part "He ascended into heaven." That was all that the soldiers needed to hear. They fired, and Rubio fell dead. Only Lieutenant Martínez referred to him as executed. Virtually all of the inhabitants of that area firmly believed that Rubio was not guilty, for a serious illness from which he suffered had left him impotent, and he was thus unable to commit the second offense of raping the bodies of the children.[11]

Moreover, it was public knowledge that Lieutenant Martínez, beginning at the rank of cadet, had served in Alta California for about forty years. During the course of the years, he had the misfortune of not being able to participate in even the slightest engagement against the Indians. (Proof of this exists in the government archives.) So that the record of his combat experience would not be entirely blank, he inserted into the record that he had apprehended a fugitive Indian named Pomponio, even though old Corporal Herrera had actually done this.[12] Also, Martínez had prepared so many criminal proceedings that for him the Rubio case was just another addition to the list of his highly esteemed and valued feats.

Don Guadalupe Vallejo was *ayudante de plaza,* but he refused to command the troop which was supposed to carry out the sentence against Rubio. However, he did go and witness it with some other people. When he heard the last words which that poor soul uttered, he decided to inquire as thoroughly as he could and discover the identity of the children's murderer. He was unsuccessful for six or seven years, during which time he was promoted to commander general and moved to Sonoma. The Indians of that area showed him a mixture of esteem, great respect, and fear. After continual requests, he finally obtained the information he desired, that an Indian named Román, from Mission San Rafael, was the one who had killed Ignacio Olivas' boy and girl. When he had verified this and had ascertained that Román was at Mission San Rafael, he ordered Sergeant Lázaro Piña to go there with a detachment of soldiers. He ordered Piña to shoot the Indian four times as soon as he found him, to leave the Indian lying there on the ground, and to return straightaway to report that he had fulfilled his duty. Two days later the order was carried out.[13]

His head swelled with pride, Commander General Victoria boasted at having ordered three people shot. Even if they were not criminals who deserved the punishment which they received, their deaths would at least serve to immortalize him as the Champion of Justice. In his conversations he liked to say that he still needed "to put a dozen more birds in the shade" if the territory were to be restored to the order he envisioned.

He shared these barbarous plans with his friend and confidant, Licenciado Don Rafael Gómez, who, with more cunning than a well-experienced fox, praised and encouraged him. This was all Victoria needed, and he began to circulate to all areas within his jurisdiction excessively detailed decrees threatening imprisonment or exile without trial.

In reaction to such conduct, three territorial delegates managed to meet at the San Francisco presidio, even though they were aware that their lives were in danger, since they were on the list of those to be "put in the shade." They faced this danger for the public good. As delegates, they agreed to send the *jefe político* a message requesting that he be kind enough to convene the *diputación,* even though the time to open the sessions had passed. Don Guadalupe Vallejo, Don Joaquín Ortega, and another person signed the petition. After waiting eight days for a response, they sent a duplicate petition to the governor, with a notice that, even if his answer was negative, they wanted a reply so that they could include it with the appeal they were sending to the supreme government. He was more angry than a snake that had been stepped on. Instead of giving a personal response, Victoria swore in a public manifesto that he would exact revenge with his own hand and would punish those three delegates for their insolence. In addition, he declared that the meeting of the *junta* of which they were members would not be permitted, because it was clear that their principal objective was the secularization of the missions, which he had thwarted. He promised to do away with that *junta,* since it comprised perverse men who opposed his authority.[14]

The delegates sent this interesting oratorical sample to Mexico along with their appeal. At the end of several months they had the satisfaction of receiving a response from the Minister of Relations. He stated that when the Excelentísimo Señor Presidente mentioned the appeal which had been sent to him, he ordered that the *jefe político* of the territory comply with the existing arrangements about the permanence and duties of the territorial assembly.

Among those exiled without trial was Don José Antonio Carillo, who was banished to the frontier of Baja California. There he was supplied with almost nothing to live on, so that the government measures which had been taken against him might seem more humane in comparison. Fortunately for him, Reverend Father Félix Caballero, a Dominican and the administrator of Mission San Miguel, offered Carrillo the warmest of hospitality in his home.[15] Despite this good treatment, Carrillo always felt like an innocent prisoner, because he was not informed of the charges against him when he was exiled. With no distractions to help him pass the time, he became depressed and consumed with desires of revenge against the *jefe político* who had sent him there and against Don Vicente Sánchez, the *alcalde* of Los Angeles who had falsely denounced him. For both amusement and revenge, Carrillo began to outline a plan of revolution. He was pleased with the final draft and wanted to put the plan into effect, but first he needed to discuss it with someone. Blessed with a dark night and a good horse, he covered the eighteen leagues which lie between San Miguel and San Diego in four hours. There Carrillo discretely met with the principal people who were generally resentful of the *jefe*'s arbitrary acts.[16]

The most notable people from the presidio crafted some amendments which they thought strengthened the plan. Then Don Pablo de la Portilla, captain commander of the Mazatlán squadron, the commander of the presidio troop, and other officers and locals adopted it.[17] Señor Echeandía did not take any part in this, probably because one of the articles stated that as soon as Lieutenant Colonel Victoria had been removed from the territorial command, he would be invited to assume the command on an interim basis, even though he was about to leave for the capital of the republic.[18] Echeandía would then be in control of both commands, and his first obligation would be promptly to convene the *diputación territorial* in the *pueblo* of Los Angeles. Without wasting time, the *diputación* would then elect or appoint the *jefe político*, the *comandante principal*, and other officers.

Soon after the plan was approved, news and copies of it were circulated. When Lieutenant Colonel Victoria learned of it, he immediately left Monterey and marched double-time to San Diego in order to surprise the insurgents before they could prepare their defenses. He intended to shoot the revolt's instigators and their accomplices. They anticipated his plans and, under the command of Captain Portilla, headed for the *pueblo* of Los Angeles. When they arrived, they discovered that the *alcalde*, Don Vicente Sánchez, was nowhere to be found. He had gone to meet Victoria to inform him who was behind the revolt. Sánchez actually was fearful, because he had imprisoned and shackled Don José María Ávila and Don Andrés Pico simply because he had the power to do so.[19] He also dreaded the revenge that Don José Antonio Carrillo wanted to take on him.

Captain Portilla's squad comprised sixty men. However, long before the start of the revolt, thirty of them had gone up to the Santa Bárbara presidio with their lieutenant, Don Juan María Ibarra. When Señor Victoria had the good fortune to pass by there, he enlisted those thirty men into his service and put them under the command of Captain Don Romualdo Pacheco.[20]

Captain Portilla assembled about two hundred armed men in Los Angeles. He knew that Victoria was approaching with a force of only thirty soldiers. He felt compassion for them but did not know how to avoid a battle which, with his larger force, meant certain death for all or most of them. Because of their integrity and courage, they deserved to be treated like adopted sons, not like common soldiers. He respected them very much because he was sure that, under different circumstances, they would sacrifice their lives to save their captain. But he knew that they would obey the man whom they recognized as their commander general, even if he imprudently led them into combat against superior forces. Therefore, considering himself as the father of sixty sons, he was faced with the possibility of ordering half of them to kill the other half. In the end, Providence proved the best commander at preventing bloodshed.[21]

Since the commander general was already near and was clearly heading for Los Angeles, Portilla left there. He intended to occupy an advantageous position at the top of one of the low ridges. Portilla positioned his force as best he could and begged all of them to return the first shot by firing a volley into the air, so as not to injure their fellow soldiers. He wanted to talk to the other side. Even though he doubted that he could convince them to come over to him, he hoped against hope that they might. Then they waited until Victoria's forces appeared, marching at a good pace, five men deep.

Shortly before they came within firing range, Captain Pacheco gave Victoria a very prudent warning, reminding him that he had but 30 men. Although they were well experienced, they were going to face 30 equally courageous comrades who were joined by an additional 150 men. It would be better to withdraw to Mission San Fernando, seven leagues away, where it was almost certain that they would not be attacked. From there they could summon the soldiers from the Santa Bárbara presidio and also persuade Captain Portilla to fulfill his duty by abandoning the rebels and reuniting with them. They could promise Portilla that he would be wel-

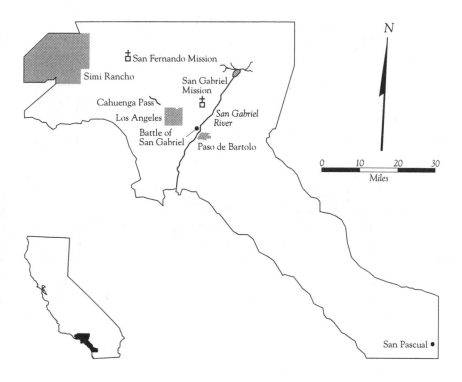

Southern California, 1846–1847

comed and pardoned. Victoria, who did not know Pacheco well, believed that this warning had been motivated more by cowardice than by prudence. He responded harshly, declaring that the officer who was "hanging on to his coattails" should not follow him. This response drew a retort from Pacheco, who told him that he was "hanging on to his own balls," as he would soon show him. He immediately positioned himself at the head of the front line, so as to be the first to enter into action.[22]

When Victoria reached the foot of the ridge, he shouted to Portilla to leave that bunch of criminals and come over and join him. Portilla ordered him to halt, and Victoria, with a rude gesture, answered that one did not order the *jefe* to halt. On that note Pacheco gave the order to advance and quickly confronted Don José María Ávila, whom he tried to strike with a saber. Both men were on very fine horses, but Ávila was more skillful in maneuvering his. With a pole on which he had outfitted a bayonet so that it would serve as a lance, he deflected the blow. When the speed of Pacheco's horse carried him past his foe, Ávila shot him in the back with a pistol. The bullet penetrated his heart, and he fell dead instantly. Ávila intended the bullet in his other pistol for Victoria, but he did not know who he was. When he was pressed hard by an artillery soldier who had joined the attackers, he refused to kill him. Instead, feeling compassion for him because he was a *californio*, Ávila only shot him in the leg. But the screams coming from this man, who looked bad and dressed even worse, in an ordinary red flannel shirt, soon made him realize that he was the *jefe*. At that moment Ávila jumped his horse as if it had sprouted wings, so he could get close to Victoria. Then he knocked him down with a bayonet that penetrated his chest. As he was doing this, Ávila was hit at close range by a bullet, which passed through his hip. He fell and was unable to get up. Seeing him thrown to the ground, Victoria approached him to thrust his sword into him, but Ávila was brave in every sense of the word. He made one last attempt to stand up and managed to catch hold of Victoria's foot. With a strong jerk he threw Victoria on his back and dragged him closer. Then he stuck his hand in his boot to take out his dagger, but fortunately for Victoria, it had fallen out. Ávila's nephew, Tomás Talamantes, saw that the soldiers were killing his uncle.[23] Although he was alone, he spurred his horse to go and defend him. He first slashed at Victoria with his saber, but one of Victoria's soldiers was alert and ready to stop such a formidable blow. He grabbed his carbine, split the chamber from the butt, and handed a small part of the tip to Victoria, who then struck Talamantes on the top of his forehead and drew blood.

Talamantes found himself amid a shower of bullets, but fortunately not one bullet struck him. When he realized that all his compatriots were fleeing, with the fastest riders in the lead, he decided that the most prudent course was to join them. So he spurred his horse and escaped before being struck by a bullet.

At that same time Don Francisco Sepúlveda appeared, but he was so full of brandy that he did not know which side he wanted to join.[24] Fortunately, he was not injured when he was fired upon, and Victoria ordered that they not shoot at him again so they could find out what he wanted. When he was questioned, he acted as if he had just awakened from a deep sleep. Finally he opened his eyes and recognized them. He told them, "Go to hell because you are not my friends," and he took off running.

When Don José Antonio Carrillo and Don Pablo de la Portilla saw first Pacheco and then Ávila fall dead, and that the thirty *mazatecos* were soldiers under the command of a good leader, they realized that their insurrection involved more than easily written words. They fled in a cowardly fashion and left the wounded Victoria, who desired confession more than combat, lord of the battlefield. In spite of the lack of spirit they had shown, they continued to boast. It should be noted that, even though they have bragged tremendously since the insurrection, they had twice as much left in reserve as their opponents. They never had the decency to say later why they had not somehow aided Ávila and Talamantes, the only two men, out of more than two hundred in the force, who joined the battle and distinguished themselves courageously. The arrogance of Portilla and Carrillo did not permit them to admit their defeat, unlike the thirty insurgent *mazatecos,* or Alférez Don Ignacio del Valle, or Don Andrés Pico, who did so openly. The *mazatecos* confessed that they should have obeyed their captain's orders. Don Ignacio del Valle confessed that, when the army had begun to disintegrate, he raced five leagues without resting his horse until he arrived at Los Nietos Ranch.[25] There, he stopped those who were arriving, encouraged them, and then sent them back to the battle. And Don Andrés Pico confessed that he did what everyone else did. Since he did not believe he would be safe in the town, he spurred his horse and went straight to a vineyard containing some narrow furrows. He placed his tired animal in one furrow and hid himself in another, underneath a very bushy grapevine, until hunger made him come out little by little to discover the outcome of the encounter with Commander General Victoria.

When this lord of the battlefield found himself lying there with two corpses, he thought that he had been mortally wounded and that his body would soon turn into a third, so he headed for Mission San Gabriel for spiritual help. There he discovered that Don Carlos Anderson, an excellent doctor from the great English Company of Calcutta, just happened to be aboard a ship anchored in San Pedro Bay.[26] They set out on fine horses to inform him of everything and to bring him back equipped with the necessary medications. They rapidly traveled the twenty-league round-trip. When Anderson dismounted and saw his patient's wound, he declared that it would be fatal if the medicine did not take effect several hours after being applied. At the end of that period of time he confirmed that Victoria was out of mortal danger.

Before the doctor gave that assurance, an urgent dispatch was sent to Señor Echeandía, summoning him to come as soon as possible to receive the territorial command. Señor Victoria stated that he was gravely ill and wanted to entrust him with the command before he died. Echeandía did

Ignacio del Valle. Courtesy of the California State Library, Sacramento.

not hesitate, and as soon as he assumed the command, he sent out a notice that the delegates were to assemble on a certain day in the *pueblo* of Los Angeles, the location designated for the *diputación territorial* to convene its sessions. Señores Don Santiago Argüello, Don Pío Pico, Don Joaquín Ortega, Don Tomás Yorba, Don Guadalupe Vallejo, and another person all attended.[27]

When more than the necessary number of *vocales* had assembled, Señor Echeandía was notified so that he could preside over the *diputación*, or at least over the opening sessions. However, he responded from Mission San Juan Capistrano that he had urgent business at hand and would come as soon as the most important matters were resolved. These included obtaining funds to pay the supercargo of an American frigate for Señor Victoria's passage from San Diego to San Blas and drawing up a case against Victoria, which would be sent to the supreme government on the same ship. When the money had been obtained and the second order of business had been finished, the *californios* began to throw corrupt officials out of the territory, telling the First Magistrate of the Republic, "Take note of why I am returning your man to you." It was known that the general government sought only two things from Alta California: first, that it not be annexed, and, second, that it not bother the government by asking for money. As long as they did not do these things, the government compensated them by allowing them to do as they pleased and govern themselves as they saw fit.

After having rid themselves of Señor Victoria, the delegates in Los Angeles waited many days for Señor Echeandía. They finally decided that the interim *jefe* no longer agreed with the plan of insurrection and wanted to delay the installation of the *diputación*. Echeandía believed that the *diputación* would begin by appointing a *jefe político* and a commander general from the military ranks. He would then be left without any official standing in the territory, precisely at a time when he did not want to obey the order to return to the capital of the republic as soon as possible.

Consequently, the *junta* was installed under the presidency of Don Pío Pico. Since he was the senior *vocal*, he was then appointed *jefe político*.[28] When Señor Echeandía was informed of this, he did not approve, for the above reason, and that refusal had far-reaching consequences. When Captain Don Agustín Zamorano learned of Pico's appointment, he also named himself *jefe político* and commander general, because he did not want to serve under Pico again. Zamorano formed a party which included people from the northern part of the territory to as far south as Santa Bárbara.[29]

He gave it the colorful, high-sounding name Division of the Supreme Government. Next he drew up a list of people whom he specifically selected from the least desirable classes, such as convicts, exiles, assassins, and thieves. He selected one of them to lead the others, and he called them soldiers of the Division of the Supreme Government. They were over one hundred strong. Zamorano dispatched them with authority to go down as far as the San Diego presidio and eliminate as many delegates, political leaders, and commanding generals as they could find.

So they left, falsely assured by Zamorano that they were part of the supreme government and not pawns of an opportunist. When they arrived at the Buenavista Ranch, five leagues from Monterey, they seized the house of the owner, Don Mariano Estrada. As a means of "assisting" the supreme government, they took whatever they felt they needed. However, they did not remove anything superfluous, that is to say, roof tiles or foundation stones. Such conduct was natural for these men. Since they repeated it along various parts of their route, Zamorano was forced to order their immediate return.[30] In their place he sent Lieutenant Don Juan María Ibarra down to Los Angeles with about one hundred men from a different class.[31] At this time the *diputación* did not recognize any *jefe político* other than the one it had appointed. Señor Echeandía, who had not surrendered the command, also wanted to be *jefe político*. However, all those gathered in San Diego maintained harmonious relations in hopes that persuasion would work.

Knowing that Ibarra was approaching with hostile intent, the southern party united. Fourteen men under the command of Captain Don Leonardo Barroso quickly set out with a cannon to occupy a crossing of the San Gabriel River called Bartolo Crossing.[32] This dangerous crossing was the only one usable during that time, because the rains and flooding had left the other crossings so full of loose and shifting sand that they were impassable. Ibarra soon found out that they were waiting for him there. In spite of his superior force, he did not dare attempt to cross. Instead, he remained on the lookout and positioned watchmen on the high point of a low ridge in order to observe their operations.

Señor Echeandía believed that all of the inhabitants of the north were bearing down upon him to divest him of a command that he viewed as his own. Since he did not want to suffer the humiliation of being stripped of the command by force, he proposed to take the most extreme measures. If necessary, these would include persuading the Indian tribes to side with

Self-portrait of Agustín Zamorano. Courtesy of the California State Library, Sacramento.

him. Since Echeandía was an obstinate man, he gave no thought to the deadly consequences which this action could produce for the territory. He sent messages to the Indians in various areas, telling them that he needed them immediately. They should come as quickly as possible to the Bartolo Crossing at the San Gabriel River with their weapons. There they would be under the command of Captain Barroso. Within five days about five hundred Indians from the immediate area arrived in various groups. After ten days, more than one thousand Indians had gathered. The best riders were issued horses and about three hundred lances and were instructed in cav-alry maneuvers. At that time Mission San Gabriel had so many horses that there still would have been more than enough left for daily work even if they had taken another thousand from the mission.[33]

Day by day that gathering of so many enemies from another class was becoming more dangerous for the territory. In order to save the territory from the threat that was building, the members of the *diputación* left Cap-tain Barroso's ranks and set up a "meeting hall" right there under the shade of a beautiful elder tree. The *junta* was convened with the required number of *vocales*. In an extraordinary session they agreed to send Echeandía a strong protest against the use of Indian forces.[34] They also asked that he appear there as soon as possible so that his presence and that of his troops and aux-iliaries might restrain the Indians. They were already seeking to set out on their own to attack Ibarra and his troops, who were quartered in the cen-ter of the *pueblo* of Los Angeles. The Indians could have accomplished this on one dark night, and it was imperative that it not be allowed to occur. Their victory would inevitably result in the atrocities of which they were capable, and general chaos would follow.

To keep Ibarra from leaving his position, they sent him another message that same day. They attached to it a copy of the protest to Señor Echeandía. As soon as Ibarra received it, he responded that he was simply a subordi-nate and unable to resolve anything himself, but he had already sent urgent communiqués to Señor Zamorano at Santa Bárbara. Two days later Señor Echeandía arrived with nearly two hundred men and seven cannons. On the following day a communiqué arrived from Ibarra, stating that he was going to evacuate the *plaza* in Los Angeles the following morning because his superior had ordered him to march to Santa Bárbara and join him there.

When Ibarra left Los Angeles, Señor Echeandía broke camp and en-tered the *pueblo* in the afternoon with more than one thousand mounted Indians and about three hundred soldiers and auxiliaries. He spent the night on the plain below the town and the following day went to Mission San Gabriel. After flattering the Indians, he sent them back to their re-spective *rancherías* and missions. He then turned to his disputes with Zamorano, which were clearly headed toward a bloody encounter and other consequences which would benefit only the general government. So one man commanded from Santa Bárbara north, while the other commanded from Los Angeles south. The *diputación* did not recognize either man as *jefe político* and continued to declare that it alone was able to resolve disagreements.

Since the only customs house was the one in Monterey, foreign merchant vessels reported there to import their cargo. The *jefe* of the north generously agreed to split evenly with the *jefe* of the south the duties which these ships paid.[35] Since neither one of them had the appropriate authorization, they abstained from granting titles of ownership to the uncultivated lands and advised people to wait until Mexico sent a governor.

During this crisis or dangerous chaos, three *jefes políticos* functioned at the same time in a territory of more than nine thousand people, not counting Indians. It was feared that crimes of every sort would multiply and administration of justice would be paralyzed. However, anxious to gain good reputations, that divided trinity of *jefes* worked incessantly to maintain tranquillity and order. This produced good results, and there were no incidents of theft or murder during their tenure.

· 7 ·

At the beginning of 1833 the national brigantine *Catalina* was anchored in the port of Monterey. It carried General Don José Figueroa, who had been appointed commander general and *jefe político* of Alta California, some officers, and about thirty infantry soldiers. It also carried a dozen Fathers from the Colegio de Guadalupe de Zacatecas and their Superior, Reverend Father Francisco García Diego, who had the title of Padre Comisario. So as not to interrupt the narrative about the Fathers and the missions, the account about the new *jefe* will follow later. The Fathers of the Colegio de San Fernando in Mexico were expecting the newcomers and waiting to be ordered to surrender some or all of the twenty-one missions to them. They allegedly wanted to destroy the missions before the newcomers could receive them, as if to say, "I do not want you serving yourself from a table that I have worked so hard to prepare for the members of my community."

It is not my intention to tarnish the conduct of those Reverend Fathers. I am only recounting the deeds. If any proof were needed, their collective discontent would be the first. The second would be that the Prefect sent an order to the Father Administrator of Mission San Luis Obispo instructing him to see how he could destroy the mission interests quickly so that the Indians could take advantage of them. For a number of days the Reverend Father pondered how he could achieve his Prelate's aims. In the end he spent more than twenty thousand pesos purchasing fine woven goods of cotton, wool, and silk and distributed them to his neophytes so that they could dress themselves.[1] The third proof would be that other missions hastened to slaughter cattle only for the hides. When they realized that they did not have enough workers to finish the slaughter quickly, they contracted out half of the work to various people. During these horrible slaughters, the animal fat had to be strewn along the ground and the meat left to rot in the fields. From 1832 to 1834 the traders who received the hides of the Mission San Gabriel steers estimated that more than one hundred thousand hides were taken and loaded onto ships in San Pedro Bay.[2]

Father García Diego had not brought a sufficient number of missionaries to administer all of the missions in the territory, so he and Reverend Father Narciso Durán, the superior from the Colegio de San Fernando, agreed that Durán would come down with his subordinates to oversee the southern missions.[3] Father Tomás Esténaga was assigned to Mission San Gabriel. Because Esténaga gave away the possessions of the Fathers, after a short time he was obliged to accept meat and lard as charity. Don Tomás Yorba would send him these items from his Santa Ana Ranch. Yorba also loaned him a cow so that he would have milk, because there were no longer any cattle at the mission.[4] A number of these Fathers suffered the hardships which they had intended for others. However, they were very good religious men and made do when they recognized that all, or at least some, of them were guilty of failing to observe the precept "Do unto others as you would have them do unto you."

To prepare the yearly general financial statement, the territorial government would ask the Father Superior to provide statistics from each of the twenty-one missions. These statistics included an inventory of goods, the number of Indians born and baptized at each mission, the number of infants and adults who by being conquered had been reborn by water and the Holy Spirit, and the number of those who had died. Equally important were the number of bushels of harvested seeds and the number of different types of livestock, although the Fathers never gave an exact number of cattle. In the statistics from Mission San Gabriel, dating from 1824 up to the beginning of its downfall, the number of cattle reported was always the same, forty thousand. However, the numbers were much higher during their years of greatest wealth. By using the approximate calculations made by various interested people along with information acquired from the *mayordomos* in charge of the mission fields, and by increasing the number of cattle branded by two-thirds, one can arrive at the following statistics.

San Diego	7,000
San Luis Rey	18,000
San Juan Capistrano	60,000
San Gabriel	110,000

San Fernando	25,000
San Buenaventura	19,000
Santa Bárbara	12,000
Santa Ynés	17,000
La Purísima	20,000
San Luis Obispo	18,000
San Miguel	12,000
San Antonio	16,000
Soledad	14,000
San Carlos	6,000
San Juan Bautista	18,000[5]
Santa Cruz	12,000
Santa Clara	13,000
San José	18,000
San Francisco de Asís	8,000
San Rafael	5,000
San Francisco Solano	7,000
	435,000

One should note that this estimate of the number of cattle was made by increasing the number of those branded by two-thirds.[6] The missions' estimates were never done with the enthusiasm or with the accuracy demonstrated by private cattle owners. Consequently, many animals were left unbranded because the missions occupied such large expanses of land.

The experience of many years has demonstrated that the Reverend Fathers were eager to convert the infidels in order to achieve two different objectives. The first was admirable and part of their obligation as true apostles to win souls for Heaven. God, who is as good as He is just, would reward them for their evangelical work. But the Indians cared very little about improving their habits while in reduction.[7] In addition, the lack of workmen to replace those who were dying affected that objective adversely, for once an Indian was baptized and affiliated with a mission, he belonged to that mission alone. So he did not have the freedom to marry an Indian woman from another mission, since she was obligated to follow her husband, and that would change the total number of Indians at each mission. In the case of an Indian woman, the mission Father would not allow one of his flock to be taken from him. In the case of a man, the Father would not want to relinquish a pair of strong arms. As proof I will recount the following incident.

Once, when Reverend Father Tomás Esténaga was the Administrator of

Mission San Carlos. From Vancouver, A *Voyage of Discovery to the North Pacific Ocean*, ca. 1798. Courtesy of the California State Library, Sacramento.

Mission San Francisco, there was an illness among his neophytes which affected the women more than the men. According to the statistics, about half the women died.[8] Since a number of young men were left unable to find women to marry, Father Esténaga was continually striving to sustain the marriages. If a wife was unfaithful, he would advise the husband to tolerate the suffering. Meanwhile, the seducer would be flogged as punishment. This had become commonplace, and the Father's advice to the poor husbands was always the same. Finally, one of the many affected Indians decided to break the silence. With desperate gestures he said, "Tell me, Father, if you were married, how many times would you tolerate being a cuckold? It has happened to me so many times that I am ready to explode from your advice. Even if you kill me I cannot take it anymore." The Father was able to contain his laughter and appear serious only because he had a terrible stomachache. He promised the poor soul that he was now going to take more efficient measures to prevent the unmarried men from stealing their women. He would send the men off to work at the mission in Contra Costa.[9]

When he revealed this plan to the guilty parties, they explained the reasons for their conduct to the Father. Some of their reasons were very sensible. They wanted to have a woman, and there were none at the mission except for very young girls. When these girls matured, there still would not be enough of them available for even half of the men. And they could not marry women from another mission because the Fathers there did not want to relinquish them. So they proposed that Esténaga lend them the barge, which was about seven tons, and give them the necessary provisions and some gifts so that they could seek out women wherever possible among the gentiles.

The Father responded to such a reasonable request by providing them with everything they needed for their expedition. They headed in the direction of Point Olompali, which was in the jurisdiction of Mission San Rafael.[10] The estuaries there offer excellent and secure landings for barges. About ten or twelve *vaqueros* had put their horses on board. As soon as they had made the crossing safely, they unloaded the gifts they had brought and headed for the interior. There they found what they were seeking. They joyfully boarded the barge to return quickly to the mission and celebrate their weddings. However, a young Indian from that tribe was bitter because his intended had rejected him by leaving with one of the Indians from San Francisco. In retaliation, he ran to San Rafael to inform Reverend Father José Altimira that the men on the barge and some *vaqueros* from San Francisco were stealing some of the gentile women.

Although these women were not affiliated with Mission San Rafael, because they were not baptized, the Father believed that he had an undeniable right to them.[11] He wanted to act as the judge in his own case and hand down a decision which would serve as an example. To achieve this, he manned a beautiful boat which he had at his disposal with a good, strong crew for rowing. He put a corporal and four armed soldiers from the escort on board and sent them off to confront the barge. Favored by a light breeze from the northeast, the men on the barge were soon sailing past the wall of rock called the Treasure.[12] The boat, meanwhile, had not even cleared the estuary of San Rafael. At that pace the Father believed that he would not be able to catch up with the barge. Exhibiting his reverend anger, he began to kick violently, without worrying about breaking a plank. He bit his lips and screamed at them to put more energy into each stroke. As soon as they cleared the estuary, the well-experienced Indian chief ordered the crew to stop rowing so he could observe the currents. This, however, irritated the Father. It seemed to him to be a malicious delay, and he hurled insults at the chief, who tolerated them in silence. The Indian who was at the front of the boat could not observe the force of the current, and it was necessary for him to stop rowing for a time. Fortunately he was confident of his skill, so he told the Father to shut his mouth because he did not know what he was saying. The current was about to change, and if they set their course in the direction of the barge, they almost certainly would catch up to it. When the Father heard this, he promised that they would be well compensated if they succeeded, but if not, he would tan their hides. Apparently the Indian slightly changed the boat's heading in order to position it in a favorable current. After sailing a while, he realized that the barge was beginning to slow down because of the countercurrent. However, his knowledge had enabled him to choose the favorable one. He let out a shout of joy and said, "Now we've got them."

The current shifted on him near the northern point of the strait of Angel Island. By circling around the opposite side of the island from where the barge was heading, he pulled ahead of it and positioned his boat parallel to the barge. They drew closer in order to speak, and the Father ordered the captain of the barge to turn around and head for San Rafael. Seeing that he could not escape because of the boat's superior speed and the soldiers' weapons, the poor soul obeyed immediately. Carried by a northeast wind and a favorable current, they arrived at the mouth of the San Rafael estuary. The tide was beginning to rise, but there was not enough water to allow the barge to pass through, so the Father ordered them all to leap ashore right there. Then he ordered that each Indian from San Francisco be given fifty lashes. After the discipline of the whip, they suffered the greater sorrow of having the women taken away from them. As a crowning indignity, the saddles were taken away from the *vaqueros* as compensation for damages and losses.[13] Finally the Father ordered them all to leave immediately and report everything to Father Esténaga.[14]

When the Indians led the life of wandering savages, they were accustomed to the fresh air of the mountains and valleys where they lived and enjoyed good health. Their subsequent confinement behind infected walls was very harmful to them. Each mission was constructed so as to include two rooms as large as parlors, where the unmarried and widowed people would sleep on the floor, with men and women segregated.[15] The walls were normally a yard thick, and there was not adequate ventilation. Imagine the stench that would emanate from those bodies, which generally were not clean. The basic reason they were soon attacked by illnesses was that they were unable to breathe fresh air. Because there was no one available who could give them the necessary medications, these illnesses soon became chronic. In addition, those who already were living in reduction were plagued by venereal diseases, which they later transmitted to the robust and healthy Indians who arrived from outside the missions. Consequently, about one-third of the few children who were born would die, and another third would die before reaching puberty. The health of the remaining third was such that a good government would have placed them in hospitals as an act of charity.[16]

Debilitated by such serious illness, it was common for them to succumb to any other minor illness which might attack them. Therefore, the annual burial and baptismal registries usually showed about two-thirds more burials than baptisms. Reverend Father Antonio Peyri also made this observation. When he was chosen to found Mission San Luis Rey, his knowledge of architecture helped him in many ways to design a structure most suitable for the church building, the different workshops, and the other mission offices. He also added a room for a *curandero* and two long rooms to serve as a hospital, for the comfort of the sick.[17] He even provided for their spiritual health by designing a chapel with doors which could be accessed from both sides and which were arranged so that the sick, both men and women, could hear mass from their beds.[18] His insistence that his neophytes keep their bodies and their dwellings clean provided him with a great challenge. To meet it he had a trench dug from an adjacent bog toward the front of the main house. There he dug two large ditches, which drained into two well-constructed reservoirs of brick and mortar. One was designated the women's bath, and the other, the men's. Once the Indians became accustomed to bathing, one would find the baths occupied from four in the morning until eleven at night.[19] He ordered the Indians' homes, a type of hut, to be constructed at a reasonably safe distance from each other, so that, once destroyed, they could be rebuilt. For example, if someone past the age of adolescence died in a hut, it would be set on fire. Immediately after the flames had consumed it, many men could build another hut for the family on the same spot. Under the threat of severe penalties, the *alcaldes* of the mission were entrusted with keeping a careful watch over the Indians to ascertain who was ill and who might have contracted a contagious disease. As soon as they detected such a case, they would take the person to the place designated for the sick, according to their sex. The Father would be notified so he could attend to the person's treatment. With these efforts Reverend Father Peyri succeeded in making his mission the only one where the Indians made progress. Until he left the territory for having sympathized with his friend Don Manuel Victoria, Father Peyri always cared for more than two thousand Indians at his mission, and they enjoyed better health than those at the other missions.[20]

About the doings of Señor Figueroa, one can say that after this *jefe* arrived in Monterey and assumed the command of the territory, Captain Zamorano, the perpetual government secretary, briefed him extremely well on the state of affairs in the country and on all that had occurred since Lieutenant Colonel Don Manuel Victoria had arrived. Figueroa also learned the names of the most important members of the southern party. He was informed that people had been hopeful that he would arrive quickly and unify everyone under his command, so he began by circulating a decree of amnesty. It did not pertain to everyone, only to those who were or might have been insubordinate to the supreme government. At the same time Figueroa sent everyone very persuasive letters in which he offered himself and his services in exchange for their friendship, advice, and cooperation. He also expressed the hope that the territory would experience beneficial reforms and improvements, given the good intentions he was bringing to such important tasks.

With great tact he managed to persuade them in his favor. From the beginning he easily was able to perceive the distinctiveness of the *californios*. They greatly appreciated the way he conducted himself and his effort to be respected rather than feared. They found in him the fine qualities they had hoped for and a good friend who was always ready to help in any manner which did not conflict with his decorum and duty. The disagreements caused by the spirit of party disappeared when he decided to assume the responsibility of being the principal agent of reconciliation. Making good use of the overall respect which people had for him, he obtained everything simply by stating that those were his desires and that everyone should work together for the good of the country.[21]

It was recommended to him that he not allow the *diputación territorial* of Alta California to hinder his work and authority. Since elections for the *diputación* had not been held yet, he gave orders that they take place. He then sent out the summons for them to meet in the capital. When the *junta* was installed, he concerned himself with the condition of the interior of the country. Later the missions' interests were the principal topic of discussion. This resulted in the divestment of the Reverend Fathers' temporal possessions and the placement at each mission of an Administrator who would receive a regular salary and whose hands would be tied only by the strength of his conscience.[22]

During that time the change of climate began to affect Señor Figueroa's health, and he petitioned the general government to be kind enough to relieve him of the political command of the territory. He would retain only the military command.[23] When this request became public, along with the fact that the temporal benefits of the missions had been taken away from the Fathers, it was like news heralded by a horrible-sounding trumpet. It injured a few ears here, but when the echo was heard in Mexico, some people felt that it was very harmonious. At once two excellent schemers of considerable influence joined forces to obtain everything that they needed from the government for the success of their project. In order to maintain appearances, they proposed to take a colony of settlers from the capital to Alta California. They put into play all of their influence to get the government to approve their plan, give them sufficient money for their transportation, and appoint Don José María Híjar as director of the colony and *jefe político* to relieve General Figueroa as he had asked.[24]

When Señor Híjar obtained some money and the desired commissions, he announced to those who wished to forsake poverty that he was recruiting people for the colony. They would be transported with all of the amenities, and it would not cost Alta California anything. When they arrived they would be given as much land as they could cultivate and as many male and female Indian laborers as they might need. With the Indians' assistance they could raise a variety of grains each year and sell the abundant harvests to foreign exporters for a good price. They could also raise cattle, but one cow was not worth more than one peso. Otter hunting was more lucrative. Not wanting to exaggerate, the directors assured the colonists that there were so many otters, even at the entrances to the ports, that some ships were actually detained by them. They had to club the otters to death in order to clear the way. During that time a fine pelt was worth 125 pesos in Mexico. When people heard those promises of making a colossal fortune in a very short time, the impresarios soon attracted a sufficient number of people whom they dubbed "colonists." They decided to send the colonists quickly to the port of San Blas to board some ships, including the national corvette *Morelos*, before someone could denounce them to the government and disillusion the colonists.[25]

However, as the directors and colonists were about to begin their march from the capital, the directors had to seek help from the soldiers in the nearby barracks. They had to be guarded as they left, because the masses attempted to scatter them with stones when the deception was revealed. Fear of the soldiers served to reduce the shower of rocks, and the crowd compensated for that with ear-splitting screams, whistles, and clapping. Those who were being taunted suffered patiently in exchange for not having their heads split open.[26]

After suffering great hardships which naturally afflict people who are unaccustomed to traveling, they arrived in Tepic. They had to wait there because the ships were not yet equipped, but Señor Híjar redoubled his determination to resolve the difficulties and to depart as soon as possible. He had maintained appearances up to that point and did not want to be discovered because of the delay. From one moment to the next, Híjar feared that someone might inform the government that his principal goals were not colonization.

His fears were well founded. In the end the government was informed that the grand colonization project would benefit only its director by furthering his premeditated plans. His main goal was to extend his power by taking control of the political government of Alta California and helping himself to the mission interests. He then would negotiate abroad with the spoils, using agents, including some of the colonists he was bringing with him, who were already prepared. Señor Híjar was therefore ordered by the ministry to stay where he was until he received new orders. This, however, merely served as an incentive to him to hasten the departure of the colony. With the money he had been able to acquire, he quickly managed to board the colonists on the corvette *Morelos* and the brigantine *Natalia,* which were anchored in the Bay of San Blas, and had them set sail for their destination.[27]

Señor Híjar's insubordination confirmed for the government the truth of the reports it had received. The reports indicated that the brigantine *Natalia* had been purchased on the company account and that the arms and munitions, taken from the capital under the pretense that the colonists would use them to defend themselves against the barbarous Indians, were actually to be used by the colonists in an uprising against the government whenever Híjar decided to carry out his premeditated plans.[28]

When the government, well informed about the entire matter, realized that in San Blas and Acapulco there was no ship equipped to take a communiqué to Alta California, it decided to risk sending an urgent dispatch by land. The man who carried the single page was promised three thousand pesos if he succeeded in personally delivering the communiqué to General Figueroa before Señor Híjar took over the political command of the territory. He was also given a general order so that he would be provided with whatever assistance he might need on his journey.[29]

Happily, the man covered the great distance between Mexico and the state of Sonora.[30] However, when he arrived at the Colorado River, he was detained by Indians who warned him every day that they would kill him the next day. In the end the Indians resigned themselves to taking his horse, the courier insignias, and his clothing. In return they made a raft for him to cross the river and gave him directions on the best way to travel so he could arrive as soon as possible at some populated point in California. He was in an unknown desert and naturally began to experience hunger and especially thirst. He realized that he was losing his strength little by little and, worse, his spirit. At midday, when he would feel the penetrating heat of the sun, he could not find water or succulent plants to moisten his throat. However, he was a man of great courage. At night he would proceed at a trot as far as he could, using a star as his compass. That way he would not tire himself as much the following day from the heat of the sun. He walked in that manner until he found water, either by accident or good fortune. Because he had gone without water for three days, he was careful not to drink too much at first. In the same spot he found shrubs laden with a small black fruit. When he tried the fruit, he found it to be bittersweet yet very tasty. Because he was fearful of it, he ate little and waited for its side effects, which, in the end, were that he ate more. According to his description, they probably were wild gooseberries. Besides providing him with nourishment, they also refreshed him. He found this type of relief for two or three more days along his route, and then he arrived at Mission San Luis Rey. After eating there, he wanted to continue traveling, so they gave him horses and a guide. By his calculations, including all his stops along the way, forty-five days had elapsed between his departure from Mexico and his arrival in Monterey. He delivered, personally and in time, the communiqué whose contents were condensed into a few words for Señor Figueroa. The document ordered Figueroa not to surrender the political command of the territory to Don José María Híjar even if he presented documents ordering it and commanding him to furnish Híjar with the resources necessary to establish the colony in the most convenient location.

Señor Híjar arrived at the port of San Diego on the brigantine *Natalia* with a portion of the colony. The rest of the colonists arrived on the corvette *Morelos* at the port of Monterey. Therefore, it took the director of the colony quite a few days to travel up to the capital. After arriving, he attempted to have the political command surrendered to him, as if he knew nothing about the communiqué which had arrived from Mexico by land.[31]

Señor Figueroa only wanted to have to take care of the general command, so that he could have more rest. Yet he had to comply with the order which he had received to retain both commands, and he informed Señor Híjar of the situation. When Señor Híjar realized that his lofty projects were being thwarted, he tried every means of persuasion which occurred to him to induce the general to surrender the government to him under any pretense. Since he was unable to obtain what he wanted, as a last resort he launched into a description of his projects. He promised Señor Figueroa a considerable portion of the profits that would be gained from speculating with the mission interests. According to his calculations, the results would be favorable and certain. Señor Figueroa used great tact in seeking to elude the proposition. He responded that he was in a good mood at that moment and Híjar's joke was a welcome respite from the serious matters which had for so long occupied his attention. Señor Figueroa assured him that, since he was a veteran soldier and a faithful follower of orders from his superiors, he would never do anything else but comply with those orders.

Señor Figueroa's refusal to surrender the political command to Señor Híjar prompted a long exchange between the two men. Figueroa stated that he needed to consult with the *diputación territorial* about the transfer of command. The *diputación* in turn stated that in light of the order from Mexico, Señor Figueroa should not surrender the government to Señor Híjar. The *diputación* decided to obey the general government, even though the reason for that government's decision had not been given.[32]

Even when Señor Híjar and Señor Padrés saw this final negative reply, they did not lose hope of getting what they wanted. They employed intrigue and sedition through agents who were scattered throughout Señor Híjar's government. These minions dispersed and began to encourage the separation of the political and military commands. They invited any *californios* of a restless spirit to form a party. When the *californios* discovered that the intentions were to appoint specific people to certain positions and that these people were incompetent, they naturally rejected the idea. The agents immediately began to provoke the gullible Indians living in the great San Gabriel Valley as far out as San Bernardino. The Indians were so provoked that they wanted to make an attempt on the life of Father Esténaga. However, someone explained the entire situation to them, and the Indians felt sorry for having made the Father suffer so much when he went out to calm them down. For example, when they took him prisoner in the field, they made him walk at their pace toward the mountains. When he became so tired that he could no longer stand up straight, they shot him in the back with an arrow.[33]

The agents' last resort was to seduce a portion of lost souls from Sonora, who were unemployed in the *pueblo* of Los Angeles and who had no occupation other than playing cards.[34] Señor Híjar's agents promised to give them enough money to revolt against Señor Figueroa and afterward to improve the lot of each one of them. Since these preparations were not secret, everyone knew what was happening, including Lieutenant Colonel Nicolás Gutiérrez, who was quartered with the Mazatlán squadron at Mission San Gabriel. Gutiérrez had been instructed ahead of time to allow the plotters to operate freely and not to fear their intrigues. Finally, when they had prepared everything, they proclaimed their revolt that night at Los Nietos Ranch. By dawn they were in the *pueblo* of Los Angeles. They promised good pay to those who wished to join their ranks, but they managed to enlist only one *californio.* After he had been with them for two or three hours, the sleep-inducing effects of his liquor wore off, and he angrily demanded to know what rogue had placed him among that riffraff. Since no one would answer him, he left.

Around ten o'clock in the morning the *ayuntamiento* met in a special session and appointed a committee to communicate with the commander of the revolutionaries and plead with him to take his troops out of the city. The commander responded that he did indeed respect the authority of the Señor Presidente very much in spite of the fact that he was being shown little respect. He said his troops were actually there to uphold public order. At two in the afternoon the *pronunciados* demanded the money which the principal instigators of the revolution had promised them, but they had depleted their financial resources. Since they had no money and were unable to obtain even a loan, their scheming became apparent. So, the very people they had tricked seized them and practically dragged them to the authorities. The *pronunciados* explained that they had recognized their mistake before having harmed anyone and that they were therefore handing over the disloyal ones with the plea that those who had been seduced be pardoned.[35]

The doctor, Don Francisco Torres, and the Spanish adventurer, Don Antonio Apalátegui, were each handcuffed and immediately placed in jail. During the night they were sent to San Gabriel with due precautions so that Lieutenant Colonel Gutiérrez could guard them with greater security.[36] That same afternoon the *alcalde* of Los Angeles sent the *jefe político* an urgent dispatch, in which he informed him of everything that had happened.[37] He also included a copy of the insurrection plan and the contrite statement by the rebels. He requested that the *jefe* grant them a pardon since the Señor Alcalde was not authorized to do so. The *jefe* replied seven days later. He expressed the appropriate gratitude to the *alcalde* for his good behavior, and he also granted the revolutionaries' request.

The government had warned Señor Híjar well in advance to restrain the revolutionaries whom he had brought to a peaceful country as colonists. Even though the government was aware of all his intrigues, the Señor Director of Colonization responded in his customary cold-blooded manner. He stated that he could not believe that a few men in a strange country, unfamiliar with the people and without resources, could be so foolish as to want to revolt. He was then told that a revolution, led by Doctor Don Francisco Torres, had broken out in the *pueblo* of Los Angeles. In addition, he was provided with the details of what Torres had managed to accomplish. Still he responded in his usual manner and acted very surprised. He said that he did not know why Torres would have been inclined to revolt, rather than fulfill his mission of delivering interesting papers that had been entrusted to him by the supreme government.[38]

To conclude, given the labyrinth of the colonization project and the aspirations of the directors and their followers, the territorial government decided to suspend the directors from their positions and return them to Mexico as prisoners. Accordingly, Señor Figueroa gave orders to disarm the colonists, apprehend the directors, and charter a ship to transport them to the port of San Blas.[39] The directors were to be delivered to the supreme government along with the charges against them. Señor Figueroa, who was now free of the immediate problem, decided to print the official communications which had been exchanged between the *jefe* of the territory, the *diputación*, and the principal director of colonization. For the satisfaction of the public, this was done in the form of a printed manifesto.[40]

When the manifesto was finished, he did not have time to have it printed, since he became seriously ill and died in September 1835. However, his secretary, Don Agustín Zamorano, attended to it. After he had compiled various notebooks, he distributed them among the friends of the deceased general. In the notebook one is given an extensive view of everything that happened during Señor Figueroa's tenure in government. Therefore, it would be advantageous for the person who is entrusted to write the history of Alta California to make use of the notebook.

With regard to Señor Figueroa's political governance, no one ever complained of having been reprimanded by him in offensive language. Although people's behavior might have merited their being treated in an offensive manner, Señor Figueroa would speak quite pleasantly to them, encouraging them to acknowledge their bad conduct, counseling them, and outlining the types of good behavior which they should follow. Consequently, Señor Figueroa had good friends even among the lower classes of society.

With regard to proper respect for the authorities, he also gave good examples in a number of cases, such as the following. When Don David Spence was the *alcalde* of the municipality of Monterey, his only desire was to fulfill his obligation and to perform the different duties of his position with prudence and sound judgment. When he arrived in the country, Spence was associated with the English company which had established contacts in Monterey before 1825. After marrying, he settled in Monterey and eventually was considered a Mexican citizen. His good behavior was a credit to his Scottish origins. Stoic in reason, honor, and deeds, he was one of those individuals described by Walter Scott before the union of the two crowns. Therefore, his judgment was never tainted by connivance, and he never failed to enforce an explicit law out of fear, as he once demonstrated during the Easter holiday festivities. The customs administrator, Don Ángel Ramírez, wanted to include a game of monte as part of the entertainment, with Señor Figueroa as his silent partner. But when Ramírez set up the gaming table in a public place, he received a discreet and polite warning from the judge, Señor Spence, that he should dismantle the table or place it where Spence would not see it and be forced to take action. The fearless monte player was accustomed to doing things his own way and did not heed the warning. Half an hour later, as the cards were about to be cut, the staff of justice fell upon the cards and upon Ramírez, who was notified that he would be fined fifty pesos. He was so surprised that he was unable to come up with one of his many splendid excuses. He could only give the real one, that he could not be fined for playing the game with the Señor Jefe Superior. For if the silent partnership were made public, the Señor Jefe Superior would have to be fined the same amount of money. When Señor Figueroa found out about the incident, he reprimanded the administrator for having publicized the silent partnership and then ordered that Señor Spence be asked to come to the government house. When Spence arrived,

David Spence house, Monterey, 1875. Courtesy of the California State Library, Sacramento.

Señor Figueroa received him with his customary good humor. He explained that he had entered into the silent partnership with Don Ángel Ramírez to placate him. He never thought that he would have to make that secret public, let alone confess it personally to a judge. He then expressed his gratitude to Señor Spence for his decision to fine them and also for his many other instances of ethical behavior. He urged Señor Spence to continue with his scrupulous administration of justice. The first time that Señor Spence was called upon to administer justice, he constructed a jail with space for a corps of guards and a room for an officer. The second time, he constructed a solid bridge across the ditch which spans the town. The third time, he constructed a stone wall around the cemetery.

Being human, Señor Figueroa was bound to have faults. In spite of the fact that his greatest desires were to do as much good as possible for the country, he was not able to achieve everything. He recognized that he did possess a defect which he could not remove, even by the power of his good intentions. He explained to a number of his friends that he was an Indian; his color and physique undoubtedly attested to that. Because he was an Indian, he sympathized with their unhappiness in being despised by the rest of society, especially by the proud class which was either pure-blooded or a mixture of European blood. For that reason, the Indians in reduction as well as the gentiles summoned the courage to steal horses without the fear of being pursued.

They first stole more than three hundred beasts outright from Don Mariano Estrada. He begged Figueroa to send out a troop, as was customary, to pursue and punish the thieves. Figueroa delayed as much as he could, but finally, and reluctantly, he gave Estrada permission to arm his neighbors so that they could try to catch up with the Indians and recover the horses.[41] Because the leader of the group lacked experience, they did not recover any horses before they crossed the San Joaquín River. Afterward Figueroa refused to give that type of permission again.[42]

The Indians preferred eating horse meat over beef. When a tribe obtained a share of horses, it would invite neighboring Indians for a banquet. The gathering and the dance afterward would last as long as was needed to finish off the stolen animals. The excellent success which they had with the first robbery served as an incentive for a second one. This time they were not even pursued a short distance. Believing that they were entirely at liberty to commit a third robbery and more, they carried on until they depleted the previously abundant stock. In the past the landowners themselves had ordered that their overabundant livestock be slaughtered, but now they were left with very few horses to operate the *ranchos*. They believed that they could prevent future robberies by constructing walled corrals next to the house. They secured the doors with iron bars and strong locks, but the Indians ridiculed these measures because they had skilled blacksmiths who could open them. If that proved to be too difficult, they would remove one adobe brick after another from the wall until they had formed a door through which the horses could come out. The Indians were so brazen that they began to attempt to kill the caretakers. After a number had been murdered, the landowners had to abandon their plans to protect the horses.[43]

The following incident demonstrates both the high regard in which Señor Figueroa held the Indians and their gratitude to him. The mission Fathers were in the habit of offering the services of eight- to ten-year-old Indian girls to homes where the owners enjoyed the finer things of life. The intent was that the girls would be taught sewing and other domestic chores. When the girls reached the age of fifteen, the same mission Fathers would persuade certain Indians to ask for the girls' hands in matrimony in order to bring them back to the mission. That was why one would always find excellent seamstresses among the Indian women. They were also familiar with the dances which were popular among those called the *gente de razón*. It so happened that the Administrator of Mission San Carlos, Father José María Suárez del Real, performed the marriage of one of his favorite *alcaldes* to an Indian girl who had been taught in a home in Monterey. The *alcalde* informed the Father that since he had invited the Señor General and his officers to the wedding, it was extremely important that the Father provide him with everything that was appropriate to honor the status of the guests. The large parlor of the main house was filled with tables upon which were served exquisite meats. This surprised the guests, since they were not expecting a banquet of such proportions. When the meal was finished, the room was immediately cleared, and the orchestra entered to take their seats to begin the soiree. With everything now ready, the Señor General, complying with the rules of etiquette, extended his hand to Madame Alcaldesa. The first selection was a waltz, and this couple stood out as the two most agile and skillful dancers.

This *jefe* tried to distinguish himself with this token of kindness and equality so that the Indians would understand him better. He was fully aware of the fatal repercussions that might result from the ignorance or malice of his favorites, the Indians. If they took advantage of him or pushed him beyond his level of tolerance, the landowners in particular and the territory in general would suffer considerable hardships.

· 8 ·

When the news of Señor Figueroa's death reached Mexico, there certainly was no shortage of candidates to replace him. However, men of integrity, reason, and knowledge, who had served the homeland, were not considered, and a congressional delegate from the state of Guanajuato was preferred. Believing that he would improve his fortune with the mission interests, he seized the opportunity and exchanged the rostrum for the political and military command of Alta California. He then set out for his destination with the necessary documents.

The biographical sketches of the representatives to the general congress which appeared in contemporary newspapers provided the *californios* with advance notice of their new governor's character. The following description was accurate to the letter: "Don Mariano Chico, a man who takes up arms, will prove for no reason at all with the tip of his sword that three plus two do not equal five. And when he has an attack of excess bile, he does not even respect the Sovereign Power of the universe."[1]

The new *jefe* of the *californios*, a lieutenant colonel, was a contemporary and friend of Don Manuel Victoria. He could have been a distant relative of Don Quixote. He wanted to take revenge on the scoundrels who had caused Victoria so much political and personal harm. With this aim in mind, he began by compiling a list of those involved, a list he intended to use at the appropriate time.

His ship arrived at Santa Bárbara Bay in April 1836, and he disembarked there because he was tired of the sea voyage. When he requested information about recent events, as was customary procedure, they told him about a treacherous murder of a husband in the *pueblo* of Los Angeles. An adulterous wife and her accomplice had been imprisoned and charged with the crime. While the authorities were in the process of drawing up the indictment against them, a large number of people rose up, armed themselves, and took the prisoners out of the jail to shoot them.[2] Chico just stood there in a trance for quite a while. Since he was from Guanajuato, it was not as if crimes of that nature would catch him by surprise. Finally, his body caught fire and exploded in its typical fashion. He wanted to leave for Los Angeles at that very moment to punish those people for their impudence, lawlessness, and the disrespect they had shown for his authority. They had committed the type of crime that would be punished severely during his tenure.

Fortunately both for him and the people of Los Angeles, Don Carlos Carrillo had known Chico for a long time. He had maintained a close friendship with him ever since they both were delegates to the national congress, and he knew how to give Chico sound advice.[3] Carrillo told Chico that he lacked authority because he had not yet assumed the command of the territory, nor had he been formally recognized as the *jefe principal*. Chico agreed and decided to hurry to Monterey to assume the command as governor. Then he could quickly decree whatever measures he pleased about the incident in Los Angeles.

During the few days that he spent in Los Angeles, he constantly tried to find out who had taken part in the conspiracy against Don Manuel Victoria and how they had proceeded. When everything had been arranged for his departure, he left for Monterey. When he arrived, Don Nicolás Gutiérrez surrendered command of the territory to him in the customary fashion.[4] Gutiérrez also circulated orders that Chico be recognized as *jefe principal*. When Gutiérrez had fulfilled that obligation, he was immediately ordered to take some troops to Mission San Gabriel, a short distance from the *pueblo* of Los Angeles, and to establish his barracks there. He was to determine who had instigated and had participated in the shooting of the man and woman who had murdered the husband. He was to imprison whomever he could apprehend and then follow up with criminal proceedings as he saw fit.

At the same time, Chico sent another order to the *alcalde* of Los Angeles, telling him, the moment he received the order, to instruct Don Abel Stearns to present himself to the authorities in the capital without wasting any time. He did not give any reason for summoning Stearns.[5] However, since his reputation for rash action was already well known, Stearns covered the 130 leagues as quickly as possible. Although he arrived after sunset, he did not want to delay his appearance, so he barely took enough time to wash up. In the company of various other people, he appeared in the government hall. The *jefe* did not know two of the men, but he received them all in a courteous fashion. He had them sit down and then took his seat.[6]

Assuming a more festive tone than usual, Chico next stated that, even though he did not have the honor of knowing two of the men present, he wished to be of service to them to the extent that his authority permitted, if indeed some issue pertaining to his official position had brought them there. But when he found out that one of those men was Don Abel Stearns, he leaped from his chair as if fifteen scorpions had stung him at once. He turned toward Señor Stearns and began the following interrogation, as he shook his index finger at him: "Are you the rogue, Abel Stearns, whom I summoned to punish because his criminal deeds warrant it? Are you the American scoundrel who rose against Don Manuel Victoria, and whom tomorrow I am going to order hanged on the flagpole in the middle of the *plaza*? Are you the impudent and dishonorable foreigner, who, without introducing himself first, had the arrogance to take a seat in my living room among decent people who honor me with their visit? Get out of my presence immediately. Tomorrow you will suffer the consequences your despicable actions deserve."

Consider the state of confusion that Chico's manner of expressing himself created for Don Abel Stearns. He left that praetorium in such a hurry that he even forgot his hat.[7] Fortunately for him, on the following day there were only a few small particles of ash left over from the huge straw fire, which is an accurate metaphor for Señor Chico's style. It seemed that Chico had been relieved of the burden of the plans he had made against Don Abel Stearns. He sent Stearns to Los Angeles and promised that he would follow him there very soon to resolve the matter for which he had been summoned.[8]

As soon as Don Nicolás Gutiérrez had quartered his troops as well as he could at Mission San Gabriel, he proceeded to carry out his orders. Don Víctor Prudón was imprisoned based on information which indicated that he was president of the council which had been formed when the *angelinos* gathered, under the command of Don Francisco Araujo, to shoot Gervasio Alipás and Rosario Villa. Don Manuel Arzaga, the council's secretary, was also imprisoned.

In carrying out his instructions, Gutiérrez determined that these three individuals bore the most guilt. He was also very determined to clarify whether Alcalde Don Manuel Requena in his judicial capacity had tried to assert his authority and stop the unlawful execution of the man and woman, or whether he had consented to, or at least not opposed, the action. Fearful that he might not be able to defend himself if charges were brought against him, Señor Requena requested that Don Mariano Romero come down from Monterey. Even though he did not yet have the title of lawyer, Señor Romero possessed a good knowledge of legal matters. He arrived in Los Angeles at the same time as Señor Chico, and he naturally busied himself with anything which could contribute to Requena's defense. However, the *jefe político* had no knowledge whatsoever of criminal proceedings, and so he reduced everything to rhetoric. With his grand eloquence he not only rudely humiliated the prisoners but also insulted other people who were not prisoners and accused them of the same offense.

Furious, he promised the guilty parties that they would shortly receive the severe punishment which he had prepared for them. Believing that he was about to be executed, Araujo almost lost his mind over Señor Chico's terrible threats. But almost instantly Chico's bile decreased, since he had drained his liver more quickly than usual. The moment he ordered the prisoners brought to him turned out to be a favorable one for them. They were in despair as they waited to hear that his threat was to be carried out. But strangely, when he received them Chico spoke to them in a moderate tone. In the end he promised them that if they acknowledged their crime and agreed to make amends, he would pardon them. They immediately provided him with more pledges than they could fulfill, and they were set free.[9] The *jefe* left at the same time on a swift march to Monterey.

The unexpected speed of the pardon and the departure piqued people's curiosity to find out the reason. Since this is something easily accomplished in small towns, it was learned a bit later that a special messenger from Monterey had brought Chico a confidential message. Upon reading it Chico became livid and wanted to leave that very hour. A few more inquiries clarified the matter. It turned out that Señor Chico had brought a "niece" with him to California.[10] She was somewhat elegant and witty, similar to Cervantes' description of Maritornes.[11] He also brought a eunuch, who was to watch over the conduct of this Dulcinea from Guanajuato during Chico's absence.[12] The eunuch performed his duty and notified his loving master that, metaphorically speaking, perhaps the girl was bored during that advent with the constant consumption of slightly rotten salt cod and had sailed out through the bay in search of fresh delights.[13] That thundering machine, propelled by the hurricane created from his own fiery

Arcadia Bandini Stearns, daughter of Juan Bandini and wife of Abel Stearns. Courtesy of the California State Library, Sacramento.

spirit, quickly reached his destination. However, in view of the evidence which surfaced, he was perverted by roguish sorcerers who transformed him into Marrimaquiz. Zapaquilda "the beautiful" had not been seen for three or four days, and when she finally appeared, it seemed that she had recovered, but she had a number of scratches on her face.[14]

Abel Stearns. Courtesy of the California State Library, Sacramento.

The man returned to his primitive behavior. Hearing about this situation from a good-for-nothing man of poor ancestry had highly offended him. Because he had been insulted to the core of his being, he ordered the eunuch jailed even before charging him with a crime. Then he tried to prove that the man had stolen some gold jewelry and a considerable number of stamped ounces of gold. Since no additional facts surfaced other than the premeditated slander of his accuser, whose hostility became more evident as he refused to reveal the real reason for the man's imprisonment, the judge set the prisoner free in due course. This started a fierce legal battle. When the *jefe* found out that two respectable and knowledgeable lawyers were advising the judge, he stopped the proceedings. He decided to take up the matter personally with the judge when the opportunity presented itself.

Chico was outraged by all types of judges because they followed legal procedures which were foreign to him and did not behave according to his whims. He recalled that he had left San Gabriel without resolving some pending matters for Don Nicolás Gutiérrez. He sent Gutiérrez an order to continue the investigation against Alcalde Don Manuel Requena. Chico ordered that Requena be imprisoned in the barracks if the investigation uncovered the slightest evidence indicating that the *alcalde* had been remiss in carrying out his obligation to prevent the shooting of the man and woman. He added that Requena should be handcuffed, and if Requena's lawyer prepared documents citing regulations or demanding compliance with the law, Gutiérrez was to handcuff the lawyer as well and place him with his client.

A few days later a husband discovered his wife in a clear act of infidelity.[15] He went and complained to the judge about her guilty accomplice's wickedness, requesting that the judge inflict the punishment which he deserved. The judge began by taking steps to arrest both adulterers, but the complainant stated that he was not pressing charges against his wife. Señor Chico wanted to get involved in this dispute, telling the judge that the woman fell under the same military jurisdiction as her husband. Therefore, the information about her case was of concern to him. Chico ordered her secluded in a respectable house, provided that they put the other adulterer in jail and prepare the case against him.

While this was going on, there was a holiday during which a company of *maromeros* put on a show in the evening.[16] The husband of the woman who was in seclusion pleaded with Señor Chico to allow her to attend the festivities, and without showing any embarrassment, she appeared at the show.[17] When a number of people in the crowd saw her, they decided to have a little fun at the expense of the *jefe político*. They thought it would be very amusing to provoke the *jefe*'s anger and force him to display it in public, since whenever Chico's anger reached its limit, he would act like a clown. So they contrived to get the *alcalde* to come to the performance, even though he had previously declined.[18] With the help of three people who were present, they decided to concoct a dispute between the two officials. As soon as the *alcalde* arrived, they gave him a seat and pointed out the woman by describing where she was seated and how she was dressed. Then they asked the *alcalde* if he knew her. He clearly recognized her and responded that it really surprised him to see her there for no apparent reason. They quickly told him everything and arranged for the prisoner, the woman's accomplice, to take part in the same festivities. While they went to pick up the prisoner, who took his time getting dressed, the *alcalde* enjoyed himself watching the *maromeros* perform some stunts. As one of the stunts ended, the people who had sent for the prisoner saw him arrive and welcomed him with great applause. Without knowing the real reason, others in the crowd joined in as if to applaud some good fortune of his.

They purposely seated the prisoner in front of Señor Chico, where he would be more visible. Chico, however, was enjoying himself conversing with a number of women, including his "niece," and had not noticed the prisoner until the husband informed him of his presence. When Chico saw the prisoner there, the blood raced through his arteries more forcefully than water spewing from a water pump used to extinguish fires. His anger made him virtually rabid. With a voice like the thunder of a violent storm, he yelled at the *alcalde*, asking him who had granted Don J.M.C. permission to be there when he was supposed to be in jail.[19] The *alcalde* responded with restraint and in a low tone of voice that he had granted the permission because two prisoners accused of the same crime were equally entitled to have a good time, and then be returned to their respective prisons. Señor Chico, already blind with rage, burst forth with a torrent of the highly obscene insults for which the miners of his country are famous. A number of officers of sound judgment and prudence quickly surrounded him. They managed to subdue him by making him understand that this was not the appropriate place for two officials to speak about matters which, if made public, would bring them dishonor, and that they were also interrupting the festivities.

This was perhaps the first time in his wretched life that Chico had heeded prudent and convincing words spoken to him. Like a volcano which spews the last of its lava before subsiding, he threatened the *alcalde* and promised that he would get even with him for everything the following day. Then he went home. After that scene, which was acclaimed by many as the best interlude thanks to the assistance of the clown, the *alcalde* pretended to act very timid. Unknown to them, he hid himself under some women's seats. When the crowd demanded that he come out, he answered

as if he were choked by fear. After the crowd had cheered the lead acrobat's finale, the *alcalde* appeared. He claimed that Chico's anger had caused
him to fear for his life, because he thought that he had overheard him say
that the rope from the swing would be converted into a noose for the harm-
less little clown's neck. Thanks to the governor's antics, this was the best
performance that the *maromeros* ever gave.

Very irritated and unable to sleep, Señor Chico spent the night contemplating how to avenge such a horrible insult. After deciding upon, and
then rejecting, one idea after another, he finally settled on one which
seemed the best to him. Without considering that every type of scandal is
reprehensible, he felt that, since the insult was public, the satisfaction
should be public as well. He summoned Captain Don Agustín Zamorano,
who served as his secretary and as major of the *plaza*. When Zamorano appeared, Chico ordered him to mobilize the available troops immediately
and have them appear before him with arms and munitions. As soon as
they were ready, Chico meticulously reviewed them himself, as if an enemy
were present and prepared to fight. Satisfied that everything was set, he ordered them to follow him to the *alcalde*'s house. When they arrived, he ordered them to line up in battle formation and to ready themselves to fire
at will. He stood by to observe the completion of these maneuvers, which,
he was sure, would guarantee his victory in such an important endeavor.
Then, without a word, he fearlessly burst into the living room and shouted
at the *alcalde*, who stood up from his chair to ask him what he wanted.
Chico replied that he had come to the *alcalde*'s house to give orders and the
alcalde was to grab his staff immediately. The *alcalde* obeyed very quickly,
since the staff was at his side. When Chico saw him with the staff in his
hand, he became like the black panther of Morocco, which pounces on its
prey ferociously and swiftly. He sprang toward the *alcalde* to snatch the staff
away from him. The *alcalde* released it without resisting. As Chico held it,
he told the *alcalde* that that judge's insignia should be in better hands. He
then proceeded to leave in the same decorous manner with which he had
entered. He wanted to show the judge's staff, which was for him a trophy
which he had won in a colossal battle, to the officers and the troops.[20]

Once the insult had been avenged by such a valiant champion, who considered himself superior to the Rolands, Amadises, and other knights of the
Round Table, he retired with his men. He ordered them confined to barracks and isolated himself in his house, fearing the inevitable consequences.

When that whole unpleasant event had ended, mounted men could be seen hurrying in every direction to alert the people to the outrageous act committed against their *alcalde*, whom they both loved and respected. As a group they could seek the appropriate satisfaction from the *jefe político*. The members of the *diputación territorial* were at hand, and its president convened an extraordinary session after he received an official communiqué from the *alcalde*. Besides notifying the president of Señor Chico's scandalous behavior, the *alcalde* expressed the general disgust of the local community, which was preparing armed retribution. He could not tell if fatalities might result, but he was warning the president ahead of time so that he would take appropriate steps to prevent a recurrence of the state of anarchy which the country recently experienced.

Since the *diputación* had been informed that groups of fifteen to twenty people, armed with the guns and munitions they were able to obtain, were already gathering, it agreed to ask the *alcalde* to use all his influence and authority to restrain the local community. It also agreed to try to handle the matter in the least disruptive manner possible for the sake of public order. By nightfall there were more armed civilians on the streets than soldiers. The *jefe* could not even count on his own troops, because the cavalry had sided with the *alcalde*, whom they had been very fond of ever since he was a child. He was the son of their former commander, whom they loved and respected as a superior as well as a father.

An enraged and caged lion does not roar as ferociously as the governor was doing in the room where he had isolated himself. Although he was extremely eager to take revenge, he found himself forced to remain behind four walls, since he did not dare stick out his head for fear of being stoned. He believed that he was in his last hours and that a fate similar to that of his friend Don Manuel Victoria would befall him. In addition, there was not a competent doctor available to heal him if one of the *californios* were to shoot him or strike him with a sword as a just punishment for his arbitrary acts.

While Chico was thus confined, he was bombarded with official communiqués from the *diputación*.[21] With due respect and great eloquence, this body informed him of the powers granted it by law. It also stated that the actions which he had taken against the *alcalde* were scandalous and disruptive. Consequently, the *pueblo* had expressed its indignation and was going to seek satisfaction by force. Since the *diputación* could not restrain the *pueblo*, he alone would be responsible for the consequences. Two well-educated *vocales* in the *diputación* gave counsel to the president.[22] Señor

Chico was choking with rage because he did not know how to respond satisfactorily to the official communiqués from the *diputación*. The communiqués actually had been sent to scare him, since he was most arrogant with those who were weak. They achieved their goal perfectly, because Chico ordered, or rather pleaded with, one of those lawyers to advise him about his final decision. He explained that he did not have adequate troops to instill respect. Therefore, to carry out his gubernatorial duties better, he planned to charter the English brigantine *Clementine*, which was anchored in the bay, and take it to Mazatlán to bring back soldiers who were not allied with the *californios* through friendship or family ties. In the interim, he would leave Don Nicolás Gutiérrez in command of the territory.

The lawyer was glad to hear this, since it accorded with his own desires. He then proceeded to overstate the soundness of that admirable idea, to try to persuade Chico not to dismiss it but rather to put it into practice as soon as possible. He promised Chico his assistance, so that he would not encounter any obstacle to his departure. With that aim in mind, he would work to insure that he could leave and that absolutely nothing would be demanded of him because of the incident involving the *alcalde*. The lawyer had considerable influence over the *alcalde* because he was his brother-in-law.[23] When Señor Chico saw that an unexpected port was opening to save him from the storm that was about to overwhelm him, he accepted everything in good faith, expressed his appreciation, and dispatched him to complete his important mission quickly.[24]

The lawyer then went to inform the other delegates of the outcome of his interview with Señor Chico. They in turn informed the *alcalde* and the alarmed *pueblo*. All agreed that, if Chico got out of the territory quickly and left them in peace, he would not have to give satisfaction for the scandal he had committed. Finally, everything was arranged so that he could set sail the next day. Everyone believed that, after the scare he had received, he would not want to return to California once he was in Mazatlán. If he had hesitated before, not knowing how to reply to the official communications sent to him by the *diputación*, he now felt that he had to reply at the last minute before his departure. He could not tolerate remaining silent while the current ruling body was acting arbitrarily right under his whiskers. Therefore, amid his continual attacks of bile, he formulated his response, using the peculiar expressions of his dialect. It consisted of but a few words, and it fit on a fourth of a half sheet of paper. He wrote the message by hand, sealed it in an envelope, and put it in the pocket of his frock coat. He then left to board the ship. When he arrived at the beach, he bid a general farewell to all those present and promised to return promptly. With one foot already on the boat and the other on the rock that served as a pier, he called out to Don David Spence.[25] Because Spence was a delegate, he gave him his written reply and asked him to tell the delegates that, besides what he already had told them in writing, he wanted to add that they were "pricks" and "sons of bitches." Since they did not deserve to be called anything better, this was his gift to them. Consider the elegant terminology that must have been used in drafting the message!

Before Señor Chico set sail, a circular was sent out calling for Don Nicolás Gutiérrez to be recognized as *jefe superior* of the territory. This admirable news was celebrated along all the populated areas through which the circular passed. Because the *californios* were generally disgusted with their governor, they were delighted to hear about the sudden change in command. Gutiérrez was a friend to all, and they held him in high esteem because of his unselfish generosity and the fact that he loved serving everyone. He had acquired that trait under the tutelage of Señor Figueroa, with whom he had served in the military since he had been a young drummer boy in a Spanish regiment. He deserted that regiment in order to follow the insurgents, and from that time on, until the general's death, they were inseparable friends.

While the circular was making its way through the territory, Gutiérrez was hurrying about to carry out the orders which he had recently received from his superior. One morning he left San Gabriel and headed for Los Angeles to attempt to resolve the Don Manuel Requena affair. As usual, he dismounted at the home of one of his friends and then summoned him. The friend appeared immediately because he was extremely afraid that Gutiérrez would be arrested, an illegal act that some people had already vowed to commit.[26] As the friend listened to the substantial charges which were being brought against Gutiérrez, he suggested that his lawyer be summoned so that he could speak on Gutiérrez' behalf and assist him with certain legal points.[27] It so happened that when the lawyer entered the room, the courier who was transporting the circular arrived and was welcomed by Gutiérrez' friend. Letters from Monterey had informed the friend that, on the day after the letters were dated, Señor Chico would set sail, because of the *alcalde* affair.[28] Don Nicolás Gutiérrez would assume both commands in his place.

Gutiérrez was unaware of what was happening around him. He was also angry because of a dispute he had with the lawyer. In a professorial manner, the lawyer was insisting that Gutiérrez judge in accord with explicit laws. Gutiérrez responded with a military directness that his responsibilities did not extend beyond complying with his orders to arrest both of them and take them to his barracks. Gutiérrez' friend was waiting out of sight in another room to see what would happen, and he overheard this conversation as he peered through a small opening in the room's thin wooden wall. Both the lawyer and Señor Requena turned pale when they heard that prospect. The friend felt sorry for them, but he was also convinced that Gutiérrez would never order such a thing on his own. However, since the order came from a superior, he knew that Gutiérrez would definitely carry it out. The friend wanted to help free them from this predicament, so, acting as if he had neither seen nor heard anything, he knocked and immediately opened the door of the room they were in. He begged their forgiveness if he was interrupting anything important, but he thought that Señor Gutiérrez needed to be informed as soon as possible about the document which had arrived from the political leadership. When he placed the document in his hands, Gutiérrez grabbed it because he was eager to know what it said. He was shocked almost to the point of paralysis when he found out. His imposing seriousness reverted to his customary friendliness. He told Señor Requena and Señor Romero that they should be grateful for their good luck because the circumstances had changed at that critical moment in their lives. The matter at hand would be dealt with on some other occasion. With this, they concluded and went to the living room, where something had been left for them so that they could have a drink.

When Gutiérrez entered the room, he asked his friend, in a tone of disapproval, knowing full well what the document contained, if he had hastened to give it to him to spare him some trouble. He responded affirmatively and then addressed the other two men, who were still deathly pale. He asked them if they would be so kind as to join him in drinking a glass of wine in honor of the *jefe* of the territory, who was there in the fullness of his power. This seemed very puzzling to them, and they both stared at Gutiérrez, as if to ask him to clarify the situation. Gutiérrez pointed his index finger at his friend and said, "This crafty fellow, without being seen by us, was aware of our business when he received the communiqué. He already knew, by letters which probably came from Monterey, that Señor Chico has some very important government business which will take him to Mazatlán. He is leaving me in charge of the command of the territory in the interim. My friend knew that I was following Chico's orders regarding you. He wanted to give me the pleasure of ordering that you be freed from the trouble which was awaiting you. This obviously was why he entered the room we were in, before he was granted permission to do so. It is time to have a drink. We can quench our thirst and enjoy what this crafty opera- tor has already laid out for us." Neither Señor Requena nor Señor Romero was fond of drinking liquor other than at the dinner hour, but this time, because of their happiness and because they knew the proper rules of eti- quette, they offered a toast to the new *jefe*.

Unfortunately for Gutiérrez, the brigantine *Clementine* was forced to call at San Pedro Bay. When the ship anchored, Señor Chico ordered that Gutiérrez be summoned. He also ordered that the treasury employee send him a ship's waybill for more than one thousand *arrobas* of tallow which Don J.M.T. of Monterey had put on board to ship to Don J.H. of Mazatlán. The employee wanted to inform Chico in person that he could not ship cargo on a foreign vessel.[29] So he went down to the beach, where he found his friend Gutiérrez. When they both found out that Señor Chico was on board the *Don Quixote*, they headed for that vessel on the first available boat.[30] When they arrived, the two *jefes* spoke privately, in low voices, for about a quarter of an hour. Then Señor Chico spoke to the employee. He asked him if he had brought the waybill which he had requested. The em- ployee responded calmly that since it was not permissible for a foreign ship to transport cargo from one port of the republic to another, he was sorry, but he would not be able to give him the waybill. Since Chico had paid no attention to the general congress for a number of years, he viewed this refusal as capricious. He became infuriated and threatened to strip the em- ployee of his job. The employee did not take this lightly. He asked Chico if he was willing to comply with regulations or if he himself would be forced to fulfill his duty. Fortunately, Gutiérrez was prepared to speak on the em- ployee's behalf. He finally convinced the man who had spilled his bile that only ships of national registry were permitted to engage in coastal trade and the waybill which he requested would be a detriment, not a protection, if he presented it to the customs authorities in Mazatlán.

A man who has the tendency to become angry for any reason can always find more than enough reasons; for the most part these reasons are base- less. Nevertheless, in this case it is important to acknowledge that Señor Chico did indeed have reason to be angry. The general opinion of those who study such matters is that the most perfect and animated young faces are commonly found among males in the United States of the North. One such individual, a striking seventeen-year-old Adonis,[31] was aboard the *Don Quixote*.[32] Self-infatuation had corrupted him, and his father wanted to keep him occupied on long voyages as a means of correcting his behavior and continuing his studies. But he felt persecuted and assaulted everywhere in different languages which he did not understand. He learned from experience to compensate for this by making himself understood only with his very beautiful and expressive eyes. He had been spending his days aboard ship very depressed until he saw another pair of lively black eyes at Señor Chico's side. The eyes sparkled when they met his, and he was almost in ecstasy. They fell in love the moment their hearts were pierced by the blind boy's arrows. But Señor Chico's vehemence in defending his honor was so apparent that even he became aware of it, to his great humiliation.

The captain served wine and brandy to the gathering. Narcissus did not believe that particular liquor was worthy of the beautiful Napea, so he quickly brought out a box filled with exquisite crystal decanters which contained some very high-quality liquors.[33] He offered her four types of liquor in delicately gilded goblets and asked her to take the one she liked best. In one of the secret compartments of the box there were assorted bottles of perfume, and he told her to choose as many as she liked. Bashfully, she took two or three bottles of perfume and paid for them with a sigh and an expressive glance. Then from another of the box's secret compartments he took out a small packet of drawings of the latest fashions. Among the drawings he was able to show her, due to the carelessness of Argos the observer, was a drawing of the latest Parisian fashion of kissing.[34] He showed her others, but no reference can be made to them because, as the time had come to dine in another room, he took the box, put it back in order, and closed it.

The excessive care with which the young man prepared and served meats to the female guest was reason enough for Señor Chico to find the meats rather tasteless, but he finally selected the ones which seemed best to him. When the meal was finished, he took hold of his "niece's" arm and escorted her up to the deck, where he spoke with Gutiérrez and gave him some orders. Gutiérrez was to carry out the orders while Chico was away on a brief trip he was planning. During that time, the brigantine *Clementine* weighed its anchors and approached the stern of the *Don Quixote* to receive its passengers. Señor Chico was notified, and he began to bid farewell. While he was shaking hands with those around him, behind his back the two passionate young people, imitating the latest fashion they had just seen, were also bidding farewell. Unfortunately for her, they were caught by surprise. The offended party took her by the arm and dug his fingernails into her. At that point Chico would have liked to have had fingernails as long as an eagle's talons. As if it were an act of courtesy, he escorted her to the gangway and walked across it behind her toward the boat. As he got halfway up the last few steps, it occurred to him to give Gutiérrez one last assignment. He went back and removed his gold watch, which had a fine gold chain. With his own hands he draped it around Gutiérrez' neck and told him that it ran a bit slow and he wanted Monsieur Praior, a watch-maker in Los Angeles, to fix it while he was away. Chico finally left in October 1836 to request additional troops in order to enable him to return and resolve his problems, but the general government was already aware of the situation and did not heed his request.

Now that Gutiérrez was free from the man who annoyed everyone, including himself, he could have been happy. However, people began to notice that he was very sad, as if his festive mood were fighting against a strong, invisible force which prevented him from dealing with his friends in his customary straightforward manner.[35] That was the way in which Captain Zamorano, Lieutenant Navarrete, and others whom he respected described Gutiérrez' behavior to him. They even urged him to admit to them if he were a victim of unrequited love, so that, if that were the case, they could help him obtain what he wanted.[36] No matter how many times they tried to discover the source of his transformation, they could not. They finally nagged him to the point that he let a few words escape inadvertently: "It is very hard to work for someone else when the burden is on you to determine if it is bad to carry out an order when it might be worse not to carry it out at all."

From this statement it was inferred that he had received secret orders which conflicted with his good judgment. The prudent Zamorano, believing that nothing else would cause such a lack of enthusiasm in Gutiérrez, took the risk of engaging him in a conversation. He told Gutiérrez that a man should be responsible for his own actions, and as *jefe político* of the territory, he should seek only fairness and justice. He should attempt to guide himself reasonably so that he could fulfill his obligations, live in peace, and maintain the trust which he always had among his friends. In addition, the fact that Señor Chico had left him in command and had acknowledged him as *jefe político* meant that Chico had yielded his authority to him. Consequently, Gutiérrez was wrong to believe that he was obligated to carry out orders which he might have received from Chico. Zamorano's sound arguments were fruitless, and he could not stir Gutiérrez from his great melancholy or change his mind.

During November 1836 the governor was forced to reprimand Don Ángel Ramírez, the customs administrator. He had more than enough reason to do so. Ramírez had been an apostolic friar from the Convent of Santo Domingo in Mexico.[37] Not happy with the convent rules, he hung up his habit to become a member of a revolutionary party. When he left the convent he was already quite adept at intrigue. So, when he received commissions, Ramírez demonstrated quite well that he was not a novice in that art. His aptitude honored the community in which he had learned from men far wiser than he. He was blessed with good luck for a few years, but then it turned bad, and he was actually jailed a number of times. However, he had influential close friends who sought for him the post of administrator of maritime customs of Alta California. The government granted Ramírez the position in order to send him far away from the capital to a remote spot, where they thought he would improve his behavior. But he was already set in his ways.[38] And a wicked friar cannot be ordered around except by one who is worse than he is. Therefore, when he assumed his post, duties paid to the public treasury became negotiable, provided that he received sufficient advances to defray the very high costs of his continual dances, gambling tables, and picnics in the countryside. Although it was already late, Gutiérrez wanted to put the Customs House in order. However, the administrator, a prototypical rebel, took from his files a revolutionary plan that suited him as poorly as a frock coat fits a uniform. When the plan was sufficiently advanced, he had the audacity to try it on, like the tailors do when they baste a garment, and he was emboldened to do things which he had been forbidden to do. For that reason, Gutiérrez, intent on giving him one last warning, summoned him. But Gutiérrez became enraged by his responses. He went so far as to tell Ramírez that if he did not behave properly, he would be forced to put a pair of handcuffs on him and another pair on the *contador* who was his assistant.[39]

Don Juan B. Alvarado, the assistant, was present.[40] He responded that if Gutiérrez tried to handcuff him, he would not allow it unless he were satisfied with the charge. Also, if Gutiérrez insisted on granting him that honor, he should be careful not to change the order when he attempted to carry it out. Angered by that reply, Gutiérrez let loose with terrible threats.

Alvarado responded that he would show him very soon that arrogance did not frighten him. He promised Gutiérrez that he would not rest until the military square or so-called presidio had been completely destroyed, down to its foundation, after everyone who lived there had been packed off to where he pleased. Fortunately for Alvarado, it was a dark night, and when he went out onto the street, they did not know where he was headed. However, based on his last words, Gutiérrez and the other officers realized that the customs administrator had found the leader for his revolutionary plan. They decided that it would make more sense to try to entice Alvarado with gentle measures. Then they could proceed against Don Ángel Ramírez, remove him from his job, bring charges against him, ship him off to the general government, and let it dispose of him. No matter how many inquiries they made as they scoured the *pueblo* to find Alvarado, no one admitted to having seen him. In fact, the same person who provided Alvarado with arms, a horse, and money so that he could leave helped to look for him until dawn, by which time he was at the Monterey River rallying the ranchers he encountered.[41] They agreed to gather others together, so that everyone would be ready when Alvarado returned from Sonoma, and they provided him with very fine horses, which did not fail him on the entire ride to Sonoma. There he met with his uncle Don Guadalupe Vallejo. He detailed his objectives and his reasons for having undertaken the trip, but he was unable to obtain from his uncle more than just a few promises, which were not as satisfactory as he had hoped. Therefore, he decided to return immediately. Alvarado was somewhat dejected, but when he crossed the Carquínez Strait and passed by ranches along the way, the landowners joined him willingly. He entered the *pueblo* of San José with everyone in formation. The citizens of San José did not want to be outdone in helping him, so in an instant they gathered together arms and horses. They included everything, even an old shotgun and a musket without a lock. When everyone who had joined was mounted on horseback, it looked as if they were very well armed, but appearances were deceiving. During the course of their march they would pass by ranches, and more people would join them. When the procession arrived at San Juan Bautista, they were met by a huge group of men with sufficient horses, some good weapons, and munitions. There was a cache of useless muskets there, but they had cleaned up the ones that still had stock and barrel. The weapons, looking as though they had just left the Tower of London, were then distributed, for their intent was to win by appearances. Since the Fathers at all the missions had taken great pains to have fine musical ensembles, they were able to obtain all the drums and bugles they needed.[42] Their sounds completely transformed the ranchers into soldiers marching in formation. When the troops arrived at the Monterey River, Alvarado saw that his first supporters had kept their promise and that a number of armed men on fine horses were ready. He learned that Gutiérrez had abandoned the small fort and assembled his forces inside the presidio. During that entire period the troops were in their barracks. Even though some, mainly cavalrymen, were unhappy, Gutiérrez always could count on the entire number, with the exception of one or two miserable ones, if the need arose.[43] Alvarado did not delay. He knew that advance parties from his side had reached the edge of the presidio with orders to detain anyone who passed so that Gutiérrez would not know that he had returned. He forged ahead until he reached the last advance party at the edge of the estuary. Since it was almost dawn, he divided his forces into various bands. They were positioned at different points and told to wait for orders.[44]

Gutiérrez had been warned by his spies of Alvarado's arrival in San Juan Bautista. They told him that Alvarado was at the head of a large detachment, which was waiting at the river, and that, when the armed citizens joined them, he would have more than enough men for fighting and lassoing. Gutiérrez' own lookouts were frightening him with this information. Since he did not expect Alvarado to be so close, he was surprised when at first light of day he heard the drums and cornets sounding reveille before his own men had the opportunity to do the same.

When it was daylight, Alvarado's division left the position which it had established between the little lake and the estuary. It filed out past the pools and took the route through the forest which passes by Mission San Carlos. From there, Alvarado stationed his large force at the edge of the pine grove in order to make it visible. That way there would be no doubt in Gutiérrez' mind of the superiority of Alvarado's numbers. In fact, when Gutiérrez peered through his spyglass, it betrayed him because it was not powerful enough. It seemed to him that everyone was armed with lances and shotguns. If he had possessed a better spyglass, he would have seen guns without locks, some poles minus iron tips, others with bayonets, and just a few lances.

At about eight in the morning Alvarado sent a demand for unconditional surrender if Gutiérrez did not want to expose himself to the horrors of a bloody encounter.[45] He received no reply, so at ten o'clock, he sent a

Soldiers' barracks, Monterey. Courtesy of the California State Library, Sacramento.

soldier under a flag of truce to Gutiérrez.[46] As the soldier neared the presidio, he was met by a patrol which blindfolded him. Leading him by the hand, they took him to appear before the *jefe*. The fearless soldier did not answer any questions put to him. Despite the many threats, he replied that he would gladly die doing his duty, in the firm belief that Alvarado and his men would avenge him in the same manner in which he was killed. His arrogant spirit induced Gutiérrez to devise a plan which was unfavorable to his own position. He refused to agree to any proposals and ordered that the flag bearer be taken back to the spot where he had been blindfolded originally and that the blindfold be removed. At noon Alvarado seized the fort, and from there he sent Gutiérrez a warning that he would open fire on him if he did not respond by three o'clock in the afternoon.

When the artillerymen abandoned the fort, they did not leave behind one single cannonball, any shrapnel, or a speck of powder. However, when Alvarado's men arrived, by sheer chance they found a small cannonball inside a rosemary bush. They placed it in different cannons of lesser caliber and found that it fit well in an old iron cannon with a broken vent which had been spiked. The cannon would be good for only one shot, but they did not have enough gunpowder to fire more than once in any event. Even to fire the one cannonball, they had to break apart various gun cartridges to obtain sufficient gunpowder. An old veteran who had served as an artilleryman for many years in San Juan de Ulúa promised Alvarado that he would make that one and only shot worthwhile for everyone by firing so it would land directly on top of the house which Gutiérrez was occupying.[47] Gutiérrez did not believe or expect that the cannons from the fort could be of any use to the insurgents, even though the artillery captain had warned him, as he abandoned the small fort, that if Alvarado knew about the cannons and had brought any ammunition from San Francisco, it would take him less than fifteen minutes to triumph.

At the presidio a group of officers, aware that they now were surrounded by a superior force and had no access to provisions, deliberated about their course of action. When no decision had been reached by three o'clock, the old veteran fired his cannon. The ball hit the slope of the roof, above Gutiérrez' living room ceiling.[48] The vines on the roof were blown away, and the tiles, along with the mortar on which they were set, fell off. Everyone in the group inside was covered with dust. They were very frightened and quickly agreed that before any more cannon shots could be fired, a flag bearer should be sent out to request an honorable surrender.[49] The people in the fort immediately saw that Gutiérrez was seeking a truce. Since this was exactly what Alvarado desired most, they immediately went out to receive the flag bearer before Gutiérrez' men could discover the real reason for the delay in firing a second shot. They quickly agreed that, as soon as Gutiérrez surrendered all arms and munitions, he and his officers would be treated with respect until they could be sent either to Mazatlán or San Blas aboard the brigantine *Clementine*. In the meantime, they could remain in their homes as prisoners of honor while preparations for the trip were being made.[50]

When the agreements were completed, part of the force went down to secure the arms and munitions and to prepare accommodations and barracks in the same building in the military square. The building could have comfortably housed twice the number of troops that were there. Alvarado informed Zamorano that naturally he was not included in the terms of the surrender because his well-known affection for the country, his large family, and his merits made him worthy of esteem and trust. Nevertheless, Zamorano wanted to accompany Gutiérrez because he had aspirations of being promoted to a higher position once he arrived in Mexico. Also, after a thirteen-year absence, Zamorano longed to see his brothers and to relax.[51] A ship was designated to transport exiled *jefes políticos*, and a few days later it was ready to take on board its passengers, who were welcomed with a very long streamer. Then the ship set sail for Mazatlán. As soon as it ar-

rived, Gutiérrez presented an account of the events in Alta California to
the general government. The report had no effect whatsoever, since it was
viewed as more of the same old story.

Don Ángel Ramírez was very happy. Since Don Juan B. Alvarado prevailed as *jefe*, Ramírez believed that he could now control the territory as
he pleased. When Ramírez was presented to him, Alvarado straightfor-
wardly explained that he was responsible for his own actions and that
Ramírez should express his opinion only when Alvarado asked him for advice. But he needed to understand that Alvarado would always do what he
considered most appropriate. The Señor Customs Administrator resented
this and decided to seek revenge with another revolutionary plan. Intending to secure a *jefe* who would be to his liking, he decided to wait for the
right opportunity to present itself.

It had already become standard practice that, if a governor preferred not
to make a decision on his own, he would ask the *diputación* to join him in
the decision-making process. The notice to call a meeting was Señor Alvarado's first order of business. The session opened with two *vocales* in
attendance, but they were declared equal to five.[52] Its first decree was to
elevate the territory to the status of a free and sovereign state. The *junta*
then appointed itself as the congress and the *jefe principal* as the governor.
Señor Alvarado was selected for that position. The new legislature promoted Don Guadalupe Vallejo to Coronel Comandante General. At this
time Don José Castro began his military career with the rank of lieutenant
colonel; he also had a territorial commission.

· 9 ·

As the congress was busy issuing decrees, Alvarado was busy circulating them. The *ayuntamiento* of Los Angeles was convinced that even though the general government was tolerating the removal of the exiled *jefes políticos,* it would denounce the decrees for the following reasons. First, it was absurd to convert a territory of fewer than nine thousand inhabitants, in which not even three hundred people were educated, into a state. Second, due to the interference or connivance of foreigners, especially from the United States of the North, attempts at annexation were becoming apparent. Third, by issuing the decree of religious tolerance, they had assumed powers which surpassed those of the general congress. For these and other lesser reasons, the municipality of Los Angeles hesitated in rendering allegiance to a government whose lofty principles would soon bring it to a quick and disastrous end.

Since it was the *síndico* who encouraged the *ayuntamiento* to involve itself in such an interesting matter, he was commissioned to leave quickly in search of a copy of Alvarado's plan.[1] Since it had not been seen yet, people wanted to know why they should support it. Certain that he would find the plan at the Santa Bárbara presidio, the *síndico* left with three friends. He stopped at Mission San Buenaventura and encountered Don Carlos Carrillo, who had the plan. When he returned with it to Los Angeles, the *diputación* studied the plan's articles and decided not to follow it.[2] They quickly decided to ask Don Antonio del Valle, the administrator of Mission San Fernando, for a loan of two thousand pesos, which he could either loan willingly or have taken from him by force. He grudgingly gave up the entire amount, and the *síndico* received it as a deposit for expenses of the counterrevolution.[3]

Since the year 1836 was coming to a close, the elections for the new

Mission San Buenaventura, 1876. Courtesy of the California State Library, Sacramento.

ayuntamiento were held. On January 1 Don Manuel Requena ceased to serve as *alcalde*, and Don Gil Ibarra assumed the position, with Don José Sepúlveda functioning as second *alcalde*. Ibarra was a very dark man, physically as well as personally. The influence of the *síndico*, who had been dismissed from his position, always remained strong, but this did not seem appropriate to the Señor Alcalde. The *síndico* succeeded in convincing the other members of the assembly to promise him that they would continue what they had begun concerning the disturbance in the north. Because Ibarra was incompetent, they agreed that Sepúlveda should replace him as leader of those who were unhappy with Alvarado's government, with the explicit condition that, since the former *síndico* was the instigator of everything, he should accompany Sepúlveda as director of operations.[4] They had scarcely arranged everything when they were informed that Alvarado had arrived in Santa Bárbara with many troops and had dispatched some of them under Don Anastasio Carrillo to quickly occupy the point of San Fernando.[5]

That was a trying day for Sepúlveda and his director of operations. Sepúlveda was engaged in outfitting the troops with arms, munitions, and horses, while the director was busy reading the decree of religious tolerance to the mothers, beginning with Sepúlveda's own mother. She, as well as the other women, did not understand very well what the tolerance of cults meant.[6] The director gave them a long explanation of the content of the decree. In the end, he told them that Protestant Fathers would be permitted to enter the territory with the authority to marry girls to a Jew or someone else who did not profess the Apostolic Roman Catholic religion. Moreover, he would not have to obtain permission from the girls' parents. The girls who were present reacted very favorably, but their mothers did not. In a very serious manner, the mothers again asked about the decree, and they were assured that the Protestant Fathers would have so much power that they would personally seek out the brides and take them to their homes for safekeeping, so that the girls' parents would not interfere with the marriages.

A snake which is seized by a falcon and dropped for the first time is not as angry as those women were at that moment. They were asking one another if men of character existed, men who would permit such a thing to happen to their daughters. They immediately turned to the devout reader of the decree and reproached him with very harsh words. They accused him of cowardice, since he was not the first to take up arms and look for other men to fight with him against Alvarado and banish him from the territory so he could take his decrees to hell. When the reader realized that his goal had already been achieved, he made a formal pact with those women as well as with some other women of influence whom they summoned. When these women of influence appeared and were informed about everything, not one of them spoke up in support of the men. They said that men had lost faith in oral promises and needed to put agreements in writing. The women, however, would not need anything in writing to make them fulfill their promises. Each woman pledged to insure that her husband, children, and grandchildren, from seventeen to sixty years of age, would take up arms for the sake of their family honor. If the reader, and the second *alcalde,* were to leave that very day with the men they could enlist, they could be certain that the women would send everyone who could bear arms to their camp.

Once the agreement was arranged, the reader left to inform his friend Sepúlveda. Without wasting time, both men agreed to invite Monsieur Charlefoux, the captain of a company of forty Shahunaoo hunters, to join their forces.[7] When Charlefoux found out what they wanted, he told them that the general government had allowed him to hunt beavers in the rivers of its domain and had never demanded a contribution or fee from him. In gratitude for such a privilege, he would be ready to meet his obligations and march on behalf of the legitimate authorities and the government which had favored him so much. He would request no compensation other than food during the campaign. The former *síndico* immediately went to Mission San Gabriel to meet with Second Lieutenant Don Juan Rocha, an experienced military man. He promised to take part in the campaign and leave as soon as possible with seventy men, most of whom were veteran soldiers. The sun was already setting quickly when the former *síndico*, that is, Sepúlveda's friend, returned to Los Angeles, where the active second *alcalde* already had readied one hundred of his own horses and an even larger number which belonged to others. About forty reputable veterans mounted some of these horses and rode ahead. The younger soldiers could then follow their hoofprints the next day. With his foot in the stirrup, Sepúlveda ordered six men who were remaining behind to leave that night. He told them to form three groups, two men per group. Each group was to go to a ranch where they would find a blacksmith who was also a gunsmith. They also were to bring horses to take the blacksmiths to San Fernando.

As they started the march from the municipal house, the friend suggested that they camp in a certain spot for the night. He advised Sepúlveda that, even though it would involve a slight detour off the road from the Verdugo Ranch, it had the advantage of providing a good grazing area for the horses.[8] In the meantime, he would take one man and head directly for San Fernando, since it was possible that Don Anastasio Carrillo had already seized the mission and positioned his soldiers in the corridor of the house, which was a natural barricade. If Carrillo had not arrived yet, the former *síndico* would send the news quickly by one of the Indian *vaqueros*, who usually had horses ready for whatever might happen. If they did not receive any news by midnight, it would be a sure sign that he had been captured or killed. Sepúlveda and a number of the older men were opposed to this plan. They stated that he would be risking his life, and if he were to have a fatal accident, it would be a great loss to them. However, Don Antonio María Lugo not only supported the proposition but also offered to be the one to accompany him. Since Lugo was one of the most respected veterans, his opinion prevailed, and they left immediately. Unfortunately, the friend happened to get one of Don Antonio Ignacio Ávila's very fine horses, which he called *gutierreños*. These horses were able to run in the rodeo or in the *plaza* for two or three days without eating or tiring. However, for lack of practice, they could not endure an eight-league gallop on the open road, and eight leagues happened to be the distance between the two points. With two leagues left to travel, the horse gave out and had to be dragged along. Consequently, they arrived at eleven-thirty at night, and Don Antonio del Valle was sleeping. The former *síndico* knocked on the window. Del Valle was startled and feared that there would be a second demand for money. When he was informed of the situation, he quickly took out writing instruments. Then the former *síndico* went out to prepare the *vaquero* who was on watch so that he would take the news to Sepúlveda that no force whatsoever had arrived from the north. He also offered reasons for his delay in communicating this information. Since it was after midnight, the respected veterans at the camp were already gathering together away from the others and discussing the possibility of sending a party to learn what had happened to the other two men. However, at that moment the messenger arrived, and they were satisfied.

At eight o'clock the following day, the two envoys arrived in San Fernando, where accommodations and barracks already had been prepared.[9] A while later the soldiers arrived with the blacksmiths. They joined with those from the mission in beginning to repair the arms and restored all of them to good condition. The next day, eighty men from Los Angeles arrived. They had left about one hundred additional recruits behind. Captain Charlefoux arrived immediately afterward with his forty Shahunaoo Indians armed with rifles, daggers, and tomahawks. He dismounted at the barracks which were assigned to him. Next, a message was received from Second Lieutenant Don Juan Rocha. He was bringing eighty-five men and wanted to set up barracks for them in the corridor of the main house. Excellent cooks, tortilla makers, and enough workers to serve the men good food from the abundant supply of choice meats, greens, and vegetables were placed in each of the barracks. The following morning ninety-five more men arrived from Los Angeles, and throughout the day about fifty more arrived in parties of five to ten. The next to last party to arrive brought a message for Sepúlveda from the distinguished mothers. They wanted him to gather their sons together and tell them on their behalf, loudly, clearly, and with no room for misunderstanding that they would rather cry for them because they had died on the battlefield than experience the sorrow of reprimanding them for a disgraceful escape.

One should not think that these women had the slightest knowledge of the zeal of the women described in accounts of ancient history. If that had been the case, they would have imagined themselves as equally heroic as the women of Gaul and elsewhere, whose exceptional feats embarrassed

Mission San Fernando in the late nineteenth century. Courtesy of the California State Library, Sacramento.

even those soldiers whose motto was "Death before dishonor." The person who saw and knew the *angelinas* well has remembered them always. He wished with all his heart, especially during the war between the two Americas, that the Mexican generals and enlisted men had been sons of these women, for then they would have fulfilled the honorable desires which they expressed.

Sepúlveda attempted to maintain as much order as possible, but with so many men gathered together, there was always someone who would create a disturbance. In this case it turned out to be a brother of the first *alcalde*. Sepúlveda publicly ordered him placed in the stocks. This proved to be example enough to restrain others from committing excesses due to drunkenness. Four companies were organized from the large group, and each company cared for its own horses. Each company had the incentive to distinguish itself with good conduct so as not to earn another humiliating punishment.

All of the arms were repaired in a short period of time, and the blacksmiths were paid well and accurately for the expenses. They also were provided with liquor, which they appreciated, because the extreme cold outside especially affected those who had to care for the horses or who composed the various advance parties which climbed Santa Susana Hill.[10] These men stoically endured the torrents of rain and the snow which fell upon them.

Sepúlveda knew that Second Lieutenant Don Juan Rocha possessed the excellent qualities that make a military man worthy of trust, so he assigned him the command as the time drew near to enter into battle. Sepúlveda would remain as second in command of the company that his friend was chosen to lead. This company comprised eighty hand-picked men.

When news arrived that Alvarado was preparing to leave Santa Bárbara and head for Los Angeles and that the community of Los Angeles had enlisted in his cause, it was also learned that each army included fathers, sons, or brothers of some of the men in the other army.[11] It was strange that no one withdrew his voluntary enlistment, not even out of respect for paternal, filial, or fraternal ties, because he did not want to provide the slightest grounds for reproach due to cowardice or not keeping his word.

Sepúlveda's friend was pondering these considerations and suggested to Sepúlveda that the friend go alone to meet with Alvarado, who happened to be a close friend of his.[12] He would go with two aims in mind. The first was to propose that Alvarado establish his government from Santa Bárbara to Sonoma and allow Los Angeles and San Diego to be governed by their local authorities until the general government resolved the situation. The intent was to avoid bloodshed among fathers, sons, and brothers. The second aim was to see and examine the opposing forces, observe their military order, and determine who would be more successful in an attack if the situation developed in that direction.

The veteran soldiers were asked to consider the plan. They were unanimously of the opinion that Alvarado would take advantage of the opportunity to seize the individual who had opposed his plans. So they absolutely refused to permit it, and even more so when they learned that this man had reached an agreement with Don Carlos Carrillo to oppose Alvarado.[13] As soon as Carrillo found out that Alvarado had arrived in Santa Bárbara, he left to inform Sepúlveda and deliver letters to him. Because he was an ally, he outlined in the letters all of Alvarado's operations. In spite of the first refusal, Sepúlveda's friend tried a second time and gained the approval of five of the most respected veterans. They eventually helped him to obtain what he wanted, but under the explicit condition that he be away for no more than forty-eight hours. If he did not return after that time, they would conclude that he had been captured by Alvarado. They would then organize a secret operation to rescue him. As soon as the force they would send spotted him, the voice of the cannon would be the first to demand satisfaction.

Don Manuel Domínguez was selected to accompany him. Both men would be served by a very energetic Indian *vaquero* acting as their squire. The Indian was provided with explicit instructions: if the two were captured, he was to flee and report everything he had seen. They left as the sun was setting. Because they were in a hurry, they were ill prepared. They had no protective clothing, not a drop of liquor, and no food for their stomachs. The cold kept them awake all night. Their horses were not from the finest stock, and they fared even worse for lack of pasture. The following day, after having suffered through strong, continuous downpours and hailstorms since the night before, they arrived at San Buenaventura at one in the afternoon.

They encountered no advance troops, sentinels, or any indication whatsoever of a military presence in the mission square, so they headed directly for the patio of the main house.[14] When they dismounted at the door of the living room, they saw that Alvarado's officers were inside, eating. The officers were kind enough to go out and welcome the guests in a very courteous manner and to offer them food. They readily accepted because they had not even had a drink of water during the past twenty-four hours. Alvarado was not there, but his secretary, Licenciado Don Cosme Peña, did the honors at the table. In keeping with his profession, he naturally began by asking searching questions. Since he was not satisfied by the replies, he got up to go and inform Alvarado of the arrival of two individuals from Sepúlveda's party whom he considered suspicious. When he mentioned their names, Alvarado replied that he knew them very well, and he was pleased that the occasion had arisen to see a friend of his. Alvarado ordered that the friend be summoned as soon as the meal was finished.

They greeted one another and followed that with some mutual, friendly chiding. Afterward Alvarado gave a long account of his reasons for pronouncing against Gutiérrez and exiling him from the territory. In turn, the friend reciprocated by attributing the counterrevolution to the highly exalted powers assumed by a so-called congress when it decreed the tolerance of cults, a decree which the general congress of the republic had never dared to issue. For this reason alone the supreme government should condemn its other deeds. In addition, the communities of Los Angeles and San Diego did not want to be blamed or reproached for having recognized a congress and a governor without legal authorization. Since Sepúlveda was determined to carry out his plan, he would try to arrange a settlement, solely for the admirable goal of avoiding bloodshed. Alvarado replied that, since the principal member of Sepúlveda's party was present and because he valued their long-standing friendship, he would ask, or rather insist, that he speak in his usual straightforward manner. Also, they could speak in the presence of his trusted secretary.

Based on that request, the friend told him that he, in fact, had helped Sepúlveda as much as he could. Since Sepúlveda had a considerable number of men, who were superior in every way to Alvarado's forces, it would be to his advantage to come to some sort of settlement with Sepúlveda. Sepúlveda's well-armed civilians mounted on fine horses would be more than enough to overpower Alvarado if they were to engage in battle. Alvarado was at a disadvantage because he had neither a leader nor a military officer, whereas Sepúlveda did have a leader and battle-hardened officers, in addition to about one hundred veteran soldiers, Charlefoux's company of excellent riflemen, and enough artillerymen to operate five cannons. About one hundred men from San Diego under the command of Don Pío Pico had arrived at San Fernando. When Pico was appointed commander of one of the companies, he instructed his men to shoot him three times to prevent him from running away, if they saw him retreat during a battle because of fear. However, no one was to shoot Señor Alvarado. Since Alvarado was his close friend, Pico believed that only he had the right to shoot him, and he would do so with the excellent two-barreled shotgun which Alvarado had sold him.

After hearing that report, Alvarado asked his secretary if the letters which he possessed might have some significance concerning the last thing he had been told. The friend was well aware that the question was a reference to the letters he had written which had been delivered by Don Carlos Carrillo. However, he decided to wait for a better occasion to ask about them. Alvarado changed the topic of conversation and said that he had sent Don Carlos and Don Anastasio Carrillo to meet with Sepúlveda, with the goal of arranging some form of agreement. However, since the commissioners from the two parties had taken different routes, they all most likely would return without a resolution.

The Señores Carrillo were detained on Santa Susana Hill by one of the advance parties from San Fernando and were not allowed to pass, despite their pleas, promises, and threats. The only concession they obtained was that one of them could leave to summon Sepúlveda. When Sepúlveda received the news, he mounted his fine horse and raced off. He arrived very quickly at the spot where the commissioners were waiting for him. These men were not only commissioners but also his uncles, *compadres,* and friends. After he greeted them, they immediately began to complain about the people in the advance party. Then, with night drawing near and a violent rain and windstorm bearing down on them, they briefly explained the purpose of their trip. Sepúlveda simply replied that he could not do or resolve anything until his commissioner returned. Even though a strong storm was obviously approaching, Sepúlveda did not even have the decency to ask them to spend the night at his camp; they were forced to ask him if they could. They explained that if they left now, the violent storm, which was threatening to break in little more than a quarter of an hour, would catch them before they could take refuge at the first ranch along the route. That ranch happened to be quite far away. Sepúlveda was inflexible and adamantly denied their request. They were forced to go back to the Simi Ranch, the property of Don José de la Guerra y Noriega.[15] They arrived late that night, drenched and frozen stiff. They resented the fact that their nephew, *compadre,* and friend would be so gracious to them in his own home yet deny them hospitality away from home.

Although the weather had not cleared, Alvarado left San Buenaventura the following day via the Cayeguas road. Even though the ranch owner was not wealthy and had a large family to support, he willingly offered whatever shelter his wretched abode could provide. This favor was greatly appreciated, since everyone had arrived drenched. The commissioners sent Sepúlveda an open letter, which was delivered to Santa Susana Hill by special messenger. They briefly stated that there were no new developments to report, and due to the bad weather, they would spend the night there and leave the next day.[16]

Alvarado received his own commissioners even though they all were soaked. They greatly emphasized their drenched state as an example of Sepúlveda's harshness. They said that they were almost certain that the governor's advance troops had not detained or refused needed shelter to the other commissioners and had treated them with the respect they and their positions deserved. They said this in order both to throw it in the face of the other commissioners and to praise Alvarado's generosity. Sepúlveda's representative was very aware of the others' intentions and anger. For that reason, to their dismay he acknowledged that he had arrived at San Buenaventura without meeting any advance troops or even a sentinel to prevent him from walking up to the door of the main building. Of course he was very grateful for the warm welcome he had received. Alvarado was offended by that reply, which to him was the equivalent of saying that he and his men were novices in the art of war and that they lacked military expertise. Alvarado turned toward Don Eugenio Montenegro (who had been promoted from customs guard to senior captain of his division) and asked him if he had paid attention to what the commissioner had said. In order to satisfy Alvarado, he shrugged his shoulders, thus avoiding a direct answer.

Sepúlveda's friend noticed that Don Carlos and Don Anastasio Carrillo were hesitant to inform Alvarado of what they had discovered about the other party while he was present. So, to give them their privacy, he went out to take a walk around the camp. Everything they had to say amounted to a long complaint. They declared that the services which they had rendered were not appreciated, especially when they had suffered greatly. They were upset that their treatment constituted an affront to the Señor Gobernador, since they were his representatives. After they had finished their report, they left for San Buenaventura. Without thinking, they took the route which Sepúlveda's friend had taken. When they met up with him, they earnestly pleaded with him to prevent a battle between the two parties; they believed he could do that. In order to increase his ranks, Alvarado had taken their sons against their wishes, and they feared that they would be killed.

After conversing for a while about the situation, they went on their way. When Sepúlveda's friend arrived at the little house, he noticed a marked change in Alvarado's demeanor. Based on advice Alvarado received from Licenciado Don Cosme Peña, he suggested to Sepúlveda's friend, who was familiar with even the smallest detail regarding Alvarado's forces, that he sign a document promising that he would not divulge any information to Sepúlveda or his men. This information would be of no use to them anyway, but Peña wanted to draw up some type of document, and Alvarado always indulged him, no matter how insignificant his ideas were. Their friendship enabled Sepúlveda's friend to respond in a straightforward manner. He told them that he thought that the document they wanted him to sign was meaningless. Nevertheless, with the approval of his superior, the *licenciado* insisted on it in a rather arrogant manner which was aimed at instilling fear. Sepúlveda's friend replied somewhat heatedly that, although it seemed ridiculous, he would sign three dozen documents of that sort, provided that he not be prohibited from commanding and giving orders in the party to which he belonged.

By the following dawn the sky had cleared, and Sepúlveda's commissioners stated that it was time to leave and they wanted to take something back with them about the objective of their trip, even if it was just one word. Licenciado Peña wanted to spare Señor Alvarado the trouble of speaking and proceeded to reply. He stated that the Señores Comisionados had yet to comply with the formalities of their duty by presenting their credentials. Therefore the Señor Gobernador had decided to press on and would not give them even the slightest indication of how he felt about the matter. If a treaty were to be negotiated, it would be arranged in Sepúlveda's presence. Peña's persistent and cunning arrogance was merely a display of self-importance intended to terrify them. He received the following reply. Sepúlveda was aware of the distance between the two points; he had not sent them to a foreign country. Therefore he did not think that someone could be so ridiculous as to demand to see credentials and then enter into the formalities of exchanging them. This procedure was an unnecessary preamble to the agreement they wished to negotiate before a war broke out pitting brother against brother or even worse. Since there were fathers on both sides whose sons were on the opposite side, the consequences would be disastrous. Fathers and sons would be stripped of their natural bonds. One would inevitably grieve when he found the bloody remains of the other, but if that were the goal, the vast San Fernando plain would lend itself well.

Alvarado wanted to avoid further discussions which could become nasty, so in a quiet tone and with a pleasant demeanor he explained that the following day he would go to the San Fernando plain, four leagues from the mission. As a compromise, he would go with his secretary and some officers to have a conference with Sepúlveda and his men. There they could negotiate the preamble which had been mentioned previously. The Indian *vaquero* who was accompanying Sepúlveda's commissioners would remain behind as a prisoner. In order to obtain the Indian's release, Sepúlveda would provide a soldier and horses to escort Alvarado and his men to within view of Sepúlveda's advance troops. There Alvarado would saddle his own horses and would return the ones he had borrowed.[17]

All agreed to the terms, and Sepúlveda's commissioners left. They rode their horses at a fast gallop over the ten leagues between Cayeguas and San Fernando. When they dismounted, everyone began to ask them different questions and demand answers all at once. For that reason, one of the commissioners climbed onto the railing on the porch and stood there like an

orator. He reported to them about his mission and said that he had promised
that he would not divulge the number of men that Señor Alvarado had
with him. However, he would not be breaking his word by telling them
that their artillery consisted of no more than three pieces of useless odds
and ends. Their men were completely inferior to those who had gathered
here under an excellent leader and combat-skilled officers. In Alvarado's
party the only person who possessed the slightest military acumen was
Sergeant Pardo. Therefore, he had no difficulty in throwing Señor Alvarado's previous offer back in his face. If he did not accept reasonable
terms, he would be the first person to shoot him. This response pleased
them, and they agreed to await the results of the conference the next day.

When everyone had calmed down, Sepúlveda showed his friend a page
of instructions which he had received from the *ayuntamiento* of Los Angeles. The *ayuntamiento*'s deceitful plot was comparable only to Don Manuel
Requena's actions and could have been written only by him. The instructions forbade Sepúlveda to fight against and defeat Alvarado.[18] However,
if he did not fight against Alvarado, he might suffer enormous consequences. He was faced with a terrible dilemma. To continue what already
had been started, it was necessary to work energetically and quickly. His
friend suggested that they both leave immediately for Los Angeles, even
though it was night. The moment they arrived they would instruct the
ayuntamiento to meet to revise its instructions, with the understanding that
the first *alcalde* and his adviser Don Manuel Requena would be shot as a
basic precautionary measure if it refused to do so. Then they could return
before dawn and resume work on the conditions that should be imposed on
Alvarado the next day. Sepúlveda wanted to reflect on the matter. He finally consulted with the elders, and they were adamantly opposed to killing
the first *alcalde*, even though they compared him to an untamed mule. Don
Andrés Pico arrived during the night with news from his brother Don Pío.
He said that Don Pío would arrive the following day, and he asked them
kindly to wait for him before taking action, so he could at least be present
for the negotiations, if there were any.[19] They wanted to respect Pico's
wishes, and they left to meet with Alvarado in the morning. During the
conference they brought up Don Pío Pico's request, and a decision was
made to hold the final meeting at eleven the next morning at the same
place. If a reasonable treaty were not negotiated, then they would have to
resort to weapons. Don Andrés Pico was at the meeting, and he took Alvarado aside in order to speak to him privately. Sepúlveda's friend watched

Pico's actions and demeanor closely. He saw Pico and Alvarado embrace one another as a sign that they were satisfied with their mutual promises. Sepúlveda's friend had been warned that there might be some sort of conspiracy, and this action confirmed his suspicions. For that reason, Sepúlveda's friend immediately spoke with Alvarado in private. He told him that Sepúlveda did not need Señor Pico or the ten other men. If Alvarado wanted a list of their names for his satisfaction, Sepúlveda's friend would provide him with one so that the men could leave immediately to increase Alvarado's ranks. Alvarado did not accept this offer because he did not want to embarrass the men or admit that indeed he would accept them.

Don Pío Pico should have arrived four days earlier, according to a previous agreement. He attributed his delay to the fact that he was transporting a large cannon which prevented him from quickening his pace. Sepúlveda, determined to comply completely with the instructions from the *ayuntamiento* of Los Angeles, decided not to wait for him and left for the designated meeting place.

Both parties arrived almost at the same time. Señor Alvarado appeared to be more complacent than the day before, but to his dismay, it was becoming apparent to him that there was little hope in obtaining the benefits which he sought. Sepúlveda was angry because the *ayuntamiento*, or rather Don Manuel Requena, who was the first *alcalde*'s adviser, had hampered his operations. Sepúlveda showed Alvarado a page of instructions and told him that they showed who favored him. However, in order to avoid bloodshed caused by the villainy of the first *alcalde* and his adviser, he would do what he was ordered even though he knew it would not turn out well at all. Alvarado seized the page of instructions and read it eagerly. When he returned the instructions to Sepúlveda, he said, "These men have destroyed the insurmountable obstacles I faced during this most critical moment. I no longer wanted to be governor of the entire territory but rather want to be allowed to govern from Santa Bárbara to the north. You should govern this region as you see fit. The tone of their document shows that these two scoundrels do not intend to support me, so I do not have to be grateful to them for anything. However, you two have not even known how to hide your intentions, so I do not have a reason to reproach you for doing whatever you could to achieve the goal which caused you to take up arms. Nevertheless, dictate whatever reasonable terms you like, based on the terms negotiated today. I shall sign them and comply with them."

Sepúlveda did not want to take advantage of that promise. Knowing that he was not on good terms with the *ayuntamiento,* he added a codicil to the instructions. It stated that in addition to conforming with and agreeing to everything outlined in the instructions, Señor Alvarado promised that no individual would be persecuted for taking up arms in opposition to his plan to banish from the territory the *jefe político,* Don Nicolás Gutiérrez.[20] The people camped at San Fernando were to leave there, return to their homes, live peacefully, and occupy themselves with their work. In addition, as soon as someone arrived at a territorial port with a dispatch from the supreme government entrusting him with the command of the territory, he was to be recognized as *jefe superior*.

After the signing of the codicil, Sepúlveda's friend appeared to be sad. Alvarado noticed this and asked him to explain why. Sepúlveda's friend told him everything, including the agreement he had reached with the very virtuous mothers. He said that he had given them his solemn promise that, if he were unable to bring them favorable news about the nullification of the Monterey congress' decree on the tolerance of cults, they would not see him again in Los Angeles. Once Alvarado learned of the active role taken by the women, he naturally wanted to side with them. He told Sepúlveda's friend to assure the women that his government would not enforce the decree.

Everything had apparently been resolved, but Don Juan Rocha and the other company commanders still needed to be convinced to agree to the terms. They were very determined to fight, and persuading the inflexible Rocha, in particular, required a tremendous amount of effort from Sepúlveda and his friend. Rocha was so enraged that he bit his hand and drew blood. When he saw that he was bleeding, he turned to his men and said that the next time he took up arms to fight among the *californios* he would bring along a skilled barber who could bleed him nonviolently. That seemed to be the only way that he would be able to spill his blood. Without a barber, a surrender or negotiated agreements would force him to bleed himself in the same way as he had just done. Also, next time, they should not bother to outfit an excellent campaign train like the one they had assembled. After his rage was finally spent, they ordered him to do what they felt was best.

Captain Charlefoux appeared to be happy. He said that he had fulfilled an obligation without running the risk of losing any of his Indians or having them kill many Mexicans. He was certain that their courage and their deadly aim would have accomplished that. Charlefoux was the first one to head back to Los Angeles. Don Juan Rocha was ordered to march the division up to the Félix Ranch and to continue on his own from there to Mission San Gabriel.[21] The other company commanders would go to various destinations and then to their homes to lay down their weapons. The army was lined up in formation. As they left they saw Alvarado's troops begin to arrive to occupy Mission San Fernando. The last ones to leave were Sepúlveda, his friend, and a number of the older men. They took the Cahuenga route, where they met Don Pío Pico and the San Diego division. Since the retreat surprised Pico, Sepúlveda showed him the instructions from the *ayuntamiento* of Los Angeles. Pico read them with disgust and stated that he would not abide by them or by the codicil, even if it meant sacrificing his own life and the lives of his men. However, his brother Don Andrés took him by the arm, led him aside, and briefly spoke with him in private. After this exchange Don Pío Pico was mollified. However, Don Martín Sánchez Cabello, who was the customs receiver in San Diego and functioned as Don Pío Pico's scribe, uttered some very insulting comments to Sepúlveda's friend about the conduct he had observed during the negotiations with Alvarado. Cabello had no other reason to do this than to make himself look important. The offended party was going to respond to these insults by drawing his weapon, but Don Andrés Pico grabbed hold of him to prevent it, and Don Pío Pico shoved Cabello aside and rebuked him for his insulting manner of speech. Cabello then proceeded to give a miserable excuse for his words. He said that he was simply agreeing with the displeasure that Don Pío had expressed when he saw the document with the instructions, but since he was resigned to it now, he asked that they forgive him for his mistake. After that, all bad feelings from that unfortunate incident were forgotten, and everyone left together for Los Angeles, three leagues away.

As they passed through the town *plaza*, they met up with Don Manuel Requena. When he asked what had been done, Sepúlveda's friend replied that they had complied with the instructions sent by the *ayuntamiento*, since they could not do anything else. Requena had the audacity to state that perhaps they had misunderstood the literal meaning of the instructions. Sepúlveda's friend responded in a loud, curt voice, which was not in keeping with his customary moderate tone. He said that the double meaning of the words had been understood very well. It was a typical device of people who knew how to avoid putting themselves in the line of fire. Instead, they preferred to stick together in small groups and denounce every-

Manuel Requena. Courtesy of the California State Library, Sacramento.

one else. As Requena walked away, he let out an icy laugh and muttered that his signature would not appear on the instructions.

The next day the *ayuntamiento* assembled in an extraordinary session and summoned Sepúlveda and his friend to account for their actions. The two had agreed that the only explanation they would provide was that they had to modify their operations in order to obey the instructions. When they responded in that manner, the first *alcalde* immediately declared that the treaty negotiated with Señor Alvarado was null and void. The remaining *vocales* voiced their approval. None of them had the courage to explain why Sepúlveda's actions were being condemned.[22]

Señor Alvarado entered Los Angeles the next day.[23] When he was informed that the *ayuntamiento* had declared the agreements null and void, he wanted proof. He ordered that the *alcalde* be told that he wished to speak to the distinguished assembly about an important matter and that he would therefore appear at the session hall within an hour. After he arrived and took his seat, he asked the *alcalde* to be so kind as to inform him if that respectable association did indeed recognize him as the territorial governor. Since there was no need for discussion, everyone said yes. He then said that he wished to see the minutes of the previous day, concerning the agreements which had been negotiated on the San Fernando plain. They handed him the book in which the minutes were written, and he read them slowly and carefully. When he finished, he thanked the distinguished assembly for declaring those agreements null and void. Actually, he had accepted and signed them because it was prudent to do so, rather than to pit his men against superior forces. Now he also was released from his promise not to persecute anyone for past deeds. So, in the sight of all, he would begin legal proceedings against the people who had worked against him because of extreme malice or crass ignorance.[24]

Sepúlveda and his friend were standing to one side, and Alvarado called them by name. He said, "Gentlemen, I know, and others have also told me, how hard you labored to have me meet with the leader of this group of fine *angelinos*. You complied with the agreement by breaking your camp at Mission San Fernando, retreating, and laying down your weapons. I, too, shall comply by not punishing anyone for having taken up arms. Even though the *ayuntamiento* has condemned our agreements, I shall not break my promise. But if, in the administration of justice, I am forced to punish a wicked man, even one whose misconduct helped me, I hope that you will be good enough to forgive me, and not ask that these men receive any special consideration." On hearing that statement, all the members of the corporation turned pale, except for Ibarra, who was dark-skinned. But his eyes began to dart around like those of a falcon, and his pupils dilated quickly, before they shrank back to a small circle.[25]

Señor Alvarado then wanted to know if there was any money left over from the 2,000 pesos that the *ayuntamiento* had borrowed from Mission San Fernando. If there was any, he wanted to use it. He had discussed this matter with the administrator, and they had agreed that the whole amount could be charged to the state government and that Alvarado could take whatever was left of it. Since the one who had received the money was present, he was ordered to deliver the funds. As soon as Señor Alvarado retired to his room, he received 1,785 pesos. He did not even ask to examine the expense account, perhaps fearing that a mistake in the calculations might entitle him to receive less money.

After receiving the money and ordering that it be put away, he asked the person who delivered it if 215 pesos were enough for him to defray expenses, since he had more than four hundred men. He answered affirmatively. Alvarado then thanked him for having safeguarded the money and took pleasure in privately calling him a *pend . . . olista*, because he should have taken half the money as fair payment for everything he had done.[26] Alvarado said that because of his conduct and the fact that he had promoted a counterrevolution against him, he deserved the punishment Alvarado had prepared for him: he was to be taken by force to Monterey. There, to atone for the crimes he had committed, he was to manage the customs as well as he had managed the 2,000 pesos from Mission San Fernando.

When the favored one expressed his appreciation for such a severe punishment, he told Alvarado that it was not convenient for him to leave Los Angeles at that time. He was operating a business in which he financed goods from ships that sailed up and down the coast. Since he had the option of returning poorly cut fabrics and unsold articles, he was bound to earn about four thousand pesos a year from this business venture alone. In addition, he had four thousand productive vines already yielding excellent fruit and three thousand more which were just beginning to produce.[27] His many years of experience had shown him that the general government never bothered to compensate a treasury employee for hard work and honesty. The various times that he had been in charge of the customs in Monterey he had the satisfaction of knowing that the public censor could not say anything negative about the way he conducted his job. However, an administrator sent from Mexico would always appear unexpectedly to take over the position. For that reason, he no longer wanted to serve in that capacity or in any other government position.

Herrera's actions as customs administrator have been described already, as well as the matter regarding the apostate Fray Ángel Ramírez. However, the story about Don Rafael González, alias "Pintito," is missing, so we shall say something about his abilities and allow others to speak of his honesty. He was appointed customs administrator of Monterey on the approval of Don José Ignacio Pavón, director general of revenue. After he assumed the position, he began his apprenticeship with the arrival of an American frigate from Boston. It was consigned to Don Alfredo Robinson, who presented the cargo manifests to customs with his typical accuracy and neatness.[28] When the Señor Administrator examined them, he thought that some serious substitutions had been made on them. Since he planned to work very diligently to curtail abuses, he asked to see the supercargo. When he entered the office, he addressed the administrator with the formalities due his position, which was standard procedure before a shipment would be appraised. Since Don Nicolás Gutiérrez and other respectable individuals came in at the same time, González composed himself in order to act with the proper demeanor of an office administrator. He took out a manifest and in a threatening voice told the supercargo that during his tenure he would not permit even one item to be substituted for another item on the list, as he obviously was attempting to do with the cotton cloth. For how could it be that, among the lines listing goods such as blankets and printed calicos, there were other items with no classification except *idem, idem*? At first, the supercargo believed that such a reprimand was nothing more than a joke. But when he saw the administrator's serious look, he took out a manifest and begged Don Nicolás Gutiérrez to show him any discrepancy he could find. When he glanced at the manifest, Gutiérrez stated in a direct and witty manner that even to an absolute *pend . . . olista* like the customs administrator, it ought to be clear that the goods were either very extraordinary or very ordinary. Therefore, it should not be surprising to find the words *idem, idem* written on a line as a way of referring to the same items as those listed on the line above. Everyone who was present burst out laughing. Only the administrator remained serious, insisting on an explanation to determine whether the duty on the goods classified as *idem, idem* should be calculated by weight or measure.

Sepúlveda's friend apprised Señor Alvarado of the situation and stated that it was the reason that he had to decline Alvarado's generous offer. Alvarado then begged him not to get involved in another revolution against the present government. He did, in fact, expect one to occur, because there were people who were unhappy with him or wanted to improve their lot. Changing the topic of conversation, Alvarado said that he should leave for Monterey soon. He had thought of taking Don Manuel Requena with him as a slight punishment for his dirty tricks. Also, he did not trust him enough to let him stay in that area. Alvarado warned Sepúlveda's friend not to request any special favors on Requena's behalf. The friend replied that he would plead with Alvarado now, to avoid having to do it later. He asked that Requena not be transferred from San Fernando because he was conducting an experiment on him. The friend wanted to see if a bad man would change his ways if, in exchange for his dirty tricks, he were treated kindly. If Alvarado did not interrupt this unusual endeavor, Sepúlveda's friend promised to provide him with a report of the results.

The day before his departure, Don Manuel Requena was ordered to accompany the governor on his march north. His political conscience was troubling him deeply, and he was unable to term that order an arbitrary one. So he asked a favor of the person whom he had offended so many times. In an anguished, or tremendously uneasy, tone of voice, he promised that he would not harm anyone in the future. Although it was after the fact, he said, he had lately realized that Don José Antonio Carrillo, the one-eyed Pérez, and other detractors, had given false reports about him. In order to convince him of his sincerity, he promised to make amends and offered his complete friendship. As Sepúlveda's friend listened to Requena, he recalled Ambrosio Lamela's proceedings with Gil Blas.[29] Because he was afraid of being far from his wife and his interests, Requena made more promises than a lover makes to his next intended victim. He achieved his goal; he was not transferred from San Fernando.

· 10 ·

About two months after Alvarado had left Los Angeles, a revolution was instigated against him in San Diego.[1] Don Juan Bandini left San Diego to see who and how many *angelinos* would take part.[2] The first person he approached was Sepúlveda's friend, who responded negatively. Bandini then begged him not to use his influence to dissuade anyone in the area who might want to join him. After Sepúlveda's friend promised that he would not interfere, Bandini remarked that Captain Don Pablo de la Portilla was the prime leader and that he was accompanied by Alférez Don Macedonio González, the frontier commander, and twenty-five or thirty men under González' command. The group included various other people from San Diego, including Don Andrés Pico and Don Santiago E. Argüello as subaltern officers. As Portilla was beginning his march from San Diego to Los Angeles, Don Andrés Castillero arrived by land. When Portilla saw that Castillero was sporting captain's epaulets, he naturally accepted him and gave him an important role in the revolution, which Castillero, wanting to endorse and support, termed the Division of the Supreme Government.[3]

They celebrated their arrival in Los Angeles by swearing allegiance to the new constitution.[4] However, after that act, to which they assigned so much importance, they did not have one real to give to the troops. Therefore they decided to ask the merchants for a loan, but some members of that group plainly stated that the plan was risky. Finally, they followed the proper procedures and mortgaged the territorial customs fees, and the merchants unwillingly gave them some blue cloth and other goods. The *ayuntamiento* was fearful that the unpaid soldiers would wreak havoc as soon as they realized that the *jefe principal* had little or no power. It sent a committee to plead that they kindly establish their camp outside the city because of the need to maintain public order. Either in obedience to the request or simply because the move was more convenient for them, they left for Mission San Gabriel. Two days later a sergeant returned with ten men to take Don José Sepúlveda prisoner.[5] He ordered that his friend be notified and provided with one of Sepúlveda's horses so he could catch up with him on the road, since they would not allow Sepúlveda to wait for him. The friend caught up with them before they reached the pass.

When they arrived at the mission, they were welcomed pleasantly. After a short conversation about various things, Captain Portilla told Sepúlveda that it had been agreed that he should be brought back there as a prisoner. He would explain the charges to him later, because some details of the suspicions about him needed to be filled in. The friend spoke to Portilla privately and begged him to clarify what he meant by suspicions regarding Sepúlveda. That simple-minded man answered with complete candor. He said that he did not know anything because these were matters which concerned Captain Castillero and Alférez Don Macedonio González. But these men also said in private that they knew nothing, since these measures had been taken by the Señor Comandante. Sepúlveda's friend was not satisfied with this, so he gathered them all together so they could give him an explanation. Each one was too embarrassed to speak, until Castillero finally broke the silence and said that there really were no charges against Sepúlveda. However, since they considered him to be one of Alvarado's converts, his presence in the town might restrain those citizens who wanted to volunteer to participate in the revolt. Therefore, they were simply trying to keep him out of circulation for two or three days. Finally it was agreed that Sepúlveda would stay with them for two days, as a friend and not as a prisoner. He would be well-cared-for and respected during that interval, and as soon as the two days were up Sepúlveda's friend could come to get him.

During the period when he was in command of the Baja California frontier, Alférez González never bothered to prepare an indictment against the delinquent Indians, since he did not know how. He would deliver only an oral judgment and would sentence them to a flogging or capital punishment. Sometimes he would sentence them to be shot, but as a means of saving cartridges he would execute them himself with his sword. When he imposed these executions, he called them justice. González found out from one of his soldiers that two Indian criminal fugitives from the frontier were somewhere in Los Angeles and ordered that they be captured. They were apprehended and placed in jail during the night, and González was told that his order had been carried out. The next day he arrived at the jail with an escort of twenty men. He asked the first *alcalde* to surrender the two Indian prisoners so that he could shoot one and whip the other. The *alcalde* replied that a judgment had not yet been rendered to determine if they were guilty and deserved the punishment González wanted to impose, especially since whipping was prohibited by any number of laws. González replied that he was not authorized to prepare dossiers, and he did not intend to worry about them when he punished Indians who came under his jurisdiction. He then ordered his soldiers to enter the jail and remove the prisoners. He then made them walk about one hundred paces toward the foot of a low ridge. The first Indian was executed there, and no effort was made to pick up the body. González returned and gave the second command while he was standing directly in front of the courthouse door, so that the *alcalde* could see that the laws could not prevent the Indian from receiving the one hundred lashings that he had ordered. Although this action was an affront to the system of public justice, he was satisfied and retired to his barracks. He felt very proud that he had proved that there were plenty of reasons that they called him the Potentate of the Frontier.

When the two days had passed, Sepúlveda's friend hurried to San Gabriel to wait out the last hour before he could claim the prisoner. Sepúlveda told him that he believed his so-called imprisonment was just a pretext for them to keep him there. They had gone to a lot of trouble to take care of him, and they really were just attempting to distract him. After they drank a few bottles of wine to celebrate, with toasts of congratulations and appreciation, Sepúlveda and his friend returned to Los Angeles. The friend had the pleasure of taking him home to his family, who had agonized over the Potentate's arbitrary acts, which Captain Portilla had condoned. Since something has been said about the lieutenant of the frontier, it would seem inconsistent if Señor Castillero were ignored. He should receive a "tribute" also.

Like many men who left the capital of the republic in search of great adventure or to work in distant places, Castillero arrived in Alta California during Don Mariano Chico's tenure in office. He made use of his limited knowledge of medicine to secure a position caring for the troops. When Governor Chico left, Castillero left the territory as well and appeared later in the manner that has been described. His ambitions to be important figured into his calculations, and a favorable opportunity arose when he discovered that some *californios* intended to play a game which they did not understand. He was able to distinguish himself as an authority in the science of intrigue, whereas the others who wanted to practice it were amateurs who were stumbling in the beginning stages. His shrewdness cautioned him to maintain a low profile, not to reveal what he knew, and to behave as meekly as a wildcat in the republic of the rabbits so that he could choose what was best for him.

He left San Gabriel after instructing poor Portilla how to operate according to the different circumstances in which he might find himself. This was Castillero's way of insuring that Portilla supported his plans. They knew that Alvarado and his sizable force were marching double-time to meet up with them. Since Castillero did not know which side would win, he used his ingenuity to remain on good terms with whichever party might prevail. Therefore, as Alvarado was approaching, he proposed to go over and see him. His pretext was that he wanted him to be the first person in the territory to see a copy of the constitution, so that Alvarado could swear allegiance to it, if he wanted to comply with the wishes of the Supreme Magistrate who ordered it circulated and obeyed. That constitutional pamphlet proved to be very useful to him. Thus he tricked the commander of the Southern Division, and then he went to see if he could do the same to the commander of the Northern Division, to determine which of the two was the more powerful and shrewd.

When he spoke with Alvarado, he recognized that he possessed a natural way with people which attracted more supporters to his side. This talent proved to be a great advantage in his being able to help himself to the customs' revenue. Castillero realized that the odds favored Alvarado and that he would most probably prevail, so he decided to side with him. In order to gain his trust and goodwill, he began to talk about the arbitrary acts committed by the military men who commanded the frontier. These men took advantage of the fact that they were so far away and that anyone who had a complaint against them had no one to whom an appeal could be made. This was the main reason for the demoralization of the *pueblos.* Even when some clever genius shook off the yoke of one of these tyrants, there were always envious people around who wanted to seize the fruits of his labor. For example, he saw with great dismay that the audacious Bandini, the idiot Portilla, and others were ganging up on him and planning to do just that. Castillero, however, was fulfilling the promise he made to the Excelentísimo Señor Presidente as he bade him farewell in his private office after having received his instructions about the territory. He would

Juan Bautista Alvarado. Courtesy of the California State Library, Sacramento.

do everything possible to prevent an outbreak of hostilities which would produce disastrous results for the country. Alvarado was not experienced enough to recognize men of cunning, and he had to complete his apprenticeship by allowing himself to be fooled by Castillero. Based on what he had been told, Alvarado believed that Castillero was a secret agent sent by the president of the republic. In the end they came to an understanding because of their ambitions and the mutual advantage of helping each other.

Castillero explained the means by which the hostile parties could avoid experiencing the terrible consequences of a conflict. He took out the constitutional pamphlet for Alvarado to read. He told him that if he found no obstacle to adopting the constitution and swearing allegiance to it, as Portilla's party had already done, that act would be viewed as an armistice, a reconciliation, and a victory worthy of celebration. Alvarado agreed to it, and Portilla agreed to do whatever Castillero did.[6] Since the revolt ended favorably, each man marched back to the place from which he had come. Castillero went with Alvarado's company.

The general government wanted to send another governor to Alta California, but it did not want him to have the same experience as the previous governors. Therefore, General Iniestra was given command of one thousand men and ordered to the port of Acapulco to board the transport vessels for Alta California.[7] Their departure was delayed considerably because of difficulties in meeting the troop's budget, which was already due, and in obtaining money for the soldiers' future wages. The delay provided enough time for the news to reach Alta California. When Alvarado received it, he decided to send a delegation to inform the government that there was no need to incur such huge expenses by sending troops to the territory, when all he needed were arms and munitions to safeguard the country. So he designated two individuals, Don Carlos Carrillo and another man, and summoned them to Santa Bárbara for instructions. From there they were to set sail for Acapulco on the schooner *California*, which belonged to the territorial government and was anchored in the bay.[8] When the two men appeared in Santa Bárbara, someone told Señor Alvarado that in light of the delegation's objective, it would not be in his best interest to send one of the men in particular. This man had a shortcoming; he always told the truth. He naturally would answer all questions truthfully, and this would not help Alvarado realize his plans. If he thought about it carefully, he would see that this advice was well founded.

Don José Antonio Aguirre was the one who gave the advice. The delegate agreed with him, since he had no desire to go to Mexico at that time. Alvarado, convinced that the situation described to him could actually happen, had to make up an excuse to satisfy those who had been appointed to the delegation. With a great display of emotion, he tried to make them understand that there was no money available to pay for their round-trip. This was quite true, and so the delegation was not sent. Don Andrés Castillero was appointed instead. He accepted because he wanted some official capacity which would enable him to speak to the president of the republic and his ministers.[9]

Don Ángel Ramírez was not content with simply allocating the customs' duties as he pleased; he also wanted Alvarado to follow his orders.[10] Alvarado had told him repeatedly that he, and he alone, was responsible for his actions, and he did not want to be given advice instead of money. Ramírez was very angry, and he proposed to instigate a revolt against Alvarado so he could seek another governor more to his liking. The spirit of provincialism in the populated areas of the north had reached such a point that the native-born wanted to be called *californios* and not Mexicans. That is why the troops adopted the practice of answering the challenge "Who goes there?" with the response "California libre." The individual who responded "Mexico" would be punished with sentry duty. For that reason, Ramírez could not attract any *californios* to his cause.[11] However, he was able to attract many who had come as soldiers, convicts, colonists, and adventurers, and he compiled a long list of names as he waited for the first opportunity to pronounce. When they received information in Monterey that Alvarado and Castro were occupied in the south, they appointed Don Francisco Figueroa as captain commander and set him up in a house within the fort.[12]

At the same time, they sent communiqués to many ranches, to San Juan Bautista, the Villa de Branciforte, and the *pueblo* of San José to report what had happened. When Alvarado's supporters heard the news, they armed themselves and headed for Monterey. Everyone met at the river. They organized an impressive force and immediately set out to seize the fort or die. They were determined that, if they triumphed, with many casualties or with only one, they would show no mercy to any of the rebels. When they approached the town, some foreigners and traders went out to speak with them and begged them to try to listen to each other's demands and negotiate a treaty before resorting to bullets. They replied that if the rebels surrendered their weapons, only their leaders would be taken prisoner and delivered to the governor for disposition. Then the foreigners and traders went back to see if the others would accept that proposal, but they totally rejected it.

The *californios* seized the fort, and from there the company of riflemen headed down the ravine.[13] They stayed hidden until they could position themselves within firing range. They ended up about one hundred yards from the battery, which due to a lack of experience or laziness had no parapet. Consequently, since the artillerymen at the battery were out in the open, they could have been attacked by the riflemen and would have been unable to fire their cannons. One of the artillerymen was the physician Don Manuel de Alva. He was the doctor who had treated the final illness of the late general Don José Figueroa. Alva wanted to kill some more people before he died, but he no longer could find patients who had faith in him. Rickets had permeated his tiny body, and it angered him that he was dying, so death mattered little to him.[14] As a result, he was the most enthusiastic participant there. When he heard talk of surrender, he lit a match to fire the cannon. His very weak condition proved to be an advantage for him and the others, for the match was blown from his hand by a shot just as he was about to light the loaded cannon. Then the rebels immediately entered into negotiations and accepted the first proposal.

The leaders of the revolt were made prisoners. During the day, as they waited for the governor to pass sentence on them, they suffered many insults hurled at them. At night the victors became so drunk that they wanted to shoot the prisoners. Fortunately for them, the merchants learned of the plan in time and quickly tried to help the prisoners by amiably advising Alvarado's people not to shoot them. In order to give their advice more force, they purchased enough liquor to finish intoxicating those most exalted captains, thus putting them in a state in which they would be unable to commit any assassinations.

Señor Alvarado received the news of the uprising via urgent dispatch as soon as the rebel leaders were made prisoners. Their fate was in his hands. When he arrived in Monterey, he decided to examine the criminal case of each individual. He released Don Francisco Figueroa and the others who were not so guilty. Licenciado Don Cosme Peña, Don Juan Ayala, and Artillery Sergeant Don José Águila were confined for a period of time at the San Simeón Ranch, located south of Monterey on a point along the coast which could serve as a presidio. Don Ángel Ramírez was sent to Mission San José, under the authority of Don José de Jesús Vallejo. As soon as Vallejo received him, he ordered him placed in irons and locked in a room, where he was held incommunicado for a long time. There Ramírez was forced to observe the monastery rules regarding abstinence which his Prelate had never been able to impose on him in Mexico. To continue the story of this wretched man, after his period of suffering at Mission San José, he was transferred to Mission San Luis Obispo, the site chosen as his prison. The Reverend Father Ramón Abella was ministering at the mission. He considered Señor Ramírez to be a woeful priest and took pity on him. He provided him with the best support possible, in order to persuade him to make amends for his very corrupt former life, but he did not succeed. In the end he experienced the sorrow of seeing Ramírez die impenitent, without accepting any spiritual comfort.[15]

The difficulties in covering the great expenses of transporting the Iniestra division from Acapulco to Monterey were presented to the general government. This problem, together with the fact that General Iniestra was uncertain that funds would be available to pay future wages, made him decide not to leave. The expedition was canceled, and the government was forced to appoint another *jefe político* for Alta California, one who would accept the position without asking for money. Don Carlos Carrillo was appointed in August 1837.[16] He received his appointment at Mission San Buenaventura, where he was acting as administrator. From there he sent a communiqué to Señor Alvarado informing him of the order and stating that he was to assume the command of the territorial government. Alvarado replied that he foresaw no problem at all in surrendering the command to him as soon as he appeared at the capital to receive it.[17]

It was the general opinion that as soon as Don José Antonio Carrillo returned to Los Angeles, there would be another revolt. Carrillo had not taken part in the revolt against Señor Alvarado because he was a deputy in Mexico at the time. When Alvarado received the document in which Don Carlos Carrillo informed him of his appointment, his first remark was that he would no longer need additional troops to go down and pacify those who were dissatisfied with his rule in the southern part of the territory. He was content that the identity of those people was common knowledge and that public opinion was judging them negatively. When Don José Antonio Carrillo arrived at the ports of San Blas and Mazatlán on his return trip from Mexico, he did not find a single ship available to sail to Alta California, so he went to Baja instead. As soon as he had gathered the necessary supplies, he began his march and arrived in Los Angeles at the same time that his brother Don Carlos was preparing to go up to Monterey to assume the territorial command. He quickly determined to persuade him that it was ridiculous and dishonorable to take the customary solemn oath before a man who was considered a revolutionary, who had no authority whatsoever, and whom the supreme government refused to recognize. In addition, Don José Antonio had conclusive information that Alvarado was preparing to rebuff Don Carlos and not surrender the government. By operating with the appropriate circumspection, Don Carlos could order that five territorial delegates be convened from among the landowners and the nearest substitutes. Then before the president of the assembly, he could be installed and take the customary oath of office in the new capital, Los Angeles. Then he could circulate his orders as governor of the territory.

That kindhearted man accepted everything that was suggested to him by his brother's cleverness or malice. He took the oath of office in the manner that has been described, and then he informed Señor Alvarado that he was now *jefe político* of the territory.[18] He ordered Alvarado to surrender the government records to the emissary he would send. When Señor Alvarado received that order, he summoned the customs administrator and told him to be prepared to turn over the office to whomever had been appointed by Don Carlos Carrillo.[19] The employee replied that he would obey any orders that he was given. Alvarado then said, "Since he refused to come and assume the command of the government with the appropriate formalities, I will make him challenge me by force. If he succeeds in taking the command away from me, he will have convinced me that his bravery exceeds his rudeness. But since the second quality is more certain than the first with him, I want to go speak to him, to see if he will wait for me or flee with the deer amid the thickets of Baja California."

Both *jefes* were busy recruiting more soldiers. Alvarado quickly organized a respectable corps, which he sent ahead under the command of Don José Castro.[20] He himself remained behind to complete outfitting another group of soldiers who were to follow. When Castro left Monterey, he sent orders ahead so there always would be horses available to them along the way. Traveling at a fast pace which allowed his men only three or four hours of rest each night, he arrived in Santa Bárbara two and one-half days later. Even though it was night, he immediately ordered an advance party to go to the point called El Rincón, a narrow pass between the ocean and the hill, to prevent anyone from crossing.[21] Shortly afterward he left, accompanied by the garrison stationed there and enough artillerymen to handle a well-mounted, eight-pound cannon. With great effort they were able to move the cannon over the rocky ground of El Rincón. This maneuver helped tremendously, for Castro succeeded in taking the high point of the ridge which dominates Mission San Buenaventura, where Don Carlos Carrillo had stationed his soldiers. Undetected, Castro had time to position his troops within firing range, and then he waited for dawn to break.

A few days earlier Captain Tovar had arrived from Sonora.[22] Don Carlos had confidence in Tovar and entrusted him with the command of his soldiers. Tovar knew nothing about the terrain other than what he had heard, but he also wanted to send an advance party to El Rincón. The officers who were accompanying him, all men of little or no foresight, assured him that it was not necessary to do this. Not enough time had passed for Alvarado to have received the documents sent by the new governor, and if Alvarado was planning on being obstinate about maintaining his command, he would not move quickly from where he was.

When day broke, Castro's cannon fire sounded reveille for the *carlistas*. They were so surprised to be jolted out of their sleep that some of the officers wrestled with the sleeves of their jackets, believing them to be the legs of their pants. Some of them thought that the situation was similar to what had happened at Troy, and soon a few began to speak of surrender. Commander Tovar, however, wanted to do his duty and to defend himself as best he could, so he positioned several sharpshooters in the church tower. One of the men was a Texan with a fine rifle, and his first shots killed one of Castro's artillerymen.[23] Castro then ordered his men to use the cannon to dislodge the sharpshooters, and that was done immediately. The defenders held out in the enclosure all day, hoping to be aided by the night. Since the nights in that area are typically foggy, they hoped to be able to escape and hide in the mustard fields. However, Castro was able to keep a close watch over them, and the following morning they surrendered unconditionally. Some men, hidden in the nooks of the vast building, believed themselves to be safely out of sight, but Castro's minions did not allow even one man to escape. They searched everywhere, even under the cloak of the great, holy teacher and Doctor, in case someone were hiding there.[24]

Then Castro set the men free and offered apologies, which Commander Tovar accepted, believing that they were sincere. The following officers were sent to Alvarado as prisoners to be dealt with at his discretion: Don José Ramírez, Don José Antonio Carrillo, Don Andrés Pico, Don Ignacio del Valle, Don Ignacio Palomares, Don Roberto Pardo, and Don Gil Ibarra. The prisoners and their escort left Santa Bárbara and spent the night at Mission Santa Ynés. They were placed in a secure and modest room. Alvarado arrived shortly afterward and was informed immediately by the officer in charge that the prisoners were at his disposal.[25] The officer wished that he did not have to do that right then, because he knew that the *jefe* was drunk and, in that condition, was known to fly into a rage. But in the end, the situation did not turn out in the way they had expected. As soon as Alvarado was informed where the prisoners were being held, he went to their door and asked them if they had belonged to the gang of scoundrels that sought to support Don Carlos Carrillo. Prudence dictated that no one answer, and their silence annoyed Alvarado even more. He reacted with a reprimand so eloquent that he was not interrupted by anyone. He concluded by saying that if he were to send them to hell, their crime would remain unpunished, and he would receive very little satisfaction. He was sending them to Sonoma instead, entrusting them to the commanding general. There they would receive the punishment he desired.

He immediately told the officer in charge to see if there was another room available for the prisoners because the one they had was too nice to be occupied by the likes of them. Also, he needed that room for his officers. There was an adjoining room, but it was extremely filthy and filled with garbage. The Indians swept it out, but to clean the room quickly, they had to throw buckets of water on the floor, and this turned it to mud. Alvarado ordered that the prisoners be placed there without a chair or even a blanket. We shall leave it to the prisoners to tell us later how much they suffered, so that we can continue the description of Alvarado's march.

He left the following morning and arrived in the afternoon in Santa Bárbara, where Castro was waiting for him. There he learned that the other governor had left Los Angeles and had headed for San Diego to recover from the defeat at San Buenaventura.[26] So Alvarado ordered that his men prepare to follow immediately in pursuit. When he passed through Los Angeles, he was informed that Don Carlos Carrillo had returned with the idea of engaging him in one last battle. Alvarado replied that he already knew this and that he hoped Carrillo would wait for him so he would have the pleasure of speaking to him before he put his plans into operation. However, if he turned into a deer and ran, he would not send his troops after him. In San Juan Capistrano Alvarado learned that Señor Carrillo was at the place called Las Flores and had barricaded himself in a square around some homes.[27] Carrillo was not the type of man who, as they say, takes up arms without military expertise. The same could be said of old Captain Portilla, who acted as leader of the force. Carrillo wavered between fear and ignorance; thus all of his preparations resulted in just the opposite of his intentions.

As soon as Señor Alvarado arrived at Las Flores, he surveyed the terrain and selected a high point which seemed most advantageous to him. From there he could attack the *carlistas* with the cannon and also cut off their source of water. Señor Carrillo did not feel safe behind the double walls of the homes. He believed that it would be better to position himself and his soldiers in a large corral. When he realized that he was even more defenseless there, he fled to the beach by himself to look for the boat that his son-in-law, Don Guillermo Dana, had sent from Santa Bárbara, just in case it might be needed. He managed to find it and set sail in the direction of the Baja California frontier.[28] His soldiers and officers remained behind and surrendered. Alvarado spoke to them in a very friendly manner and advised them to keep busy with work and not allow themselves to be seduced by others who might want to revolt. The only retribution that he imposed on them was to wish them well, and then he sent them back to their homes. That is how Don Carlos Carrillo ended his tenure in government. As was promised earlier, the description of the suffering of the *carlista* prisoners will be completed.

As previously recounted, since the room where the prisoners were placed was filled with mud and they were denied a chair or even blankets, they were forced to spend the entire night standing up. The next morning they continued their march closely supervised by Captain Don Santiago Estrada. He took them to a spot near Monterey where Don José de Jesús Vallejo met them. He then was to take them to Sonoma and surrender them to the commanding general. When they arrived at the San Pablo Ranch, where they were supposed to set sail for their destination, they found that Don Joaquín Castro had gone to great lengths to prepare a meal for them in his home. Since the food was ready, he begged Señor Vallejo to allow the prisoners to enter his home to take some refreshment. Vallejo adamantly refused, saying that they did not deserve the food. However, he did ask Castro for permission to slaughter a bull on the shore of the estuary, so they themselves could grill the amount of meat they wanted to eat.

When they arrived in Sonoma, the commanding general refused to stoop to their level and speak with any of them. He ordered them confined, without the right to communicate with anyone outside. Their daily rations consisted of split peas, which were not very well cooked, and a few pieces of meat, which they tolerated only because they had suffered from the hunger pangs of an empty stomach for two or three days. Once a woman felt sorry for them, and she had a boy take them two watermelons. When the boy was near the door, the commanding general saw him and immediately ordered the sentinel to smash the watermelons into pieces on the floor. He also ordered him to keep a close watch to prevent the prisoners from receiving more food than had been allotted to them. Alvarado had

Jail on Mariano Guadalupe Vallejo's Sonoma *rancho*. Courtesy of the California State Library, Sacramento.

not been mistaken when he told them at Mission Santa Ynés that if he were to send them to hell, he would not be satisfied because he would not receive news from there about their suffering.

When Castillero arrived in Mexico, he learned that the government had appointed Don Carlos Carrillo *jefe político* of Alta California. Shortly afterward the news arrived that Alvarado did not want to transfer the command to him. This was attributed to Don José Antonio Carrillo's meddling. Either because it was weak or because it wanted to avoid a greater evil, the government issued two appointments for the position of *jefe político*. One appointment was for Don Juan Bautista Alvarado, and the other for Don Carlos Carrillo. Señor Castillero was commissioned to return to California with both appointments and was instructed to deliver one to the person who could garner the most support.[29]

The commissioner arrived in San Diego, where he encountered the angry *carlistas*.[30] They immediately informed him of Alvarado's actions and his obstinacy in not respecting the decisions of the general government. Castillero listened to everything, apparently showing great concern. He told them that he very much wanted to be able to favor Carrillo by helping to exonerate him before the Supreme Magistrate of the Republic. But by his actions, Carrillo already had shown himself to be a habitual criminal. Under those circumstances Castillero would be ashamed even to consider helping him because the attempt would earn him a well-deserved reproach. If he attempted to restore Carrillo's honor, he certainly would run the risk of damaging his own reputation, since the dishonor would be transferred to him. Castillero said that, even though he had not arrived in time to avert the troubles which Don Carlos Carrillo was experiencing, simply because he obeyed an order instructing him to assume the territorial command, he still hoped his persuasion could bring Señor Alvarado under control. However, it was important not to waste time. It would be difficult for him because the two-hundred-league trip had been prepared hastily, and he did not have enough horses.

This was merely an excuse to ask for some horses, which were provided quickly and willingly. The horses were up to the journey, and he managed to meet with Señor Alvarado. When he was introduced to Alvarado, Castillero warmly congratulated him for being the legitimate governor of Alta California and placed the appointment in his hand.[31] After he gave Alvarado that pleasant surprise, he showed him Don Carlos Carrillo's appointment. Castillero assured Alvarado that, from the moment he had received it, he was determined to keep it secret. When he returned to Mexico, he would give Carrillo's appointment back to His Excellency the President and inform him that he considered Carrillo a fool and not worthy of receiving the honor that the President wanted to bestow on him. He then gave Alvarado a complete account of his conversations in San Diego with members of Don Carlos' party. He mentioned the promise he had made to them to go quickly to see Alvarado and persuade him to render obedience to the supreme government. He told Alvarado that he wanted to be sure that he had tricked them into believing that he was on their side, so when he spoke about Alvarado, he used some offensive and dishonorable language to describe the Señor Gobernador. He also took great care to hide the fact that he was the bearer of the appointments.

Señor Alvarado considered himself the legitimate governor, and he wanted to discharge the obligations of that position by reestablishing order in the territory and doing whatever possible for its inhabitants. He usually worked by lamplight from four in the morning until seven. At that time he would eat breakfast as he waited for his secretary to arrive so they could determine which matters needed attention on that day. Then he would read and sign papers that were ready to be sent. He never was criticized about that aspect of his official duties. The funds of the national treasury were based solely on the income generated by the customs' revenues. Alvarado ordered the collector's office to manage the funds in the following way. The expenses of the collector's office would be covered first. Then the balance would be passed to the office of distributions, which would divide the amount in half. One-half would be designated for the military register, and the other for the civil register. Alvarado did not want to be personally involved with collections and payments or be the one to decide what should be allocated for extraordinary expenses. His main objective was that everyone dedicate himself to honest and productive work. He hoped that they all would become rich and he alone would remain poor. Thanks to his good friends, who used the salary he earned as governor, his home was completed, and a small ranch was purchased for him. It also was necessary to build a proper home for him at the ranch. Perhaps from time to time he might share his wise advice with others and provide them with the resources that would enable them to acquire even more of what they needed to live comfortably. [Next, he ordered the release of the prisoners who were sent to the purgatory of Sonoma to atone for their crimes. They had waited in limbo for more than two months for their release. One can just imagine the excitement they felt when they heard the news. They left Sonoma as happy as a sailor who awakens to fair skies after having spent the night in a violent storm.][32]

Alvarado wanted the person whom he had previously nominated in Los Angeles for the position of customs administrator to accept that position. Therefore, he repeated his request and even called upon their long-standing friendship to try to persuade him. He finally convinced him to come up to Monterey and assume the position, but under the condition that he not be obligated to acknowledge any official communications from Don José Ignacio Pavón, Director General of Revenue. Alvarado's friend knew from experience that the treasury laws and the orders issued by that ministry did not apply to various points far from the capital. That was especially true in this territory, where the *jefe político* managed his employees and the treasury as he saw fit. In the rivalries which ensued because of this, Alvarado emerged victorious when the general government suppressed the complaints about the management of revenue and thus implicitly condoned the actions of the *jefe político*. Therefore, the customs administrator would always lose because he was supposed to obey Señor Pavón, the eternal

Residence of Juan Bautista Alvarado, Monterey, 1912. Courtesy of the California State Library, Sacramento.

Director General of Revenue. First he would lose his position, then his reputation, and finally all credibility.

At the end of each year the customs administrator would send the Señor Director of Revenue the financial statements, monthly cash balances, a general account of debtors and creditors, and cargo manifests of goods that had entered the country. He would also attach a very brief official letter to the manifests. But to irritate the Señor Director even more, he would send him a long letter informing him of the *jefe político*'s official orders to reduce the abuses committed by the treasury branch. Señor Pavón would have fits of rage whenever he received those documents. Then he would proceed to waste time sending harsh reprimands to everyone. It would take so long for the customs employee to receive them that by the time they arrived they would have no effect, so they would be thrown away, unopened and forgotten. That particular employee worked in the customs office for six consecutive years, during which time he achieved his goal of irritating the Señor Director General of Revenue whenever possible. He succeeded because he did not fear him and because it was the only form of revenge that he could exact on him. In 1831 he tricked Pavón by sending him an official document which stated that all the customs administrators from the different ports had been removed. However, the administrator in Monterey deserved to keep his temporary position, since it was known, and Pavón had been well informed, that he had managed the office well and had conducted himself properly. Therefore, his appointment should be given to him in a timely fashion, without fail. The joke was complete, at the expense of some embarrassment for the general government. In 1832 Señor Pavón arranged for his illustrious *compadre*, Don José Rafael González, alias Pintito, to be sent to Alta California. Reference has been made to this man already.

From 1838 on, the customs revenue increased on a yearly basis by about seventy thousand pesos. The line infantry had decreased by two-thirds, and the revenue was sufficient to cover their expenses. Because the territory was in need of foreign goods whose importation was technically prohibited, everyone accepted a fairly high duty's being placed on them. The *jefe político* informed his superiors that he was forced to violate several treasury laws and that this had required him to become involved in the administration of that branch. To avoid reprimanding Alvarado, the general government did not respond. By keeping silent it implicitly condoned what was being done. Therefore the territorial governor was never censured for not observing those laws, and he despised the Director General of Revenue for the trouble he caused.

The custom of accepting goods from merchant ships as payment of duties prompted corruption. The duty on these goods would be increased by more than 25 percent of their actual worth; therefore, the customs administrator asked the *jefe político* to establish a regulation banning this practice. He also requested another regulation stating the duty that would be paid in hard currency on a graduated scale. The administrator drafted the decree, and it was approved by the *jefe* and went into effect six months after it was published. The decree stated that any ship whose duties did not amount to six thousand pesos had to pay the entire amount in silver. If the total was between six and twelve thousand pesos, it had to pay half in silver. If the total was between twelve and eighteen thousand pesos, it had to pay two-thirds in silver. And if the amount was eighteen thousand pesos or more, it had to pay one-third in silver.[33] This decree was important because there was so little money in circulation and most of that was acquired in exchange for crops. The decree also stated that people who were holding Customs House orders for payment in goods by ships that had not paid their duties in full should understand that only certain goods, such as hides and tallow, would be included. If they were not satisfied with the price of

Customs House form, June 8, 1841. Courtesy of The Bancroft Library, University of California, Berkeley.

cloth, they could discuss the matter with the supercargo at the time of payment and take cattle hides or tallow instead. The current rate for cattle hides and tallow had been set at two pesos per hide and ten reales per *arroba* of tallow. This procedure produced the desired results, because the payment orders issued by the *comisaría* attained the acceptability they should have had to begin with. With this, there was enough money to apportion to the individuals on the military and civil registers. It even was possible to lower the prices on goods so that the hides and tallow would not have to be given away, forcing people to purchase goods on other ships.

Don Guillermo A. Gale, who had represented the trading company from Boston since 1824, always behaved with the utmost integrity. It did not matter if he was presenting cargo manifests from the frigates or managing the accounts of the people from different points along the coast who had business dealings with him; he did it all in good faith. It might take two to three years to gather enough hides to load his cargo, yet no one ever complained that Gale had taken advantage of him. After a period of time he was invited to become a partner in the company. Don Alfredo Robinson took over Gale's position as director of the West Coast operation. Like his predecessor, he acted in good faith. Because of his friendly and generous nature, he eventually earned the friendship of the most prominent people in the territory. Robinson later was succeeded in that position by Don Enrique Mellus. He too followed the good example of his predecessors until the day the Mexican flag ceased to wave over the territory.

Among the trading fleet there were a number of wretched vessels which would arrive from Callao, Lima, the Sandwich Islands, and Central America. For that reason the utmost care and vigilance was taken to prevent fraud.[34] There were a number of cases in which goods were confiscated because they had not been declared. Even though these merchants deserved to be completely ruined, the customs administrator took pity on them and did everything possible to save their ships from being confiscated. He was certain that such people smuggled for the enjoyment of it, for the insignificant items they were hiding were hardly worth the risk. They engaged in smuggling because they enjoyed it and because they loved to brag that they were more shrewd than the expert traders. In addition, they said they knew how to take advantage of the clumsiness or foolishness of the narrator.

· 11 ·

At the beginning of April 1840 Señor Alvarado received a secret warning that an uprising by foreigners who intended to take over the country was about to occur.[1] The uprising would be led by the American Isaac Graham, a beaver hunter who had arrived by land. He had grown up in the forest and had received no formal education. He did not even know one letter of the alphabet. However, he had learned how to use a rifle. Graham had settled in the Monterey area on the Natividad Ranch.[2] He and the Englishman William R. Garner, who had married one of the owners of the ranch, were planning the conspiracy.[3] Don José Castro was informed by Señor Alvarado of the wickedness of those foreigners and ordered his soldiers to be prepared to march as soon as night fell. Under cover of darkness Castro and his men raced to different places and in different directions undetected. The first leg of their race measured ten leagues, and their goal was to surprise Graham and William Garner asleep in their beds. When they captured Garner, he was so frightened that he immediately asked them to show him mercy by not shooting him and pardoning him for his crime. He also promised to denounce all the conspirators, but Castro already knew where he should go to find them, and he took off so fast that it seemed as if he were fleeing. At dawn he returned to Monterey with the ungrateful foreigners, strung together with a long rope.[4]

They were informed of the charges against them with the same speed with which they had been captured. As soon as that formality was concluded, the *Guipuzcoana* was outfitted.[5] This small ship had been chartered to transport them to San Blas, where they would be put at the disposal of the supreme government. When everything was ready, Don José Castro and the soldiers who were to guard the prisoners also boarded. Seven days after their departure they anchored in San Blas. As soon as possible, the prisoners were sent to Tepic, where they were received by the commander, Don Manuel del Castillo Negrete. He released them and took Castro prisoner to oblige the British consul, Eustace Barron.[6] Experiencing such injustice, Castro immediately informed the supreme government of the situation. When the government received the news about Commander Castillo Negrete, it concluded that his actions showed that he undoubtedly deserved the reputation that he could be bought with money. The government severely reprimanded him and ordered him to release Castro immediately and provide him with whatever assistance he needed to come and appear at the capital.[7] Barron's agents were paid well and followed Castro to the capital. They persecuted him cruelly and took great pains to make it appear that the prisoners were innocent. In the end they managed to convince the wretched government that the prisoners were innocent and that the government should pay the expenses of their return trip to Monterey. And since Castro was the guilty party, he should be judged by a council of war.

General Micheltorena defended Castro and worked hard to help his client. In the end Micheltorena clearly proved to the council that the government had acted unjustly in its judgment.[8] Micheltorena succeeded in securing Castro's release, but the vile persecution from the House of Barron forced Castro to leave the capital. He traveled on back roads through the Durango Mountains and eventually arrived in Mazatlán. He then boarded one of the small coastal trading ships and sailed to Baja California.[9] From there he continued his journey on land. His expenses increased to fifteen thousand pesos. In order to cover expenses and pay the moneylenders, Señor Alvarado had to raise money by ordering cattle killed solely for their hides. In doing this, he sacrificed what would have amounted to more than fifty thousand pesos.[10]

If one were to consider today the veil of schemes which was drawn to hide the uprising by foreigners in 1840, an uprising which finally took place in 1846, one would come to realize that the government of Mexico only slightly attended to or halfway realized what was happening behind the scenes within the capital. The government never considered the advantages to be gained by stimulating development in different parts of this territory, which was so ready for it. That is why today those people with their *considerandos* need to be reminded of a familiar story about two people who inherited vast expanses of adjoining lands.[11] When the landowners met, following the rules of etiquette they congratulated one another and pledged

José Castro. Courtesy of the California State Library, Sacramento.

their friendship. But their habits forced an end to their friendship. The heir to the northern part was a very clever old man and an excellent strategist, especially on economic matters. For example, he would secretly test his servants by paying four reales to a servant who was supposed to earn twenty pesos. He always managed to have excellent servants who would come from everywhere to fill his jobs. Everyone liked him because he would reward deserving individuals well. They agreed with him in large matters and overlooked what was not essential. In this manner he brought progress to them without having to speak of it repeatedly. That inheritance was divided into a number of prosperous *haciendas*. The owner took pleasure in the fact that the workers held him in high esteem. They never referred to him as Master; they called him Uncle Samuel instead.

This old man had a very large telescope, which he used to observe his neighbor from afar as he worked in his usual greedy manner. One day, after admiring the way he had tastefully and symmetrically planted his own fields with choice seeds, sugarcane, wheat, cotton, and other crops, some of which he needed and some of which simply struck his fancy, the old man went to see his neighbor to give him some friendly advice on how to plow his land. He suggested that he first plow his land very superficially, in accordance with the strict style and rules of art in vogue, and then plant the canes, tip down. The rest of the seeds should be selected, preferably, from those found along the seashore. Another time, he saw that his neighbor owned a little pig which he fed only fruit peelings, in the hope that it would grow somewhat so he could sell it to the highest bidder. From afar Señor Clever noticed that the little animal had natural horseshoes which were not made of yellow brass. He immediately went to see his neighbor and offered to buy the pig for fifteen *tlacos*, nine of which were fake, and an agreement was reached. Next he calculated the value of the purchase. After doing so, he was astonished to see how much wealth those fifteen *tlacos* had allowed him to accumulate so quickly. He then pulled out a small, useless nail from the little pig's left shoe. He desperately wanted to buy his friend a beautiful, large bell from Sonora, so he could have the pleasure of ringing it to announce the rosary, or in honor of San Sebastián and the other saints to whom he was so devoted. But I see that I am digressing completely from the story I wanted to tell.[12] Therefore, I shall proceed without interruption.

Ever since the period of Spanish rule, the separation of the political from the military command did not function smoothly in the territories or in places far from the capital. The commanders generally regarded the conflict as inevitable and attributed it to the different jurisdictions assigned to their positions. This was not the case during the last periods of revolution in the territory, when the political and military commanders were Don Juan Bautista Alvarado and Don Guadalupe Vallejo. Vallejo was Alvarado's uncle, and the two had always maintained a very close friendship, ever since Alvarado was a child. When Señor Alvarado triumphed over Don Nicolás Gutiérrez, he wanted his uncle to become commander general, and he promoted him from the rank of lieutenant to chief colonel of arms. During the various pronouncements against Alvarado's government, Señor Vallejo never personally volunteered to help him pacify the revolutionaries in the south. According to Señor Alvarado, Vallejo would always give the excuse that the Indian tribes in the north were threatening to revolt and the only way to contain them was for him to remain in Sonoma. Every time a revolt would break out against him, Alvarado would repeat his uncle's excuse and laugh, saying that his uncle did not want to be disturbed for some half-grown revolution. He preferred to let his nephew handle those and would wait for a ripe one to come along.

The general government recognized these men as equals in their respective positions but made the mistake of sending confidential correspondence to each of them. They were told somewhat cautiously that if they acted in a manner which best served the country's interests, the government would approve their measures. Because of this, each one believed that the first magistrate of the republic favored him over the other, and disagreements began.

In attempting to carry out his responsibilities, Señor Alvarado appointed Don Salvador Vallejo to the position of civil judge to the Sonoma and San Rafael area. Don Guadalupe reacted by asserting, in a battle of words with Alvarado, his preference for rule by the military, of which Don Salvador Vallejo was a member. However, this was simply an obstacle, for he was actually trying to prevent the civil court from functioning.[13] More than anyone else he knew very well that a military man was permitted to accept a municipal post. He was also perfectly aware of the advantages for himself and for the landowners in the area if the military remained in control. To be as brief as possible, the military's power to prohibit vagrancy permitted it to decree that only workers were to remain in an area. The military had the authority to remove everyone from the area who lived by gambling, swindling, or drinking. These and other differences triggered the quarrel between the two *jefes*. It reached such a point that they stopped communicating with one another entirely. Each man was intent on bringing about the downfall of the other and counted on the support of a powerful advocate.[14]

In his role as commander general, Señor Vallejo drew up a captain's commission on behalf of Don Víctor Prudón, a Frenchman who had joined the Híjar colony as an instructor. Prudón was then sent to Mexico as a messenger or commissioner to try to have Señor Alvarado removed from the political command of the territory and replaced by the commander general.[15] When Señor Alvarado found out about this, he commissioned Don Manuel Castañares to go to Mexico and sabotage Prudón's plans.[16] Cas-

Mariano Guadalupe Vallejo in his study at Lachryma Montis.

tañares originally had come from Mexico in search of a customs position, but he had not been able to obtain one. Now, if he could outwit Prudón, he would have the opportunity to secure the position of customs administrator. So he left to obtain what he wanted. When he arrived in Mexico, he was unable to carry out his orders. But in the end it turned out well. Prudón obtained for Señor Vallejo promotion to the rank of lieutenant

Native Californian woman of the Fort Ross area. "Inhabitant of Rumiantsev Bay," watercolor by Mikhail T. Tikhanov, 1818. Courtesy of the Scientific Research Museum, Academy of Fine Arts, St. Petersburg, Russia.

Native Californian man of the Fort Ross area. "Balthazar," watercolor by Mikhail T. Tikhanov, 1818. Courtesy of the Scientific Research Museum, Academy of Fine Arts, St. Petersburg, Russia.

colonel, and Castañares was appointed customs administrator, a position which he so desired. However, neither Alvarado nor Vallejo received any satisfaction.[17]

By 1842 the Mexican government was convinced that the United States wanted to acquire the territory of Alta California either peacefully or by force.[18] Therefore it decided to send a sizable squadron under the command of General Don Manuel Micheltorena. The government provided him with several chain gangs, made up primarily of thieves and assassins from different jails, and told him to transform them into soldiers. When they sailed to Mazatlán, the commander general of that town did not permit them to go ashore. He was fearful that they would corrupt or pervert the inhabitants who lived on the edge of town, especially those who worked on the docks, in the shipyard, and in the slaughterhouses. Therefore, to prevent these problems, the soldiers were permitted to land only on the island while the transport ships were being prepared to receive them and the money which Señor Micheltorena was supposed to have brought.

The general was inexperienced in matters regarding ships. Instead of chartering the ships, he contracted them on a per diem basis to transport his men to San Diego. Each ship captain calculated how much water would be needed during the voyage and loaded just enough barrels of it on board. The intent was to ration the water carefully so that the last barrel would be emptied the day that they arrived at their destination. The voyage was prolonged for almost two months so that the ships would run out of water on the day they arrived in San Diego. Many of the soldiers and officers, including Lieutenant Colonel Don Agustín Zamorano, were dying from the hardships of the voyage and constant seasickness. Barely strong enough to go ashore, Zamorano died surrounded by his family after having been away from them for seven years. But even more incredible was the fact that his companions stole everything of value that he had in his trunks, even his gold watch and chain, which mysteriously appeared on one of the most respected Señores Jefes.[19]

The moment the general set foot on the beach at San Diego, he expressed his fears that the governor of the territory would not surrender the command to him and would order him to leave immediately. However, some people assured him that the command would be surrendered to him as soon as he appeared in the capital to assume it. Nevertheless, he still was very uncertain as he began his march. Don Manuel Castañares marched on ahead of him because he was more eager to assume his own post than to

The *Cyane*. From *Frank Leslie's Illustrated Newspaper*, May 9, 1862, 100. Courtesy of the California State Library, Sacramento.

have to report to Señor Alvarado that he had not been able to secure him the position of perpetual governor of Alta California. The incumbent customs administrator began to prepare to surrender his post as soon as he found out that Alvarado had been tricked. As soon as Señor Castañares appeared, he immediately surrendered the position to him.[20]

A few days later the frigate *United States* and the sloop *Cyane*, commanded by Commodore Jones, anchored in Monterey.[21] Jones then sent a message to Señor Alvarado, informing him that he would take possession of Monterey since war had been declared between Mexico and the United States. He advised Alvarado not to expose his people to the horrors of war, because he did not have sufficient soldiers to oppose Jones's troops. He also stated that he expected Alvarado to comply with his demands by eleven o'clock the following day. The message was delivered by the commodore's secretary and Don Juan Armstrong, the commander of the frigate. Señor Alvarado was in shock as he read the note, which was written in Spanish. After a period of silence his face suddenly became pale and then immediately turned red, as if blood were about to burst from his eyes. In a voice choked with emotion he told the commodore's secretary, who was a Spaniard, that if he had only half the number of men in the commodore's force he would consider their forces equal. Then he would not have needed to try to frighten him with threats. It would bring him pleasure as well as honor to fight him in defense of his country. However, since he could not do this, he would comply.

It was almost sunset when the commodore's representatives left Señor Alvarado's house. That night Alvarado sent a communiqué post haste to General Micheltorena, informing him of the unexpected arrival of the American warships under the command of Commodore Jones. Alvarado attached a copy of Jones's demand and the reply he would give the commodore the following day. It stated that he was compelled to surrender because his force was not large enough to oppose Jones and because he and his men wanted to protect his people from bombardment. Jones could accordingly take possession of Monterey at the appointed hour or before. Alvarado also informed Jones that he had sent an urgent communiqué, dated that day, to the commander general of the territory to advise him of the situation.

Flying flags of truce, yet with their guns aimed at the town, the ships maintained their positions as they waited for the appointed hour to arrive. At ten o'clock on that ill-fated day, all the small boats were lowered into the water to transport the soldiers, who were commanded by Captain Armstrong. Once ashore, Armstrong headed for the governor's home. There, the true *californios*, people who loved their country and were proud of their nationality, were forced to witness a painful ceremony for the very first time. The national flag of the three guarantees was lowered from its native flagpole so that it could be replaced by the stars and stripes. This flag was alleged to be the symbol of liberty, but that was actually a lie. It belonged to an oppressor who displayed arrogance against the weak. As he was inspecting the papers in the government archives, the commodore found some recent newspapers which completely convinced him that Mexico and the United States were not at war. Therefore, since he had acted wrongly, he promised that he would evacuate the town at four in the afternoon, and as soon as the Mexican flag had been raised, he would honor it by firing his cannons in salute.

Marching to Monterey, General Micheltorena received Señor Alvarado's communiqué at Mission San Fernando. He then returned to Los Angeles to prepare to defend the territory against the invader Jones. If the worst should happen, he could flee quickly from there to the state of Sonora. The following day Micheltorena received another communiqué informing him of the commodore's mistake and that the town had been deserted after Jones had taken possession of it. Jones promised to satisfy

Micheltorena and offered unconditionally to come down to the port which was closest to his residence. The general knew that he had arms and munitions which the Mexican government had provided for his expedition, but he was not aware of the specific contents because he had never bothered to inspect the crates. When he did open them, he found that the caliber of the shotguns was fourteen drams while the cartridges were one ounce. So he had to order the soldiers to take the weapons apart and rebore them. He also had to spend the entire day teaching his would-be soldiers how to handle the weapons.

The general used that problem with the weapons as a pretext to tell the governor that serious difficulties in preparing the country's defense prevented his going up to the capital to assume the political command. Micheltorena humbly asked Alvarado to come down and surrender the command in Los Angeles, since he had established his headquarters there. When Señor Alvarado received that communiqué, he said that he was too ill to travel to Los Angeles and entrusted the transfer of power to Don Manuel Jimeno, the senior member of the *diputación territorial* and the government secretary. Jimeno did indeed go down to Los Angeles to surrender the command to the new *jefe*.[22]

Even though the *californios* received very little formal education because there were no schools, they had a natural talent for assessing the capabilities of their governors at first sight. They viewed Micheltorena as a man of many theories, not a man of action. He would be better suited for a teaching position in a public school than the governorship, but even then, he probably would not have enough energy to punish the children who misbehaved.

Commodore Jones sailed to San Pedro Bay on the *Cyane* and then went to Los Angeles, nine leagues away.[23] There he met with the general as he had promised and tried to apologize for the outrage committed in Monterey. At the same time, it happened that three coastal trading ships were sighted. The lookout in San Pedro decided to increase the number of ships he had seen, so he hurried to Los Angeles and reported that four ships were approaching the anchorage. The general immediately concluded that they were American warships and that the commodore intended to surprise and seize the *jefe*, the *jefe* of the territory. Therefore, as a precaution he decided to stay awake with his staff the entire night. At about two o'clock in the morning Micheltorena received a report that someone's house at the edge of the town was on fire. He believed that the resident had been bribed by

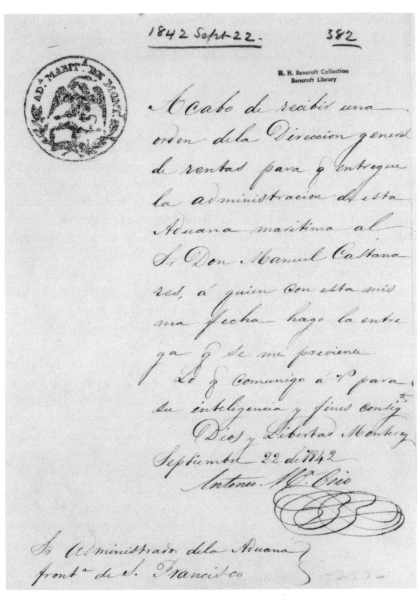

Osio's letter of resignation from the Customs House, Sept. 22, 1842. Courtesy of The Bancroft Library, University of California, Berkeley.

Commodore Jones to set fire to his own home in order to divert Michel-torena's attention so that the commodore and his men could seize the arms and munitions depot. He immediately took action. First, he ordered that the owner of the burning house be seized. That poor soul already had been burned on various parts of his body; yet when the soldiers arrived, he still was trying to salvage his most valuable possessions from the flames that were devouring his miserable shack. They quickly seized him, took him to their barracks, and locked him up in a prison cell, where he practically suf-focated. This sudden imprisonment caused him tremendous anxiety be-cause he did not know why he was there. He thought about everything that he had lost in the fire and about his wife and child, who had been left alone to defend themselves from such depraved soldiers. He hoped that the sol-diers would just steal what little he had been able to salvage from the fire and spare his family.

As the general was vigorously giving orders to prevent a Yankee attack, Commodore Jones remained sound asleep in his quarters. The following day, when he was informed of what had happened the previous night, he and his countrymen shared a laugh. He quickly returned to his ship before his presence caused the *jefe* of the territory any more problems.[24]

General Micheltorena began his tenure as governor with optimistic wishes of doing as much good for the country as possible. His good inten-tions were joined to an inability to deliberately harm anyone. He was the only governor vested with authority so broad that it was similar to that granted to the first magistrate under the Bases de Tacubaya.[25] He was granted this authority before he left Mexico so he could operate freely and not be compelled to consult with the capital on serious matters when a delay might impede the resolution of an issue. There were other advantages as well for the *californios*, but the governor did not know how to take ad-vantage of them. He lacked forcefulness and strength of character, qualities which were so essential in a political and military commander. Since he al-ways obeyed all his wife's orders, he was better suited to be a subordinate.[26]

Micheltorena's apathy in restraining the criminal activity of his sol-diers, who committed robberies and stabbings daily, simply exacerbated the problem and increased the number of citizen complaints. He responded by saying that he already had arranged to prescribe the remedy, even though everyone knew that he had not even studied the prescription. With one or two exceptions, his officers were worse than the soldiers. These officers would encourage the other men to commit robberies and insist that they

Manuel Micheltorena. Courtesy of the California State Library, Sacramento.

treat them as knights by giving them a share of the loot. They also would borrow money with no intention of paying it back. The public constantly complained loudly to the general about the bad conduct of his soldiers and officers. A number of officers were angered by the conduct of their fellow soldiers, and they too complained to the governor. They requested that he impose the appropriate punishment on the guilty parties so that the public would receive some satisfaction and not confuse them with the bad officers who had accompanied the governor.[27]

In 1843 Micheltorena went up to Monterey, where he continued to hear complaints about the misconduct of his soldiers and officers, but he lacked the courage to reprimand them. The citizens understood his silence to be his way of condoning their vile acts and encouraging them to commit even worse atrocities. Colonel Téllez, the general's assistant, was desperate because the governor was not heeding the citizens' demands that he do his duty and punish the guilty soldiers or officers. So Téllez decided to take the matter into his own hands. He visited the barracks frequently and ordered that any guilty soldier be whipped one hundred or two hundred times. He also ordered the arrest of any officer who tolerated or was an accomplice in criminal activity. Téllez would provide the governor with a full report each time he did this, but the general reacted merely by lowering his head and shrugging his shoulders, without approving or disapproving. Téllez interpreted the general's silence as an approval of his methods. This encouraged him to continue the whippings, which had produced good results.

However, this did not please the corrupt soldiers and officers, and they held a meeting. They came to an agreement that the men who had been punished most recently should go with an officer to the governor and show him, as if he were their common father, the bruises and wounds on their bodies. They believed that the colonel's harsh punishment was too severe for their petty crimes and that so many whippings would eventually kill them. The complainants needed to have an officer represent them. The first officer they turned to said that he first wanted to treat his tongue with liquor so he could speak better, but he exceeded the recommended dosage of medicine and could not say anything. So, without any words, the men showed the governor their backs, which had been scarred by the blows from the rod. As they had hoped, he felt compassion for them.

The general was one of those men who becomes terrified at the sight of blood. When he saw the effects of Téllez' sternness, he was disgusted. He consoled the malcontents, advised them to behave, and then sent them away, telling them he was certain that the colonel would not be forced to punish them again for any crimes committed. Then he summoned the colonel. As soon as he received the summons, Téllez appeared before the governor, who told him that he had seen a soldier who had been completely disabled because of the excessive beatings which Téllez had ordered as his punishment. Therefore, he should refrain from ordering such beatings in the future. Téllez respectfully replied that the governor should accept his resignation if he was not going to permit him to do his duty or, since his services were no longer necessary, send him back to Mexico to continue his career in the artillery. The general refused both requests. Téllez' face turned completely pale from a fever induced by an attack of bile, and he left.

He was gravely ill for more than twenty days, and his pallor was similar to the color of a squash blossom. Fortunately for him, the troops did not have a doctor, so he was treated with folk remedies. When he finally began to recuperate, he was able to leave his barracks, and no one sought retribution. He visited the general, who naturally was surprised to see him, especially because he was so yellow. Téllez replied that the governor's heart was even yellower from the cowardliness buried there, which led public opinion to believe that he and other officers tolerated the robberies and other atrocities committed by the soldiers. In his mind the governor's conduct was equal to that of the officers who were still encouraging others to steal and give them a share of the spoils. Astonished by such a startling response, the general could think of nothing to say, so he kept quiet. When he finally spoke, he advised the sick man to have patience so he could recover his health more quickly. When the two men parted, their long-standing friendship was severed. Since the general no longer wanted to hear annoying reproaches from Téllez, he decided to send him on a mission to Mazatlán or Acapulco, with the intention that he would never return to give his report.[28]

The general issued an order restricting Colonel Téllez' authority. It produced results which should have been expected: the soldiers, no longer fearing punishment, went completely out of control and committed all types of excesses. The general's tolerance of everything and his ignoring of the public's complaints sparked attempts at revolution. Many trading houses were robbed, and one robbery even took place next door to the general's own home. As he walked by that trading house with Téllez and some other officers, he could not stop laughing after he saw the hole which had been made in the wall. He said it seemed as if the owner of that house had no idea how to create an opening for a window. Téllez replied that the soldiers were the ones who made those holes so they could go in and rob the house. It should therefore be obvious why the homeowners were resorting to a new way of covering the holes, by obtaining lead for bricks and gunpowder for mortar. There was no doubt how things would look when all this was completed. When the general heard that, he turned pale, lowered his head, and silently began to walk with long strides.[29]

Chapter 11

Another time when the general went for a stroll, he was pleased to see that a number of his soldiers, who said they were married, had constructed small homes along the wall away from the barracks. All the homes, except for two, had tile roofs. Those two little shacks belonged to two very poor residents who had been too lazy to imitate the soldiers' ingenuity and had used tule instead, thus exposing their homes to fire. Again it was Téllez who had to reply. He told the general that in reality, those residents' ingenuity could not be compared with that of the soldiers, for the soldiers had privileges that were denied to those poor men. The soldiers could steal tiles without running the risk of the local judge finding out. Téllez' comment was a blow to the general, who understood the clear meaning of that reply.

The audacity of the soldiers reached such an extreme that they would assault anyone who was alone at night, and even in broad daylight. They would take any money the person had or his best article of clothing. If he resisted, they would kill him or leave him near death. During that time, the French frigate *Angelina*, under the command of Captain Monsieur N. Yena, anchored within the bay, intending to hunt whales. As soon as the captain had become acquainted with some of the townspeople, he would stay in town until eight o'clock at night. At that hour, the pilot on watch was ordered to send a boat, and a sailor would go to notify the captain and his men that they were ready to pick them up. On the third night, the first pilot, who had gone out to hunt during the afternoon, went to the beach to wait for the boat at the appointed hour. He arrived at the shore at the same time that two sailors disembarked and went in search of the captain. After walking a short distance, they raced back, pursued by soldiers. The pilot had his shotgun cocked and ready to fire, but he believed that the mere sight of the weapon would be sufficient to restrain the soldiers, so he and a sailor went to look for the captain. The sailor did not want to go unarmed and took one of the harpoons. After they had walked a short distance, the soldiers fired on them. In the confusion the pilot fired his weapon, killing a soldier, and the sailor drove the harpoon through another soldier's back. The sailor ran to the town to inform the captain that the pilot was in danger and then, accompanied by some officers from the troop, went back to the beach. They found the pilot lying unconscious on the ground, bleeding from different parts of his body and missing a few fingers. They also found the dead soldier and the other man who had been stabbed with the harpoon. They immediately went to inform the general of the situation. He had the audacity to accuse the captain of being the cause of those tragedies because he had not returned to his ship before nightfall. How-ever, Captain Yena, a shrewd and courageous man, vigorously told Michel-torena that he alone was the cause of the problem, since he had not main-tained order or commanded the respect of his subordinates. The captain also said that he would have to provide the admiral of the French squadron in the Pacific with a full account of the situation. He planned to set sail that night to find him and inform him about how his countrymen were being treated. As evidence, he was going to show him the body of his pilot who had been mutilated and brutally wounded as he was being robbed in-side the town. The weak-spirited general was frightened by such a threat, but he managed to maintain his composure.[30]

In December 1844 the small groups of people who were discussing the possibility of a revolt were no longer maintaining secrecy. The general was frightened, and he tried to make people believe that very soon he would send about 150 of the worst soldiers back to Mazatlán. Since people did not have faith in his promises, they proceeded with the preparations for the up-rising. The Monterey River always had been the spot where the revolutions broke out, and it was there that Don Manuel Castro and Pico pronounced against the government of General Micheltorena.[31] Señores Alvarado and Castro agreed to lead the revolutionaries, but it was not yet time to reveal themselves.[32] Alvarado left his ranch in Alisal and headed for San Pablo, where he spoke with his uncle, Don Guadalupe Vallejo, and requested that he join him in the revolution to overthrow General Micheltorena.[33] Vallejo gave Alvarado so many excuses that he interpreted them as a negative re-sponse and left for San José to join Don José Castro. The general had wanted to prevent Castro from taking part in the revolution, so he sent him on official business to the San Joaquín River, but he misjudged the situation, and this tactic worked against him.[34]

When Micheltorena learned of the pronouncement at the river with only about thirty individuals involved, he sent Colonel Téllez to pursue them. He gave him explicit orders indicating exactly how far he should go. Téllez fulfilled the order by going to the exact spot which Micheltorena had indicated and then returning. However, the general was very upset that Téllez had not advanced any further.[35] Téllez responded that he knew very well that in matters of war a subordinate officer must strictly observe orders from a superior. The general then ordered the troops to prepare so that he could go out in person and teach the rebels a lesson. Since he was no longer friendly to Téllez, he would be accompanied only by Battalion

Commander Valdez. The general and his soldiers did not march very far each day, which was an indication that he had very little desire to fight. When they finally arrived at the Laguna Ranch, which is five leagues from San José, he was very tired.[36] When Alvarado found out, he advanced to within one-quarter of a league of the general and set up his own camp in a beautiful forest. From there Alvarado's riflemen could fire easily.

It was the middle of winter, and the cold, constant snow and heavy rain showers made a battle impossible. The general occupied the ranch house, and even though he was well protected and comfortable, he complained that he was freezing. He also was upset because the bad weather had brought everything to a halt, and he could not go out to survey the field to prepare the battle plans. He was trying to make everyone believe that he was eager to fight when his actual intentions were quite different, as the following facts will prove. In the forest, Señor Alvarado and his soldiers, exposed to the bad weather conditions, braved the steady downpours. No one complained of being cold, sleepy, hungry, or wet, because each man was more concerned with protecting his weapon and ammunition from the rain. The storm lasted all night and subsided a bit the following day. After suffering through such a powerful storm, everyone agreed that it would be very painful to die from the cold because their blood could not circulate. So in order to warm their bodies, they would have to fight.[37]

As the time of battle drew near, Alvarado's troops withdrew and repositioned in a better location, but the general did not order his troops to pursue them as he previously had stated he would do. Because it was bitterly cold, the back of the soldiers' legs had gone numb, and it was difficult for them to fight. Therefore, the general immediately ordered an honorable surrender which would be beneficial to both sides. The greatest benefit was that no Mexican blood would be shed. For if there was to be bloodshed, it should be in defense of their country against the common enemy who was lying in wait: the United States.

Alvarado did not want to accept the surrender, but to appease his friend and *compadre* Don José Castro, he had to acquiesce. Because Castro had never forgotten what the general had done for him in Mexico, he felt that he owed him a debt of gratitude, so they waited for the terms of the surrender to be negotiated. The principal condition concerned the bad soldiers and officers whose actions had provoked the collective feelings of dissatisfaction among the *californios*. The general would go to Monterey to prepare to send the corrupt soldiers and officers back to Mazatlán, and he would verify that this had been done. Alvarado's division established its winter quarters at Mission San José, with the help of the administrator there. The surrender was based on these terms. Micheltorena and Valdez signed it on one side, and Alvarado and Castro on the other. Then each battalion immediately left for its destination.[38]

When the general arrived in Monterey, Téllez already had been completely informed of the situation. He also was quite prepared to condemn Micheltorena for not having done his duty as general because he had signed an exceedingly shameful treaty without having lost a single man or having fired one cartridge. Téllez told him that he was ashamed to be one of the soldiers under his immediate command. Even though the general was endowed with great eloquence, his shame stopped the blood from flowing through his arteries and caused him to blush in embarrassment so that he could not speak. Finally, he completely renounced the treaty and promised Téllez that he would send him on a mission to Mexico as soon as possible. Unfortunately for Téllez, a ship which was sailing to Mazatlán appeared, and he took advantage of the opportunity and boarded it. The general was left with officers who were incapable of reproaching him for the tremendous mistakes he made.[39]

Because Señor Micheltorena was a weak and cowardly man, he sought advice from the dregs among his military associates on how to punish Alvarado, without considering the dishonor which would result. On his own he decided that he was authorized to declare the treaty he had signed invalid. He then asked Don Juan Sutter, who owned an establishment on the Sacramento River, to call together all the foreign residents who had settled in the area. If they were discreet enough, they could decide on a day to mount a surprise attack on Alvarado in his quarters, with one group coming down from the north and the other coming up from the south. Micheltorena swore on his honor that each individual who took part would be compensated for his services with a land grant which he could select and colonize. The adventurers who had gathered naturally jumped into the ring after hearing that promise, which the general had no intention of fulfilling. However, Alvarado and Castro had a keen eye and were expecting the general to commit just such a vile deed. They intercepted one of several suspicious communications and cleared up any doubts they might have had about the general's vile behavior. Then they immediately left for Los Angeles.[40]

The general was waiting for Sutter to come down to join his forces so he could pursue the rebels. Sutter, equipped with chains and handcuffs for the principal rebels, soon arrived. When Castro and Alvarado arrived in Los Angeles, their supporters were ready and waiting, and they also managed to sway a number of foreigners to their side. Together, they formed a sizable force which had no reason to fear Micheltorena's troops. As the general was approaching, Castro went out to scout the area and encountered thirty foreigners.[41] When they saw him and realized that his force was greater, they ran to seek refuge on higher ground. Castro wanted to speak to them, not fight them, so he dismounted and walked alone toward them. When he came within rifle range, a few men wanted to fire half a dozen rounds at him, but the majority preferred to wait to find out what he wanted to say. So they watched him approach them fearlessly with no other weapon than his sword.

When he arrived he respectfully saluted them and immediately explained that he intended not to attack them but rather to dispel their illusions about the general's promise. He assured them that, while the general would make them fight against the country's native sons, he would not fulfill his promise. Castro believed that it was his duty to inform them of this so they would be free to leave the area immediately and go wherever they pleased. After listening to Castro, they conferred among themselves and decided not to take sides. Instead, they would return to where they started, even though they had no money to cover their expenses. Castro solved this problem by giving them stamped gold he was carrying. The foreigners were grateful and pleased, and they began their return march.[42]

The general continued his march to the great Cahuenga plain, where he encountered Alvarado's force. As they approached to within cannon range, both sides opened fire. The older soldiers and veteran officers on both sides watched in amazement as the cannonballs passed right through the ranks without injuring anyone. The only cannonball that did hit something struck a horse in the chest and killed it. The horse belonged to one of Alvarado's soldiers, who, since he was luckily standing to one side when the horse was thrown back by the blow, was not injured. When the fear produced by the first whiff of gunpowder had passed, Alvarado's riflemen shouted that it was time for them to enter into action. They divided into groups and took possession of a deep ravine to position themselves so that they could fire from close range without exposing themselves to the havoc of the enemy grapeshot. The cavalry took up a new position, and the artillery took possession of a more advantageous spot. That one maneuver caused Captain Sutter to waver. He told the general that the only way he could save his life was to go with the foreigners under his command and surrender to Alvarado. Waving his white handkerchief as a sign of truce, the general did this immediately.[43] Micheltorena was convinced that the first rifle shots would be aimed at one individual in particular as punishment for the bad faith he had demonstrated in the previous surrender. He knew very well that, although Castro had many faults, he did possess the virtue of being able to forgive even the most despicable actions of his worst enemy. So he asked Castro to negotiate a new treaty and promised to honor all its conditions. Castro's influence among the members of his party was strong; but for all his persuasiveness, he found it very difficult to calm them down and have them accede to his patron's wishes. He finally managed to arrange the surrender, and the treaty was signed. The terms were the following: since the commander general and *jefe político* of the territory urgently needed to go to the capital of the republic, he would leave Don Pío Pico, the senior member of the *diputación territorial,* with the political command and Don José Castro as commander general, until the supreme government could resolve the situation.[44] The general would march to the port of San Pedro (twelve leagues away) with his entire supply train and surrender everything to the designated official there. Then they all would board the *Don Quixote,* which would be anchored there, and sail to Monterey. There they would board the general's wife and his belongings, but the soldiers would not be allowed to go ashore. Around the middle of February 1845 the general left with every intention of not returning to the territory to avenge any offense.

The fact that Don José Castro remained behind as commander general was an affront to the most senior officer, Don Guadalupe Vallejo, who was not considered for the position solely because of favoritism. Castro began his command intending to work closely with Don Pío Pico. However, the infamous Castillero again showed up and suggested that he oppose Pico. He told him confidentially that it would suit the supreme government if the two of them worked together to prepare the territory for an attempted annexation. For if they feared an invasion, no foreign government would aid them simply out of a generous desire to help the weak against the strong.[45] At that time Don Pío Pico convened a meeting in Santa Bárbara of all the important people from all over the territory, and he invited Don José Castro to attend.[46] The clever Castillero assumed that the meeting probably had been arranged as a reaction to his efforts to create dissension between the commander general and the *jefe político*. He was so brazen that he abused the power that he had over Castro by suggesting that he act as Napoleon I did when he threw the senate out the window.[47] This news traveled quickly and discreetly, and as a result, no one who had been called to the meeting in Santa Bárbara came, except Don Diego Forbes, the British vice-consul. He had the British corvette *Juno* anchor in Santa Bárbara Bay, but he could not authorize it to do anything.[48] According to some people, the *Juno* set sail and headed for the South Sea to inform Admiral Seymour of the *californio jefe*'s plans.

· 12 ·

Those who aspired to possess the territory had their suspicions about what might happen, so they accelerated their plots to acquire it by force or by purchase. They prepared to try the first option, as long as they retained the chance to try the second before trouble began. Colonel Frémont was on an overland expedition and came to the Monterey area on the pretext that he needed to replenish his supplies. His true motive was to convince the inhabitants that they should view his armed intrusion into a foreign territory as a beneficial rather than a hostile act. Don José Castro was somewhat inclined to tolerate this outrage, but at that moment he received a message from his uncle, Don Ángel Castro, who stated that three of Colonel Frémont's soldiers had arrived at his ranch (near San Juan Bautista).[1] When they saw that he was alone and unarmed, they had dared try to rape his daughters.[2] Don Ángel was one of many people who prided themselves in saying that they had been loyal subjects of His Catholic Majesty. As a veteran presidio soldier, he knew how to protect his honor under any circumstances. When Frémont's soldiers threatened this honorable old man by placing a pistol at his neck so the others could commit the intended crime, the old soldier found energy and courage from the knowledge that his strong fists would not fail him. He told his aggressor that he preferred death to dishonor. Then he grabbed him by the neck, yanked the pistol from his hand, and threw it to the ground. This quick and vigorous action prevented the soldiers from committing their barbaric act. They retreated immediately to Frémont's camp but promised to return again.

This change in the relationship between Frémont and Castro prompted Castro to leave Monterey to attack Frémont. When Frémont found out, he headed for one of the high hills in the Natividad Mountains, where he planned to barricade himself and resist Castro. In a letter written in pencil

Thomas O. Larkin. Courtesy of the California State Library, Sacramento.

from there to Don Tomás O. Larkin, United States Consul in Monterey, Frémont vowed to fight until death as long as his nation's flag was flying in Monterey. He knew that the government would be grateful for his sacrifice and would avenge his death by inflicting an appropriate punishment on those who so unjustly took his life.[3] Castro approached the camp just as darkness was drawing near, so he decided to stop and seek comfort and security by spending the night on a hill before engaging in action the following morning. Frémont knew very well that he was in a dangerous position. When nightfall came, he escaped by descending the hill along one of the most rugged paths. The next day Castro could find only the prints left by the horses as they slid down the hill. Frémont traveled all night in the direction of Captain Sutter's Sacramento River establishment, but Castro no longer wanted to pursue him.[4]

A few days later the corvette *Cyane*, with Captain Archibaldo Gillespie aboard, anchored in Monterey Bay.[5] Gillespie was in the territory on a mission, and he stayed at the home of Consul Larkin. When Frémont sent word, Gillespie hurried for the Sacramento River to reach an agreement with him on how they should proceed in accordance with their instructions. When he arrived at Sutter's establishment, Frémont already had left for the United States. However, Gillespie really wanted to catch up with him, so he took enough horses and men to defend himself from the Indians. By traveling at a fast trot, they were able to cover a very long distance, but this tired the horses, and Gillespie realized that he would not catch up with Frémont as quickly as he had hoped if everyone rode together. Therefore he decided to send two or three men ahead on the best horses. As soon as they caught up with Frémont, they delivered Gillespie's message and warned him that Gillespie was in danger of being attacked by the Indians. They undoubtedly would kill him at some point during the night if reinforcements were not sent quickly. Frémont immediately ordered a squad of soldiers to go back without stopping so that they would arrive in time to assist Gillespie. They traveled all day and arrived when it was already dark. They found Gillespie waiting for either death or help. He used Frémont's men to strengthen his defensive position, since he believed that an Indian attack was inevitable. The Indians, however, were unaware that Gillespie had been reinforced and thought they could finish him off with only one attack.

Since the Indians believed that they would catch Gillespie and his two or three men off guard, they decided to attack. The chief boasted that he was the bravest of his tribe, since he was expecting that he would be completely shielded from the bullets by a type of coat of mail that was made with little panels of wood instead of chain and blue drill. Confident that their opponents were few in number and inspired by the chief's examples of courage and skill, the Indians attacked vigorously. But in the end the superiority of Gillespie's firearms told in his favor. The Indian chief was killed by a bullet which passed through his body. He and his bravest warriors were left there on the ground, and the other Indians fled.[6]

When Frémont and Gillespie finally met, they discussed different ways they might initiate hostilities without implicating their government. It was imperative that the United States government not be accused of taking over a defenseless foreign territory solely by force, and it did not want to appear to be acting in bad faith, since both nations were bound by treaties and war had not been declared between them. Therefore, in order to conceal their true intent, or color it so that it would be more in keeping with public opinion, they decided to camouflage the flag of stars and strips with a temporary flag which depicted a brown bear on a white field and a star in the top corner.[7] Captain Montgomery, commander of the corvette *Portsmouth*, which was anchored within the port of San Francisco at Sausalito, sent them supplies.[8] Troops came down from Sacramento and arrived in Sonoma at dawn. They surprised Don Víctor Prudón and the brothers Vallejo, Don Guadalupe and Don Salvador, in their beds. After they had seized them and informed them that they were prisoners, they forced them to march to Sacramento.[9] Don Jacobo P. Leese, an American who had arrived in 1833 and was married to a woman from the Vallejo family, wanted to accompany his brothers-in-law to see if he could somehow help them by speaking with his countrymen. When they arrived at Colonel Frémont's camp, they claimed that Leese was not a true descendant of Uncle Samuel and imprisoned him with the others. For more than three months they were fed worse food than the other prisoners in Sonoma, to whom reference has been made, received. Señor Vallejo was being measured with the same yardstick that he used to measure others.[10] Vallejo begged them to allow him to have provisions and his favorite food brought down from his home in Sonoma so he would not go hungry, but they denied his request because they wanted to humiliate him. He was imprisoned for about four months and was released when the war between Mexico and the United States ended, but his health had been shattered.

After the Americans took possession of Sonoma under the command of Mr. Ide, or Don Cuero, which means the same thing, they raised the bear flag because they were not supposed to raise their national flag.[11] It is important to speak about Mr. Ide with respect. He was an honorable man, and he behaved like one by preventing disorderly conduct among the men of lower rank. The first thing he did was to pour out all the liquor they had

Francisca Benicia Vallejo, wife of Mariano Guadalupe Vallejo. Courtesy of the California State Library, Sacramento.

Adela Vallejo, the second daughter of Mariano Guadalupe Vallejo and Francisca Benicia Carrillo. Adela married Levi Cornell Frisbie, brother of one of her father's business associates. Courtesy of the Solano County Historical Society.

obtained. Then he took great pains to insure that all women would be respected, especially those who were suffering because their husbands had been taken prisoner. Despite Mr. Ide's recognized attempt to preserve order in his jurisdiction, one of the *californios* went from San Rafael to Sausalito and asked Don Guillermo Richardson to accompany him on a journey to plead with Commander Montgomery to send one of his best lieutenants to take charge in Sonoma.[12] At first Montgomery gave excuses, trying to imply that he knew nothing about the claims of those from Sacramento and that he could not side with them even if he wanted to. However, he finally acceded and sent a first lieutenant, Mr. Misroon, to Sonoma.[13]

After the *californio* had pleaded with Señor Montgomery, he returned to San Rafael and remained on the alert for hostile maneuvers. He soon spotted two boats and a launch from the *Portsmouth* in the strait of San Pedro and San Pablo. His suspicions were confirmed when a young clerk from one of the merchant ships anchored in San Francisco told him that when he had passed through the strait with his boat loaded with hides, he was pursued by three vessels which he recognized as belonging to the *Portsmouth*. Many of the men were armed, and the launch was equipped with a cannon on the bow. The vessels had been sent to prevent Commander General Castro's troops from crossing, because they were expecting him to go to Sonoma and attack Ide.

Just as had occurred in the revolution plotted by foreigners in 1840, some peaceful artisans were arrested purely on suspicion, and they were included with those who were actually guilty. The just-mentioned *californio* was determined to secure their release from jail because he knew they were innocent. He succeeded in doing so because of his friendship with Señores Alvarado and Castro. He took the prisoners to his own home and accepted the responsibility of being their jailer. They stayed with him until the revolutionaries tried them and found them innocent, and then they were released. They promised the *californio* that they would show him their appreciation as soon as possible. They did not forget. When the *californio* was in San Rafael observing the progress being made by the Bear Flaggers, one of his former prisoners was in Sonoma following Mr. Ide's orders against his will. This man, a carpenter, told Mr. Ide that he needed to travel to San Rafael on urgent business. However, his main reason for going was to warn his former benefactor that he should go to San Francisco as soon as he possibly could, because an order already had been issued that he be arrested and taken to Sacramento. He received a similar warning at the same time from a lumberman who worked far away and had left his job sawing wood to go see the *californio*. He did not underestimate these warnings and immediately prepared to escape.

When he arrived in San Francisco, he stayed as usual at the home of the United States vice-consul, Don Guillermo Leidesdorff. The *californio* filled his words with a powerful emetic and made Leidesdorff spit out what information he wanted to know about the doings of Montgomery, Frémont, and Gillespie. Leidesdorff also told him that if he did not leave San Francisco immediately and head for Santa Clara, where he knew Commander General Castro was located, he would be arrested along with Ridley and a number of others who were supposed to be taken to Sacramento.[14] The *californio* did not waste any time; he mounted a good horse and traveled the eighteen leagues from San Francisco to Santa Clara in three and one-quarter hours. Señores Castro and Alvarado were there and, when they saw him, congratulated him for not having been taken prisoner. Then they asked him to tell them what he knew about events from Sacramento to San Francisco. They were particularly interested in hearing how Señor Montgomery had acted in the affairs with Colonel Frémont, and they listened with satisfaction.

When Castro had learned that Sonoma had been taken, he had gone to Mission Santa Clara to establish his headquarters. As soon as possible, he ordered sixty men under Captain Don Joaquín de la Torre to cross the strait of San Pablo and land on the San Rafael side. From there they were to take the horses that had been readied for them and go as quickly and discreetly as possible to surprise the Americans who had taken possession of Sonoma. Since it was known that Commander Montgomery had a blockade in place, he entrusted the squadron's passage to one of the owners of the San Pablo Ranch who had a reputation as an excellent pilot. He skillfully maneuvered the boats through the crossing and outwitted the men who were keeping watch from the *Portsmouth*'s vessels.

De la Torre took the horses which his men had ridden and went to spend the night at the Camilo Ranch Olompali, which was halfway between Sonoma and San Rafael. Possessing neither the military expertise nor the wisdom necessary for an operation such as had been entrusted to him, he did not take any precautionary measures that night. At sunrise on the following day, before he had ordered the horses saddled, he received word from an Indian *vaquero* that about thirty Americans from the Sonoma side were close by. The Indian told him that he had raced at full speed to bring him the news and that the Americans were following close behind at a fast gallop. Located in an area of low ridges, ravines, and forests, Olompali was a good site to plan an ambush. Any other commander would have taken advantage of this, but de la Torre did not have the necessary experience. The only thing he did well was brag.

Alférez Cantúa, a very prudent and courageous man, could ride a horse faster than anyone. Accompanied by a few soldiers, he intercepted the Americans who were approaching. They were so surprised to see him that, without realizing what they were doing, they rode into a corral. Since it was constructed only of poles tied together, it offered very little protection. When the shooting began, a bullet hit Cantúa, passed through his side, and killed him. The Bear Flaggers soon realized that they were trapped in the corral and that they would all surely die if de la Torre attacked them with redoubled zeal. Just as they began to consider surrender, they heard de la Torre's drummer sounding the retreat. In fact, he retreated so quickly that he left Cantúa's body behind.[15] Unable to decide on a safe spot from which he could defend himself or simply rest, de la Torre traveled for days and nights, up and down the hills.

Three or four days later, news of Colonel Frémont's arrival in Sonoma reached San Rafael. Frémont was preparing to pursue de la Torre with the troops that had come down from Sacramento and the garrison in Sonoma. Someone took pity on the people who were with de la Torre and quickly left to find him and prudently advise him to go immediately to Sausalito.[16] There he was to seize Don Guillermo Richardson's large launch and as soon as his soldiers were on board, sail for the anchorages at the San Pablo Ranch. When the helpful adviser encountered de la Torre, he found it very difficult to persuade him that this was the only recourse he had left and that he should take advantage of it as soon as possible. Perhaps for the first time in his life, de la Torre managed to do something at the right time. Once he was convinced that the advice was sound, he and his troops headed for Sausalito. As soon as they arrived, de la Torre boarded his men on the launch. Just as they had cast off, Señor Frémont and his men came racing toward the shore to try and catch them on land.[17] After landing at the San Pablo Ranch, de la Torre met with the commander general and gave him a full report of his expedition and its sad consequences. Later, everyone left for Mission San Juan Bautista.

During the afternoon of July 6 the frigate *Savannah*, under the command of Commodore Sloat, anchored in Monterey Bay. At seven o'clock the following morning he sent the military commander a formal demand to surrender to the United States naval forces, since war had been declared be-tween Mexico and the United States. The town garrison consisted of Don Mariano Silva, an old man who was the artillery captain. He replied that the town was defenseless. Since he could not oppose them alone, the com-modore could take the town whenever he pleased.

At eleven o'clock the inhabitants of Monterey experienced the sorrow of seeing the stars and stripes wave for the second time from the flagpoles that had been erected for the tricolor flag of the three guarantees. How-ever, this time it seemed worse, as they began to think about the loss of their nationality and of everything they had worked so hard to create. For experience has always shown that conquerors never have been able to maintain a brotherhood with those they have conquered.

After Captain Silva sent the commander general a copy of the com-modore's order to surrender and his own reply, an officer from the frigate appeared with a sealed document from the commodore to the commander general. In it the commodore stated that it would be in the best interests of the people of California to avoid the terrible consequences of a bloody and destructive war. Therefore he was inviting the commander general to meet with him to arrange terms for an honorable surrender which would guarantee the rights and privileges of the inhabitants.

After reading the communications, Don José Castro believed that the commodore's true motive was to capture him. So he refused to meet with him and instead headed for Los Angeles. There he planned to take measures to defend the territory from a possible attack. When he arrived at the Santa Margarita Ranch, which belonged to Mission San Luis Obispo, he en-countered troops which outnumbered his own.[18] These soldiers had been ordered by the *jefe político*, Don Pío Pico, to oppose Castro and take the military command from him by force. At the ranch the members of the southern party learned that the Americans had taken possession of Mon-terey and Sonoma. However, that was not a strong enough reason for them to unite in a common cause. The discord between the two *jefes* was too deeply rooted. Castro had declared that the territory was in a state of siege due to the foreign invasion and that in accordance with the law he had assumed both commands. But the *jefe político* was stronger than the *jefe militar*, and Pico did not want to be stripped of his authority. He preferred to settle their differences with arms before attending to the invaders. The two men clearly demonstrated their enmity, as they kept their distance from each other while they headed to Los Angeles. After they arrived, the

Pío Pico. Courtesy of the California State Library, Sacramento.

commander general found himself with no support or resources, so he decided to disband his military force. He then left with a few soldiers who wanted to accompany him to the state of Sonora.[19]

With the commander general now gone, Don Pío Pico replaced him with Don José María Flores, who undertook the responsibility of organizing the country's defense.[20] Many people around Monterey and San Francisco were willing to defend with one last effort the nationality which they held so dear. In several skirmishes with the American troops, they fought like true Mexican soldiers and courageous victors and served as a model for those at Cerro Gordo, Angostura, and other points.[21] Without worrying about being outnumbered and poorly armed, they fought with the enthusiasm which only the defense of one's native country can inspire. Examples of this were demonstrated by Don Manuel Castro at the Natividad grove, and Don Francisco Sánchez at the edge of the oak grove at Santa Clara.[22]

The population of Los Angeles was so large that the commander general could have recruited three hundred capable men there with fine horses. However, since there were not enough weapons and munitions, he could outfit only eighty men. Meanwhile, the corvette *Cyane*, under the command of Captain Mervine, anchored in San Pedro Bay. He and about four hundred men went ashore and began the nine-league march to Los Angeles. The *angelinos* had acquired a very small cannon which they would fire to celebrate special occasions. Unfortunately the vent on the cannon was too wide, and those who wanted to play artilleryman would be injured and might even lose their thumbs when they fired it. Even though the cannon had this defect, the *angelinos*, aware that it could do more damage through its mouth than through its vent, believed that it was an excellent defense. However, it was not mounted on a gun carriage. So to make it more powerful, they mounted it on a cart made from a tree trunk and left to engage Captain Mervine's forces.

Mervine had confidence in the size of his corps of well-armed soldiers, and he did not deem it necessary to unload any large pieces of artillery. He advanced to the Domínguez family ranch, where he was approached by Flores and his eighty men. Much to his dismay, Mervine began to experience the little cannon's adverse effects. He was forced to place his dead and wounded men in the large carts he had brought as a precaution or for use in the campaign. The *californios* used the few shotgun cartridges they had to fire their cannon; it performed so successfully that Captain Mervine was forced to retreat quickly to the beach.[23]

The war frigate *Savannah*, under the command of Commodore Stockton, also had anchored in San Pedro Bay. When Stockton learned what had happened to Captain Mervine, he ordered that various pieces of artillery be unloaded so he could march to Los Angeles. When the *californios* saw the preparations being made by Stockton, all the satisfaction they had received from their encounter with Mervine disappeared. They knew that they could not oppose such a superior force, let alone hinder their march. They knew that they had to devise some plan as a last resort, and their first idea proved to be a good one.

The eighty men walked halfway around San Pedro Hill. Then, one after the other, they climbed up to the top, where they could be easily seen by the warships, and then they climbed down. The first man to arrive at the base of the hill would run halfway around to catch up with the formation that was coming down, and he would position himself behind the last man. Thus they gave the appearance that there were more than six hundred soldiers. Then, leaving lookouts behind on dominant points to observe the commodore's maneuvers, they went down to hide in a ravine near the *embarcadero*.

Even dogs knew instinctively that the *californio* troops never carried provisions since there always was a ranch somewhere along the routes they traveled. It was easier for them to take a steer from a ranch, kill it, and eat as much meat as they wanted. One time a mixed-breed dog, probably part hound, that lived in a warehouse along the beach, appeared in the *californios'* camp looking for scraps of meat. The dog was treated well by a soldier, who spoke, thought, and acted in typical barracks fashion. He fed the dog because he had an ulterior motive. He told his comrades that it was extremely important that he send a note post haste to Commodore Stockton, but that he did not have any paper. In order to keep him in a good mood, they provided him with a dirty half sheet. He composed his message in the form of an official letter, using the vocabulary of troopers, wheelwrights, and soldiers. He ended the letter with great bravado and challenged Stockton to a colossal battle. He signed, sealed, and addressed that meaningless hodgepodge which had been written by hands washed in the sewer. He tied the paper to the dog's neck and whipped him a few times. The dog ran home, and someone there let him in.

The soldier who was the author of that farce assured his companions that he had given the commodore some very sound advice to which he would not be able to respond. To preserve his honor, the commodore would have to leave, and the soldier expected him to do that very soon. About two hours later, one of the lookouts came down to report to Commander Flores that the Americans were reboarding their soldiers and artillery train. This unexpected news pleased everyone. They were even happier when they saw that the two warships were apparently setting sail for San Diego. The commodore thought it would be better to retreat to San Diego because it might have been difficult for him to walk nine leagues from the *embarcadero* to the city, even though he was a fairly robust man. He also believed that after he had taken San Diego by force, it would be easier to obtain the horses, pack mules, and draft animals he would need for his trip back to Los Angeles. This idea proved to be more successful than he had hoped.[24]

Because I am a *californio* who loves his country and a Mexican on all four sides and in my heart, as a point of honor, I should keep quiet about the following event or let it go unnoticed or be forgotten, but this would not be in keeping with the purpose of my narrative.

When the commodore arrived in San Diego, he encountered some corrupt *californios* and some Mexican traitors. They strongly hoped to improve their conditions. They offered themselves and their supplies to the commodore so that he could increase his ranks and resources in the war he was fighting against the men whom they should have regarded as their brothers. They were blinded by their selfish ambition to sell a small number of cattle and horses for a good price. Señor Stockton definitely should have had misgivings about the gratuitous offers of those wretched people, but when their actions demonstrated to him that they had shiny black leather hearts, he deemed it wise to praise them. However, if those men had been Americans, Señor Stockton, a patriotic and upright man, would have hanged them like bunches of grapes from every yardarm of his frigate's main mast. These spurious *californios* were not ashamed to act as spies or even to provide the invader with any information he wanted. Señor Stockton did not expect and could not have asked for better assistance at such an opportune time. When he had all the horses, pack mules, and draft animals he needed and more, he began his march to Los Angeles with a sizable force, a large artillery train, ample ammunition, arms, and other supplies.

The *diegueños* who were loyal and trustworthy sent Commander Flores a report detailing the commodore's preparations, including a list of his converts and the type of war machinery he was transporting. Because there was an extreme shortage of resources for the defense of the country, Flores did everything possible to build an arsenal from the useless and barely serviceable weapons that were available. He also was able to obtain some gun-powder and balls of lead and two mounted cannons, which would not be very effective against the enemy at long range. Their courageous determination to defend and preserve their nationality offset the disparity of weapons, munitions, and numbers of soldiers. Even though they were at a disadvantage, they were not frightened as they were lying in wait to see if they could strike a decisive blow when the commodore approached. Nothing had yet impeded his march to the San Gabriel River.

There were two different routes which could be used between Los Angeles and the San Gabriel River, a distance of slightly more than four leagues. One was through the low hills, and the other, a more direct route, was through the lower portion of the mustard field. Because this route was more heavily traveled, they waited for the commodore there. Since Commander Flores was aware that his adversary had all the advantages, he carefully considered several plans of attack and decided that he would be most successful if he concentrated his operations at the mustard field. He planned that his men would set the field on fire as soon as Stockton's soldiers entered it. Driven by the prevailing south wind, the fire would then affect Stockton's rear guard and force him to change formation. At that point, with Stockton's forces cut off from each other by dense smoke, the cavalry would charge with their lances and join Flores in a battle which they would surely win. That plan was never to be realized. The commodore was a very shrewd man; one of the spurious *californios*, who had joined him in San Diego and with whom Stockton shared his doubts and fears, had familiarized him with the terrain. They placed themselves in formation at the entrance to the mustard grove. From there they formed a curve, went halfway around the right side, and took possession of the upper pass, which was completely level and smooth.

That maneuver absolutely destroyed Flores' plan, and now he was in a predicament. He could not devise another plan without risking defeat, because the enemy artillery would overpower his troops if they were to engage in battle in an open area. But they had to do just that, because the enemy already was positioned in the surrounding area. He advanced his force as close as possible so his small cannons could have an effect, and then he opened fire against the commodore and his square formation. When the commodore saw that his main artilleryman's aim was not accurate and that he was missing his targets, he immediately ran over and removed the artilleryman from the cannon so he could aim and fire the cannon himself. The commodore

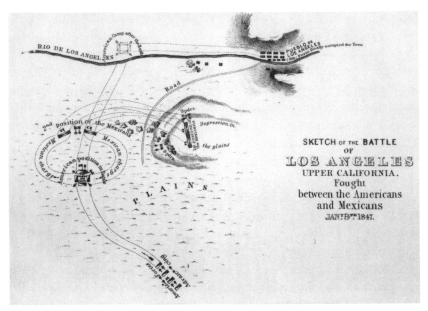

Lieutenant William H. Emory's map of the battle of San Gabriel. Courtesy of The Bancroft Library, University of California, Berkeley.

demonstrated his excellent marksmanship by dismantling Flores' best little cannon with his first shot. Flores took that as a sign of impending doom and decided that he would either win or lose with one last cavalry charge. So he ordered one, but, oh, what bad luck! A number of his subordinate company commanders were his rivals and aspired to take over the general command, so they opposed or ignored his orders. These commanders refused to move when the other company commanders ordered an advance. Without their support, these other commanders did not have enough soldiers to break the square. Consequently, they were driven back with some cavalrymen wounded, including the flag bearer, who eventually died.[25]

When Commander Flores saw that he also was being attacked by the spirit of discord, he surrendered the battlefield to his enemy and gave him all the honors of victory. He resigned from the general command and left the territory as soon as he could obtain the provisions he needed to begin his journey along the Sonora route. The commodore entered Los Angeles with the triumphant display of one who had conquered by force. He had some meetings with the *jefe político*, Don Pío Pico, about how they could arrange a settlement and establish among the people an order that would be in the best interests of the country. However, Don Andrés Pico did not want any part of this. He decided to act on his own and lead his sixty men into battle to show the enemy that there were some sons of California who were still willing to prove their mettle. He also wanted to demonstrate to the good Mexican people that he was the only person left who truly respected their nationality. Therefore, after retreating from Los Angeles, Pico wandered about for a few days and then arrived at a place called San Pascual. Convinced that he was far away from the enemy and in dire need of rest, he decided to spend the night there. An Indian soon appeared and informed him that a big American captain, traveling with more than two hundred men, had established his camp nearby. The Indian also said that the captain was carrying a cannon and that another captain had left San Diego with more than fifty men and many horses to join up with him.

According to the Indian's account, the big captain was General Kearny, who recently had come from New Mexico. While he was in San Diego, he had received news from Don Archibaldo Gillespie and then had left to join him. They had been informed by another Indian that Don Andrés Pico and his soldiers were close by, and so the general wanted to take precautionary measures. Captain Gillespie told Kearny not to bother, because the *californios* were not worth the trouble. He assured the general that he could sleep very peacefully and early the next morning they could go and watch the *californios* try to escape as quickly as possible.

The Americans were anxious to see if what they had been told about the *californios'* courage was true, so they prepared to surprise them at dawn the following day. When they began their march, an Indian devoted to Don Andrés Pico slipped away and ran as fast as he could to warn him that the American troops were about to arrive and wanted to fight. Señor Pico was very fortunate to receive that warning, because he had not heeded the previous one. He immediately ordered his men to prepare to mount their horses quickly. Then he pondered what defensive and offensive strategies he should use, since his soldiers would be facing a well-organized army that outnumbered his own by four to one. The Americans also had a general in command, assisted by two brave captains who knew their duty.

After Señor Pico had made his decision and conveyed it to his troops, they were not discouraged by the overall superiority of General Kearny's troops nor by the fact that all the odds were in his favor. When Pico saw that the enemy was near, he rode away quickly, as if he were retreating. He wanted to lure Kearny's troops to a specific spot where his lancers could exercise their skill accurately and without any obstacles. When Pico left his camp, a young boy had remained behind. He was a prisoner of his own fear, so frightened that he could not move a muscle, unable to follow his companions. This poor soul, alone and unable to defend himself, stood as still as a statue, not even able to beg for mercy from the executioners. Their passion and desire to shed blood was satisfied as they rode past the boy, as some shot him and others stabbed him. They should have taken pity on him because he was a weak young soul. Instead, they boasted about the heinous murder they had just committed as they continued riding to catch up with Commander Pico. Pico let them ride into the area he had selected for the battle and shouted, "Halt. Face the enemy. Charge!"

Pico, positioned at the head of his small troop, was counting on the power that the force of the horses and well-aimed lances would have. He was the first man to charge, and he collided with the captain of Kearny's troop, who fired at Pico and missed, but Pico thrust his sword through the captain's body from one side to the other, killing him. At the same time the man named Güero Higuera confronted Captain Gillespie and stabbed him twice with his lance. Gillespie let himself fall to the ground and pretended to be dead, because he did not want to be stabbed a third time. Señor General Kearny acted in a manner which was contrary to what would be expected of a man of his rank and nationality. He received two lance wounds in the back, but thanks to the speed of his horse he was spared any other injuries. He fled from the battlefield in disgrace, leaving behind a number of dead soldiers along with a cannon and munitions. Señor Pico immediately reviewed his troops to see if any of his men had been killed and to examine the wounded. He was pleased that all but one had survived the clash uninjured. This one person received a very peculiar injury, and it is a story which is worth telling. A bullet from a pistol which fires five rounds struck him in the neck next to his Adam's apple. Then the bullet turned around between the skin and flesh and came to rest exactly next to the spot through which it had entered. The bullet and the wound resembled a button and buttonhole which needed to be fastened.

As General Kearny was fleeing, he noticed that the top of one of the hills would be an excellent defensive position for his troops. Kearny climbed the hill and was followed by all the men who were able, including Captain Gillespie, who was suffering greatly from his injuries. Señor Pico was so overjoyed by his victory that he immediately decided to lay siege to the general without stopping to consider that his troops were outnumbered and thus doomed to fail. With the arrogance befitting one who sees himself in the stronger position in a siege, he sent the general a formal demand for unconditional surrender. The general replied that he would not surrender. His reply was written by Captain Gillespie in Spanish so there would be no misunderstanding. When Commander Pico read the message, he recognized Gillespie's handwriting and immediately summoned Güero Higuera. He reprimanded Higuera for deceiving him about having killed Captain Gillespie, and he showed him the message as proof that Gillespie was still alive. However, Higuera was like other men of his rank who were accustomed to playing tricks on their commanders. He replied that he believed his lance had penetrated Señor Gillespie's body sufficiently to have killed him. Gillespie, however, was a clever man, and he acted with the shrewdness of a coyote in pretending to be dead when he fell from his horse. Just then another enemy soldier approached Higuera, and he had to stab him twice with his lance; then he chased after the rest of those who were fleeing.

After Señor Pico pondered the situation with cold-blooded calculation, he realized that it would be impossible to carry out the intended siege. Instead, he decided to try to frighten the general's horses, which had climbed up the hill and were loose, and then capture them. With that goal in mind, he ordered his men to rope a wild mule and hang leather rings and other noisy objects on it. The loud clatter would frighten the horses and make them head toward the bottom of the hill. The American officers knew that if they allowed the mule to approach their horses all havoc would break loose, so they immediately dispatched a squad of riflemen to shoot it. Afterward a few men jokingly thanked Señor Pico for sending them enough fresh meat for that day. During the night they left for San Diego.[26]

General Kearny should have been appointed *jefe superior* of the territory, because he was the highest-ranking officer. However, his disagreements with Colonel Frémont escalated to such a point that Frémont challenged him to a duel. The general did not accept. According to the story his supporters circulated, he left the country to comply with instructions he had received from the federal government. On the other hand, Señor Frémont's supporters claimed loudly that the general had been stabbed in the back and had fled because he feared that Frémont would kill him in a duel.

The flag of the North Americans waved in all the populated areas of Alta California, but the Mexican tricolor still flew in a few places as it wandered about its own country, passing through the deserted fields, unable to find shelter from the bad weather. It seemed as if the flag were revealing its

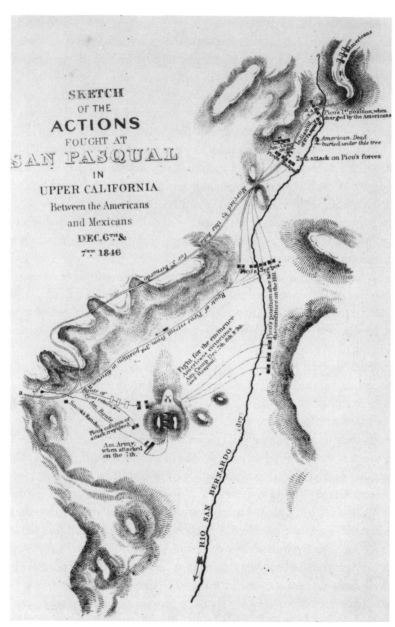

Lieutenant William H. Emory's map of the battle of San Pascual. Courtesy of The Bancroft Library, University of California, Berkeley.

despair. Its brilliant colors had been faded by the strong rays of the sun, it had been torn by bullets and thorny branches, and worst of all, it had been orphaned with no hope at all of being helped. Nevertheless, the flag proudly waved in the wind, sensing the courageous heartbeats of the brave men who supported it. If they could not obtain an honorable surrender, they vowed to fight to the bitter end and die defending the flag. Let it be known for all time that even though they were unable to do more for their native land and for the country of their birth, these men should serve as an example for other places invaded by forces from the United States.

The Americans had the greatest confidence in the troops commanded by Colonel Frémont, and they were the ones that pursued Don Andrés Pico. Pico, who had ample warning, decided not to avoid combat. He looked for a level area, free of obstacles, where he could lead his young soldiers into battle. They wanted an area where they could spur their horses freely, thrust their lances, and either triumph or die after a brave fight. In a very short time Colonel Frémont found Pico. When the two *jefes* encountered each other, it seems that they both wanted to have a meeting before resorting to weapons. Señor Frémont was recognized for his military expertise, and he correctly esteemed the courage of his opponents. Because he also was a shrewd man, he was convinced that these courageous Mexicans would be of use to the territory after it became a state. To their dismay, these Mexicans would be viewed as foreigners in their own country, but they would make excellent citizens of the United States. With this in mind, Frémont proposed terms for a surrender to Señor Pico, but he did not accept them. He then suggested other terms to him, and Pico again refused. This negative response almost led to a confrontation; but since Señor Frémont was more experienced, he wisely waited until he could convince Señor Pico with good and benevolent judgment. He explained to Pico that he believed his reasons for not accepting the surrender bordered on fear because he found himself in a very critical situation. He had no support from the Mexican government, and none would be forthcoming, since the enormous distance rendered assistance impossible.

The commanders had lingered too long in their discussion. Since Señor Frémont was needed elsewhere, he wanted to conclude the negotiations for the surrender. Frémont was generous in granting Pico everything that his military honor permitted. The surrender finally was negotiated with the following terms: Señor Pico would march to Los Angeles and enter the city in formation, with drums beating and flag unfurled. After arriving at the *plaza*,

Andrés Pico. Courtesy of the California State Library, Sacramento.

he would order his troops to disband. Each soldier would return home, put away his weapons, and live as a peaceful, good, hard-working citizen. The cannon and remaining ammunition, which had been taken from General Kearny, would be surrendered immediately, since they were the property of the United States government. After the terms had been agreed upon and the document was signed, Pico complied with all details of the surrender.[27]

Now that the Americans were in possession of the territory, a number of different naval officers assumed the command in succession until Colonels Mason and Riley were appointed by the government. When they assumed the

John C. Frémont. Courtesy of the California State Library, Sacramento.

command, they conducted themselves with the enthusiasm typical of fine military men and the benevolence of excellent citizens. Many other officials and staff people were appointed after the Mexican government sold the territory to the United States and it became a state.

It is evident that this unfortunate country's many riches were hidden from her. A very old legend of unknown origin stated that a number of rivers in the north in both Californias contained sands of gold. Reverend Father Juan Ugarte, who succeeded the distinguished Father Salvatierra in Baja California, said that he had gone to visit the beaches at the mouth of the Colorado River on the first boat that was built in the territory, and he had found nothing.

The Franciscan Fathers from the Colegio de San Fernando in Mexico took over the administration of those missions when the Jesuit Fathers departed. Later, the Franciscans received orders from their superiors to surrender the missions to the Dominican Fathers. After the Dominicans took possession of and established these missions, they always were occupied with their apostolic work and never endeavored to explore the meadows along the rivers to determine what was in the sand. Lately, there has been speculation that the Fathers already were aware of the sands of gold. This cannot be true, because, if it is difficult to keep a secret when three people know about it, it would be impossible to do so when more than forty people are involved. Therefore, the most likely if not indisputable scenario is that when a small quantity of gold was discovered in 1844 on land belonging to Mission San Fernando, it became apparent that there was a deposit of gold in this region.[28] Later, in 1848, gold was discovered in abundance at Sutter's establishment in Sacramento.

As one who has experienced the sufferings of the *californio* landowners, which the political change has caused, I would ask that you please allow me to conclude the present letter here. Another friend of yours, with a very small pen, might continue the story. Please accept this brief work which your dear, devoted servant [S.Q.B.S.M.] dedicates to you as a token of our friendship.

Antonio Mª. Osio

Epilogue

On February 2, 1852, less than a year after completing his manuscript, Osio filed a claim before the U.S. Land Commission in San Francisco for Angel Island. Testimony on his behalf was offered by former governor Juan Bautista Alvarado, former San Francisco harbor master William A. Richardson, and Jean Jacques Vioget, who had made the first survey of San Francisco. Vioget told the commission, "I have never heard the title of Osio to the said Angel Island questioned or disputed."[1] Osio left for San José del Cabo soon after filing his claim; by July 1 he had arrived at his place of birth. His land interests in California were handled by Edward Vischer. Both Osio and his son Salvador lost their *ranchos* to a land speculator named Andrew Randall, and Vischer sold Osio's claim to Angel Island to future San Francisco mayor C. K. Garrison, who at the time was the agent of Cornelius Vanderbilt's steamship company. Vischer apologized to Osio for only being able to obtain twelve thousand dollars for the land, but he told Osio that he hoped that the money would help him recover the losses sustained in Osio's dealings with Randall.[2]

Osio spent the rest of his life in San José del Cabo, where he and Narcisa Florencia lived until their deaths. Between 1852 and 1860 she bore five more children: Manuel (1852), María Plácida (1853), Juan Manuel (1855), María Josefa de Jesús (1859), and Josefa Antonia Nemesia (1860). Antonio María Osio remained in public life. He served as *alcalde* at San José del Cabo in the 1860s and as a *juez* in the 1870s. On November 5, 1878, he died.

The fate of Osio's manuscript after Savage reported in 1883 that it was in the possession of Osio's daughter Beatrice is not entirely clear. Beatrice Osio de Williamson continued to live in the San Francisco Bay Area for some time after her father's death. As late as 1900 she was living in Oakland.[3] We do know that the manuscript eventually came into the possession of Vallejo Gantner, son of John Gantner, of the firm of Gantner and Mattern in San Francisco.

John Gantner had married Adela Frisby, the granddaughter of Salvador Vallejo.[4] Gantner was quite active in the Native Sons of the Golden

West.[5] Among their other concerns, the Native Sons of the Golden West were quite interested in the preservation of historical documents. For instance, in 1915 they backed a bill in the California legislature to undertake a complete survey of all materials in California which affected the study of local history. In a letter to the membership urging them to support the bill, Grand Secretary Fred H. Jung said, "There is much miscellaneous material . . . invaluable material for local history in private hands in the form of diaries, collections of correspondence, and so forth, the knowledge of the location of which is of the highest importance."[6]

We speculate that the manuscript became known to John Gantner as a result of this effort or of a similar one undertaken under the auspices of the Native Sons. Since the manuscript mentions both Mariano and Salvador Vallejo, it stands to reason that Gantner, whose wife was a Vallejo, would have been interested in it. Gantner's son Vallejo certainly had possession of the manuscript in the early 1950s, when he gave it to Margaret Mollins and Virginia Thickens, who planned to translate and edit it. When Herbert Eugene Bolton, for whom they worked, became ill and died, however, they had to return to teaching and were not able to complete the project. They arranged for the manuscript to be deposited at the archives of Mission Santa Clara, its original home.[7]

Notes

Biographical Sketches

Glossary

Bibliography

The Family of Antonio María Osio

Index

Notes

Introduction

1. What is now known as the peninsula of Baja California was often referred to as Antigua California until 1800 (Crosby, *Antigua California*, xv).

2. The quotes in this and the previous paragraph are taken from two reports prepared by the *diputación*, both written by Antonio María Osio. See Archivo General de la Nación, Mexico City, Gobernación, Legajo 129, Expedientes 15, 18.

3. Gates, "California Land Act."

4. On the Land Act and its effects, see Pitt, *Decline of the Californios*, 83–103.

5. No biography of Osio exists. The most convenient compilation of the events in his life can be found in Bancroft, *History of California* 4: 761–62. Bancroft states, "But for the record of offices held by him, there is a remarkable lack of information about the man." The information about Osio's life that we offer in this introduction generally comes from the manuscript itself and from various other manuscript collections in The Bancroft Library at the University of California, Berkeley, and the Archivo General de la Nación (hereinafter AGN) in Mexico City.

6. Maynard Geiger, O.F.M., in *Franciscan Missionaries in Hispanic California, 1769–1848* (249–51), gives biographical information on Suárez del Real. Osio's 1864 trip is inferred from a letter from Edward Vischer to Osio at Santa Clara, Sept. 30, 1864, Osio Papers, The Bancroft Library.

7. Bancroft, *Literary Industries*, 647. On Savage and Cerruti, see Mollins and Thickens, *Ramblings in California*; H. Clark, *Venture in History*, 17; and C. S. Peterson, "Hubert Howe Bancroft," 55–56.

8. See F. J. Weber, "John Thomas Doyle."

9. Bancroft, *Literary Industries*, 647–48. At the head of the copy of the manuscript made by Savage for Bancroft, which is now in the Bancroft Library, is this note from Thomas Savage:

San Francisco (Calif.)

January 8, 1883

I have this day examined a copy of the history of California, whereof the annexed is another copy; or rather, the former is, to the best of my knowledge and belief in the handwriting and bears the signature at the end of its author, Antonio María Osio, occupying about 162 pp. of paper of about fool's cap length. Sewed onto the first page is what purports to be the rough copy of a letter without a signature, from said Osio to Fray Jose Ma. Suárez del Real, dated at Santa Clara April 4, 1851, from which I conclude that Real had asked Osio for facts to enable him to write a history of California, and for the earlier parts of the history of the Californias, and the administrations of the various governors to Arrillaga inclusive, he refers to the works of Piccolo and others.

> The original alluded to is in the possession of Mrs. Williamson, a Mexican lady who I understand is a daughter of the late Ant. M. Osio and lives now at 326 Polk St in this city, her husband being in Mexico.
>
> Thos. Savage

The original of the manuscript is now in the archives at Santa Clara University. The Doyle copy is at the Huntington Library, and the Forbes copy is at the Beinecke Rare Book and Manuscript Library, Yale University.

10. In the Archivo General de la Nación, there is, for instance, a collection of copies of the minutes of the 1832 *diputación*. At the bottom of a number of the copies is the phrase "Es copia, San Diego, 15 de mayo de 1832. Juan B. Alvarado." On the top lefthand side of the first page of the same proceedings, we find written, in Osio's hand, "Como de oficio para los años de 1832 y 1833, Osio." This indicates that at a later date Osio was asked by someone—or perhaps took it upon himself—to verify the accuracy of the copies. On the top of another document dealing with trade, again in Osio's hand, is written, "Havilitado provicionalmente por la comisaria provisional de la alta California para el año de 1832, Osio." This indicates the same type of verification on Osio's part. AGN, Gobernación, Legajo 120, Caja 191, Expedientes 2–4.

11. David G. Gutiérrez has said, "Ultimately the critical aspect of the annexation of the West proved to be the power that conquest bestowed on Americans to explain what had occurred there. As Reginald Horsman notes in his analysis of the Mexican War, 'total Mexican defeat convinced the Americans that their original judgment of the Mexican race had been correct. . . . Americans were not to be blamed for forcibly taking the northern provinces of Mexico, for Mexicans . . . had failed because they were a mixed, inferior race' " (Gutiérrez, "Significant to Whom?" 522).

12. In fact, the Mexican dictations and reminiscences in Bancroft's *History of California* were used in procrustean ways that made them serve the conquerors' notions of the superiority of what they termed Anglo-Saxon progress and development over what they were certain were Mexican indolence and laziness. On the denigration of Mexicans in Bancroft, see the comments of Genaro Padilla (*My History, Not Yours*, 254-55) and Antonio Ríos-Bustamante (*Mexican Los Angeles*, 176). On Osio's manuscript and the Mexican reminiscences in general, Bancroft says, "It [Osio's manuscript] is a work of considerable merit, valuable as a supplement to those of Vallejo, Alvarado, and Bandini, as presenting certain events from a different point of view; but like all writings of this class, it is of very uneven quality as a record of facts. None of them, nor all combined, would be a safe guide in the absence of the original records; but with those records they have a decided value" (Bancroft, *History of California* 4: 762). This statement and others like it seem unobjectionable until they are contrasted with statements like the one in *Literary Industries* about Andrés Pico: "There were several of the brothers Pico, all, for native Californians, remarkably knowing. Whether they caught their shrewdness from

the Yankees I know not" (Bancroft, *Literary Industries*, 490). In *Popular Tribunals*, which was dedicated to "William T. Coleman, Chief of the Greatest Popular Tribunal the World has ever Witnessed"—Coleman gave Bancroft a dictation—the vigilante reminiscences are fairly consistently treated as the gospel truth, and the givers of the dictations are congratulated for throwing brilliant light on difficult points. Vigilante Chauncey Dempster's reminiscence, for instance, is characterized as "able and eloquent . . . prepared for me with great care, in which the heartbeats of the movements seem to pulsate under his pen" (Bancroft, *Popular Tribunals* 2: 73; see also 1: viii, 191). In the *History of California*, on the other hand, the Mexican narratives are subject to a seemingly endless series of critiques in extensive footnotes (it should be noted that both critiques and footnotes are absent from *Popular Tribunals*). Thus the reader is informed, for instance, that Osio's account of one scene is "amusingly absurd" (Bancroft, *History of California* 3: 208). Bancroft simply takes a figure of speech which Osio used ("In the end, Providence proved the best commander at preventing bloodshed"), interprets it literally, and then patronizingly denigrates it. The vigilante reminiscences were also at times inconsistent with each other, but Bancroft did not feel compelled to point this out to his readers. See Senkewicz, *Vigilantes*, 193–94.

13. U.S. Commission for Ascertaining and Settling Private Land Claims in California, Papers (hereinafter cited as Land Commission Papers), Angel Island, MS, The Bancroft Library; Livingston, *Ranching*, 4–11.

14. Mollins and Thickens, *Ramblings in California*, 109.

15. On this point, see especially Padilla, *My History, Not Yours*, 77–152.

16. Examples of Chase's editing include the random creation of new paragraphs, arbitrary substitution of the imperfect tense for the preterit tense (which in some cases slightly changed the meaning of the sentence), arbitrary changes in prepositions and direct and indirect object pronouns, spelling correction of proper names, insertion of quotation marks around proper names, addition of definite and indefinite articles, and placement of accents where required.

17. The Doyle copy did include a portion of text material which is missing from the original manuscript. In the original manuscript (p. 101A), Osio indicated with a # symbol, as he had done in a previous section, that the rest of the paragraph on that page was written on a separate sheet. This particular sheet must have been lost or inadvertently discarded after 1876, because it is not with the original. Fortunately, Chase had access to that extra sheet and included the information in his copy.

18. The Forbes copy, not dated, is housed at the Beinecke Rare Book and Manuscript Library at Yale. Of the three known copies, this is the least accurate, because the scribe took wide liberties with the text, beginning with the title "Memories of Alta California." He then proceeded to make changes throughout the body of the manuscript. The Forbes scribe perhaps viewed his task more as that of an editor than that of a scribe. He changed syntax and vocabulary, paraphrased the material, added clauses at random with the intent of clarifying a point, and

omitted words and complete paragraphs. For example, note the following discrepancies between Osio's description of Mariano Chico's personality traits and the same information as it appears in the Forbes copy:

Osio: "A man who has the tendency to become angry for any reason can always find more than enough reasons; for the most part these reasons are baseless. Nevertheless, in this case it is important to acknowledge that Señor Chico did indeed have reason to be angry. The general opinion of those who study such matters is that the most perfect and animated young faces are commonly found among males in the United States of the North."

Forbes: "If an irritable man becomes angry for any reason, and most of the time the reasons are unfounded, what next happened to Chico gave him just cause to become angry. It is the general opinion that in the United States, the most perfect and animated young faces are found among the male sex."

As in the case of the Doyle and Bancroft copies, the Forbes scribe made corrections in spelling, but instead of striking out the original and writing the correction in the space above, in some instances he simply rewrote the words, and other times he left the original spelling. If the scribe had been conscientious, the Forbes copy of the Osio manuscript could have been more accurate, since the scribe was working with the original.

19. Bancroft, *History of California* 1:55.

20. Ibid. In his biographical sketch of Osio, Bancroft claimed that Osio wrote his manuscript "in his later years," despite Savage's clear statement to the contrary. See 4: 762.

21. This information comes from the superb study of Baja California by Harry W. Crosby, *Antigua California*, 318–28, 351–68, 389–90.

22. Ibid., 363. We are indebted to Harry W. Crosby for personally providing us with additional information on Osio's family.

23. When he married Narcisa Soto at Mission Santa Clara in 1838, Osio reported that he had been born in 1804. However, we accept Martínez' statement that Osio was seventy-eight years old when he died on November 5, 1878, which would put his year of birth at 1800. See Mutnick, *Some Alta California Pioneers* 2: 2, 1708–11; and Martínez, *Guía familiar*, 447.

24. Martínez, *Guía familiar*, 13, 264; idem, *History of Lower California*, 316; Bancroft, *History of California* 2: 701.

25. Mutnick, *Some Alta California Pioneers* 2: 2, 1708–11.

26. Bancroft, *History of California* 1: 291, 716; 5: 728; Mutnick, *Some Alta California Pioneers* 1: 3, 1082–85.

27. A. P. Bowman, *Index*, 330.

28. Land Commission Papers, Aguas Frías, MS.

29. Bancroft, *History of California* 4: 407, 409, 423.

30. Hammond, *Larkin Papers* 4: 326.

31. Land Commission Papers, Angel Island.

32. McKevitt, *University of Santa Clara*, 33.

33. Ong, *Orality and Literacy*, 38.

34. Couser, *Altered Egos*, 17.

35. Alvarado, "History of California" 1: 108–9; Vallejo, "Historical and Personal Memoirs" 1: 136.

36. Although, as Rosaura Sánchez says, Vallejo and Alvarado maintained authorial control over their memoirs by dictating the conditions of the sessions, they did not have the degree of control that Osio had over his manuscript. In his case no one else was involved. There was no interviewer and no list of questions. See Sánchez, "Nineteenth-Century Californio Narratives," 283.

37. Sánchez states, "The manuscripts were always re-copied and carved up by topics, periods, etc., to create files of notations, excerpts, and documents for the various writers hired to write Bancroft's California history" (ibid., 286).

38. There is evidence in the manuscript that Osio acted as his own editor, for he at times crossed out words and placed corrections in the space above.

39. Osio's sources included the Bible, Sir Walter Scott's works, the epic poem *Amadís de Gaula*, *Lazarillo de Tormes*, Cervantes' *Don Quixote*, Lope de Vega's epic poem *La gatomaquia*, Samaniego's *Fábulas*, and Lesage's picaresque novel *La historia de Gil Blas de Santillana*.

40. In another episode, Osio re-creates a meeting between Mariano Chico and Abel Stearns and uses a biblical reference as metaphor. Recalling the Gospel of Mark (15. 15–16), Chico is cast in the role of Pontius Pilate, administering bad justice.

41. Janet Gurkin Altman writes: "The *I* of epistolary discourse always situates himself vis à vis another; his locus, his address, is always relative to that of his addressee. To write a letter is to map one's coordinates—temporal, spatial, emotional, intellectual—in order to tell someone else where one is located at a particular time and how far one has traveled since the last writing. Reference points on that map are particular to the shared world of writer and addressee" (Altman, *Epistolarity*, 87; see also 119).

42. Osio recounts at least one event at which he and Suárez del Real were both present: a wedding of an indigenous *alcalde* performed by the priest, which Governor José Figueroa also attended.

43. Mutlu Konuk Blasing observes, "The *I* and the *YOU* whom the *I* addresses are both on stage; consequently, the work should not be seen as an object, because one cannot simply speak for oneself. Whom else one is speaking for depends upon which stage one is speaking from, what the props are, and who one's audience is" (Blasing, *Art of Life*, xxvi). We might also note that Osio's clear division of the narrative into two parts, events before and after 1825, indicate that he was aware of the distinction between a *crónica* (chronicle) and a *memoria* (memoir). In the *memoria*, the author explicitly states that he will only narrate what he has seen and experienced, but he will highlight the narration with appropriate commentary. The *crónica*, on the other hand, may include material of which the author has no

personal experience, and no attempt is made to distinguish between the two. The inclusive nature of Osio's own personal experiences as well as those of his family and friends expands the structural dimensions of the text. Now the reader sees that the exterior epistolary framework is supported by a substructure, the *memoria*, which can be classified as both a personal and a collective autobiography.

44. Osio suggests that Suárez del Real consult the work on Serra by Palóu and, at another point in the manuscript, suggests that the author of the full history of California should take into account another published source, the work of Governor Figueroa on the abortive Híjar-Padrés colonizing effort: "Señor Figueroa, who was now free of the immediate problem, decided to print the official communications which had been exchanged between the *jefe* of the territory, the *diputación*, and the principal director of colonization. For the satisfaction of the public, this was done in the form of a printed manifesto.

"When the manifesto was finished, he did not have time to have it printed, since he became seriously ill and died in September 1835. However, his secretary, Don Agustín Zamorano, attended to it. After he had compiled various notebooks, he distributed them among the friends of the deceased general. In the notebook one is given an extensive view of everything that happened during Señor Figueroa's tenure in government. Therefore, it would be advantageous for the person who is entrusted to write the history of Alta California to make use of the notebook."

45. Altman, *Epistolarity*, 144–45, 162.

46. Blasing, *Art of Life*, xxiv.

47. See D. J. Weber, *Mexican Frontier*, 240–41.

48. A major theme of the section of the manuscript which deals with the U.S. invasion is the loss of *nacionalidad*. For instance, in describing the U.S. capture of Monterey, Osio writes, "At eleven o'clock the inhabitants of Monterey experienced the sorrow of seeing the stars and stripes wave for the second time from the flagpoles that had been erected for the tricolor flag of the three guarantees. However, this time it seemed worse, as they began to think about the loss of their nationality and of everything they had worked so hard to create. For experience has always shown that conquerors never have been able to maintain a brotherhood with those they have conquered." In the same vein, Osio describes the resistance to the invasion: "Many people around Monterey and San Francisco were willing to defend with one last effort the nationality which they held so dear. In several skirmishes with the American troops, they fought like true Mexican soldiers and courageous victors."

Chapter 1

1. The viceroy during the period 1813–16 was Félix María Calleja del Rey. A native of Valladolid, he arrived in New Spain in 1789 as an infantry captain. He was active in New Spain and defeated Miguel Hidalgo in 1811 and José María Morelos in 1814. After serving as viceroy, he returned to Spain and served as gov-

ernor of Cádiz and of Valencia before he died in 1828. See *Diccionario Porrúa;* and Briggs and Alisky, *Historical Dictionary of Mexico,* 30.

2. The Colegio de San Fernando was a Franciscan seminary in Mexico City which trained priests for the Indian missions. It was founded in 1734, and by the 1760s it was already staffing five missions in the provinces of New Spain: San Luis Potosí, Guanajuato, and Querétaro. After the expulsion of the Jesuits in 1767, the Colegio agreed to the request of the viceroy, Joaquín de Monserrat, that it take over the missions in California. Accordingly, all the missions in Alta California, which were started in 1769, were staffed from this seminary. See Engelhardt, *Missions and Missionaries* 1: 289–90, 614–17.

3. Solá had the reputation of being a strong disciplinarian. One of his aides, José Canuto Boronda, recalled that he tended to be serious and formal and that he would reprimand officers and men publicly if he noticed anything out of order (Boronda, "Notas históricas," 5). But the governor did have a slightly milder side. Esteban de la Torre, whose father was Solá's secretary, recalled that once, when he was a young boy, the governor was playing games with him. Solá ordered Esteban to open his mouth, and then he struck Esteban so hard that he bit his tongue. In reaction, Esteban struck Solá in the face. The governor pretended to be highly upset and told Boronda to take the boy home to his mother, María de los Angeles Cota, for a severe whipping. The mother seemed to be about to do so when Boronda hurried him back to Solá, who took him into a room and lectured him about showing respect for one's elders. Then he told Esteban to go to the dispensary and pick out some fruit to take back to his mother (Torre, "Reminiscencias," 2–3; Boronda has essentially the same story, 5).

4. For more than forty years after their inception in 1769, the missions of Alta California were governed by a president, appointed by the head of the Colegio de San Fernando. In 1812, however, the Franciscans divided the governance of the missions into two distinct spheres by the creation of the office of prefect. In general, the prefect was responsible for the temporal affairs of the missions, including relations with the government, while the president confined himself after 1812 to the spiritual governance of the mission staff. The prefect when Solá was appointed was Father Vicente Francisco de Sarría. See Engelhardt, *Missions and Missionaries* 3: 4.

5. The Bay of Biscay, from which the Biscay region gets its name, is between northern Spain and western France. Sarría's birthplace, San Esteban de Echébarri, and Solá's, Mondragón, are both in that region.

6. Juana Machado described Argüello as tall and husky, with a big round white face, black eyes, and extremely black hair. In his demeanor, she said, he gave the impression of being friendly and generous. See Machado, "Los tiempos pasados," 6.

7. The four Spanish presidios in Alta California were at San Diego, Santa Bárbara, Monterey, and San Francisco. The best general treatment of this institution in Spanish colonial America is Moorhead, *Presidio.* As David J. Weber writes, "By the 1760s, presidios or military bases, most of them fortified, had eclipsed the mis-

sions to become the dominant institution on Spain's North American Frontiers" (Weber, *Spanish Frontier*, 212). A discussion of the difficulties of defining the term *presidio* precisely can be found in Weber, *Spanish Frontier*, 438. See also Faulk, "Presidio." On Alta California, see Whitehead, "Alta California's Four Fortresses."

Osio is here most likely referring to a series of renovations made at the San Francisco presidio in the middle to late 1810s. See Bancroft, *History of California* 2: 372; Langellier and Rosen, *El Presidio de San Francisco*, 91; and Schuetz-Miller, *Building and Builders*, 178.

8. Corte de Madera, modern Corte Madera, was located north of the Golden Gate, in what is now Marin County. During the Spanish and Mexican periods it was used as a logging site for various construction projects in and around San Francisco. See Beck and Haase, *Historical Atlas of California*, 98.

9. The barge was launched at the end of 1818. Juan Bautista Alvarado, with the embellishment that is characteristic of his later recollections, claimed that the barge was built by *three* English carpenters. Bancroft says that it weighed about five tons (Bancroft, *History of California* 2: 373).

10. In the 1840s Osio was granted all of Angel Island and a *rancho* at Point Reyes, also north of San Francisco. He visited both of these places frequently. This description of the tides and currents encountered on the sea voyage from San Francisco out into the bay is most assuredly firsthand and based on his frequent journeys through these waters in the 1840s.

11. A league was approximately 2.6 miles.

12. Marín had been captured and brought to San Francisco at some point in the 1810s. He was captured again in 1824, after which date he apparently worked as some sort of boat master in San Francisco Bay. See Vallejo "Historical and Personal Memoirs" 1: 110.

13. Point Bonetes formed the northwestern tip of the mouth of San Francisco Bay. It was variously termed Bonete, Bonetes, Boneta, and Bonetas during the Spanish and Mexican periods. See Gudde, *California Place Names*, 34–35.

14. Point Año Nuevo is located about forty miles south of San Francisco on the Pacific coast. Point Reyes, also on the Pacific coast, is about an equal distance north of San Francisco.

15. The incident that Osio is describing here occurred in May and June 1811. The four ships were the *O'Cain*, the *Mercury*, the *Albatross*, and the *Isabella*, which Davis commanded. See Ogden, *California Sea Otter Trade*, 53–55.

16. The Spanish regularly captured and, according to the Aleuts, sometimes executed those who were engaged in hunting the sea otters without permission. In November 1810 Davis had left a note for Argüello on a stick in the sand, in which he asked Argüello to return some "poor Indians" to him, since he claimed that they had entered San Francisco Bay to hunt without his knowledge. See Ogden, *California Sea Otter Trade*, 54.

17. Drakes Bay, so named because Francis Drake allegedly anchored there in

1579 on his circumnavigation of the globe, is on the Pacific coast north of San Francisco. Point Reyes forms its tip.

18. The source of this particular story, like so much else in the manuscript which occurred before Osio's arrival in 1825, was probably Argüello himself, since he was Osio's brother-in-law. Or perhaps Osio is narrating a tradition that was preserved in the Argüello family. It is impossible to corroborate this account, although there were repeated instances of tension between Solá, who ordered that all commercial legislation be strictly observed, and Argüello, who, as his dealings with Davis indicate, favored a more relaxed and flexible approach to foreign ships, especially in the absence of regular supplies from Mexico. See Bancroft, *History of California* 2: 288–91. The Russian trader Kiril Khlebnikov said that Argüello would allow the Russian-American Company to hunt in the waters of San Francisco Bay so long as the company gave him half of the catch. Another reason Argüello valued the presence of the Russians was that he was occasionally able to purchase ammunition from them. A frequent complaint of the Spanish military in Alta California was that the colonial administration in New Spain would not outfit them properly. See Shur, *Khlebnikov Archive*, 98, 155. Solá apparently softened his views as he came to appreciate the great poverty of the troops. See Langellier and Rosen, *El Presidio de San Francisco*, 90, 101.

19. The priest whom Osio calls Magín was Magín Matías Catalá.

20. San Bruno Hill is slightly south of San Francisco, on the coast of the bay.

21. A *chalupa* is a kind of narrow canoe.

22. Osio is referring here to William Smith.

23. The *Mercury* was captured by *La Flora* in June 1813. There is a record of a U.S. ship, the *Sultan*, engaged in trade along the California coast in 1816. The discrepancy in dates gave Bancroft enough ammunition to attack the veracity of Osio's account. He says, "Osio . . . writing, probably from memory, an account of the smuggling operations of those years, in which the details are inextricably confused, says that the captains of the *Sultana* and *Urbana*, then at San Francisco, offered to aid Capt. Davis, owner of the *Mercury,* to recapture the vessel, but he declined. This is all wrong, and no such vessels were on the coast." Yet less than twenty pages later, Bancroft states that, in a list of vessels trading on the coast from 1810 to 1814—the time frame within which the *Mercury* was captured—the *Sultan* is included and that it was captained by a man named Reynolds. This does not stop him from fuming that, in Osio's account, "chronology and fact go for nothing." See Bancroft, *History of California* 2: 268–69, 282.

24. Jessie Davies Francis concluded that the *californios* "never really had a chance at their own fur fisheries." Others, notably the Russians and the North Americans, came in and overhunted the herds, eventually wiping them out. Some *californios* in the 1820s organized a mercantile concern, the California Fishing Company, to enable them to gather some of the profit to be made in this venture. But they often found that they were dependent on the Russians for boats, indige-

nous fishermen, and the marketing of the catch. See Francis, *Economic and Social History*, 583–601.

Chapter 2

1. The most complete account of Bouchard's life we have found is Hector R. Ratto's book *Capitán de navío Hipólito Bouchard*. According to Ratto, Bouchard was born around 1785 in St. Tropéz, France. This Mediterranean location gave him both a love of the sea and a feeling of enmity toward Spain, and it may help to explain his decisions to take to the sea and to fight against the crown in South America.

By 1811 he was sailing and fighting on behalf of the revolutionaries of the La Plata River region in modern Argentina. In command of the *25th of May*, he participated in a battle against royalists in February of that year, and he helped defend Buenos Aires against a Spanish bombardment in July. He joined José de San Martín in April 1812 and was granted Argentine citizenship a year later for having "unequivocally supported the liberty and happiness of America." In 1815, commanding the *Halcón*, he was a part of a Pacific expedition, under the overall leadership of the Irishman Guillermo Brown, which attempted to disrupt Spanish shipping and to spread word about the independence movement. See Elías, "Cruceros de Brown, Bouchard, y Cochrane." In July 1817 he was given command of the *Argentina*, which was to pursue Spanish shipping where the Argentine flag had never flown.

Displacing almost seven hundred tons, with forty-two cannons and a crew of 250, the *Argentina* left Buenos Aires in July 1817. By September it was at Madagascar, where, according to his account, Bouchard attempted to disrupt some English and French ships engaged in the slave trade. In November Bouchard fought some Malaysian pirates in the East Indies, and by March 1818 he was harassing Spanish merchant ships in Philippine waters. He spent several months engaged in this activity, and by August he had landed in the Hawaiian Islands.

In Hawaii, Bouchard encountered the *Santa Rosa*, a Buenos Aires privateering vessel whose crew had mutinied and sold the ship to King Kamehameha. Bouchard showed the monarch a forged document ostensibly from the government in Buenos Aires, commissioning him to track down and bring back the *Santa Rosa*. The king, promised compensation, agreed, and he turned the ship over to Bouchard at the end of August.

Bouchard recruited Peter Corney, an Englishman who had been first mate on the *Columbia*, a schooner of the North West Company which had engaged in the Astoria, California, Hawaii, and China trade from 1814 until it was sold in Hawaii in 1817. He put Corney in command of the *Santa Rosa* and decided to head for California to harass Spanish interests there, and perhaps to spread the revolution as well. See Bealer, "Bouchard in the Islands of the Pacific"; and Barry, "Peter Corney's Voyages."

2. Monterey was defended by a fort, called El Castillo, situated on the cliffs at

the southern tip of Monterey Bay, slightly to the south and west of the Customs House, on what Vancouver called "a small eminence that commands the anchorage" (Spencer-Hancock and Pritchard, "El Castillo de Monterey," 231). El Castillo was constructed in 1794 and was not militarily impressive. An American seaman commented in 1804 that it consisted of "a miserable battery . . . altogether inadequate to what it is intended for" (ibid., 234).

Corney, whom Bouchard had recruited in Hawaii, had visited Monterey at least twice in the middle 1810s. In 1815 he penned a relatively detailed description of the site, including El Castillo, in his journal: "The fort stands on a hill, about one mile to the westward of the town; and just above the landing place, it is quite open on the land side, and embrasures thrown up on the sea side mounting ten brass twelve pounders, with a good supply of copper shot" (Corney, *Early Voyages*, 130).

Accounts of what occurred during the day after Bouchard's ships entered Monterey Bay are varied. Most authorities agree that the *Argentina* and the *Santa Rosa* entered the bay either toward dusk or at night, and that, as Osio says, the *Santa Rosa* came in close to the shore while the *Argentina* stayed out of range. See, for example, Bancroft, *History of California* 2: 227. They remained in those positions until the next morning.

3. The Rancho del Rey was the government *rancho* which was supposed to supply meat and horses for the presidio companies. The *rancho* proper was about twelve miles northeast of Monterey. Other *ranchos del rey* were located near the three other presidios: San Diego, Santa Bárbara, and San Francisco. See Bancroft, *History of California* 1: 621–22.

4. The *Santa Rosa* refused to identify itself. As Corney, on board that ship, wrote, "The Spaniard hailed me frequently to send a boat on shore, which I declined" (Corney, *Early Voyages*, 217).

5. Defenses had been increased along the California coast during the month preceding Bouchard's visit. On October 6, 1818, Captain Henry Gyzelaar of the U.S. ship *Clarion* arrived at Santa Bárbara with the news that two insurgent ships were being outfitted in Hawaii for an expedition against Alta California. The commander there, José de la Guerra y Noriega, informed Governor Solá of the news, and the governor ordered increased vigilance. See Bancroft, *History of California* 2: 222–24. Most likely, part of the increased vigilance at Monterey was the erection of a temporary battery dug out on the beach, just north of the Customs House and a bit to the south of the fort. Alvarado, who was a child in Monterey at the time, recalled in the 1870s that the temporary battery was "to the south of the main battery on the site of the present steamer wharf" (Alvarado, "History of California" 2: 120).

6. Osio was here voicing a complaint common among those born in California, who called themselves the *hijos del país*. In the 1870s, after describing the bravery of Sergeant Dolores Pico in a campaign against the indigenous peoples near Mission San Miguel, Juan Bautista Alvarado wrote: "It is a pity that the Spanish laws placed obstacles before a sound and experienced military man like Pico, preventing him

from going up the ranks to captain or colonel. My grandfather has told me that Sergeant Pico had fought singlehandedly against six Indians whose bodies served as mute witnesses to the bravery of their longtime adversary, but Pico had not been born into the nobility. He had not been educated in the royal schools at the expense of His Majesty, and that was enough to close the doors of honor to him, of which he was worthy because of his bravery" (Alvarado, "History of California" 1: 171). That this neglect of Alta California by Spain and Mexico ended up harming both Alta California and Mexico is one of the major themes of Osio's work.

7. Accounts about what happened after dawn on this day are very confused. Some recent authorities maintain that an artillery duel between the *Santa Rosa* and El Castillo ensued. For instance, Spencer-Hancock and Pritchard write of a "barrage of fire" from El Castillo ("El Castillo de Monterey," 236), and the most recent account of the Bouchard affair says that "from the *castillo* Sergeant Gómez poured shot down on the deck of the crowded ship" (Burgess, "Pirate or Patriot?" 44).

This version of events is problematic. It assumes that Bouchard, who had just circumnavigated the globe and had fought a good number of sea battles in his life, was such a novice that he would put his ship in the direct line of fire from a fort directly above it. How, under such withering and direct fire, could the *Santa Rosa* have possibly survived? And how, after all this, did Bouchard manage to take Monterey?

To their credit, those who present this version are not unaware of these issues and are also somewhat uncomfortable with their account. Bancroft confessed, "The result of this artillery duel was certainly well nigh inexplicable" (*History of California* 2: 228), and Spencer-Hancock and Pritchard added, "It is not clear why Bouchard and Peter Corney, English captain of the *Santa Rosa*, subjected their force to this barrage of fire from *El Castillo*" (236).

Most likely, the confusion stems from an inadvertent lack of precision in the retelling of the story. Bancroft summarizes Solá's report to Viceroy Félix María Calleja as follows: "The Santa Rosa opened fire on the shore battery. The . . . Spanish guns . . . were not all serviceable, but returned fire, and with so much skill and good luck were they aimed by the veterans and amateurs under Gómez [the Castillo commander], that after a two-hour battle during which they kept up a constant and effective fire, they did much damage to the frigate" (Bancroft, *History of California* 2: 228). The report actually referred to two different sites, with the "veterans" under Gómez and the "amateurs" under Vallejo. As the commander, Gómez had overall supervision. Since only Gómez was named, Bancroft most likely assumed that the artillery battle took place between El Castillo and the *Santa Rosa*. However, Bancroft was not entirely comfortable with that scenario. Two pages later, he says that he is "disposed to believe . . . that it may not have been the guns of the regular battery, the *castillo*, which did such execution . . . but those of a new battery on the beach" (230).

Osio's account is clearer and makes greater sense. He states that the *Santa Rosa* entered the harbor and positioned itself close enough to the bluff and the shore that defenders in the fort could do nothing but helplessly lob cannon over the ship, without causing any damage. This placement is consistent with Corney's account, for he says, "Being well acquainted with the bay, I ran in and came to at midnight, under the fort" (Corney, *Early Voyages*, 217). He is describing a deliberate positioning of his vessel. When Corney opened fire the next morning, it was on the town and the presidio, not on the fort, from which he correctly figured that he had little to fear. The firing was meant to provide cover for a landing party.

Corney, however, was unaware of the temporary battery manned by José de Jesús Vallejo on the beach, since that battery had been set up only a month earlier.

8. Vallejo's fire was able to do considerable damage to the *Santa Rosa* and also prevented a landing. As Vallejo recalled, "Captain Bouchard was unaware that Governor Solá had notice of his approximate arrival and was prepared for defense much better than what he thought. In fact he had placed cannon at a place near the beach. The insurgent chiefs, unaware that such a precaution had been taken, were approaching the place in which I, in command of the improvised battery, was awaiting to have the order imparted to me to fire. Finally the anxious messenger arrived. I did not give him time to refer the message, took aim at the black frigate and hit it with various volleys, one after the other at water level. . . . The insurgents yelled 'Mercy, Mercy.' I paid them no attention and continued loading cannon" (Vallejo, "Historical Reminiscences" 1: 57–58).

9. Many contemporaries were severely critical of Gómez' decision to order Vallejo to cease fire. The more extreme criticism spilled over into accusations that he was a traitor, that he had secretly sent Bouchard the plans of the Monterey defenses, and that he had a cousin in Bouchard's crew. Solá, noting that Gómez' own house had been hit by the insurgents, dismissed the criticism and recommended that Gómez be promoted to lieutenant. The promotion took effect the following year, and Gómez remained in Alta California until he returned to Mexico in 1822, after he had married into the Estudillo family. See Bancroft, *History of California* 2: 230, 470; 3: 759. Vallejo and Alvarado were still repeating these criticisms of Gómez in the 1870s: Vallejo, "Historical and Personal Memoirs" 2: 142; Alvarado, "History of California" 1: 122. Alvarado even claims that Bouchard himself, pretending to be an English scientist, had visited Monterey in 1817. However, Alvarado said the ruse was not entirely successful, since Ignacio Vallejo and Dolores Pico figured out that Bouchard's crew was actually Spanish by the way that they drank their brandy and rolled and smoked their cigarettes (111).

Osio's account helps us understand why Gómez would have ordered a cease-fire. Even though the *Santa Rosa* was damaged, the larger *Argentina* was still sitting offshore, beyond cannon range. Besides not wishing to increase the number of casualties, Gómez probably calculated that the damage inflicted on the *Santa Rosa* gave the Spanish enough leverage to be able to negotiate the departure of both ships.

10. The insurgents landed, according to Vallejo, at the beach of Doña Brígida, which was named after Brígida Armenta, whose family owned a house and a farm

in the neighborhood of the beach. The farm grew most of the vegetables that were consumed in Monterey. Osio is correct on the location: the beach of Doña Brígida is indeed in a cove which is bounded by Point Almejas on the east. It is about two and a half miles from El Mentidero. See Clark, *Monterey County Place Names*, 406.

11. Solá sent a small detachment led by José María Estrada to try to prevent Bouchard's landing, but it was unable to do so. See Bancroft, *History of California* 2: 232.

12. Women among the *californio* elite started families very early. María Inocente Pico, for instance, later complained that girls were not able to finish even rudimentary studies because their mothers would take them out of school to marry them off when they were still very young. She herself, she said, was taken out of school when she was fourteen, and she married only a year later. See Pico, "Cosas de California," 14. Using the data collected by Northrop, Gloria Ricci Lothrop calculated that the average family in California at the time had 8.84 children. See Lothrop, "Rancheras," 61.

Recent local studies have tended to discover somewhat smaller families. Katharine Meyer Lockhart found that fertility in San José was "higher than comparable figures for many populations during the same time period." The average number of children per marriage over the Spanish and Mexican period was a bit under eight. See Lockhart, "Demographic Profile," 60–67. In an investigation of Santa Bárbara and Los Angeles, Gloria Miranda has found that the average family sizes there were smaller. In 1834, Santa Bárbara families had 4.4 children, and Los Angeles families 3.9. In addition, over the Mexican period the average age of women at marriage slightly increased. See Miranda, "Hispano-Mexican Childrearing Practices," 308; and idem, "*Gente de Razón* Marriage Patterns," 7. The infant mortality rate is also an important demographic variable. Robert Wayne Eversole has found that it was comparatively low throughout the Mexican period. See Eversole, "Towns in Mexican Alta California," 169–78.

13. The evacuation of Monterey was hurried and, by most accounts, rather chaotic. José Fernández wrote, "The women and children were running around trying to gather up things they would need, but they did not have enough time to take food and clothing. It was a pitiful sight to see them in that condition" (Fernández, "Cosas de California," 16). Jacinto Rodríguez added that few women and children had time to dress (Rodríguez, "Narración," 7). María Inocente Pico, who was about seven years old at the time, remembered that "the families were so scattered and confused that it took a large number of men on horseback to get them back together and especially to learn if any were still wandering about lost" (Pico, "Cosas de California", 15).

14. José María Amador reported that Solá met Argüello with open arms and that Argüello spent the next four days integrating the Monterey and Santa Bárbara troops into his command and drilling the combined force (Amador, "Memorias," 5).

15. El Refugio, located about twenty-five miles west of Santa Bárbara, was granted to José Francisco Ortega or members of his family in the late 1790s. According to José de Jesús Vallejo, the ranch had a reputation for being a center of smuggling operations (Vallejo, "Historical Reminiscences," 11). William Heath Davis, for instance, stopped there and conducted illegal trade with the Ortegas in August 1818, only a few months before Bouchard arrived (Ogden, *California Sea Otter Trade*, 78).

16. The detachment from Santa Bárbara was led by Sergeant Carlos Antonio Carrillo. Relying on letters from Father Ramón Francisco Fernández de Ulibarrí, who was at Mission La Purísima, Bancroft says that the Spanish soldiers simply apprehended three of Bouchard's men who had wandered too far away from the main band in search of a cart. See Bancroft, *History of California* 2: 237.

After leaving El Refugio, Bouchard stopped at Santa Bárbara and arranged a prisoner exchange with the commander there, José de la Guerra y Noriega. Rafael González, a member of the military detachment at Santa Bárbara, recalled the beginning of the negotiations: "We saw that a boat was leaving the larger frigate seemingly headed toward Voluntario Hill. Then Capt. Guerra ordered Ensign Maitorena to take two soldiers and find out what that boat wanted. Lucas Olivera and I went with the Ensign, and, on reaching the hill, we saw that the boat was now fairly close to the shore. They shouted to us to go back, that they had a letter for the Commander 'of this little fort.' We retired to give the boat a chance to land on the shore. A man jumped into the water (which was up to his chest) from the boat. He had the letter on a stick in the form of a baton; he came running ashore and buried a part of the stick to which the letter was attached in the sand. Then he went back, climbed into the boat and pulled away, and when they were fifty or sixty yards from shore, they shouted to us, 'Take the letter.' We went up and the Ensign took the letter, which was for the Captain. I learned afterward through Don Domingo Carrillo that the letter was from the leader of the insurgents, Hipólito Bouchard, and it said that he had prisoners on board and would like to exchange them for his men who had been taken on land" (González, *Spanish Soldier*, 9).

According to Father José Señán, resident at Mission San Buenaventura, "these captives were instrumental in preventing an attack on San Buenaventura, for Bouchard swore repeatedly, while the rebel frigates lay anchored off Santa Bárbara, that he would release our people he held prisoner (he had only one, a disreputable individual named Molina) and would immediately leave these coasts without giving further trouble if we would hand over the three prisoners. After a good deal of bargaining we released them to avert serious consequences" (Señán, *Letters*, 116).

17. Many of the *californios* apparently thought that Bouchard continued down to Baja California and sacked Loreto and San José del Cabo. Vallejo even said, in the 1870s, that Osio, "at present a resident of San José del Cabo," told him that Bouchard's men sacked Loreto and were driven off by outraged residents of that town when they began to plunder the church there (Vallejo, "Historical and Per-

sonal Memoirs" 1: 180). Alvarado has substantially the same story (Alvarado, "History of California" 1: 133). However, Osio does not have this account, for he knew full well that Baja California was sacked by Cochrane's insurgents in 1822. A full account of this action is López Urrutia, *La escuadra chilena en Argentina*. Cochrane's account of ordering the ships to Baja California is in Dundonald, *Narrative of Services in the Liberation of Chile, Perú, and Brazil from Spanish and Portuguese Domination* (178–208).

18. After Bouchard left San Juan Capistrano, he continued south until he reached Vizcaíno Bay in Baja California on December 24, 1818. He spent a month repairing his ships on Cedros Island off the bay. He had no contact with any ships except an English vessel which he visited on January 15. Bouchard set sail on January 17 and reached San Blas on January 25. As Osio recounts, he made his headquarters at the Three Marías. He took at least one prize, the Spanish vessel *Las Animas* out of Nicaragua, and had a hostile encounter with another vessel flying the Spanish flag. Bouchard spent more than a month blockading San Blas, finally leaving for Acapulco on March 1. During his journey he kept "the authorities in the various ports in a state of excitement for weeks," in the words of Lewis Bealer. At Realejo, Nicaragua, the ship that Bouchard was commanding, the *Santa Rosa*, was attacked and disabled by the vessel he had encountered at San Blas, which turned out to be a Chilean privateer. See Bealer, "Privateers of Buenos Aires," 139–72; Caillet-Bois, *Historia naval argentina*, 174–75; and Carranza, *Campañas navales de la República Argentina* 3: 128–33. We have been unable to corroborate the specifics of Osio's story about Bouchard. It is true, however, that Bouchard did spend five weeks off San Blas and that a vessel he commanded was hit by enemy fire. The manuscript indicates that Osio's source was Yndart or Martija. A José D. Yndart was identified by Bancroft as being engaged in the Acapulco trade in the 1840s when Osio was administrator of the Monterey Customs House, but we have been unable to identify him further. Whatever its origin, the story allows Osio to draw a moral lesson from the Bouchard affair. This was his purpose in all the sections of the manuscript that describe Alta California before his arrival.

19. According to Ratto, when Bouchard reached Valparaíso, he was imprisoned by Cochrane on charges of having illegally seized a Danish ship in Realejo, Nicaragua. After the matter was finally resolved—Bouchard served less than five months in prison—he was again given command of the *Argentina*. The ship, along with the *Santa Rosa*, served as a transport carrier for San Martín's expedition to Peru in 1820. Bouchard served for a while under Cochrane in this campaign and was apparently given some land in Peru at its conclusion. He settled there and died in January 1837, killed by one of his slaves.

20. This is one of the passages in the manuscript which indicates that Osio did at least rummage among the documents in the various archives to which he had access. He was something of a historian.

21. The content of this note is metaphorical. By saying that he had "pots of food

with one hundred or so ingredients," he means that he had a defense prepared, that is, cannons and cannonballs, muskets, and so on.

22. The communiqué proves that he was a cunning man, somewhat Machiavellian. Osio's description of the governor as behaving like a descendant of the Borgias demonstrates that he was at least somewhat familiar with Renaissance Italy.

23. The phrase means that one need not be too deferential.

24. The reconstruction of Monterey is described in Schuetz-Miller, *Building and Builders*, 164–66.

25. The *californios* generally detested the Mexican soldiers sent to them, who were often *mestizos* and whom they termed *cholos*. Alvarado recalled, "The majority of these soldiers were corrupt and lustful, and so audacious that not even their officers dared to impede their mutinies and other demonstrations. Quarrels and struggles among themselves were daily occurrences. . . . their conduct displeased the meritorious veterans who still wore the uniforms of the veterans of Hernán Cortés. The *cholos* wore their hair so short that it hardly showed one inch down their necks, while the old soldiers wore long hair down their backs. . . . This manner of dress contrasted clearly between a presidial soldier of California and one of the *cholos*" (Alvarado, "History of California" 3: 12–13).

26. According to José Fernández, the appointment of Agustín Fernández was made because the Mexican authorities felt that the major opposition in California to Mexican independence would come from the missionaries, many of whom had been born in Spain (Fernández, "Cosas de California", 47). María Inocente Pico described Canónigo Fernández as a fleshy man of average height, who had a flushed, but fair, complexion (Pico, "Cosas de California," 15). Juana Machado remembered above all his brightly colored red vestment (Machado, "Los tiempos pasados", 2). Vallejo remembered him and his retinue as being monte players and heavy drinkers (Vallejo, "Historical and Personal Memoirs" 1: 226).

27. Fort Ross, the headquarters of the Russian-American Company, is approximately fifty miles north of San Francisco on the Pacific coast. The settlement was founded in 1812 and was suspended in 1841. The establishment at Bodega Point, about eighteen miles south of Fort Ross, was called Port Rumiantsov, and it was used as an outpost by the Russians. See Beck and Haase, *Historical Atlas of California*, 40. José Fernández stated that the *canónigo* toyed with the idea of trying to drive the Russians out but came to the conclusion that the indigenous people of the area supported their presence and would not countenance a Mexican attempt to drive them out (Fernández, "Cosas de California," 46). On the fort, see Tikhmenev, *Russian-American Company*, 132–44, 224–33; and Gibson, *Imperial Russia*, 112, 174–98. Fernández was accompanied on his visit to Fort Ross by Father Mariano Payeras, whose account of the journey can be found in Mathes, "El comisionado"; and Cutter, "Franciscan Visit."

28. Solá was chosen delegate from Alta California to the national congress (Bancroft, *History of California* 2: 471). An interesting example of the way the *ca-*

lifornios still living in California in the 1870s were alert to U.S. misreadings of their history is in José Fernández' "Cosas de California," a dictation given to Bancroft's staff. Describing Solá's departure, Fernández says, "I want to mention that a few years ago I read a work written in English in which it was said that the first delegate sent to the Mexican congress by the *californios* was one of the sergeants from the presidio companies, a real brute of a man, the best that they could send. This statement is completely false" (Fernández, "Cosas de California," 48).

Chapter 3

1. Those who lived in the missions in the middle of the mission chain were the Chumash. In 1791 Alejandro Malaspina, who had a very low opinion of most of Alta California's indigenous peoples, excepted the Chumash from his strictures about the native peoples' lack of intelligence (Rawls, *Indians of California*, 41). At the beginning of the period of Spanish colonization in the 1770s, there were probably 18,500 people living in the Chumash region. By the 1820s almost all of the Chumash had been incorporated into the mission system, and by 1832 there were fewer than 1,400 at Santa Bárbara, La Purísima, and Santa Ynés. See J. R. Johnson, "Chumash and the Missions," 365. In the case of the Chumash, serious population decline preceded missionization. In fact, their decision to move into the mission system may have been a strategy for coping with that demographic catastrophe. See Larson, Johnson, and Michaelsen, "Missionization."

2. The Chumash revolt of 1824 was the largest organized indigenous uprising in the history of the California missions. The best account is Sandos, "Levantamiento! The 1824 Chumash Uprising Reconsidered." (A more popular version of the same essay appeared as Sandos, "Levantamiento! The 1824 Chumash Uprising.") Sandos emphasizes the indigenous roots of the rebellion. He interprets it as an attempt on the part of the Chumash to preserve their culture against the attempts of the missionaries to uproot it.

The missionaries tended to interpret the revolt as an uprising against the cruelties of the soldiers, in spite of the missionaries' attempts to restrain such acts. "Who gave the power to Corporal Cota to render such a despotic punishment?" cried Father Ripoll. "Why are the complaints of these unfortunate people made by the Fathers in their behalf not heard?" (Geiger, "Fray Antonio Ripoll's Description," 355). The Guardian of the Apostolic College of San Fernando argued, "The revolt was not against the missionaries; on the contrary, the revolting Indians wanted to have the fathers go along with them, and told them that they would care for them" (F. J. Weber, *Mission of the Passes*, 23). Doubtless such desires partly contributed to the revolt. But Osio's explanation, that the revolt aimed at freeing the participants from Mexican and church rule, was a more expansive view that turns out to be largely consistent with Sandos' later interpretation.

This larger significance was given to the event by contemporary *californios* and by later ones as well. In a report to the general government, Governor Argüello stated, in terms close enough to those Osio used to give rise to the strong suspicion that the two of them had talked about this affair, "Their plan . . . was no other than to rid themselves of all of us, that is, the *gente de razón*, and remain in their old gentile liberty" (Thompson, *El Gran Capitán*, 81). This interpretation persisted in Mexican California. Alvarado stated, for instance, "The object of the uprising was the extermination of all the white people resident at the missions, cities, towns, estates, and *ranchos* of Alta California" (Alvarado, "History of California" 2: 43).

3. The best introduction to conflict among the native populations of Alta California is McCorkle, "Intergroup Conflict." McCorkle emphasizes the limited nature of these conflicts. The desire to seize territory and exploit peoples was not present on a permanent basis among several of the native peoples. There were, he says, "no native California conquest states." He also notes that at least two regions in native California "appear to have developed effective methods for limiting armed intersocietal conflicts" (700). See also Moriarity, "Accommodation and Conflict Resolution." In the same vein, José Fernández, who fought against the native peoples while he was in the military, wrote, "They fought with valor and sometimes they proved very clever in their assaults or in preparing ambushes but they were neither treacherous nor bloodthirsty" (Fernández, "Cosas de California," 14).

There was some tension in central Alta California between the Chumash and the Yokuts (Phillips, *Indians and Intruders*, 30). Angustias de la Guerra reports that tension existed between the Chumash at San Buenaventura and those at the other missions, and between the Chumash and the Gabrieliño people to the south (Guerra, "Ocurrencias," 7). On Angustias de la Guerra, see Sánchez, "Angustias de la Guerra de Ord," in Sánchez, Pita, and Reyes, *Crítica*.

4. Tensions were apparently running fairly high in the Chumash region. In 1822 Father Mariano Payeras had drawn up some elaborate plans, apparently never put into effect, for the defense of La Purísima (Hageman and Ewing, *Archeological and Restoration Study*, 257). According to an oral tradition collected by anthropologist John P. Harrington in 1914, rumors of violence to come were widespread among the soldiers and the indigenous people (Blackburn, "Chumash Revolt of 1824," 223–24). The soldiers and the neophytes were both hearing that the other group was going to kill them at mass.

5. Alfred Robinson later noted that Uría had a certain number of "eccentricities," such as "constantly annoying four large cats, his daily companions," or when "with a long stick [he] thumped upon the heads of his Indian boys, and seemed delighted thus to gratify his singular propensities" (Geiger, *Franciscan Missionaries*, 258). Osio's account of Uría's actions that day at Santa Ynés cannot be verified, but it is consistent with what is known about this man's behavior. Engelhardt reports that in the early twentieth century a story about Uría's shooting an Indian was still widely circulating at Santa Ynés. In addition, it is agreed by all that the buildings were burned as Osio recounts. See Engelhardt, *Missions and Missionaries* 2: 195–96.

The revolt began on a Saturday because an indigenous man had come to Santa

Ynés to visit an imprisoned relative and the corporal of the guard there, Valentín Cota, had ordered him whipped. The date of this whipping is unclear in the sources, but apparently the plotters at La Purísima were so incensed at this episode that they began the revolt sooner than they had planned. See Bancroft, *History of California* 2: 528; and Engelhardt, *Missions and Missionaries* 2: 195.

6. Eibar is a city in Guipúzcoa, Spain, and is famous for its weapons factories. It is located about fifteen miles southwest of Bilbao.

7. Spanish soldiers began their conquests in the Americas wearing the heavy armor that they had used in Spain. From an early date, however, they began to imitate the indigenous peoples they were fighting and substituted more flexible and cooler animal skins and cotton batting for their armor. See D. J. Weber, *Spanish Frontier*, 43.

8. The two priests at Mission La Purísima were Antonio Rodríguez and Blas Ordaz, and the corporal was Tiburcio Tapia.

9. Osio is being ironic here, for Ordaz had an unsavory reputation among his brethren as being a priest of notoriously loose morals and one who was intimate with a number of women. In 1832 Narciso Durán, the president of the missions, issued a circular letter in which he denounced an unnamed friar for not conducting himself properly as a Franciscan priest. Engelhardt thought that Durán was referring to Ordaz. Bishop Alemany confided to his diary in 1850 that he had discovered that Ordaz had fathered three children. See Geiger, *Franciscan Missionaries*, 173–74. Perhaps Osio is implying that the women were saying things about themselves and Ordaz that their husbands should not know!

10. Ordaz accompanied the group, while Rodríguez remained with the Indians. See Engelhardt, *Missions and Missionaries* 3: 196.

11. The member of the Sepúlveda family was Dolores Sepúlveda. According to Bancroft, his traveling companion, Ramón Sotelo, was also killed. Sotelo was a religious freethinker who was once sentenced to a chain gang for having expressed views "not even a Protestant would have dared to entertain" (Bancroft, *History of California* 2: 412). Engelhardt reports that the other two victims were named Simón Colima and Mansísidor de Loreto. Little else is known of them. See Engelhardt, *Missions and Missionaries* 3: 196.

12. Pacomio, one of the indigenous leaders at Mission La Purísima, was credited by some later accounts with being the main planner and instigator of the entire revolt. According to Vallejo, he was a great favorite of the clergy and the military at the mission, and he received training in carpentry from the missionaries and in musketry from the soldiers. In the early 1820s he sent emissaries to all the indigenous peoples living in the vicinity to organize the revolt. He is supposed to have told Father Rodríguez, who had stayed at La Purísima, "Better a hundred casks of blood should flow than that it should be a hundred thousand. If in this war I kill all the whites, not over four thousand persons will perish, but if the whites win and kill off all the Indians, many hundreds of thousands of human beings with souls made in

the likeness of God, as I have been told by the missionary fathers who educated me, will lose their lives" (Vallejo, "Historical and Personal Memoirs" 2: 279).

13. The most direct account of what happened at Santa Bárbara is Ripoll's report to Sarría, in Geiger, "Fray Antonio Ripoll's Description." If Osio is correct that the Santa Bárbara plotters were determined to go ahead with a predetermined plan even though it had been discovered, the rebels showed themselves able to improvise quite well. The local indigenous leader, Andrés Sagimomatsee, told Ripoll that he had heard that the soldiers were going to shoot them while they were attending Sunday mass, and so Andrés evacuated the women from the mission. He got Ripoll to go to the presidio to inform Guerra y Noriega and, in the interest of calming things down, to persuade the commander to remove the mission guard (which consisted of only three soldiers). Andrés and his people took advantage of Ripoll's absence to arm themselves. On Andrés, see Sandos, "Christianization Among the Chumash."

According to Angustias de la Guerra, Ripoll emotionally and tearfully begged the commander not to send troops against the Indians (Guerra, "Ocurrencias," 8). Guerra y Noriega consented. When Ripoll returned, with the order for the guard to withdraw, a scuffle ensued. In Ripoll's words, "But as it always happens when a large crowd is involved, there are some who are bolder than others, despite the care exercised by those in charge who intend no harm—one of them [Andrés Sagimomatsee's men] told the soldiers to leave their muskets and to proceed to the presidio without them. When he said this, others took the muskets from the soldiers' hands and the Indians wounded two of them with chopping knives because they did not hand over their arms willingly" (Geiger, "Fray Antonio Ripoll's Description," 349). Guerra y Noriega then left the presidio for the mission to investigate and avenge this scuffle.

14. *Guerra* means "war," and thus Osio was implying that the captain was not a very fine warrior. The fact that Osio uncharacteristically states his source for the following story about Guerra y Noriega's stopping the battle for the meal probably indicates that he does not believe it. (The brother-in-law was probably one of the Carrillos mentioned in the manuscript: Guerra y Noriega was married to María Antonia Carrillo, sister of Anastasio, Carlos, and José Antonio Carillo). According to his daughter, who was nine years old at the time, Guerra y Noriega received news about the revolt on Saturday afternoon. See Guerra, "Ocurrencias," 7.

15. Angustias de la Guerra says that the rebels at Santa Bárbara used the other priest at the mission, Father Antonio Jayme, as a human shield to protect themselves from the shots of the soldiers. See Guerra, "Ocurrencias," 9.

16. According to Angustias de la Guerra, her father broke off the fight after about five hours, when the hour to eat arrived. When the Mexicans returned, most of the Indians had already left. See Guerra, "Ocurrencias," 9. Ripoll agrees that the soldiers broke off the engagement and returned to the presidio and that then the Indians left (Geiger, "Fray Antonio Ripoll's Description," 350).

17. Soldiers scoured the countryside looking for any indigenous people they could find. Ripoll has accounts of them murdering some nonparticipants whom they stumbled upon. See Geiger, "Fray Antonio Ripoll's Description," 351.

18. Estrada described the approach to the mission in this way: "On the 16th, at two o'clock in the morning, after we had overcome indescribable obstacles on account of the declivity of the mountain, we succeeded in ascending and in dragging the cannon by hand. Observing that it was about time to operate it, after having placed it under cover for protection along with the munitions in charge of twenty-eight horsemen under a corporal, I commanded that two advance guards, each composed of fifteen horsemen under the command of Corporals Nicholas Alviso and Trinidad Espinosa, to separate to the right and the left, and in a circular movement to proceed toward the mission in order to prevent the flight of the rebels, and make them meet our forces. In this manner, step by step we approached the mission until we were within shooting distance of our cannon. Protected by thirty-three infantrymen, this firing began at about eight A.M., always advancing until we reached within shooting distance of our muskets. From their loopholes, the Indians poured out a lively gunfire at us with their one-pound cannon, and also sent out a shower of arrows. Boldly despising that resistance, the artillery replied with brilliantly directed shots, and the musketry with a not less active firing" (Engelhardt, *Mission La Concepción Purísima*, 51–52).

19. This is the judgment of many modern historians. Phillips, for instance, says, "That Christianity was only superficially adopted by many neophytes is quite apparent." Phillips quotes Father Gerónimo Boscana, who, speaking of the neophytes, remarked, "As all their operations are accompanied by stratagems and dissimulation, they easily gain our confidence and at every pass we are deluded" (Phillips, *Chiefs and Challengers*, 31). On Boscana, see also Haas, *Conquests and Historical Identities*, 29. Francis F. Guest has recently written, "The converted Indians, if they and their children remained faithful to the form of Christianity they had learned, tended to live a spiritual life that was largely artificial" (Guest, "California Missions," 267).

20. An *hechicero* is a shaman or witch doctor.

21. Estrada reported, "It seemed that the Indians wanted to take to flight, but, seeing that the cavalry had completely surrounded them, and that Don Francisco Pacheco with twenty horsemen and drawn sword hastened to intercept them, the Indians could not help seeing that they were completely cut off. They then availed themselves of the advocacy and favor of Fr. Antonio Rodríguez, the missionary of said mission. He agreed to their clamors and sent a written supplication that the firing cease, and then he appeared openly in person. I commanded that the firing stop" (Engelhardt, *Mission La Concepción Purísima*, 52).

22. Seven men were executed. They were actually shot for alleged complicity in the killings of the four Mexicans. See Engelhardt, *Mission La Concepcíon Purísima*, 53.

23. Vallejo identified this Pacomio with a José Pacomio, a carpenter, who lived

at Monterey in the 1830s and served in public office there. See Vallejo, "Histori-cal and Personal Memoirs" 2: 279, 290; and Bancroft, *History of California* 3: 675. Alvarado said that with the single exception of Solano, Pacomio was "the most intelligent Indian ever produced in Alta California" (Alvarado, "History of Cali-fornia" 2: 67).

24. The fugitives had gone to a place about twelve miles past San Emigdio Ranch, to a village near the shore of Buena Vista Lake, about sixty miles from the Santa Bárbara coast (Cook, *Expeditions*, 204). Sarría described the site as "an islet in a large lagoon surrounded by dense tules along its shore. The path to the lagoon was defended by a muddy and marshy area. People on horseback could not pass through without experiencing extreme difficulty and danger" (Sarría, "Carta al Obispo de Sonora").

25. This was actually the second offensive against the fugitives. The first, led by Lieutenant Narciso Fabregat, was defeated by the fugitives, although the Mexican sources tend to blame bad weather. See Bancroft, *History of California* 2: 534. The force of which Osio is speaking comprised two parts. One force left from Santa Bár-bara, but it was actually commanded by Captain Pablo de la Portilla. His diary is in Cook, *Expeditions*, 154–56. Another force, commanded by Antonio del Valle, left from San Miguel. The two contingents joined up before finally setting out for the tules. See Bancroft, *History of California* 2: 535.

26. Ripoll did not want to go on the expedition. Fearing that the soldiers would butcher the runaways, he did not want to be associated with that in any way. See Geiger, "Fray Antonio Ripoll's Description," 363. Sarría convinced him to go, after Sarría had seen Governor Argüello. As Sarría recalled, "I appeared before the governor of the Province. . . . I negotiated with this *jefe* and requested that he grant the Indians a general pardon, if they returned to the mission. I easily achieved my goal, because when the Señor Gobernador heard this account, he felt the same way about it that I did" (Sarría, "Carta al Obispo de Sonora").

27. Portilla wrote, "Having observed that they [the fugitives] hoisted a white flag (which according to previous arrangement was the signal that they would re-ceive me peacefully), I halted the troop at a gun-shot and went toward them in the company of the Reverend Fathers [Sarría and Ripoll]. Seeing my intention, some of them came to greet me, among them one named Jaime who had some authority among the Indians. I delivered to him the pardon which I had brought from the governor. He said that they would accept it and that they were ready to return to their mission, but they were obliged to call attention to the reasons which had led to their uprising as well as to their apprehension lest, if they surrendered their weapons, they would be treated like the Indians of La Purísima. I realized immedi-ately that they were possessed by great fear and so I undertook to relieve their feel-ings, using whatever methods were dictated by good judgment. In the afternoon I succeeded, when there was another conference with the chiefs" (Cook, *Expeditions*, 155). One of Portilla's soldiers, Rafael González, thinks that the priests had more

effect on the fugitives than his commander did: "Father Sarría and Father Ripoll conquered the Indians with well chosen words" (González, *Spanish Soldier*, 21).

The Jaime mentioned by Portilla appears in another oral tradition collected by Harrington. Luisa Ygnacio, a Chumash born a few years after the revolt, called Jaime a "doctor, singer, and teacher." He was clearly a person of authority in the community. See Hudson, "Chumash Revolt of 1824," 124.

28. Sarría reported, "After a five-day journey we arrived at the valley of the tules. After a day's rest, Captain de la Portilla, Reverend Fr. Antonio Ripoll, the administrator of Mission Sta. Bárbara, and I went to speak with the fugitives. The three of us were unarmed and kept ourselves at a fair distance from the soldiers so that the Indians would not be afraid to speak with us. They came out to receive us, displaying much distrust and fear. They did not want to lay down their weapons, mainly bows and arrows and a few firearms which they had taken from the mission. All of this was overlooked, and they proceeded to reveal their complaints, to their satisfaction. Their complaints were respectfully heard, and they were granted safe conduct. They met with us a number of times at the same spot, and with peace, mutual joy, and satisfaction, they were convinced to return to the mission, taking advantage of the general pardon that was being granted to all, without exception.

"On June 13, a mass of thanksgiving was celebrated in a very beautiful wooded area at the place where we had met with the Indians. This year, the date coincided with the Feast of the Holy Trinity. The same Indians who had fled displayed their musical talent as they sang under the direction of their choir master, Jayme, one of the first ones to have taken part in the uprising. We remained there for three more days so that many families from nearby areas, who had become separated, could be reunited. On June 16 we left for Mission Sta. Bárbara, accompanied by many neophytes, male and female, of all ages, who previously had been fugitives. We walked very slowly so they could follow us, and the trip took seven days. Others then followed, coming in large groups. Very few are still missing; therefore, the mission is back to the way it was before. The fugitives from Sta. Ynés and La Purísima returned to their respective missions in the same manner, and to date, there are very few missing still" (Sarría, "Carta al Obispo de Sonora").

29. As J. Frank Dobie has summarized the matter, "The horses of the Californians multiplied astoundingly" (Dobie, *Mustangs*, 41). On the large numbers of wild horses, see Bancroft, *California Pastoral*, 336, 339, 346. Horses were periodically slaughtered to prevent their numbers from increasing too much. See, for example, Bancroft, *History of California* 2: 133, 182, for instances of this during the first decade of the nineteenth century.

30. John Begg was the agent in Santiago, Chile, for the British trading firm headed by James Brotherton. Begg and Company opened South American offices in Lima and Guayaquil in 1820 and 1821, before two of its employees, William Hartnell and Hugh McCullough, established a business concern in Alta California in 1822. See Dakin, *Lives of William Hartnell*, 19; and Ogden, "Hides and Tallow,"

255. According to Vallejo, Hartnell was known to the indigenous people and to the missionaries as *pestaña blanca*, white eyelash (Vallejo, "Historical and Personal Memoirs" 2: 20).

31. Speaking of the U.S. trading presence in the 1820s. José Fernández later wrote, "The majority of those who established trading houses in Alta California were citizens of the state of Massachusetts, and, when the Indians asked them where they had come from, they would answer Boston. . . . The Indians believed that all the white men or 'güeros,' as they called them, came from just one place, so whenever they saw an Englishman, or German, or an American, they would say, 'There goes a Boston' (Fernández, "Cosas de California," 45).

32. This was not a unanimous opinion. José Fernández, admittedly more of a soldier than a merchant, stated, "Señor Robinson did not have the pleasant manners that were so necessary to charm the *californios* who always preferred to do business with people who would flatter them, and they paid no attention to philosophers or stern people" (Fernández, "Cosas de California," 59). On Robinson's important *Life in California*, see Churchill, "Adventurers and Prophets," 18–45.

Chapter 4

1. The Point of Pines is on the tip of the Monterey peninsula, about four miles from El Mentidero.

2. The word *carajo* means something like prick, or stronger.

3. The *Asia* had been involved in the events of 1821. It was the vessel that carried Viceroy Juan O'Donojú to Veracruz and Conde de Venadito to Havana. See Bancroft, *History of California* 3: 25.

4. Bancroft has a full account of the incident: see *History of California* 3: 25. This incident is also referred to in Worcester, *Sea Power and Chilean Independence*, 10, 25, 35, 81. The episode became the basis of an early Jules Verne novella, *The Mutineers*.

5. The "three guarantees" is a reference to the 1821 Plan of Iguala drawn up by Agustín de Iturbide and Vicente Guerrero. The guarantees were independence (Mexico would become a constitutional monarchy), religion (Roman Catholicism would remain the state religion), and equality (all inhabitants were to possess equal rights). The "castles and lions" (*castillos y leones*) refers to the flag of Spain, which contains castles, symbolizing Castilla, and lions, symbolizing León.

6. The wedding was on April 30, 1825.

7. See John 19. 26–27.

8. The "three initials" were SMC. They stood for Su Majestad Católica, "His Catholic Majesty."

9. Bancroft (*History of California* 3: 26) cites Vallejo's account that the quarrel was between Arnaldo Pierola from the ship and Juan López from the town.

10. This was true at some points in the history of Alta California, but not during the turbulent revolutionary years of the 1810s. José Fernández recalled, "During the time that Mexico was fighting for its independence, the rulers of the

mother country had completely forgotten California and had stopped sending the missionaries their pay, and the soldiers had received no clothing. . . . Truthfully, if it had not been for the missionaries who provided the troops at the four presidios with provisions, California would have reverted back to the Indians, because many times the soldiers expressed the desire to return to avoid dying from hunger or cold" (Fernández, "Cosas de California," 44).

11. Admiral Isidro Atondo y Antillón led an attempt to conquer and populate Baja California, which lasted from 1683 to 1685. The attempt failed because of the hostility of the indigenous people and because the peninsula was suffering from an extreme drought. See Martínez, *History of Lower California,* 106–14. According to Martínez, the expedition cost 225,000 pesos. See also Crosby, *Antigua California,* 11. Documents relating to the expedition can be found in Mathes, *Documentos.*

12. Salvatierra wrote a series of reports to New Spain seeking crown funding for the missions. Some of these reports made it to Madrid. One even reached the Council of the Indies and was read there in the presence of Felipe V. When the authorities in New Spain proved reluctant to send to California the funds that the crown had ordered, the Jesuits began to pressure the government, and the provincial ordered Salvatierra to travel to Mexico City to help in the negotiations. See Crosby, *Antigua California,* 67–68, 78; and Venegas, *Salvatierra,* 181.

13. When Serrano asked Rodríguez about the property, Serrano was probably not at that time *alcalde* but had a more subsidiary position, such as clerk or secretary. The fact that Osio specifically attributes the story to a ninety-six-year-old veteran indicates that he himself was not ready to vouch for the particulars, but only for the general moral of the account.

14. Osio is referring here to Echeandía, who, he thought, was unfairly critical of Argüello. In the last half of the 1820s Argüello occasionally argued that he had been awarded the rank of lieutenant colonel but that the commission had never been delivered to him. See Bancroft, *History of California* 3: 12.

Chapter 5

1. According to Juana Machado, Echeandía was tall, thin, and somewhat pale. He was possessed of elegant manners, was extremely friendly, and was fond of dancing and other diversions. See Machado, "Los tiempos pasados," 6.

2. Texcoco was one of the lakes surrounding the Aztec capital of Tenochtitlán, the site of Mexico City. Osio is being ironic here, for it was far smaller than the Sea of Cortés or the Gulf of California.

3. After independence the *San Carlos* was renamed the *Morelos.* Osio's use of the older name is significant. It points to the ambivalence felt by the *californios* of Osio's generation toward the Mexican government.

4. Bancroft and Hutchinson give the name of the vessel as the *Nieves.* See Bancroft, *History of California* 3: 9; and Hutchinson, *Frontier Settlement,* 127. The *Constanza,* the vessel to which Osio refers here, was a schooner, as he says. It sailed out

of San Blas and had made at least one trip to Alta California in 1824, the year before it took Echeandía to Loreto (Bancroft, *History of California* 2: 519).

5. The *comisario* was José María Herrera.

6. After being replaced as governor by Echeandía, Argüello remained in San Diego for a time before he eventually returned to San Francisco, where he resumed his service as commandant. He was never able to establish good relations with his successor, and apparently he began to drink more heavily. His health was described as "broken" in 1828, when Echeandía relieved him of his command. His antipathy to Echeandía was so well known that he was offered the leadership of the Solís revolt in 1829. This he declined. He died at San Francisco on March 27, 1830. See Bancroft, *History of California* 3: 12.

7. Echeandía's opinions were representative of Mexican liberalism, which emphasized the liberty and equality of all, including the Indians. Angustias de la Guerra later told Bancroft's staff, that "when he [Echeandía] arrived in California in 1825 he came speaking of the republican and liberal principles which filled the heads of Mexicans in those days" (Monroy, *Thrown among Strangers*, 122). Forty years after Echeandía had left Alta California, Alvarado remembered him as the one who had most helped his generation understand the "true principle of republican liberty" (Alvarado, "History of California" 2: 133). Echeandía's liberalism struck a chord among the younger generation. Mariano Guadalupe Vallejo recalled that he, Alvarado, and Castro had secretly collected and read books which dealt with "the goddess we called Liberty" when they were growing up in Monterey and that they had gotten into trouble when they were discovered (Vallejo, "Historical and Personal Memoirs" 3: 90–93).

8. Osio was well aware of the sad state of the supplies for the military. In 1844 he wrote to Governor Micheltorena that, on his arrival at San Francisco in 1830, "I noticed the lack of clothing of the company of soldiers to the extent that the only means to tell they were soldiers was the *fusil*. The clothing worn by a soldier who was carrying a message was a dirty shirt made of woolen blankets, and for pantaloons he had a blanket tied to the waistline crossing the legs so as to make a man's way of dressing. The misery filled me with compassion for these poor people, and at the same time Señor Mariano G. Vallejo as commander of that company asked me to help give better clothing to these soldiers, so I gave him hats, clothing, and money amounting to 216 pesos. Afterward he was in need of meat, and I gave him eight bulls" (Osio to Micheltorena, June 12, 1844, in Osio Papers). On the generally poor state of the military supplies, see Langellier and Peterson, "Lances and Leather Jackets," 6–7.

9. Herrera was the first treasury official appointed by the independent Mexican government to work in Alta California. As *comisario* he reported directly to the *comisario general* of the western states of Sinaloa and Sonora, whose office was in Arispe, Sonora. He was thus independent of the governor. This arrangement was bound to cause controversy. Before Herrera's arrival, finances had been handled by

the Monterey presidio commander, Mariano Estrada, on the authority of an appointment by the *diputación*. Estrada would hardly have welcomed Herrera. In addition, Estrada was also responsible for the administration of the *rancho nacional* in Salinas. He probably was not in the habit of keeping the presidio, territorial, and *rancho* accounts sufficiently separate from his personal accounts to please the new *comisario*. See Bancroft, *History of California* 3: 59; and Tays, "Revolutionary California," 64.

10. As Osio makes clear, the quarrel between Herrera and Echeandía revolved around jurisdictional disputes, with Herrera claiming an independence from the governor which Echeandía found intolerable. In September 1826 Herrera's superiors rebuked Echeandía for not supporting Herrera. Finally, on his own authority, Echeandía along with the *diputación* toyed with the idea of suspending Herrera, but they were unable to convince José Antonio Carrillo, José Antonio Estudillo, or Osio to assume the post. They finally appointed Pablo González *contador* and severely limited Herrera's functions to the performance of banal and routine matters. Herrera then resigned and decided to go to Mexico to plead his case, but Echeandía refused to allow him to leave Alta California and appointed Manuel Jimeno Casarín as acting *comisario*. See Bancroft, *History of California* 3: 60–65; and Tays, "Revolutionary California," 81–83.

11. The Codornices mountain range is located on the eastern side of San Francisco Bay and stretches south to the Monterey area.

12. El Toro is one of the highest peaks in the mountains behind Monterey. It rises to 3,650 feet. See Clark, *Monterey County Place Names*, 346.

13. The details of this affair are murky, but the account that Osio relates here is also told by many of the Bancroft memorialists, indicating that the *californios* believed that Herrera was implicated in what was basically a work stoppage by a segment of the military. All these accounts possess a basic pattern. On the one hand, the *californios* generally regarded the Mexican government's inability to pay the California soldiers as an indication of Mexico's lack of concern for Alta California. On the other hand, when the soldiers reacted normally to this state of affairs, the *californios* then blamed Herrera—a clear symbol of the Mexican government in their eyes—for fomenting revolution. Since Mexico created the situation in which instability was the only possible outcome, it seemed only logical to the *californios* to blame a representative of the Mexican government when the instability actually occurred. In other words, this story points to the profoundly suspicious attitude of the *californios* toward the central government. As we shall see, Osio himself came to the conclusion that these attitudes were ultimately self-destructive, since they prevented the *californios* from recognizing their true interests.

14. The *corifeo* is the leader of the chorus in the Greek theater. This classical and literary reference perhaps indicates that Osio, in hindsight, concluded that, even as early as 1828, Mexican Alta California was on the road to a tragic end and that the Solís revolt symbolized the direction in which the territory was moving.

15. The revolt of Estanislao is one of the most famous in the history of Alta California, yet it remains difficult to piece together the various episodes which made up the whole. What is clear is that two large expeditions were sent against the rebels. One, led by José Sánchez in the beginning of May 1829, was beaten back by the indigenous forces, and the other, led by Mariano Guadalupe Vallejo at the end of May and the beginning of June, finally defeated them.

Yet most contemporaries, including Osio, speak of still another expedition. They say that it took place in the fall of 1828, although they differ on the question of who led it and what happened. Most modern scholars who have studied the matter, notably Cook and Holterman, believe that a fall expedition was sent out, but they are unable to fix its outcome precisely.

What happened in the fall was the following. In November 1828, when it became obvious to Father Narciso Durán that Estanislao and some other Indians from Mission San José were not going to return to the mission from a visit to their *ranchería*, he wrote Ignacio Martínez, the commander of the San Francisco presidio, and asked him to send out a force under "Sergeant Soto" against the runaways. Martínez wrote Governor Echeandía a week and a half later, "I have arranged that a party of twenty men go out." But there is nothing in the record to indicate what, if anything, this expedition accomplished. To further complicate matters, Osio insists that Soto died a few days after the return of the expedition, yet the records at Mission Santa Clara unequivocally state that Soto died on May 27, which would mean that he was wounded on the Sánchez expedition.

We believe that there were three forays against Estanislao and that Osio's account inadvertently confuses the first two. This confusion is understandable when it is recalled that Antonio Soto was the father of Osio's second wife, Narcisa Florencia Soto, and Osio's account can be understood as that preserved in the Soto family tradition. Naturally enough, this tradition would emphasize the role of Antonio Soto and portray him as heroically as possible.

The following version seems to us to make the most sense and to take into account most of the available evidence. The first expedition should be understood as a reconnaissance expedition, sent by Martínez to satisfy Durán. Running away from the missions was hardly unusual, and when Martínez heard about Estanislao from the priest, he sent out a small party to investigate the matter. Soto was an obvious choice to lead this foray, since, as Osio says, he could get along in the indigenous language (at least well enough to understand that he was being insulted). Then, on the basis of information provided by the Soto party, the Sánchez expedition was sent out in May. Soto was on this expedition and was mortally wounded in battle.

We think it is significant that there is a close correspondence between Sánchez' account of the second expedition and Osio's account of the first. For instance, the tactics which Osio has Soto employ in the first expedition—sending some men through the forest and some around it—are exactly those which Sánchez reports as having been utilized on May 8, 1829, by his men in the second expedition. In his report, Sánchez states that Soto fought valiantly and was "severely wounded." Over the course of twenty years, the Soto family probably—and naturally—began mistakenly to place the time of Soto's bravery during the expedition he himself had commanded, rather than during the expedition in which he was merely a participant.

The best treatments of this whole affair are Holterman, "Revolt of Estanislao"; and Cook, *Expeditions*, 165–80. A very fine and accessible account of Estanislao is contained in Rice, Bullough, and Orsi, *Elusive Eden*, 45–59.

16. Estanislao was a member of the Lakisamnes, a part of the Yokut group. (The spelling of the name varies tremendously. We follow that given in Heizer, *California*, 470.) Many years later Juan Bojorques, who participated in the campaigns, offered this description: "He was about six feet tall, his skin was more white than bronze, and he was very muscular like a horse. He had a very masculine-looking face" (Bojorques, "Recuerdos," 21). The *ranchería* was located by the Lakisamne River (now the Stanislaus River, which, like Stanislaus County, is named for Estanislao), some fifty miles to the north and east of Mission San José (Beck and Haase, *Historical Atlas of California*, 22).

17. The proverb literally means "There is no better wedge than one made from its own pole." Its general meaning is "There is no worse enemy than an alienated friend." In this instance Osio is implying that the most cruel punishment is that which is given to you by your own people.

18. Osio uses the word *sumaria*, which we have rendered as "dossier." In a legal investigation, a judge would collect oral statements from the defendant, victims, and witnesses. These statements were collected into a document known as a *sumaria*. See Langum, *Law and Community*, 63.

19. This was Mariano Estrada, who retired in 1829. See Bancroft, *History of California* 2: 608.

20. The *Danube* was a vessel from New York consigned to Hartnell by Daniel Coit, a U.S. trader doing business from Lima. It was supposed to arrive in March 1829 but did not make Monterey until September. During the fall it engaged in a very successful coastal trade before it was wrecked off San Pedro early in 1830. See Dakin, *Lives of William Hartnell*, 144–46.

21. Vallejo and Rocha were sent to San Diego aboard the *Brookline*, a vessel from Boston consigned to William A. Gale. See Bancroft, *History of California* 3: 73, 82, 135, 137.

22. Solís offered the leadership of the revolt to Luis Argüello. José Fernández, one of Argüello's soldiers, stated, "I witnessed Solís offer to surrender his command to Argüello and serve under him." Fernández attributed his old commander's unwillingness to assume command to his reluctance to take unfair advantage of Echeandía. In this account Argüello "was not on good terms with Echeandía, and he believed that it would not be right to make him suffer from the weight of his revenge at the moment in which other enemies were on his back" (Fernández, "Cosas de California," 59–62).

23. Bancroft suggests that the artillery sergeant was Lázaro Piña (*History of California* 3: 76). Piña was a career military man who served at Monterey, San Rafael, San Francisco, and Sonoma. He went to Mexico during the war with the United States and was killed at the battle of Cerro Gordo in April 1847 (Bancroft, *History of California* 4: 780).

24. La Cieneguita was a small *rancho* a few miles directly west of Mission Santa Bárbara, on the border of the Santa Bárbara *pueblo* lands.

25. María Inocente Pico, whose brother, José de Jesús Pico, was involved in the revolt, stated that Pacheco promised that he would do everything he could to assure them of better treatment in the future (Pico, "Cosas de California," 17).

26. The American ship was the *Volunteer,* under the command of John Coffin Jones Jr. Bancroft states that fifteen prisoners were on board. Herrera was confined to a room constructed for that purpose on deck, and Solís and the rest were in irons. See Bancroft, *History of California* 3: 85.

27. *Plana mayor* refers to officers who were not assigned to a specific company, that is, the general staff.

28. Jimeno resigned in November 1830. See Bancroft, *History of California* 3: 86.

29. Osio never had the opportunity to try out this double bookkeeping scheme, for he was not *contador* long enough to work it out.

30. The legal emancipation of the Indians, which accompanied secularization, was a gradual process that stretched from 1826 to 1840. See Jackson and Castillo, *Indians, Franciscans,* 90–93.

31. Echeandía's secularization decree was issued on January 6, 1831. It provided that the missions, beginning with San Gabriel and San Carlos, would be converted into towns to be settled by the mission Indians and other Mexicans who wished to do so. Each indigenous family was to be given a house lot, eight acres of land, farm animals, and tools. Undistributed items and land were to be managed by an appointed administrator. Two schools for educating the Indians were also to be established. See Hutchinson, *Frontier Settlement,* 130–34; and Geary, *Secularization.* Historiographically, the modern discussion of secularization was initiated by the influential 1965 article of Manuel Servín (Servín, "Secularization").

32. Gómez was appointed to the Customs House in January 1831, and Osio moved to San Francisco at the same time. Osio was not especially happy there, and he became frustrated when the switch he thought had been arranged did not materialize. Bandini, who was acting *comisario* at the time, also tried to have the governor effect it but was unsuccessful. See Bancroft, *History of California* 3: 376.

Chapter 6

1. The appointment and rule of Victoria inaugurated a period of great political instability in Alta California, a period which is very well covered in Tays, "Revolutionary California." There were many causes of this instability. In our judgment, the opinion of Mariano Guadalupe Vallejo's brother-in-law, Julio Carrillo, comes

close to the correct explanation. He told Bancroft's staff, "I, who have always watched very carefully the most important changes which have transpired in my country . . . can assure you that the secularization of the missions was the prime mover of every one of the civil wars which caused so much mischief in my native California from the year 1829 to 1846. (I however make an exception of the revolution which José Castro and Juan B. Alvarado led against Governor Micheltorena.) The desire to dispose of the lands and cattle belonging to the ex-missions was undoubtedly the incentive of every revolution, though as a pretext most of the leaders were in the habit of telling their followers that they had taken up arms with the object of setting up on a sound basis the customs house, which, if truth must be told, was the focus of corruptions with very few exceptions. The parties in charge of it always aided and abetted our wealthy foreign merchants, who day and night made a study of the art of smuggling" (Carrillo, "Statement of Julio Carrillo," 132–33).

2. José Boronda remembered Victoria as having "light brown hair" and being "tall, thin, and well built. He acted in a very military fashion and was strict with everybody" (Boronda, "Notas históricas," 11).

3. This scene, of course, deliberately reenacts the opening scene of the work, in which Sarría made the gesture to which Osio refers. Osio's description of Peyri here should be understood symbolically: the absence of another Father points to the fundamental weakening of the mission system, even though the missionaries had a temporary ally in the new governor.

4. Victoria was appointed by the conservative administration of President Anastasio Bustamante in 1830. He arrived at San Diego in November 1830. He expected to find Echeandía awaiting him but instead received a letter saying that the outgoing governor thought it better to wait for him in Monterey, so that the power could be transferred in the capital. Victoria started north and received another letter on the way saying that Echeandía would come down and meet him in Santa Bárbara. Victoria reached Santa Bárbara on December 31, but Echeandía was not there. It seems clear that Echeandía was stalling so that he could prepare and issue the secularization decree before transferring power to Victoria. See Harding, *Zamorano*, 45–46; and Gómez-Quiñones, *Roots of Chicano Politics*, 112–13.

5. Victoria intercepted the mail carrying copies of the decree to points south. He immediately ordered it countermanded and wrote an angry letter to Echeandía. Then he hurried the rest of his journey. See Harding, *Zamorano*, 50. Victoria may have encountered one or more of the commissioners heading for the missions, for the Monterey *ayuntamiento* chose commissioners for the missions between San Luis Obispo and Santa Cruz on January 8 (Bancroft, *History of California* 3: 307). So Victoria would have encountered the commissioners after he reached San Luis Obispo, as Osio says.

6. Victoria was described by Vallejo as "of black complexion . . . and of less than medium education" (Vallejo, "Historical and Personal Memoirs" 2: 112). If he was a

dark-skinned *mestizo*, as this characterization would imply, that may well have provided another reason for the *californio* elite's dislike of him.

7. Victoria arrived at Monterey on January 29 and took the oath of office on January 31.

8. Rubio was a soldier at San Francisco from 1824 and had also served at Missions Santa Ynés and San Francisco Solano. Little else is known of him. See Bancroft, *History of California* 3: 191–93; 5: 706.

9. The Indian's name was Atanasio. He had stolen items worth about two hundred dollars from *sub-comisario* Jimeno's warehouse. He was under eighteen years of age and was employed in the warehouse. Ibid., 3: 190.

10. This event took place in May 1831. The servant's name was Simón Aguilar; he was executed on May 28. Ibid., 191.

11. Rubio was executed on August 1, 1831. Ibid., 192.

12. Pomponio, who had run away from Mission San Francisco, was wanted for a number of crimes, including the killing of a soldier. According to Bancroft, who used the official records, he was captured by Martínez with "a corporal and two men." The corporal may well have been José Herrera, who is the "old Corporal Herrera" referred to by Osio. Herrera was an Indian fighter who had been wounded in an engagement against the Indians near San Francisco in 1810. Also wounded in the same campaign was Francisco Soto, the grandfather of Osio's second wife, Narcisa Florencia Soto. Ibid., 2: 91, 537.

13. Versions of this story are in many *californio* accounts, (ibid., 3: 193). What recommends Osio's version is that he freely offers his source, Lázaro Piña.

14. The first petition was sent on July 30, 1831. It was signed by Tiburcio Castro as well as Vallejo, Ortega, and Osio. The second petition was dated September 11, and Victoria's reply was issued on September 21. The memorial to the general government was sent on November 7. Ibid., 187–89.

15. Mission San Miguel de la Frontera, about forty miles south of San Diego, was founded in 1787 by the Dominican priest Luis Sales. Father Caballero had a good number of contacts in Alta California. See Engelhardt, *Missions and Missionaries* 1: 522; and Bancroft, *History of California* 2: 739.

16. Signed by Pío Pico, Juan Bandini, and José Antonio Carrillo, the *pronunciamiento* was issued on November 29. It called for the suspension of Victoria and for the *diputación* to choose separate political and military commanders. See Harding, *Zamorano*, 55–56.

17. The amended Plan of San Diego was signed on December 1 by Carrillo, Portilla, Bandini, Pico, and others. It supported the *pronunciamiento* and called for Echeandía to resume both commands until the *diputación* or the general government could act. The text appears in Bancroft, *History of California* 3: 202–4.

18. Even though Echeandía may not have been directly involved in drawing up the amended plan of December 1, his name headed the list of signers. Ibid., 204.

19. Ávila was involved in a series of quarrels in Los Angeles, but it is not clear

why either he or Pico was jailed. Ibid., 204, 207. One of Ávila's sisters was married to José Sepúlveda, later a close associate of Osio's in the political controversies of 1837. Ibid., 5: 716.

20. José Fernández remembered Pacheco as "a strict disciplinarian and a man blessed with tremendous courage" (Fernández, "Cosas de California," 64).

21. In a typical denigration of Osio, Bancroft says that Osio's account of "the interposition of providence in the interest of an *economía de sangre* is—though given in sober earnest—amusingly absurd" (*History of California* 3: 208). As the text makes abundantly clear, Osio was employing a simple figure of speech, not speaking literally.

22. The battle took place on December 5, 1831, at Cahuenga, a mountain pass about ten miles northwest of Los Angeles on the way to San Fernando.

23. For reasons that are not clear, Talamantes and his uncle Ávila had been jailed in 1831 by Victoria and Sánchez.

24. Sepúlveda had also been jailed by Victoria and Sánchez. Bancroft, *History of California* 3: 196.

25. Los Nietos Ranch was one of the earliest land concessions in Alta California, granted to Manuel Nieto in 1784. The original grant was a sprawling 150,000-acre site which began about ten miles southwest of the *pueblo* of Los Angeles. To accommodate Nieto's heirs, the grant was divided into five parts: Santa Gertrudis, Los Coyotes, Los Cerritos, Los Alamitos, and Las Bolsas. See Pico, *Historical Narrative*, 52.

26. Alvarado later said that a Doctor Anderson had once told him that he should drink some liquor every six months to improve his health. He quipped that, if every six months was good, then more frequently must be better! See Alvarado, "History of California" 2: 110.

27. The *diputación* met on January 10, 1832, in Los Angeles. See Osio, "Minutes." Bancroft summarizes some of its sessions in a long footnote. (*History of California* 3: 216–18).

28. Pico says that as the next most senior delegate, Vallejo administered the oath to him. See Pico, *Historical Narrative*, 54.

29. Zamorano was supported by many in the foreign mercantile community in Monterey. Much of the correspondence between him and Echeandía is reproduced and translated by Harding. See Harding, *Zamorano*, 70–102.

30. Zamorano's biographer strongly denies this story and calls it "an example of the attempts by the Californians to slander Zamorano" (ibid., 101). He may well be right.

31. Ibarra left on February 12, 1832. Ibid., 100.

32. This crossing of the San Gabriel River was at the intersection of the river and the "old road" (*camino viejo*), about ten miles to the east of Los Angeles. See Gudde, *California Place Names*, 24.

33. Bancroft, while admitting that this story of Echeandía's recruiting Indians

was widely current and is even to be found in Robinson's 1846 *Life in California,* is less than convinced of it. However, in a report penned by Osio, dated May 15, 1832, the *diputación* recalled the great peril it said was created at the gathering of so many gentile and neophyte Indians in Echeandía's force ("en número considerable se reunen diariamente a la fuerza militar del Señor Echeandía"; AGN, Gobernación, Legajo 120, Expediente 15). The report was signed by Pío Pico, Mariano Guadalupe Vallejo, Antonio María Osio, and José Joaquín Ortega.

34. The warning was sent on April 18, 1832. Pío Pico wrote Echeandía and sent a copy to Zamorano. Pico warned Echeandía that public uproar against his decision to recruit Indians was increasing daily. See Pío Pico to Echeandía, April 18, 1832, AGN, Gobernación, Legajo 120, Expediente 21.

35. The two *jefes* Osio is speaking about here are Zamorano and the *diputación.* Zamorano appointed Mariano Estrada as *sub-comisario* at Monterey to replace José Joaquín Gómez. Estrada was close to Osio, and they probably worked out an informal arrangement. On the other hand, in San Diego Echeandía did not receive anything from Monterey. See Harding, *Zamorano,* 139–40.

Chapter 7

1. According to José del Carmen Lugo, "Every year both male and female Indians would receive a blanket, and if it were torn before the year was up, they would be given another. Every man was given a loincloth and some cotton cloth. Every woman received cotton cloth for a skirt. When the missions were better stocked with the trade that they had, they began to give the Indian women printed calico, blankets, shawls, and material that had broad stripes or vibrant colors, which was what they liked best" (Lugo, "Vida de un ranchero," 99).

2. This slaughter of cattle has been very controversial in the historiography, and the fact that Osio uncharacteristically runs through a series of "proofs" indicates that the controversy was acute even during his time. In the 1870s José Fernández admitted that the story "was hard to believe." But he insisted that "more than 100,000 head of cattle were slaughtered" (Fernández, "Cosas de California," 73).

Engelhardt attacks Osio's account, along with those of Pío Pico and Juan Bandini, as coming from "members of the gang who engineered the confiscation of the missions, and consequently bitter enemies of the missionaries." That Osio favored the secularization of the missions is clear from the manuscript; that he was a bitter enemy of the missionaries is just as clearly not the case.

Engelhardt specifically attacks Osio's version. On the question of the discontentment of the San Fernando Fathers, he says that "the whole territory was dissatisfied," so the priests' discontent was not unusual. Osio was not the only one who spoke of the *Fernandinos'* being unhappy with the transfer. Robinson says basically the same thing. See *Life in California,* 189. On the events at San Luis Obispo, Engelhardt states that there is no evidence that "such an order was issued." In another place, however, he speaks of "the almost entire lack of local documents

on the period preceding the transfer of Mission San Luis Obispo" to the secularization commissioner in 1835, so it is not clear what weight ought to be given to
the lack of one specific document from the period. The priest at Mission San Luis
Obispo was José Ramón Abella, who went there from Mission San Carlos. Osio
would have known him while both were in the Monterey area in the late 1820s
and early 1830s. The *comisionado* at San Luis Obispo was Manuel Jimeno Casarín,
with whom Osio worked in the Customs House at Monterey. The twenty-thou-
sand-peso figure seems very high, especially since there were only 253 neophytes
at the mission. See Engelhardt, *Mission San Luis Obispo*, 126, 131. On the slaughter of the cattle, Engelhardt disputes the figures given by Osio and others. See Engelhardt, *Missions and Missionaries*, 3: 656–57.

Hutchinson offers the most reasoned explanation of the affair. On the slaughter of the cattle, he writes, "The available evidence does point to such an occurrence, but it is by no means clear that there was anything reprehensible about it or
that the missionaries were responsible for all the killing that took place." It was not
the case that the cattle were slaughtered for the benefit of the missionaries. It appears to have occurred either so that the missionaries could sell the hides to buy
food for the Indians or because the missionaries feared that the Indians would not
receive very many cattle in the secularization process. So they sold as many hides
as they could for the Indians while they still had the chance. See Hutchinson,
Frontier Settlement, 249–50. Osio specifically says that this was the case at San Luis
Obispo.

3. The Zacatecans took charge of Missions San Francisco Solano, San Rafael,
San Francisco de Asís, San José, Santa Clara, San Juan Bautista, Santa Cruz, and
San Carlos. See Engelhardt, *Missions and Missionaries* 2: 452.

4. Geiger writes, "When he [Esténaga] had first come to San Gabriel in 1833,
he found that all of the cattle had been killed in resentment against secularization.
He himself went to the extreme of allowing neighbors to enter the mission property, unroof the buildings, convert lumber into firewood, dispose of tools and uten-
sils" (Geiger, *Franciscan Missionaries*, 80).

5. The Doyle copyist apparently did some quick calculations and thought that
Osio's figures added up to 434,000, not the 435,000 he said. So the copyist added
1,000 cattle to San Juan Bautista, giving it 19,000 and making the figures add up
in his own mind. The Bancroft copy, based on the Doyle copy, also has that in-
correct figure.

6. Many visitors to the missions of Alta California estimated the numbers of
cattle in the herds at the various establishments at quantities far higher than those
given in the official annual reports. Alfred Robinson, for instance, reported that
Mission San Gabriel was thought, at one time, to have between 80,000 and
100,000 head of cattle. The highest figure ever officially reported was 26,300. But
Robinson was hardly alone in this. In 1826, when the official count was slightly
over 15,000, Harrison S. Rogers reported that the mission had "over 30,000" head

of cattle (Engelhardt, *San Gabriel*, 149, 157). In 1827 Duhaut-Cilly said that Mission San Diego had 12,000 head of cattle, when 9,120 were reported (Engelhardt, *San Diego*, 216).

The official statistics of cattle at San Gabriel were lower than Osio states: 1824, 13,304; 1825, 13,895; 1826, 15,300; 1827, 18,400; 1828, 26,300; 1829, 25,000; 1830, 23,500; 1831, 20,500. Thus it can be seen that the missionaries reported that the herds grew dramatically in the mid-1820s, leveled off at the end of the decade, and began to decline at the beginning of the 1830s. See Engelhardt, *San Gabriel*, 279. Osio's total estimate is almost three times the reported number of cattle: in 1832, all of the missions reported a total of 151,200 head (Engelhardt, *San Gabriel*, 199).

7. By "improving their habits," Osio meant becoming more like Mexicans. David J. Weber pungently states that the object of the missions was to turn the Indians into "tax paying Christians," but they generally did not perform this function well. He writes, "It seems likely that exposure to the market economy and the workaday world of Hispanic frontier society did more than the missions to alter Indian society and culture" (Weber, *Spanish Frontier*, 306–7). See also Sandos, "From 'Boltonlands' to 'Weberlands,'" 604.

8. Nothing like the story Osio tells is extant in other records. The manuscript indicates that his source was Esténaga, and the incident would have occurred in the 1820s, when Esténaga was at San Francisco de Asís. Altimira, stationed at San Francisco Solano, was also an associate priest at San Rafael.

The greatest recorded decline in the population of Mission San Francisco de Asís occurred in 1822 and 1823; the number of neophytes present dropped 83 percent, from 1,252 in 1820 to 208 in 1823. Part of the decline, especially in 1823, stems from the fact that, with the opening of Mission San Francisco Solano in 1823, San Francisco de Asís neophytes who were from the northern part of San Francisco Bay were allowed to go there or to San Rafael if they wished. But this would account for only about half of the decrease in population. Beechey, who visited San Francisco de Asís in 1826, commented on the dramatic decline of the neophyte population and attributed this partly to the move of some to San Rafael and partly to "sickness and death [which] have dealt with an unsparing hand." In addition, the sex ratio of the mission population changed, as Osio states. From 1816 to 1822, for instance, 42 percent of the recorded neophytes were women; but from 1823 to 1832 women accounted only for 35 percent of the neophyte population. See Engelhardt, *San Francisco*, 192, 271; Bowman, "Resident Neophytes," 145–48; and R. H. Jackson, "Gentile Recruitment," 226–28. In his thorough study of Indian population at the missions, Jackson noted "consistently high death rates" and "frightful mortality" at San Francisco. He attributed it to "overcrowding and the related problem of poor sanitation in the adobe Indian housing; polluted water; dehydration among children, caused by diarrhea; syphilis; chronic respiratory ailments; and the practice of locking up women and girls at night in unhealthy dormitories" (R. H. Jackson, *Indian Population Decline*, 100–101). In sum, enough collateral evidence exists to make Osio's story plausible. Most likely, some of the neophytes who went to San Rafael attempted to take some gentile women and were expelled from the northern shore of the bay for their efforts.

9. After the mid-nineteenth century, the term "Contra Costa" referred to the eastern shore of San Francisco Bay. Before then, however, its meaning was less precise, and the term could also refer to the northern shore. This is the sense in which Osio uses it here. See Gudde, *California Place Names*, 177. The mission in Contra Costa to which Osio refers is either San Rafael, of which the priest at San Francisco Solano, José Altimira, was an associate missionary, or San Francisco Solano itself. When San Francisco Solano was established, neophytes from San Francisco de Asís were allowed to go there if they were originally from that area. See Engelhardt, *Missions and Missionaries* 2: 184.

10. Point Olompali was at the mouth of Novato Creek, approximately seven miles north of Mission San Rafael. It was named for a nearby Miwok village. See Gudde, *California Place Names*, 242.

11. Altimira had a bad reputation among the local indigenous people. Many of them ran away, and in 1826 his mission was burned. See Engelhardt, *Missions and Missionaries* 2: 184; and Geiger, *Franciscan Missionaries*, 9.

12. The Treasure is a rock approximately one acre in size in the bay. It is about five miles north of Angel Island. It received its name from legends of sunken treasure which were associated with it. The current name is Red Rock. See Hoover, *Historic Spots*, 183.

13. José del Carmen Lugo observed that, among the *vaqueros*, some rode with a saddle, and others rode bareback. The former were provided with a saddle, bridle, spurs, boots, and shoes. The latter were given the same things that the other Indians received: cotton shirt, loincloth, and blanket. See Lugo, "Vida de un ranchero," 102.

14. During his first few years at San Francisco Solano, Altimira often complained that Esténaga was insufficiently supportive of the new mission. See Smilie, *Sonoma Mission*, 19.

15. Many descriptions of these arrangements survive. For instance, speaking of San Gabriel, one of the larger missions, José del Carmen Lugo said, "The single men lived in a separate building, and at night, when they retired to their dwelling, the door was locked and the key was given to the priest. The single women lived in another building that was called *el monjerio* [the convent], and an old woman watched over them all the time, day and night. When they gathered together, they were put under lock and key, and this key was given to the priest every night" (Lugo, "Vida de un ranchero," 104).

16. Osio's remarks on indigenous population at the missions are generally consistent with recent scholarship. See R. H. Jackson, *Indian Population Decline*.

17. In his response to the *Interrogatorio* of 1814, Peyri offered a detailed de-

scription of different herbal remedies employed by the indigenous people to treat various illnesses. See Engelhardt, *San Luis Rey,* 28; and Nunis, "Medicine in Spanish California," 47–48.

18. In his 1827 visit to the mission, Auguste Duhaut-Cilly spoke of "an infirmary with a special chapel." As he told it, "The infirm could enter the church through the inside corridor without stepping from under cover; thus gracious and superabundant solicitude looked above all to their convenience. Attractive and elegant is the cupola that surmounts that little temple, said Fr. Antonio [Peyri], delighted in letting his good taste shine forth in ornamenting it" (Engelhardt, *San Luis Rey,* 56). Pablo Tac remembered that there were two infirmaries, one for the men and one for the women ("Onís, *Las misiones españolas,* 25.)

19. Peyri describes the construction of the dam in an 1827 report, and Duhaut-Cilly spoke in that same year of "two beautiful lavatories in stucco" (Engelhardt, *San Luis Rey,* 51, 57).

20. Jackson reports that "the population of San Luis Rey grew rapidly" from "its founding in 1798 until 1811, when its population stood at 1,601." He continues, "The Franciscans achieved considerable success in their recruitment campaign over the next twenty years. . . . In 1834, on the eve of the secularization of the missions, the population of the mission was 2,844, making it the most populous Alta California establishment" (R. H. Jackson, *Indian Population Decline,* 88). Peyri left Alta California on January 17, 1832, on board the *Pocahontas,* which also carried Governor Victoria into exile. See Bancroft, *History of California* 3: 210.

21. Two months after he arrived, Figueroa was able to report that he had calmed the territory by the general amnesty he had offered to those who had attacked Victoria. See Hutchinson, *Frontier Settlement,* 216.

Vallejo's reminiscences offer a good example of Figueroa's approach. He relates that he, along with Alvarado and Osio, journeyed to Monterey to confer with the new governor after Figueroa's amnesty offer became known. They made a point of telling him that they were not seeking to avail themselves of the amnesty but simply to "lend our cooperation in assuring public order." Figueroa let that pass and urged them to give him any ideas that they had about the future of the territory. The three were pleasantly surprised when "he listened to us attentively, and made notes on all that was explained to him." Vallejo, Alvarado, and Osio stayed with Figueroa for dinner, and "when we left his house, the leavetaking was frank and cordial on the part of all, and the relations we maintained with him to the hour of his death never failed in their friendship" (Vallejo, "Historical and Personal Memoirs" 2: 163).

22. The most detailed discussion of the secularization process, and one which pays close attention to events in Mexico City as well as in Alta California, is in Hutchinson, *Frontier Settlement,* 216–66. Hutchinson argues that the *californios* were much more interested in the question of how the mission lands were to be divided than they were in anything else. If that was their interest, the *californio* elites

were not disappointed. In 1844 William Hartnell, who had inspected all the missions in 1839, reported, "The missions are almost entirely gone to ruin and can never be brought back to their former state, and there is no doubt that the temporal welfare of a great portion of the inhabitants has been much improved by their ruin" (Rojas, "California in 1844," 24). The *diputación* passed the secularization decree on August 2, 1834, and the governor proclaimed it a week later. See Geary, *Secularization*, 151.

23. Figueroa made this request on March 25, 1833, two months after he arrived. See Hutchinson, *Frontier Settlement*, 217.

24. Virtually the entire *californio* elite opposed this colonizing effort, both at the time it occurred and in later reminiscences. They interpreted it as a conspiracy to put all the mission lands under the control of Mexican speculators, led and symbolized by Padrés and Híjar. Most historians, with the notable exception of Bancroft, have accepted that view, but Hutchinson's important work, *Frontier Settlement*, contests this interpretation. He views the colony as the realization of a long-standing desire on the part of some in the Mexican government to populate and strengthen California so that it could be better defended against Russia, England, and the United States. He sees *californio* opposition to the colony as a manifestation of hunger for the mission lands.

25. After completing his book, Hutchinson discovered an official list of the members of the colony, and he published it in 1973. See Hutchinson, "Official List."

26. In 1878 one of the members of the colony, Agustín Janssens, told Thomas Savage, "In the afternoon, rumors began that the colony would not be allowed to leave Mexico City; that there was much opposition on the part of the public because some ill-intentioned and ignorant persons had noised it about that those who came with the colony had joined under duress and against their will. The matter reached such lengths that the crowd, to the accompaniment of insulting words, removed the traces of the carts in which our people traveled. . . . Finally the government, recognizing the violence of the mob, provided a squadron of gendarmes as an escort for the colonists. The local authorities, assisted by police, quieted the populace" (Janssens, *Life and Adventures*, 11). This seems to be the most likely explanation, although one congressman from Oaxaca said that the mob attacked the party because it feared that such a group would cause the loss of California. See Hutchinson, *Frontier Settlement*, 208–9.

27. The departure of the colonists occurred at a time of political instability in Mexico, the beginning of a long period of bewildering political maneuvering which would last until 1855. As Hutchinson demonstrates, the colonization effort was supported by Valentín Gómez Farías, a liberal who was elected vice-president in 1833. General Antonio López de Santa Anna, then known as an upholder of liberal principles, was elected president. He soon withdrew from public life and left executive power in the hands of Gómez Farías, under whose leadership the 1833

secularization bill was passed. Gómez Farías' forces got a colonization bill passed by the lower house of the congress, but the bill did not make it through the senate before political instability increased, as military units began to pronounce against the current government and in favor of the return of Santa Anna. At that point Gómez Farías proceeded to complete the organization of a colonization effort he had begun the year before on his own authority. Given the rush—the instructions were not ready until April 23, 1834, only one day before Santa Anna returned to Mexico City—the instructions he gave to Híjar and Padrés were inevitably vague, and this increased the suspicions of the *californios*. The two ships set sail on August 1, 1834. See Hutchinson, *Frontier Settlement*, 181–215.

28. The *Natalia* was a ship owned by the Cosmopolitan Company, which had been organized to supply the colonists with provisions. The company was headed by Juan Bandini, and its secretary was José María Herrera. See Hutchinson, *Frontier Settlement*, 203–4. The relation between the colony and the company was unclear in the minds of the *calfornios*, and the reputation of the colony suffered by being too closely associated with Bandini. Juana Machado remembered, for instance, that whenever people spoke of the colony, it was always referred to as "Bandini's colony" (Machado, "Los tiempos pasados," 30).

29. When Santa Anna returned, he did so as the conservative champion of the army and the church. Híjar was an appointee of Gómez Farías and, as such, would not have been someone that Santa Anna would have wanted in office. See Meyer and Sherman, *Course of Mexican History*, 324–28. The order countermanding the appointment was issued on July 25, 1834, a week before the colonization ships left San Blas for Alta California. See Bancroft, *History of California* 3: 270–71.

30. The name of the courier was Rafael Amador. He left Mexico City on July 26 and handed the note to Figueroa on September 11. See Hutchinson, *Frontier Settlement*, 265.

31. Osio implies here that Híjar had learned something about the communiqué. He was correct, for Híjar had picked up rumors of it on his trip from San Diego to Monterey. Ibid., 284.

32. The specific point at issue was whether Híjar could continue to function as director of colonization and, if so, whether the mission property should be made available to him as seemed to be called for in the first articles of the instructions he had received. The *diputación* decided that Híjar could continue to function as director of colonization but that the colony should not receive any mission property. That property, the *diputación* piously stated, properly belonged to the Indians. Ibid., 288–92.

33. These indigenous people were the Cahuilla. Apparently a member of Híjar's party, Buenaventura Araujo, invited them to a meeting to explain the colonization effort to them and assure them that the newcomers were not after their lands. Some of the Cahuilla apparently stole some horses from the San Bernardino *rancho*, which belonged to Mission San Gabriel. The next day, Father Esténaga went

out with a few others to try to get the horses back. The Cahuilla seized the wagon in which the priest was riding and the few things he had in it, such as a chalice, his breviary, his hat, and a crucifix. Esténaga was released the same day. Ibid., 278–79.

34. On Saturday, March 7, 1835, a band of about fifty recent arrivals to Los Angeles from Sonora, led by shoemaker Juan Gallardo and cigar maker and merchant Felipe Castillo, armed themselves and marched on the town hall. Their *plan* denounced Figueroa for various misdeeds and called for his removal. Ibid., 355; Bancroft, *History of California* 3: 284–90.

35. Osio was living in Los Angeles by this time. Along with *ayuntamiento* members Vicente de la Ossa and Rafael Guirado, he was appointed to a committee to tell the *pronunciados* that the *ayuntamiento* had rejected their call and to ask them to move their men away from the town hall. See Bancroft, *History of California* 2: 283.

36. Osio was asked to defend Apalátegui in the legal proceedings against him, but he declined. Ibid., 285.

37. The *alcalde* was Francisco Javier Alvarado. Ibid., 3: 635.

38. Torres had been on his way to Mexico with some papers that Híjar had asked him to deliver. Ibid., 284.

39. Padrés, Híjar, Torres, Apalátegui, and others left from San Pedro on the U.S. brigantine *Loriot* on May 10.

40. Figueroa's *Manifiesto a la república mejicana* was published in Monterey in 1835 by Zamorano. It has been translated and republished, with an excellent introduction, by Hutchinson. See Figueroa, *Manifesto*.

41. Traders from New Mexico and trappers from the United States began to enter the territory at the beginning of the 1830s in search of mules and horses. Thefts from the missions and *ranchos* on the part of nonmission indigenous people dramatically increased, and priests and *rancheros* called on Victoria and then Figueroa to put a stop to this activity. Figueroa issued an "Order and Decree Concerning Robbers of Horses and Other Livestock" on November 18, 1833. The order stated that each presidio should send out each month an expedition to "scout those places where the robbers shelter themselves and hide their stolen animals." But the governor's order also insisted, "The natives are to be treated with gentleness and charity. They shall be caused to realize that it is a delinquency to steal cattle" (Lawrence, "Mexican Trade," 29; Cook, *Expeditions*, 188; Phillips, *Indians and Intruders*, 82–85; Hurtado, *Indian Survival*, 46).

42. In early 1834 the Walker party of trappers from the United States encountered a group of *californios* chasing some Indians who, the *californios* said, had stolen three hundred horses from Mission San Juan Bautista. When the *californios* caught up with the Indians, they found only some feeble older men and some women and children, but no horses. Enraged, they massacred the Indians and cut off their ears. See Phillips, *Indians and Intruders*, 90. For a good general overview of the situation, see Broadbent, "Conflict at Monterey," 88–90.

43. In 1841 William Dane Phelps reported a "scarcity" of horses because "the Indians on the frontiers for a number of years back have stole all the horses they could lay their hands on" (Phelps, *Alta California*, 114). In the next year a French traveler observed, "The supply of horses is now diminishing in California, for the Indians carry on endless raids" (Phillips, *Indians and Intruders*, 114–15).

Chapter 8

1. Chico came to Alta California with Santa Anna's appointment. He had a mission to introduce the new centralist administration to that area. That in itself would have turned the *californios* against him. In addition, the recent decision in Mexico to make Los Angeles the capital of the territory would have made the northerners hostile to anyone from Mexico. See Tays, "Revolutionary California," 575.

2. In Los Angeles on March 26, 1836, Domingo Félix was killed by Gervasio Alipás. Félix's wife, María del Rosario Villa, had been living with Alipás for two years, and Félix finally had her arrested. After the *alcalde*, Manuel Requena, had tried to reconcile the couple, she was released, and as the two were on their way back to their *rancho*, Alipás ambushed them. Assisted by his lover, he then murdered Félix. When the body was discovered, Alipás and Villa were arrested. A group dominated by foreigners soon organized a vigilance committee, which took the prisoners from the jail and shot them. See Bancroft, *History of California* 3: 416; idem, *Popular Tribunals* 1: 62–66.

3. Carrillo had served in the Mexican congress in 1831–32. See Galvin, *Coming of Justice*, viii–ix.

4. When Figueroa became ill in August 1835, he had José Castro, as the senior available member of the *diputación*, assume the political command and Nicolás Gutiérrez, as senior military officer, assume the military command. Castro surrendered the political command to Gutiérrez on January 2, 1836. See Harding *Zamorano*, 165–67.

5. Stearns held the office of *síndico* during the vigilante episode. Since Stearns was the highest-ranking person of U.S. birth in the city government, Chico may well have suspected that he had sympathized with the vigilantes. Also, Chico may have thought that Stearns might prove to be a good scapegoat for the movement against Victoria. See Tays, "Revolutionary California," 543.

6. The vividness of the following description indicates that Osio may have been the second person. Osio's own relationship to Stearns was an interesting example of the complex web in which an official like Osio could be caught as he tried to attain the twin objectives of enforcing the Mexican laws and increasing the overall prosperity of Alta California. Stearns was generally regarded as being involved in smuggling, yet his trade contributed to the economic well-being of the Los Angeles elite. In 1835, when Osio was *receptor* at Los Angeles, word apparently reached Ángel Ramírez, administrator of the Monterey Customs House, that Stearns was being

allowed to get away with too much. Osio, somewhat defensively, wrote Ramírez that Los Angeles, where Osio was stationed, was too far away from the coast for him (Osio) to exercise sufficient vigilance over the coastal trade in general, and over Stearns in particular. This was probably an example of the behavior Osio explicitly acknowledges later in his manuscript: he was willing to condone such activity since he did not think that it harmed Alta California. Such behavior would obviously have made him close to Stearns. In fact, in 1840 Osio, then working as administrator at Monterey, investigated charges of falsifying records brought against Stearns and pronounced them baseless. See Wright, *Yankee in Mexican California*, 54–55, 61.

7. This is a reference to Mark 15.16, where Jesus, having been condemned before Pilate, is led away by soldiers to the praetorium.

8. Chico arrived in Los Angeles on June 15 and left on June 28. See Tays, "Revolutionary California," 540-41.

9. Apparently, all were released except Prudón and Arzaga, whom Chico had decided to send off to Mexico City for punishment. See Wright, *Yankee in Mexican California*, 80.

10. Her name is given in the sources as Doña Cruz, and little else is known about her. See Bancroft, *History of California* 3: 421. Vallejo, in his reminiscences, says that Chico's inaugural ball was sparsely attended, since the more respectable elements of Monterey society had conceived as great a distaste for Doña Cruz as they had for Panchita Arancibia, the supposed former nun who was living with customs administrator Ángel Ramírez (Vallejo, "Historical and Personal Memoirs" 3: 68). By the 1870s, Teresa de la Guerra, wife of William Hartnell, mainly remembered that Chico was called *oso chico* (little bear) and that he was "crazy and lustful" (Guerra Hartnell, "Narrativa," 25).

11. Maritornes is the Asturian servant in Cervantes' *Don Quixote*. Don Quixote meets her at the inn where he stayed after having been beaten by the herders. Maritornes is an outgoing person who is fascinated by men. In her relationships with men she demonstrates that she can be both compassionate and cruel to them at the same time. Her physical appearance is rather ordinary and somewhat masculine. Chico's "niece" exhibits some of Maritornes' personality traits; she, too, is attracted to men, and Chico is very aware of this.

12. Dulcinea is the name that Don Quixote bestows upon the peasant woman from Toboso, Aldonza Lorenzo. In his imagination, Don Quixote elevates Aldonza to the status of the perfect or idealized woman (Dulcinea) whom he can love from afar. The name Dulcinea has become synonymous with the concept of the "beloved one" or "mistress."

13. Advent is the season in the Catholic liturgical year which immediately precedes Christmas. It is a season of waiting for the appearance of the Savior. Osio uses the term ironically here, much as he ironically alluded earlier to the trial of Jesus by Pontius Pilate. Chico's "niece" may have been bored with him and was restless as she awaited her "savior," that is, another man.

14. Marramaquiz and Zapaquilda are two protagonists in Lope de Vega's burlesque poem *La gatomaquia*. They did not originate with Lope de Vega, however, for they appear in the fables of Aesop. They also appear in a fable by La Fontaine, *La chatte metamorphosée en femme* and in three fables by Félix María Samaniego— *Los ratones y el gato*, *La gata mujer*, and *Los gatos escrupulosos*—who took his inspiration from La Fontaine and Lope de Vega. Osio's reference to Marramaquiz and Zapaquilda is yet another example of his familiarity with a wide range of authors and literary genres. In Lope de Vega's poem the action centers around the turbulent relationship between Marramaquiz, who is an old, brave, and extremely jealous tabby cat, and Zapaquilda, the beautiful, young cat who is adored by all of the male cats in the vicinity. Eventually, a foreign cat arrives on the scene and seduces Zapaquilda with gifts and exquisite food. Marramaquiz flies into a rage when he witnesses Zapaquilda's interest in the foreigner. She later engages in a fight with another cat and is clawed brutally. Marramaquiz then kidnaps Zapaquilda and locks her away in a tower. Osio is drawing obvious parallels between specific incidents involving these cats and Chico's jealousy and quick temper as demonstrated later by his brutality toward his "niece," when he digs his fingernails into her arm as if his nails were eagle's talons. Osio here seems to imply that it is quite possible that Chico physically abused his "niece," since she, like Zapaquilda, was not seen for three or four days and had scratches on her face.

15. The husband was José María Herrera, who had returned to Alta California in 1834. His wife was Ildefonsa González, who had become romantically involved with José María Castañares. The case had originally been brought to public attention by Ana González, the wife of Castañares. By the end of May, Herrera had become involved and had secured the imprisonment of Castañares in the jail and the seclusion of González in the house of Francisco Pacheco. See Bancroft, *History of California* 3: 437; and Fernández, "Cosas de California," 96).

16. The *maromeros* were acrobats who generally performed their stunts while swinging from ropes around a large pole.

17. By the latter part of July, Herrera was softening his position. On July 30 he agreed to withdraw his suit on the condition that Castañares leave Monterey. See Tays, "Revolutionary California," 561.

18. The *alcalde* was José Ramón Estrada.

19. The initials J.M.C. refer to José María Castañares.

20. Chico removed Estrada from office and replaced him with Teodoro González, a member of the *ayuntamiento*, on July 27, 1836. González proceeded immediately to rouse the people of Monterey against Chico. According to some accounts, Chico also insulted Mariano Estrada, the former commander of Monterey, who was still extremely popular. That served further to incite the populace against him. See Tays, "Revolutionary California," 566.

21. In this and the next few paragraphs Osio confuses the two representative bodies in Monterey which were involved in the removal of Chico. The body which

called for the people to rise against him was the town *ayuntamiento*. The two men who conducted the negotiations with Chico were members of that body. The body to which Chico formally indicated that he was going to leave Alta California was the *diputación*. Ibid., 566–72.

22. The two were members of the *ayuntamiento*. They were most likely Teodoro González and Bonifacio Madariaga. Ibid., 566.

23. Bonifacio Madariaga was married to María Josefa Vallejo de Estrada, who was the widow of José Mariano Estrada's brother and José Ramón Estrada's uncle. See Bancroft, *History of California* 4: 727.

24. The *diputación* demanded that Chico turn over the political command to Alvarado, the most senior member of the *diputación* who happened to be present in Monterey. It also demanded that the governor turn over the military command to the senior military officer. If he did that, the body promised, it would do its best to protect him until he left the territory. Chico did not split the commands. Instead, he turned them both over to the senior military officer, Nicolás Gutiérrez. Ibid., 3: 441. The concentration of power stemming from the union of the civil and military commands was one of the most basic complaints the *californio* elite had against Mexico at this time. For instance, it appeared in a speech which Carlos Carrillo delivered to the Mexican congress in 1831. See Galvin, *Coming of Justice*, 49–60.

25. Spence was serving on the *diputación*.

26. Osio had succeeded Stearns as *síndico* at the beginning of July. See Bancroft, *History of California* 3: 636.

27. The lawyer was José Mariano Romero.

28. The *Clementine* sailed from Monterey on July 31 with Chico aboard. The letters which Osio received, accordingly, would have been dated July 30. This episode, then, occurred toward the beginning of August. The *Clementine* sailed from San Pedro on August 10. See Bancroft, *History of California* 3: 442.

29. The *Clementine* was an English brigantine. Ibid., 3: 382.

30. The *Don Quixote* was a U.S. vessel which engaged in trade between Alta California and Hawaii in the 1830s and 1840s. Ibid., 3: 382; 4: 10. The U.S. trader William Sturgis Hinckley was associated with both it and the *Clementine*, and it would not have been unusual for Chico to have been invited to dine aboard the *Don Quixote* while that vessel and the *Clementine* were both in San Pedro Bay. See Wright, *Yankee in Mexican California*, 80; and Bancroft, *History of California* 3: 382.

31. In Greek mythology Adonis was so handsome that the goddesses Aphrodite and Persephone quarreled over him. Zeus settled the issue by having Adonis spend one-third of the year with each of them, and the remaining third with whomever he chose. See Grimal, *Dictionary*, 13–14.

32. Whatever the basis of the following story, the fanciful fashion in which Osio relates it and his extensive use of mythological characters give it a clearly deliberate air of unreality. He turns the story into a symbol of the self-satisfied United

States being able effortlessly to seduce an unsuspecting resident of Alta California with an easy display of luxurious possessions. In another section a bit further along in the manuscript, Osio will try his hand at yet another allegorical story along the same lines and with equally unsatisfactory results, as he himself admits. Both stories indicate that he was trying to make sense of the attraction that the United States obviously had for some *californios,* and he was unable to come up with an explanation or an allegory that accounted for what he thought was such ill-advised behavior.

33. Narcissus was a very handsome youth who one day happened to see his own reflection in a stream and was so taken by its beauty that he remained in that spot gazing upon himself until, due to lack of food and sustenance, he died. Napea is simply a Spanish transliteration of the Latin Napaea, the name for the wood nymphs in Latin bucolic poetry. See Grimal, *Dictionary,* 286. By using the classical form instead of the generic term *ninfas,* Osio is able to maintain the more fantasy-filled tone that he is seeking here.

34. Argos is a mythological character who has one hundred eyes and is constantly vigilant.

35. When Gutiérrez arrived in Monterey, he was not greeted with the unanimous relief Osio suggests. Rafael Gómez, for instance, stated in his diary on September 8, "At present it seems that his intention is to carry on the unjust procedures that [Chico] committed. God grant that it be untrue, since with that conduct he causes us to be disorderly" (Gómez, "Diary of Rafael Gómez," 268).

36. Gutiérrez had a reputation for becoming intimately involved with indigenous women. The *californio* elite was greatly upset at this. One suspects that the major reason was not the moral question but rather that the women were indigenous. Alvarado, for instance, made a point of telling Bancroft's people that Gutiérrez' women were not the kind "whose degree of perfection" hit the eighteen-carat mark (Alvarado, "History of California" 3: 115).

37. In Spanish, the word *convento* refers to a religious community for either men or women.

38. Osio writes, "Pedro era viejo para cabrero," a proverb which literally means "Pedro was too old to be a goatherd."

39. The final quarrel between Gutiérrez and the *californios* probably concerned something relatively insignificant, such as the proper protocol for placing guards around the harbor to prevent smuggling. But the roots of the quarrel were that, after expelling Chico, many of the *californios,* especially those around Monterey, did not want to be ruled by another person appointed by the central government. The *diputación,* which had wanted Chico to separate the military and political commands when he left Alta California, maintained this position and stated that Gutiérrez should turn over the political command to its senior member, José Castro. See Harding, *Zamorano,* 174; and Tays, "Revolutionary California," 605.

40. At this time Alvarado was also a member of the *diputación.*

41. Among those recruited by Alvarado was Isaac Graham, a hunter from Kentucky. (Tays, "Revolutionary California," 607). Alvarado later insisted that he did this only because "we were determined to treat the foreigners as friends and brothers" (Alvarado, "History of California" 3: 134). Osio ignores the role of foreigners in this movement.

42. The musical instruments and the mission choir at Mission San José, under the leadership of Father Narciso Durán until 1833, were reputed to be very fine. See Geiger, *Franciscan Missionaries,* 69.

43. The cavalry were generally *californios,* and Gutiérrez wrote that he did not trust them. See Tays, "Revolutionary California," 614.

44. The forces reached Monterey on the night of November 3. Ibid., 609.

45. Alvarado later said that he had to attack as quickly as he could, for he was afraid that any delay would give Gutiérrez' supporters in San Diego time to organize and assist him. He feared that "the delay might prove fateful to our party and to me because the foreigners generally served those that paid them the best and they could have gone over to the enemy camp, taking with them the weapons and munitions we needed so badly" (Alvarado, "History of California" 3: 143).

46. This soldier was José Antonio de la Guerra. Among the demands he delivered to Gutiérrez was one that the territory of Alta California "shall be governed by a native of the country" (Tays, "Revolutionary California," 615–16).

47. San Juan de Ulúa at Veracruz was the last Spanish fortress to surrender to the Mexicans, on November 18, 1825 (*Diccionario Porrúa,* 1640). The soldier was named Balbino Romero (Bancroft, *History of California* 3: 461).

48. José Castro, who was actually the overall military commander, sent Gutiérrez a note saying that the cannon had been fired "against my orders." Soon afterward he sent another note saying that he was finding it difficult to control his troops and urging Gutiérrez to surrender immediately if he wished to avoid hostilities. See Tays, "Surrender of Monterey," 344.

49. Negotiations took some hours. The surrender was completed in the evening and actually occurred the next morning. Full details are in Tays, "Surrender of Monterey," 345–49.

50. The *Clementine* sailed from Monterey on November 11 and had arrived at San José del Cabo by November 28. Ibid., 352–53.

51. Zamorano actually went first to San Diego, where he participated in the movement against Alvarado in 1837. He left Alta California, most likely with Juan José Tovar, in 1838. See Harding, *Zamorano,* 211–50.

52. The *diputación* had seven members. Osio is regarding Alvarado as the political chief and José Castro as the military chief. That left five other members, but there were only two present. They were Antonio Buelna and José de la Guerra. The other three members, David Spence, Manuel Crespo, and José Joaquín Gómez, were absent and did not participate in these actions. See Bancroft, *History of California* 3: 469–71.

Chapter 9

1. Alvarado grudgingly admitted that Osio's opposition to the actions of the *diputación* was effective. He wrote that Osio "disapproved of the plan for the independence from the Mexican nation. He based his argument on the fact that we did not have sufficient troops to repel an invasion in case the president of Mexico thought it convenient to punish our audacity. Osio's ideas were circulated little by little, and it was due to this that I lost most of my fainthearted sympathizers" (Alvarado, "History of California" 3: 178).

2. The Los Angeles *ayuntamiento* decided not to support the north in a special session on November 25 and 26, 1836. See Harding, *Zamorano*, 213.

3. In a letter to Antonio del Valle on November 25, 1836, Osio had proposed that they work for a type of coalition arrangement, with Vallejo and Carlos Carrillo sharing the commands. In a letter to Mariano Guadalupe Vallejo the next day, Osio reported on his trip to see Carlos Carrillo. He also stated that one great danger facing Alta California was the general instability which the northern revolution might unleash throughout the entire land. Mexico might attack and use the Sonora ruffians in the attempt to reconquer the area. He urged Vallejo to go to Mexico and try to work out some peaceful compromise before things got out of hand. He reminded Vallejo that during the 1831 troubles the two of them had discussed the ultimate independence of Alta California and that Vallejo had quipped that it would not happen before their great-grandchildren were old. See Tays, "Revolutionary California," 653–54, 666–67.

4. Osio clearly regarded these few months as the most exciting time of his life, and he gets a bit swept away here in describing his own military acumen. Almost four decades later, Alvarado was probably closer to the mark when he said of Osio, "That he came to figure at all in our political life was due to his education and probity, not his military valor" (Alvarado, "History of California" 3: 233).

5. Alvarado and his forces, which apparently consisted of about sixty-five *californios* and twenty-five foreigners from Isaac Graham's group, arrived at Santa Bárbara on January 3, 1837. They were warmly received by José de la Guerra y Noriega and Father Durán, as well as by Carlos Carrillo. Alvarado's own party did not leave until January 11 or so. See Tays, "Revolutionary California," 691, 693.

6. The plan of the new government stated that Catholicism would be the only religion allowed to hold public services but that no one would be harassed for private religious opinions. Osio's playing on the fear of family disintegration is significant, in light of the increase in single, unattached foreigners who were entering the land from the United States as he was composing his manuscript in 1851.

7. The name is spelled in a variety of ways. This man was apparently a French Canadian trapper who entered California from New Mexico with a group of indigenous people and engaged in trapping and horse stealing. A number of such groups were operating in southern Alta California in the late 1830s. Agustín Janssens, who spoke French, did the actual negotiating with the Canadian. See

Bancroft, *History of California* 2: 758; Phillips, *Indians and Intruders*, 82; and Janssens, *Life and Adventures*, 74–75.

8. The Verdugo *rancho*, San Rafael, was directly north of Los Angeles. It consisted of 36,403 acres. Mission San Fernando was about twenty miles from the southern part of the *rancho*. See Beck and Haase, *Historical Atlas of California*, 37.

9. The camp was set up on January 16. See Tays, "Revolutionary California," 695.

10. Santa Susana Hill was a ridge on the hills separating the San Fernando and Simi Valleys. It is approximately ten miles to the west of Mission San Fernando. See Gudde, *California Place Names*, 318.

11. On January 16 Alvarado dispatched a letter to the Los Angeles *ayuntamiento*. He urged reconciliation but said that his forces could easily defeat any thrown in their path. The *ayuntamiento* discussed the letter the next day and decided to attempt reconciliation. It authorized Sepúlveda and Osio to bargain with Alvarado. See Tays, "Revolutionary California," 695–96. Alvarado later described Osio as "a citizen of Los Angeles, the wealthiest landholder of that day, and a man for whom I had respect and affection" (Alvarado, "History of California" 3: 219).

12. A message from Osio proposing this reached the *ayuntamiento* on January 17. See Bancroft, *History of California* 3: 496. Alvarado later fumed that Osio had convinced Carrillo not to support him. See Alvarado, "History of California" 3: 178.

13. The type of agreement between Osio and Carlos Carrillo, to which Osio refers twice in this section, is not clear. It should be remembered, however, that in November Osio had suggested to del Valle that Carrillo might serve as a compromise political commander. Perhaps Osio had hinted or suggested this to Carrillo.

14. These negotiations were conducted at Rancho Cayeguas, about fifteen miles to the east of San Buenaventura. This meeting took place on January 17. See Tays, "Revolutionary California," 696.

15. The Simi *rancho*, a huge expanse of 113,009 acres, was on the other side of Santa Susana Hill from San Fernando, about ten miles from San Fernando. Its southwestern corner touched Cayeguas, where Alvarado was headquartered. See Beck and Haase, *Historical Atlas of California*, 31.

16. This happened on the night of January 17. Osio and Domínguez accompanied Alvarado and his party from Cayeguas on the morning of the eighteenth.

17. Alvarado identifies the *vaquero* as an indigenous man named Mauricio. He says that Mauricio and he came to an agreement while they were together, and that Mauricio (after Alvarado released him) spread the story at San Fernando that Alvarado had been reinforced by José Castro. According to Alvarado, this caused the rebels at San Fernando to lose heart. See Alvarado, "History of California" 3: 220-24.

18. The *ayuntamiento* authorized Sepúlveda and Osio to negotiate on its behalf on January 17. As the manuscript makes clear, Osio and Domínguez' trip to Cayeguas on the night of the sixteenth was made without the authority of the *ayuntamiento*,

which had not as yet authorized negotiations. It was a decision made by those at San Fernando. The *ayuntamiento*'s negotiating instructions consisted of five items, which can be found in Bancroft, *History of California* 3: 496. The third item said that Catholicism must be the only permitted religion and that other religions must be prosecuted as before. But the first item, which was the controlling one, put the avoidance of conflict above everything else. Osio had not seen those instructions before he initiated negotiations.

19. As a result of the delay of the San Diegans, negotiations were in fact postponed one day, from January 19 to January 20. See Tays, "Revolutionary California," 698.

20. Alvarado added the phrasing that the commissioners requested. Apparently, Osio and Sepúlveda then tried to convince Alvarado that he should go back to the north and rule there (the intent of the words Osio puts into Alvarado's mouth), but Alvarado refused and told them that, if San Fernando was not abandoned, he would take it by force. Ibid.

21. The Félix *rancho*, also called Los Felis, contained 6,647 acres and was on the northern border of the *pueblo* of Los Angeles. See Beck and Haase, *Historical Atlas of California*, 37.

22. The *ayuntamiento* met on January 22 and annulled the agreement that Sepúlveda and Osio had made with Alvarado. The *ayuntamiento* doubtless hoped, as Osio had, that Alvarado would agree to rule only in the north. Osio and Sepúlveda claimed that they had shown Alvarado the instructions only "through fear of being attacked then and there by the opposition" (Wittenburg, "Three Generations," 226). Osio thought that the *ayuntamiento*'s instructions had given away too much and that a stronger stand might have induced Alvarado to be content to rule only in the north.

23. If Alvarado did enter the city on January 23, as Osio says and as Bancroft and Tays are inclined to agree, there is no record of a formal meeting of the *ayuntamiento* on that day. However, if Alvarado demanded that the body meet with him, and if the session went anything the way Osio describes it, it is unlikely that it would have been recorded as a regular meeting. There must have been some sort of contact between Alvarado and the *ayuntamiento* on January 23 or very soon afterward. On January 26 Alvarado was present at the *ayuntamiento,* and he and its members agreed to a vague plan, which called for the restoration of federalism to the nation as a whole and for the election of a new *diputación*. Osio was on the committee to hammer out the details of the plan, and some negotiations between the various parties had to have occurred before the actual legislative session. See Bancroft, *History of California* 3: 501–2.

As part of the general reconciliation, Osio gave a speech in which he said that "sooner than submit to another Mexican tyrant, he would retire to the forest and be devoured by wild beasts." Even though Alvarado presents himself in his reminiscences as a man who understood the necessity of negotiation and of giving the southerners a sense that they were full-fledged partners in the cause, he remembered the rituals of accommodation with impatience and distaste. He said, "Antonio María Osio reached the extremity of saying that he approved of my conduct in every particular; that he was satisfied that I was working in the interests of the general welfare and that his friends and he, rather than allow themselves to be ruled by unprincipled men, would prefer to bury themselves in the forests and let themselves be devoured by the wild animals of the wilderness" (Alvarado, "History of California" 3: 233).

24. According to Julio Carrillo, Alvarado's style in writing was greatly inferior to many other *californios*, but he was the best orator among them. See Carrillo, "Statement of Julio Carrillo," 136.

25. Ibarra was a *mestizo*, and Osio mentions it—pejoratively—whenever he refers to him. On this strong color consciousness, which Osio shared with others in Alta California, see Miranda, "Racial and Cultural Dimensions"; Servín, "California's Hispanic Heritage"; D. J. Weber, *Mexican Frontier*, 214–15; and Mason, "Alta California's Colonial and Early Mexican Era Population," 171.

26. Alvarado starts to toy with Osio, pretending that he is going to insult him by calling him a *pendejo* (which might be politely, but inaccurately, translated as "idiot"), but instead of pronouncing the entire word, he pauses for a second and then finishes the word with the ending—*olista*. The actual word that he utters is *pendolista*, which means "penman" or "calligrapher," or refers to someone who spends all his time keeping records, a stereotypical accountant. Osio successfully conveys the tone of Alvarado's speech by placing the dots between *pend* and *olista*.

27. A good collection of information on the various types of agriculture is in Francis, *Economic and Social History*, 568–77. By 1831 more than one hundred thousand vines were reported as being cultivated in southern Alta California (McKee, "Beginnings of California Winegrowing," 63). The *californios* were very sensitive to the U.S. insinuations that they had kept Alta California in a state of agricultural underdevelopment. José Fernández, for instance, insisted that "wheat, corn, beans, grapes, wool, and olive oil" were abundantly produced (Fernández, "Cosas de California," 7).

28. Robinson has this same story in his memoir. He says that González was "as well-calculated to discharge his duties as he was to navigate a steamboat through the Straits of Magellan" (Robinson, *Life in California*, 176).

29. As in his description of Mariano Chico, Osio again draws parallels between well-known literary figures and a political official to highlight a severe character flaw in Requena. Osio mentions the names Gil Blas and Ambrosio Lamela. Both are characters in the picaresque novel *La historia de Gil Blas de Santillana,* by Alain René Lesage. Originally written in French, the novel was translated into Spanish in 1756 and was extremely popular with the public. The main character, Gil Blas, is a young boy who sets out to make his way in the world and finds himself pulled along by a series of adventures. He is exposed to the very lowest and most corrupt

elements of society, including the rogue Ambrosio Lamela, who befriends Gil Blas yet robs the unsuspecting boy of his possessions. In the end, Gil Blas realizes that Lamela is a disreputable person who is motivated only by personal and private interests and that therefore he must sever his ties with Lamela to protect his own reputation. Osio characterizes Requena as having personal and private motivations similar to Lamela's and is not convinced of his sincerity.

Chapter 10

1. Alvarado left Los Angeles at the beginning of February. According to the agreement, an election was soon held, and a new *diputación* was chosen. Osio was a member, but he did not attend the opening sessions in Santa Bárbara on March 25. When he did appear in April, he and Pío Pico offered a plan which called for the reestablishment of departmental affairs to the state in which they had been before the expulsion of Gutiérrez, for all the laws of Mexico to be observed, and, somewhat incongruously, for the Treaty of Los Angeles to be upheld. This plan was not adopted, and by the beginning of May, Alvarado had consolidated his power in Los Angeles. The *ayuntamiento* there formally voted to recognize his government on May 2. See Bancroft, *History of California* 506–9.

2. Bandini came to Los Angeles in May 1837 to try to enlist prominent citizens in the cause. He spent a few days trying to garner support, and on May 26 he and a group of eight others seized the military garrison and its arms. See Killea, "Political History of a Mexican Pueblo," pt. 2, p. 22.

3. Castillero had been appointed frontier commander by the *comandante general* of Baja California, José Caballero, on April 12, 1837. Caballero was concerned that the instability in Alta California might spread to the south, and he authorized Castillero to "take such action as you see fit, according to the circumstances that present themselves to you due to the difficulties, so I am informed, in which the factions in California are involved." Acting creatively on these vague instructions, Castillero proved to be, in Tays's words, "a shrewd diplomat" (Tays, "Captain Andrés Castillero," 236–39).

4. This was the constitution of 1836, which went into effect on December 29, 1836. It was a strongly centralist document. The states of the federal republic which had been organized by the constitution of 1824 were abolished and replaced by military departments. The territory of California also became a department under this system. See Meyer and Sherman, *Course of Mexican History,* 328; and D. J. Weber, *Mexican Frontier,* 32.

5. The San Diegans seized weapons from the garrison on the evening of May 26. Sepúlveda was taken at his home, where he was entertaining Pío Pico, who was himself a sympathizer of the movement. Sepúlveda was taken because he had been appointed a captain of the militia. See Tays, "Revolutionary California," 704, 709.

6. Castillero convinced Alvarado that California had nothing to fear from the centralist system. In fact, now that California was a department exactly like the

other former Mexican states, it had been elevated to a level of equality with them. As modern historian Juan Gómez-Quiñones has summarized the matter, it was true that Alta California was converted into a *departamento*, but since it was "already under the central agreement in theory, the change in practice primarily affected the titles of the offices" (Gómez-Quiñones, *Roots of Chicano Politics*, 149). Castillero also convinced Alvarado that only *californios* would be appointed governor and probably that he himself would be able to continue as chief executive. Alvarado concluded that the constitution "offers us the guarantees to which we aspire" (D. J. Weber, *Mexican Frontier*, 259).

7. The Mexican congress issued a decree on April 1, 1837, authorizing a loan of sixty thousand pesos for "the pacification of the department of California." On June 6 a naval captain, Lucas Manso, submitted to the War Department an estimate of the cost of a six-hundred-man expedition to Alta California. The expedition was to be led, as Osio says, by General Iniestra. Tays thinks that "this is as close as México ever came to sending an expedition to reconquer California at this time" (Tays, "Revolutionary California," 678, 683; Tays, "Captain Andrés Castillero," 235). Iniestra was also reported as being assigned to come north to support Micheltorena in 1845. See J. M. Flores, "La carta de Flores," 152.

8. The *diputación* was meeting at Santa Bárbara in July 1837, and Alvarado was there for its sessions. After the 1836 constitution, the name of the *diputación* was changed to *junta departamental*. In 1843 another constitutional change renamed it the *asamblea*. For purposes of consistency, we continue to refer to it in our notes as a *diputación*.

9. Castillero sailed from Santa Bárbara on the *California* on August 25. See Tays, "Revolutionary California," 684.

10. The series of events which Osio now recounts occurred in July 1837, mainly while Alvarado was in Santa Bárbara for the meeting of the *diputación*. Osio, as he often does in the course of relating these events, finishes off one story—in this case that of Alvarado's dealing with the southerners—before beginning another, even though the strict chronological order needs to be sacrificed for coherence.

11. This movement was a movement of Mexicans who were afraid that their own livelihood would be threatened by the new government. This is why Osio puts the remark about the "California libre" password immediately before his account of the revolt. See Bancroft, *History of California* 3: 523.

12. This happened on July 1, 1837. A band of some thirty or forty seized the fort. The affair is narrated in Bancroft, *History of California* 3: 523–26.

13. The riflemen were from Isaac Graham's group.

14. Alva was ill and finally received a discharge on the basis of disability in 1840. See Bancroft, *History of California* 2: 692.

15. Abella reported that he tried to induce Ramírez to go to confession but that he was unsuccessful. See Engelhardt, *Mission San Luis Obispo*, 137–38.

16. The appointment was actually issued on June 6. There was a certain logic

in it. The *californios* had long agitated for an *hijo del país* to rule them, and Carrillo had been born at Santa Bárbara. He had also served in the Mexican congress, where his brother, José Antonio, was currently a deputy. José Antonio engineered the appointment. See Bancroft, *History of California* 3: 534–35.

17. Alvarado at first indicated that he was ready to surrender the governorship to Carrillo, but he was also interested in stalling the transfer as long as he could, in the hope that Castillero might be successful in his mission in Mexico City. For the same reason, José Antonio Carrillo, who had just returned from the congressional session there, urged his brother to assume the governorship immediately and dispense with the traditional transfer ceremony. See Tays, "Revolutionary California," 725–28.

18. Carrillo took office in the presence of the Los Angeles *ayuntamiento* on December 6, 1837. See Bancroft, *History of California* 3: 539.

19. The administrator was William Hartnell, with whom Osio had been associated. See Dakin, *Lives of William Hartnell*, 212.

20. Alvarado sent Castro south after Carrillo had sent troops north to San Buenaventura in March 1838. See Tays, "Revolutionary California," 732.

21. El Rincón is on the coast, approximately halfway between San Buenaventura and Santa Bárbara, which are twenty miles from each other. See Beck and Haase, *Historical Atlas of California*, 36.

22. According to both Bancroft and Tays, Tovar did not arrive until April 4. He was placed in command after that time. The battle at San Buenaventura, however, occurred at the end of March, and the commander of the Carrillo forces was Juan Castañeda. See Bancroft, *History of California* 3: 554–55.

23. Castañeda, the *carlista* commander, was from Texas.

24. The search was so thorough that they even checked behind a statue of St. Bonaventure. St. Bonaventure, a professor at the University of Paris, is considered a Doctor of the Church.

25. The battle was concluded on March 28, and Alvarado arrived at Santa Ynés on April 5. See Tays, "Revolutionary California," 733–35. Those whom Osio describes as being arrested here were probably released and arrested again at Los Angeles on May 20, and sent to Sonoma then.

26. When Carrillo was informed about the defeat at San Buenaventura, he left Los Angeles for San Diego before April 1. See Bancroft, *History of California* 3: 556.

27. Las Flores was just north of Mission San Luis Rey. See Beck and Haase, *Historical Atlas of California*, 39.

28. Osio is dramatically telescoping events here. At Las Flores, Carrillo surrendered to Alvarado, and the two of them signed a treaty, which is reproduced in Bancroft, *History of California* 3: 562. They agreed mutually to reduce their forces and to go together to San Fernando to work out their differences. The talks there proved fruitless, and Carrillo left for Los Angeles, promising to keep the peace. On May 10 Alvarado left for Santa Bárbara. He soon heard that Carrillo and his friends

were continuing their plotting. On May 20 he sent a force to Los Angeles and had Carrillo, his brother, and a number of their supporters arrested and brought to Santa Bárbara. Some of them were sent to Sonoma (See n. 25 above). Carlos Carrillo, however, was allowed to remain in Santa Bárbara. It was from there that he escaped in Dana's boat. See Tays, "Revolutionary California," 742–43.

29. This story of the double appointment was current at the time. Its roots are probably that Mexican president Anastasio Bustamante had said that he did not really care who the governor of California was and had suggested at one point that perhaps the *diputación* should offer some expression of its own wishes. See. T. H. Hittell, *California* 2: 253.

30. Castillero arrived at Santa Bárbara on November 15 aboard the *California*, a vessel which was engaged in the coastal trade. It is not recorded as stopping at San Diego on its way back from San Blas. See Bancroft, *History of California* 3: 574; 4: 101.

31. Castillero also bore other documents, including one giving a general amnesty to all who had participated in the events of the past few years and another appointing Vallejo *comandante general*. Ibid., 3: 575.

32. In the original manuscript, this passage, which we have bracketed and which describes the release of the prisoners and their reaction to being set free, was written on a half sheet of paper. This loose page was inserted between pages 88 and 89 of the original. Perhaps as Osio was rereading his manuscript, he realized that he had forgotten to include this detail and inserted it later.

33. This decree was issued in April 1839. Osio gets the scale confused in his account. The actual scale was if the duty was 3,000 pesos or less, it all was to be paid in silver; if the duty was between 3,000 and 6,000 pesos, two-thirds was to be paid in silver; if the duty was between 6,000 and 12,000 pesos, one-half was to be paid in silver; and if the duty was more than 12,000 pesos, one-third was to be paid in silver. See Bancroft, *History of California* 4: 91.

34. Faxon Dean Atherton, for instance, described a situation on November 9, 1837, in which Osio refused to let some goods be landed because of irregularities in the documents. See Nunis, *California Diary of Faxon Dean Atherton*, 74. José Fernández related a normal way of avoiding part of the duties: "Every ship captain was permitted to include in his manifest a list of rations, and since all of these captains were supposedly carrying provisions for voyages of three years, they would list an enormous amount of provisions on the ration list and before leaving our ports they would sell the provisions for cash" (Fernández, "Cosas de California," 50).

Chapter 11

1. Whether there was a conspiracy or not and, if so, what its aims were are unclear in the sources. The fullest treatment remains Bancroft, *History of California* 4: 1-42. The significance of Osio's treatment of this matter is that he had fairly consistently ignored the political and military presence of non-Mexicans up to this

point. Isaac Graham's part in the events of 1836–38, for instance, is generally only obliquely acknowledged in the manuscript. From this point forward, however, the presence of foreigners in Alta California gradually comes to dominate Osio's writing and his concern.

2. La Natividad was inland from Monterey Bay, about fifteen miles northeast of the Monterey presidio. See Beck and Haase, *Historical Atlas of California*, 31.

3. Garner was married to a daughter of Manuel Butrón, grantee of La Natividad. See Bancroft, *History of California* 2: 738; 3: 754.

4. Garner was captured first, on April 5 or 6. Graham and some of his companions were captured on April 7. By April 11 thirty-nine people had been arrested. Ibid., 4: 12.

5. The *Joven Guipuzcoana* was a Mexican brigantine, which had been purchased by José Antonio Aguirre in March 1840. Ibid., 104.

6. Some of those arrested were British citizens, and some were citizens of the United States. Barron acted on behalf of all of them, since either the U.S. consul at Tepic was absent or the office was not filled when the prisoners arrived. Ibid., 32.

7. The *californios* who were guarding the foreigners were themselves jailed for a time in Tepic, and they were released after a few weeks of captivity on orders from the capital. Castro himself was locked up for only a few days. Alvarado had instructed him to go to Mexico City as soon as he could, to report on the state of affairs in Alta California and to work with Castillero to try to obtain some financial assistance for Alta California. Ibid., 13, 29–30.

8. Castro had to face charges brought by the U.S. and British ministers. He was eventually acquitted, in April 1841, and he left the capital in May. Ibid., 34.

9. Castro's trip back to Alta California was indeed largely by land, although there does not seem to be evidence that the trip was more difficult than usual because of the hostility of Barron. But here Osio sees Castro as a type of *californio* to come: harassed by foreigners and reduced to the back roads and alleys of his own country.

10. On October 1, 1841, Alvarado ordered that Castro be paid what was due him. The method by which the money was raised is not stated. See Bancroft, *History of California* 4: 34. Osio sees Alvarado as being forced by foreigners to do exactly what he thought those involved in the slaughter of the cattle in 1832–34 had done: to act against the overall best interests of Alta California.

11. A *considerando* is a "whereas." Osio is most likely referring to the 1851 session of the California legislature, which was meeting in San José, just a few miles from Santa Clara, where Osio was composing the manuscript. This session of the legislature dealt extensively with land and mining issues, and this did not bode well for the *californio* elite, who, like Osio, were having difficulty in holding on to their lands in the face of pressure from squatters. Also, by 1851 it was becoming excruciatingly clear that the *californio* presence in California was regarded by the Anglo newcomers as something of an irritant. The governor's opening message, for in-

stance, called for repeal of the constitutional provision that all laws be published in both English and Spanish. It was, the governor stated, just too expensive.

12. As Osio admits at the end of this somewhat clumsy effort, his attempt at this long analogy about the United States and Mexico does not really make the point that he wanted to make. Osio was apparently well read, and his manuscript often benefits from the classical and literary allusions he inserts into it. But he was an accountant, not a novelist, and when he attempts to create a story on his own, he does not succeed very well.

A possible interpretation of the symbolic elements of Osio's story is as follows: The two landowners represent the United States (the northern landowner) and Mexico. The northerner, called Uncle Samuel, was clever and knew how to win trustworthy people to his side. His loyal servants would work for a lesser wage and not complain, knowing that if they proved themselves they would be rewarded well. Osio mentions that the landowner brought progress to these workers, who in turn helped the landowner divide his inheritance into *haciendas*, a possible metaphor for the westward expansion. The landowner is described as a greedy and meddlesome person who has a keen interest in his neighbor's crops. The friendly advice he gives his neighbor on how to improve his crops is but a pretext to overtake the neighbor's lands. Osio again appears to equate the northerner's character traits with encroachment on foreign territory.

The poorly fed pig symbolizes California and the manner in which it was mistreated and ignored by Mexico. After the northerner discovers that the yellow horseshoes on the pig are made not of brass, but rather of gold, he offers to buy the pig from its owner and eventually swindles him. The fifteen *tlacos* symbolize the fifteen million dollars which in the Treaty of Guadalupe Hidalgo the United States agreed to pay Mexico. The useless nail that he takes from the pig's shoe may represent the *californios* who felt as if they no longer belonged after the U.S. invasion.

13. Salvador Vallejo was appointed *juez de paz* at Sonoma in January 1839 and took the oath of office in May. He was also commander of the troops there. In June, Mariano Guadalupe Vallejo ordered Salvador not to serve as *juez*, since Alvarado had no right, he said, to appoint a military officer to a civilian position. This was inconsistent, since Salvador Vallejo had served in other civilian offices, such as that of *alcalde*, while a member of the military. As Osio says, the quarrel concerned who had the power to name officeholders in Sonoma. Mariano Guadalupe Vallejo argued that Sonoma was basically a fort, and that gave him, as *comandante general*, an exclusive power of appointment. See Tays, "Mariano Guadalupe Vallejo and Sonoma," 369.

14. Vallejo's position, which he expressed to the general government, was that the two commands should be united under one person who was not connected by blood with the leading *californios*. He was not calling for Alvarado to be replaced with himself, although Alvarado and his circle assumed that that was his true in-

tent. The developing tensions between Alvarado and Vallejo are well summarized in Tays, "Mariano Guadalupe Vallejo and Sonoma," 50–61.

15. Prudón served as Vallejo's secretary. According to José Fernández, he knew four languages (Fernández, "Cosas de California," 166).

16. At this time Prudón was serving as Vallejo's secretary. Vallejo set him his task in December 1841, and he arrived in Monterey on January 1, 1842. Alvarado's circle, including Osio, suspected that his true mission in Mexico City was to plot against Alvarado, so they at first attempted to delay his departure. They finally decided to send Castañares with him. The two sailed together on the *California* from Monterey on January 20 and arrived at Acapulco on February 14. See Bancroft, *History of California* 4: 204, 281–84.

17. When Prudón and Castañares reached the capital on March 2, they discovered that Micheltorena had been appointed governor a month earlier. But Santa Anna tried to assuage the situation by giving everyone a promotion: Vallejo to lieutenant colonel, Prudón to captain, Castañares to customs administrator, and Alvarado to colonel of the militia. See Tays, "Mariano Guadalupe Vallejo and Sonoma," 61.

18. On this point, see Brack, *Mexico Views Manifest Destiny*, 88-101.

19. The ship left Mazatlán on July 25, 1842, and arrived at San Diego exactly a month later, on August 25. Zamorano probably died on September 16. See Harding, *Zamorano*, 256.

20. Osio resigned on September 22, 1842. See Provincial State Papers, Tomo XVIII, 382, The Bancroft Library.

21. This was on October 19, 1842. Thomas ap Catesby Jones had heard in Peru that three British ships were on their way to Alta California, and also that war between the United States and Mexico was likely. He had also picked up rumors that a French fleet was heading for Alta California. As he later put it, he decided that he had to risk taking Alta California "by right of conquest in war" rather than letting the British or French gain it. On the other hand, if there was not war, "the responsibility of the act at first might seem to rest on me, certainly not on our government, who gave no orders on the subject" (Bancroft, *History of California* 4: 306). Jones specifically regarded himself as implementing the Monroe Doctrine. See Smith, "Thomas ap Catesby Jones."

22. Jimeno surrendered the political command to Micheltorena in Los Angeles on December 31, 1842. From Sonoma, Vallejo had issued orders transferring the military command on September 19. See Tays, "Revolutionary California," 753.

23. Jones left Monterey on the *Cyane* on January 9, 1843, and arrived at San Pedro on January 17. See Bancroft, *History of California* 4: 320.

24. The most complete account of Jones's visit to Los Angeles is in Wright, *Yankee in Mexican California*, 105-10.

25. The Bases de Tacubaya was a thirteen-point armistice imposed by Santa Anna on September 28, 1841, to end a struggle within centralist ranks between

Bustamante and Paredes. By its terms Santa Anna was given power to name an interim president who would enjoy what Ramón Eduardo Ruiz has called "dictatorial" powers. Santa Anna named himself to the post. See Ruiz, *Triumphs and Tragedy*, 180; and *Diccionario Porrúa*, 186.

26. Micheltorena had brought a mistress with him to Alta California. He married her in 1843. See Juárez, "Notas," 8.

27. Fernández wrote that "Micheltorena had arrived in California accompanied by hundreds of soldiers who had dressed themselves in honorable military uniforms the very day they had left the presidios where they had been imprisoned for robbery, assault, and murder" (Fernández, "Cosas de California," 105).

28. The opportunity to do so arrived in December 1844. See n. 39 below.

29. Micheltorena's convict soldiers were poor and even more underpaid than Mexican soldiers in Alta California normally were. The governor was aware of this, and once he plaintively said, "It was hard to shoot a hungry, unpaid soldier for pilfering food" (Bancroft, *History of California* 4: 367).

30. This episode happened in 1844, when the *Angelina* was at Monterey. In 1845 the newly arrived French consul tried to investigate the matter. Ibid., 563, 590.

31. This was on November 15, 1844. The Pico was José de Jesús Pico.

32. According to Rafael Pinto, who worked at the San Francisco Customs House, Osio tried to proselytize for the revolt among the employees there. See Bancroft, *History of California* 4: 463.

33. Alisal is about twenty miles to the northeast of the Monterey presidio. The distance from there to San Pablo, on the eastern shore of San Francisco Bay, is about eighty-five miles. See Beck and Haase, *Historical Atlas of California*, 30–31.

34. Castro had been sent on an expedition against the indigenous peoples of the interior. See Bancroft, *History of California* 4: 462.

35. Apparently the expedition went only to the Salinas River, which empties into Monterey Bay a scant dozen miles north of the presidio. Ibid., 461.

36. Rancho Laguna Seca was about ten miles southeast of San José. See Beck and Haase, *Historical Atlas of California*, 30.

37. The Germán brothers describe an unsuccessful attempt that night by Alvarado's men to steal Micheltorena's horses (Germán and Germán, "Sucesos," 12–13).

38. In a report to the War Department, Micheltorena said that he agreed to this only to gain time: "I have put them off by offering to send away the bad men for three months, in order to gain this time, while I await the schooner *California*." The agreement, called the Treaty of Santa Teresa, was signed on December 1. See Bancroft, *History of California* 4: 467.

39. Téllez was sent south in December 1844, ostensibly to bring back more troops. Ibid., 471.

40. Sutter led a force of about 220—about half foreigners and half indigenous

people—from New Helvetia on January 1, 1845. The rebels left San José on January 2 and departed for the south on January 6. Ibid., 485, 489–90.

41. Castro went out with an advance party to San Buenaventura, and Micheltorena's forces were just to the south of Santa Bárbara. During the second week of February, it seems that Micheltorena's forces lost almost half of their numbers, as some people decided to return to the north. Ibid., 500–501.

42. According to José Fernández, Castro "harangued them with the intent of making them understand that they should not get involved in matters that did not concern them. . . . he gave each an ounce [of gold] and sent them home" (Fernández, "Cosas de California," 112).

43. The battle of Cahuenga lasted two days, February 20 and 21, without casualties. It ended on the second day after some overnight maneuvering, when Micheltorena's forces appear to have found themselves in an untenable field position. See Bancroft, *History of California* 4: 503–6.

44. On February 15, the *diputación*, meeting at Los Angeles, had declared Pico, its most senior member, governor. Ibid., 499.

45. Castillero was sent to Alta California to prepare for the arrival of a military force which the Mexican government had decided to send, so that California would not be lost as Texas had been. However, the plans were a casualty of a change of the Mexican government at the end of 1845, and the force never was actually sent. The trouble between Pico and Castro did originate, as Osio says, in differences over military policy and over Castro's insistence that the danger Alta California faced meant that higher military expenditures and a general military reorganization were necessary. Pico opposed both measures. See Tays, "Revolutionary California," 769.

46. This meeting, called for June 15, never occurred. The delegates from the north refused to attend. See Harlow, *California Conquered*, 88–89.

47. Osio is making reference to Napoleon Bonaparte's coup d'état of 18 Brumaire (November 9, 1799), when members of the senate reportedly escaped through the windows in an attempt to save their lives. See Palmer, *Encyclopedia of Napoleon's Europe*, 57.

48. On the background to the proposed Santa Bárbara meeting, see Jackson, *British Ranchero*, 93–99. The *Juno* was at Santa Bárbara in June 1846. See Bancroft, *History of California* 5: 217.

Chapter 12

1. The Castro *rancho*, Ciénega de los Paicines, was about twelve miles southeast of Mission San Juan Bautista. See Beck and Haase, *Historical Atlas of California*, 31.

2. Thomas O. Larkin's report simply said that one of Frémont's men, who was drunk, wanted one of Castro's daughters to have a drink with him. The event happened around the beginning of March. See Larkin, *Papers* 4: 272.

3. Castro ordered Frémont out of Alta California on March 5. Frémont instead moved six miles northward to the highest point in the Gavilán Mountains and

raised the U.S. flag there, in a calculated insult to the *californios*. In the letter to which Osio refers, Frémont wrote Larkin, "If we are hemmed in and assaulted here, we will die every man of us under the flag of our country" (Hammond, *Larkin Papers* 4: 245). At the time, Osio was serving as captain of the Monterey militia. See Bancroft, *History of California* 4: 652; and Garnica del Castillo, "Recuerdos," 9.

4. Frémont left during the night of March 9–10. See Harlow, *California Conquered,* 72.

5. The boat arrived on April 17. Gillespie had a set of papers on his person which identified him as a merchant who was traveling for reasons of health. Ibid., 77.

6. This attack took place on the night of May 9–10, 1846, near Klamath Lake in Oregon. See Bancroft, *History of California* 5: 25.

7. The Bear Flag Revolt was undertaken by a group of U.S. settlers in the Sonoma area, not by the U.S. army or navy. Technically, the U.S. military forces were not involved, but neither Osio nor many other *californios* believed that the technical reality corresponded to the actual state of affairs. After the meeting with Gillespie, Frémont returned to Alta California from the Oregon Territory. By June 12 he was camped close to Sacramento. See Harlow, *California Conquered,* 96.

8. On the *Portsmouth,* Montgomery sent an official letter to William Ide, leader of the Bear Flaggers, denying his request for weapons. However, some *californios* insisted that the vessel was providing the insurgents with supplies. Manuel Castro, for instance, wrote the minister of war in Mexico City on June 19 that the ship was giving weapons to the rebels. Ibid., 103–5.

9. Vallejo and the others were seized on June 14, 1846. They left for Frémont's camp on that day and reached it on June 16. Frémont had them sent to Sutter's establishment at New Helvetia, where they were kept until August. Ibid., 101.

10. This is a reference to a saying of Jesus, in Matthew 7.2, Mark 4.24, and Luke 6.37–38: "The measure with which you measure shall be used to measure you."

11. Osio is making a joke here. In Spanish, the *h* is silent, and when Osio heard Ide's name, he assumed that it had an *h* in front of it and that it was spelled more or less like U.S. citizens spelled the part of the cattle they traded for: *hide*. In fact, Osio spells the name phonetically: "Haid." In Spanish, *cuero* means "hide." In addition, Spanish and Mexican soldiers in Alta California were often called *soldados de cuera,* because of the protective leather jackets that they wore, and Osio is also poking fun at Ide's military exploits in "seizing" the undefended Sonoma.

12. Osio is talking about himself here. He and Richardson had known each other for years. Richardson managed Angel Island for Osio in the 1840s and lived at Sausalito. Osio, meanwhile, was spending more and more time at San Rafael.

13. Vallejo had also sent a messenger, José de la Rosa, to Montgomery and asked for help. Misroon was sent on the morning of June 16. See Harlow, *California Conquered,* 104–5; and Bancroft, *History of California* 5: 129–31. When Osio heard Misroon's name, he assumed that the first syllable was actually "Mister" and that the second syllable was the man's name. So he wrote it as "Mr. Rum."

14. Osio met Leidesdorff on June 22, and then Leidesdorff gave him a letter to give to Larkin in Monterey. Whether Osio gave the letter to Larkin himself or had someone deliver it to Monterey is unclear. See Hammond, *Larkin Papers* 5: 68. Ridley was arrested on July 2. Bancroft thinks it was at the instigation of Leidesdorff. (*History of California* 5: 136).

15. The battle took place on June 24, 1846. It is described in Harlow, *California Conquered*, 109.

16. It seems that this person was Osio, who was probably back at San Rafael and who certainly would have known the whereabouts of Richardson's boat.

17. The escape took place on June 29. See Harlow, *California Conquered*, 111.

18. The Santa Margarita *rancho* was about ten miles northeast of Mission San Luis Obispo. See Beck and Haase, *Historical Atlas of California*, 35. Castro and Pico met on July 12. See Bancroft, *History of California* 262.

19. Both Pico and Castro left Los Angeles on the night of August 10 after the *diputación* had dissolved itself. Castro immediately went to Sonora, and Pico hid out until September 7, when he slipped over into Baja California. Both men petitioned the Mexican government for assistance in the struggle, but of course it had its hands full with the U.S. invasion. See Harlow, *California Conquered*, 149–50.

20. After Pico and Castro had abandoned Los Angeles, it was occupied by U.S. forces, and eventually Gillespie was made military commander of the southern area. His rule in Los Angeles was harsh, and resistance to his regime grew. Flores was a leader of that resistance, and Gillespie was forced to leave Los Angeles and set up headquarters in San Pedro on September 30. Ibid., 163.

21. The battle of Angostura was fought south of Saltillo on February 22 and 23, 1847. The U.S. forces held the pass for two days of intense attacks by the Mexicans. After the second day of battle, the Mexicans retired to the south. U.S. histories generally refer to this engagement as the battle of Buena Vista. The battle of Cerro Gordo was fought on the road from Veracruz to Jalapa on April 18, 1847. Despite fierce Mexican resistance, the U.S. army managed to outflank the Mexicans and drive them from the field. See Eisenhower, *So Far from God*, 272–83, 181–91; Bauer, *Mexican War*, 209–17, 263–68; and *Diccionario Porrúa*, 87, 328–29.

22. The battle of Natividad took place on November 16, 1846, outside of San Juan Bautista. The *californios* and the U.S. forces fought each other to a standoff, although the North Americans suffered higher casualties than did the *californios*. The battle of Santa Clara occurred on January 2, 1847. A group of *californios*, incensed at the plundering of their *ranchos*, had seized Washington Bartlett, *alcalde* of San Francisco, and five or six others. U.S. marines came to the scene, and battle was joined. After a brief engagement, an armistice was arranged, and the U.S. authorities agreed to respect the *californios'* property. See Harlow, *California Conquered*, 195–97; Regnery, *Battle of Santa Clara*.

23. Four of Mervine's men were killed by the *californios*, and another four to six were wounded. See Harlow, *California Conquered*, 167–68.

24. Stockton arrived at San Pedro on October 25 and left for San Diego on October 30. Ibid., 170–71.

25. The battle of San Gabriel was on January 8, 1847. The U.S. forces crossed the San Gabriel River at the Paso de Bartolo instead of by the more direct ford at Los Nietos. Ibid., 209–13; Bancroft, *History of California* 5: 389–90.

26. The battle of San Pascual took place on December 6–7, 1846. Osio describes it after the battle of San Gabriel, which took place a month later, so that he could end his account with a *californio* victory. The attempt to stampede the animals occurred on December 10, and Kearny's troops headed for San Diego on that same day. See Harlow, *California Conquered,* 182–88; Clarke, *Stephen Watts Kearny,* 195–232.

27. The Treaty of Cahuenga was signed by Frémont and Pico (Flores had turned the command over to him after the battle of San Gabriel) and other commissioners from both sides on January 13, 1847. The major *californio* commissioner was José Antonio Carrillo. The treaty's terms were generous to the *californios.* See Harlow, *California Conquered,* 232; the terms are in Bancroft, *History of California* 5: 404–5.

28. Gold was first discovered at San Fernando in 1842. See Bancroft, *History of California* 4: 297.

Epilogue

1. Testimony of Jean Jacques Vioget, in Land Commission Papers, Angel Island.

2. Many of the letters from Vischer to Osio are preserved in the Osio Papers at The Bancroft Library. See, for instance, Vischer to Osio, Oct. 31, 1852, and June 24, 1853. The Land Commission upheld Osio's claim in 1854, and the district court in San Francisco upheld that judgment in 1855. See Hoffman, *Report of Land Cases,* 100–101, and p. 3 of appendix. However, in December 1859, the U.S. Supreme Court threw out the claim in the case *United States v. Antonio María Osio,* 23 Howard 273.

3. According to the 1900 census, she lived in enumeration district 357 on Maple Street.

4. Adela Frisby was the daughter of William Edward Rose Frisby and María Inés Telecilla Vallejo. María Inés was the daughter of Salvador Vallejo and María de la Luz Carrillo. See Gantner, "Notes on the Life of My Father."

5. Gantner, "Gantner and Mattern," a brief appendix to Gantner, "Notes on the Life of My Father." The information on Gantner's involvement in the Native Sons of the Golden West comes from the obituary of John Gantner, which is appended to the end of the "Gantner and Mattern" essay.

6. Fred H. Jung, Grand Secretary, to all members, March 8, 1915, Native Sons of the Golden West Papers, The Bancroft Library.

7. This information comes to us through correspondence with Mollins and Thickens.

Biographical Sketches

José Ramón Abella was born near Zaragoza, Spain, in 1764. He came to New Spain as a Franciscan in 1795 and entered Alta California at Santa Bárbara in 1798. He served at San Francisco from that date until 1819, and during that time he participated in two important exploratory journeys into the interior of California. After his stay at San Francisco, he moved to Mission San Carlos at Carmel, where he remained until 1833. With the arrival of the Zacatecan friars, he then moved south, to San Luis Obispo, where he ministered until 1841. He died at Santa Ynés in 1842. See Geiger, *Franciscan Missionaries*, 3–6.

José Antonio Aguirre was born about 1793 in Spain. He established a very successful trading concern in Guaymas, Mexico, and engaged in the California coastal trade. He lived in Santa Bárbara from at least 1838 and married María del Rosario Estudillo. He was still living in Santa Bárbara in the 1850s. See Bancroft, *History of California* 2: 688.

Gervasio Alipás was involved in the San Diego phase of the movement against Victoria in 1831. He was executed by the Los Angeles vigilantes in 1836. See Bancroft, *History of California* 2: 690.

José Altimira was born in Barcelona in 1787. He entered the Franciscan order and was ordained a priest in his homeland. He arrived in Monterey in 1820 and was assigned to San Francisco, but he quickly grew to dislike the cold, damp climate. In apparent complicity with Luis Argüello, he petitioned the *diputación* in 1823 to transfer the missions in San Francisco and San Rafael to a new site in Sonoma. When the *diputación* approved, Altimira quickly established the mission. His superiors strongly objected to this, and finally a compromise was reached whereby all three missions, including Altimira's new mission, San Francisco Solano, were allowed to remain active. He stayed there until 1826. After the mission had been burned, he retreated to San Rafael with a small band of neophytes. He was then posted to San Carlos and San Buenaventura. He secretly fled Alta California with Father Antonio Ripoll in 1828. He was last reported to be in the Canary Islands in 1860. See Geiger, *Franciscan Missionaries*, 6–10.

Manuel de Alva came to Alta California with Governor Figueroa in 1833 as surgeon for the military. He took part in the northern revolt against Alvarado in 1837 and sided with Carlos Carrillo in 1838. He left Alta California in about 1840. See Bancroft, *History of California* 2: 692.

Francisco Javier Alvarado was born in 1808, the son of another Francisco Javier Alvarado, who had served as a soldier and official at San Diego and Santa Bárbara from 1780 until his death in 1818. The mother of the younger Alvarado was María Ignacia Amador, daughter of Pedro Amador. Alvarado served as *alcalde* of Los Angeles in 1835 and as a substitute member of the *diputación* in 1833 and 1837. See Bancroft, *History of California* 2: 692.

Juan Bautista Alvarado, the son of José Francisco Alvarado and María Josefa Vallejo, was born in Monterey in 1809. His father died shortly after his birth, and his mother married José Raimundo Estrada, brother of José Mariano Estrada. He served as secretary of the *diputación* from 1828 to 1834 and was a member of that body for the next three years. During that period he also worked in the Monterey Customs House. He led the revolution against Gutiérrez in 1836 and served as governor until 1842. He was a leader in the move against Micheltorena in 1844–45 and was subsequently appointed administrator of the Customs House at Monterey. He died in 1882. See Alvarado, *Vignettes*, vii–xiv; Meier, *Mexican American Biographies*, 5; and Sánchez, "Juan Bautista Alvarado," in Sánchez, Pita, and Reyes, *Crítica*, 76.

Antonio Apalátegui was born around 1801. A clerk, he was part of the Gómez Farías colonization effort in 1834. He was apparently refused a position by Governor Figueroa and took part in a movement against the governor in Los Angeles in 1835. He was exiled for his part in the affair. See Bancroft, *History of California* 2: 699.

Francisco Araujo arrived in Alta California as a soldier with Governor Figueroa in 1833 and served for a time in Monterey. In 1836 he was commander of the vigilante armed force in Los Angeles. He may have been sent out of the territory by Chico. See Bancroft, *History of California* 2: 699.

José Darío Argüello was a native of Querétaro, New Spain. He joined the army at around the age of twenty and arrived in California in 1781. He served as commander in both San Francisco and Monterey in the 1790s and early 1800s. He became acting governor upon the death of Arrillaga and was named to the same office in Baja California when Solá was appointed governor of Alta California. He held that office until 1822, when, after San José del Cabo and Loreto were sacked by insurgents, he moved to Guadalajara, where he died in the late 1820s. On November 28, 1822, Antonio María Osio married his youngest daughter, Dolores. See Bancroft, *History of California* 2: 701.

Luis Antonio Argüello was born in San Francisco in 1784. His father, José Darío Argüello, was then serving with the military at the Santa Bárbara presidio. Luis Argüello entered the military at an early age and quickly rose through the ranks, no doubt aided by his father's eminence. A cadet in 1799, he became a lieutenant in 1806, and by 1818 he had risen to become captain of the garrison at San Francisco. He was selected acting governor in 1822, and he held that office until the appointment of Echeandía in 1825. After leaving office he filled a number of military posts, but apparently he began drinking heavily. He died at San Francisco in 1830. See Bancroft, *History of California* 3: 9–13.

Santiago Argüello, younger brother of Luis Antonio Argüello, was born at Monterey in 1791. He entered the military at an early age and served at Santa Bárbara from 1806 to 1817 and at San Francisco from 1817 to 1827. In 1827 he was transferred to San Diego, where he served as commander and as a member of the *diputación.* He retired from the military in 1834 and served as *alcalde* of San Diego in 1836, acting against Alvarado. He was commissioner of San Juan Capistrano from 1838 to 1840 and prefect of Los Angeles from 1840 to 1843. He received a number of land grants and died in 1862 on his *rancho,* Tijuana, near the California-Mexico border. His wife was Pilar Ortega. See Bancroft, *History of California* 2: 702.

James Armstrong was commander of the *United States* at Monterey in 1842, and of the *Savannah,* which visited Alta California in 1844–46. See Bancroft, *History of California* 2: 703.

José Joaquín de Arrillaga was born at Aya, Guipúzcoa, Spain, in 1750. He entered the army at an early age and served in northern Mexico and Texas in the 1780s and 1790s. He was appointed lieutenant governor of the Californias in 1783 and served as interim governor from 1792 to 1794. The governments of Alta and Baja California were separated in 1804, and he was appointed the first governor of Alta California in that same year. He served until his death in 1814. Bancroft portrayed him as a competent official, one who could obey orders so well and tactfully that he made no enemies but who also lacked originality, vision, and "enthusiastic confidence in the future of the province." See Bancroft, *History of California* 2: 204–7.

Manuel Arzaga served as secretary of the Los Angeles *ayuntamiento* in 1834 and 1835 and as secretary of the vigilante organization in Los Angeles in 1836. See Bancroft, *History of California* 2: 704.

Antonio Ávila was a convict who had arrived in California in 1825 after having been convicted of robbery and murder in Puebla. He sided with the authorities in the Solís revolt and again in 1832, in the apparent hope of gaining an early release. His hope was unrealized, and he remained in California until about 1838. See Bancroft, *History of California* 2: 705.

Antonio Ignacio Ávila was the son of Cornelio Ávila, a native of Sonora, who settled in Los Angeles in 1783. In 1804 Antonio married Rosa Ruiz. In 1822 he was granted a *rancho,* Sausal Redondo, on the Pacific coast, directly north of Los Palos Verdes. Between 1835 and 1848 he often served as *juez de campo.* He died in 1858. See Bancroft, *History of California* 2: 705.

José María Ávila, a native of Sinaloa, was the son of Cornelio Ávila and Isabel Urquides. He became the owner of extensive property in Alta California and was elected *alcalde* of Los Angeles in 1825, but he was evidently suspended for being an overbearing official. He was jailed by Vicente Sánchez in 1831 and was killed later that year in the battle of Cahuenga. See Bancroft, *History of California* 2: 705; 3: 207.

Juan Bandini was born in Peru in 1800 and came to Alta California with his father, a trader, in the 1820s. He served in the *diputación* in 1827 and in the customs service for four years after that. He was active in the movement against Victoria in 1831. In 1833 he represented Alta California in the Mexican congress and became involved in the colonization efforts being organized at the time. He headed the Cosmopolitan Company, a trading concern established in conjunction with the Gómez Farías venture. The company failed when its supply ship was wrecked. He opposed Alvarado from 1837 to 1838 but later received an appointment as administrator at San Gabriel. In the 1840s he was *síndico* of Los Angeles and secretary to Governor Pío Pico. He died in Los Angeles in 1859. See Bancroft, *History of California* 2: 709–10.

Eustace Barron was a British businessman who served as British consul at Tepic, Mexico, in 1840. He was involved in seeking freedom for those sent there as a result of their alleged participation in the 1840 foreigners' plot. See Bancroft, *History of California* 4: 30–33.

Leonardo Díaz Barroso was sent to Alta California in 1830 as a lieutenant and was soon promoted to captain. He was at Los Angeles in 1831 and saw action during the military campaigns of 1832. He returned to Mexico in 1833. See Bancroft, *History of California* 2: 711.

Hipólito Bouchard was born around 1785 in St. Tropéz, France. By 1811 he was sailing and fighting on behalf of the revolutionaries of the La Plata River region in modern Argentina. In July 1817 he was given command of the *Argentina*, which then circumnavigated the globe. By August 1818 he had reached Hawaii, and he proceeded to raid the coast of Spanish Alta California. On his return to South America, the *Argentina* was used as a transport vessel for San Martín's 1820 expedition to Peru. At the conclusion of the campaign, Bouchard was given some land in Peru, where he settled. He died there in January 1837, killed by one of his slaves. See Ratto, *Bouchard*.

Manuel Cantúa was a soldier in the San Francisco company from 1832. He was at Sonoma in 1844 and with Sutter in 1845. He was killed at Olompali in 1846. See Bancroft, *History of California* 2: 741.

Anastasio Carrillo was born at Santa Bárbara in 1788. His father was José Raimundo Carrillo, who had come to Alta California from Loreto in 1769, and his mother was Tomasa Ignacia Lugo. He entered the military at an early age. He engaged in many expeditions against the Indians during the 1820s. He retired from the military in 1836 but negotiated with Alvarado in the south in 1837. He served on the *diputación* in 1839. He was married to Concepción García, and he received a number of land grants, including an 1845 grant to Rancho Cieneguitas, a few miles west of Santa Bárbara. See Bancroft, *History of California* 2: 743; 3: 518–19.

Carlos Antonio Carrillo, the son of José Raimundo Carrillo and Tomasa Ignacia Lugo, was born at Santa Bárbara in 1783. He served in the military at Monterey and Santa Bárbara from 1797 to 1825. In 1828 he served in the *diputación*, and he was a delegate to the Mexican congress in 1831–32. He served again in the *diputación* in the mid-1830s. In 1837 he was appointed governor of Alta California, but he was never able to force Alvarado from office. He died in 1852. See Bancroft, *History of California* 2: 743.

José Antonio Carrillo, son of José Raimundo Carrillo and Tomasa Ignacia Lugo, was born in San Francisco in 1796. He served in the *diputación* from 1822 to 1824, as Echeandía's secretary in 1826, and as Los Angeles *alcalde* in 1827. He was exiled to Baja California in 1831 as a result of a quarrel with Los Angeles *alcalde* Vicente Sánchez. From 1831 to 1832 he opposed Victoria and favored Pico. After serving as a delegate to the Mexican congress, he opposed Alvarado in 1837 and was jailed at Sonoma as a result. He participated in the resistance to the U.S. invasion in 1846 and signed the Treaty of Cahuenga in 1847. He attended the constitutional convention in 1849 and died in 1862. See Bancroft, *History of California* 2: 745.

José María Castañares was born in Puebla, New Spain, and came to Alta California in 1833 to clerk for Rafael González at the Customs House. He was married to Ana González, Rafael's daughter. His affair with Ildefonsa González, the wife of José María Herrera, caused a sensation in Monterey in 1836, and Castañares soon went to Mexico. He returned to Alta California in 1840 and served on the staff of the *tribunal*. He went back to Mexico in 1845 and remained there. See Bancroft, *History of California* 2: 748.

Manuel Castañares, brother of José María, came to Alta California in 1840 and served as secretary of the Monterey prefecture until 1842. He was sent by Alvarado to Mexico in that year and was then appointed administrator of the Customs House at Monterey. He served in the Mexican congress from 1844 to 1845 and never returned to Alta California. See Bancroft, *History of California* 2: 748.

Juan Castañeda was a Mexican officer serving in Baja California who came to Alta California in 1837 with José Antonio Carrillo. He played a major role in the Carrillo fight against Alvarado. In 1839 he was named secretary to General Mariano Guadalupe Vallejo, who sent him on a mission to Mexico City. He returned to Alta California in 1842, perhaps with Governor Micheltorena. He testified in some land cases in the 1850s. See Bancroft, *History of California* 2: 748–49.

Andrés Castillero was a soldier on the frontier in Baja California. He was in Alta California with Governor Chico in 1836 and left the territory after the expulsion of Gutiérrez. Sent by José Caballero, the military commander of Baja California, he returned in 1837, to try to settle the civil conflict between north and south. He was successful and later served as Alvarado's emissary to Mexico City. He returned to Alta California in 1845 to try to strengthen its defenses against a possible U.S. invasion. He was living in Mexico as late as 1861. See Bancroft, *History of California* 2: 749; and Tays, "Captain Andrés Castillero."

Ángel Castro was a native of California. He was born around 1791 and married Isabel Butrón. He commanded military companies at both San José and Branciforte in 1842 and was the grantee of Los Paicines *rancho* near San Juan Bautista, where he was *juez* in 1844 and 1846. See Bancroft, *History of California* 3: 749–50.

Joaquín Castro was the son of Francisco María Castro, a soldier who settled at San Francisco before 1800 and was granted the San Pablo *rancho* on the eastern shore of San Francisco Bay in 1823. Joaquín lived at San Pablo and served in various civic and military offices. See Bancroft *History of California* 2: 750–51.

José Castro, the son of José Tiburcio Castro, was born around 1810. He served in the *diputación* in the 1830s and served as acting governor for four months after the death of José Figueroa in 1835. He took part in the resistance to both Chico and Gutiérrez in 1836 and served again as acting governor after Gutiérrez' expulsion. He took an active role against the foreigners' revolt in 1840 and also against Micheltorena in 1845. After Micheltorena's exile, he became military commander and led part of the resistance against the U.S. forces. He fled to Mexico in 1846 but returned to Alta California in 1848. He went back to Mexico in 1853 and was appointed military commander of Baja California in 1856. He held that office until he was killed in 1860. See Bancroft, *History of California* 2: 751–52.

José Tiburcio Castro was a native of Sinaloa, New Spain. His father, Macario, was a soldier at San Diego and San José. Tiburcio followed in his father's path and entered the military. He also served as *alcalde* of both San José and Monterey in the 1820s and as a member of the *diputación* in the 1830s. He participated in the movement against Governor Victoria in 1831. In the later 1830s he was the administrator at Mission San Juan Bautista. See Bancroft, *History of California* 2: 752–53.

Manuel de Jesús Castro was the son of Simeón Castro and María Antonia Pico. Born in Monterey in 1821, he served as secretary to the prefect of Monterey in

1842–44. He was one of the instigators of the revolt against Micheltorena. He was made prefect of Monterey in 1845 and supported Pico against José Castro. He fought with Flores in 1846 and fled to Mexico in 1847. From 1852 until his death he lived mainly in San Francisco. See Bancroft, *History of California* 2: 753.

Magín Matías Catalá was a native of Catalonia, Spain. He went to Mexico in 1786 and to Alta California in 1793. After a brief stay at San Francisco, he moved to Mission Santa Clara in 1794. He worked there until his death in 1830. He suffered greatly from rheumatism, which constantly bothered him as he aged. Toward the end of his life he could only feebly hobble along as he visited the sick, but he insisted on continuing his work. He gained a reputation as "the holy man of Santa Clara." See Geiger, *Franciscan Missionaries,* 42–46; and Engelhardt, *Holy Man of Santa Clara.*

Mariano Chico was born in 1796 in Guanajuato, New Spain. He served in the Mexican congress and was appointed governor of Alta California in December 1835. Arriving in April 1836, he was expelled by the *californios* on July 31 of that same year. He served as governor of Guanajuato in 1846 and participated in the war to repel the U.S. invasion. He died in 1850. See Bancroft, *History of California* 2: 759; and *Diccionario Porrúa,* 464.

William Goodwin Dana was a native of Boston who reached Alta California in 1826 on the *Waverly*. He married Josefa Carrillo, the daughter of Carlos Carrillo. He engaged in trade and agriculture in the Santa Bárbara area and served as *alcalde* there in 1836. In 1837 he was granted the Nipomo *rancho* near San Luis Obispo, where he lived until his death in 1858. See Bancroft, *History of California* 2: 774.

William Heath Davis was a Boston merchant involved in the China and Hawaii trades. He began trading and smuggling in Alta California in the 1810s. He died in Honolulu in 1823. His son, William Heath Davis Jr., became a prominent merchant in gold rush San Francisco. Toward the end of his life the younger Davis published the important work *Sixty Years in California*. See Bancroft, *History of California* 2: 776.

Manuel Domínguez was the son of Cristóbal Domínguez, a San Diego soldier from before 1800. He served on the Los Angeles *ayuntamiento* in 1829 and as *alcalde* in 1832. He opposed Alvarado in 1837 and was second *alcalde* of Los Angeles in 1839. U.S. troops occupied his *rancho* at San Pedro in 1846. In 1849 he was a member of the constitutional convention. He died in the early 1880s. See Bancroft, *History of California* 2: 783.

Narciso Durán was born in 1776 at Castelló de Ampurias in Catalonia, Spain. He arrived in Alta California in 1806 and served at Mission San José from that date until 1833. At San José he organized the neophytes into a mission choir, wrote an elaborate choir book, and composed the music for two masses himself. Robinson, who heard the choir in 1831, called the music "well-executed." At San José Durán extended hospitality to Jedediah Smith and Kit Carson, among others. He became president of the missions in 1825, but his stand against the emancipation of the native Californians made him unacceptable to the Mexican officials, and he stepped down in 1827. However, he was elected president again in 1830 and was appointed vice-commissary prefect soon after. In 1833, with the arrival of the friars from Zacatecas, Durán went to Santa Bárbara, where he remained until his death in 1846. He served as president of the San Fernando missions until 1838, when he was chosen commissary prefect. He remained in that office the rest of his life. Angustias de la Guerra said that in 1833 he was of "regular stature. Somewhat gray, white in color. He was blue-eyed. He did not wear sandals like the other friars because he suffered from rheumatism in his feet." See Geiger, *Franciscan Missionaries*, 68–75.

José María de Echeandía, a lieutenant colonel of engineers, was engaged in surveying the boundaries of the newly created Federal District in Mexico when he was appointed political and military governor of Baja and Alta California in 1825. He disliked the chilly and foggy climate of northern California and made his headquarters in San Diego. Little is known about him except for his service in Alta California. He returned to Mexico in 1833 and was reported to be practicing his profession as an engineer in the 1850s. He died sometime before 1871. See Bancroft, *History of California* 3: 243–45; and Hutchinson, *Frontier Settlement*, 124–25.

Estanislao was a member of the Lakisamne tribe, which lived in the central valley of Alta California, about fifty miles east of Mission San José. He was the indigenous *alcalde* at the mission, an indication that he enjoyed the favor of the local clergy. Alvarado said that he was able to read and write. Along with a number of companions, he refused to return to the mission after visiting his *ranchería* following the 1828 harvest. His forces defeated those of veteran fighter José Sánchez in 1829, before being defeated by a combined Monterey-San Francisco expedition led by Mariano Guadalupe Vallejo. Estanislao was pardoned after this and continued to live at Mission San José until his death in the 1830s. The only physical description of him comes from Juan Bojorques, decades after his death: "He was about 6 feet tall, his skin was more white than bronze, he was very muscular like a horse. . . . born and reared at Mission San José, employed as a *vaquero* and a trainer of mules." See Holterman, "Revolt of Estanislao"; Alvarado, "History of California" 1: 52; and Bojorques "Recuerdos," 21.

Tomás Eleuterio Esténaga was born in Vizcaya, Spain, in 1790. He was ordained in Mexico around 1810 and came to Alta California in 1820. He worked at San Francisco until 1833. When the Zacatecan friars took over the northern missions, Esténaga was assigned to San Gabriel, where he presided over the decline of that once flourishing institution. Discouraged, he left Alta California in 1835 but returned a year later. He died in 1847. See Geiger, *Franciscan Missionaries*, 78–81.

José Mariano Estrada was born in Loreto, Baja California, in 1784. He came to Alta California in the late 1790s and served in various positions at the presidio at Monterey, including *habilitado* and acting commander, until he retired from the military in 1829. He was close to the Argüello family and was the executor of Luis Argüello's will in 1830. In the early 1830s he worked briefly in the customs service but spent most of his time managing Buena Vista, his *rancho*, outside of Monterey. Bancroft was unable to place him after 1845 (Bancroft, *History of California* 2: 792–93). From internal evidence it appears that Estrada was one of the major sources for Osio's manuscript.

José Ramón Estrada was the son of José Mariano Estrada. Born in 1811, he hunted otter in the early 1830s, was the grantee of El Toro *rancho* outside of Monterey in 1835, and served as *alcalde* at Monterey in 1836. He served as administrator of Mission Santa Clara in the late 1830s and as a member of the departmental *junta* from 1842 to 1845. Like his father, he dropped from public view after 1845. See Bancroft, *History of California* 2: 793.

Santiago Estrada was a son of José Mariano Estrada. He served as *síndico* at Monterey in 1833 and as auxiliary *alcalde* there from 1835 to 1836. He served as commander in 1837 and as captain of the auxiliary company from 1839 to 1845. See Bancroft, *History of California* 2: 793.

José Fernández was born in Spain around 1803. Before arriving in Alta California aboard a French ship in 1818, he had been living in Lima. A sailor by trade, he became an artillery soldier and served at San Francisco from 1819 to 1827. He then settled in San José, where he served as secretary to the *ayuntamiento* and as *síndico*. He fought with José Castro against the United States in 1846 and then lived in Santa Clara until his death in the mid-1870s. See Bancroft, *History of California* 3: 737.

Agustín Fernández de San Vicente was a priest from Durango sent by Agustín Iturbide to manage the change of government from Spain to Mexico in Baja and Alta California. He arranged the appointment of Luis Argüello as governor. He had the reputation of being a bon vivant and a gambler. In 1825 he was appointed vicar in New Mexico. See Bancroft, *History of California* 3: 737.

Francisco Figueroa was the brother of Governor José Figueroa and came to Alta California with him in 1833. He was *contador* at the Monterey Customs House in 1834 and was involved in the northern movement against Alvarado in 1837. In the mid-1840s he served in the *diputación* and was city treasurer of Los

Angeles in 1850. He lived at the Alamitos *rancho* his brother had purchased and was married to María de Jesús Palomares. See Bancroft, *History of California* 3: 738.

José Figueroa was born in 1792 in Jonacatepec, New Spain. He participated in the Wars of Independence, fighting with José María Morelos and Vicente Guerrero. He served as military commander of Cuernavaca in 1823 and in the congress of the state of Mexico in 1824. In 1824 he was appointed military commander of Sonora and Sinaloa, where he subdued rebellions of the Yaqui and Mayo peoples. He arrived in Alta California as governor in 1833 and served there until his death in 1835. He is best known for the secularization of the missions and for his opposition to the Híjar-Padrés colonization effort of 1834. See Hutchinson, *Frontier Settlement*, 154–55.

José María Flores came to Alta California in 1842 as Micheltorena's secretary. He was sent to Mexico in 1844 but returned the next year. In 1846 he directed *californio* resistance in the last phase of the war against the United States. He returned to Mexico in January 1847 and remained in the Mexican army, becoming a general. He died in 1866. See Bancroft, *History of California* 3: 741; and Layne, "José María Flores."

James Alexander Forbes was born in 1804 in Scotland. He arrived in Alta California in 1831, after having been rescued from a shipwreck by a vessel heading for San Francisco. He lived as a trader and farmer in the Santa Clara Valley and married Ana María Galindo. In 1842 he was appointed British vice-consul at Monterey. After the conquest, most of his wealth was eaten up in litigation concerning the New Almadén mine in San José. He died in Oakland in 1881. See Bancroft, *History of California* 3: 743.

John Charles Frémont was born in Georgia in 1813. He was a lieutenant in the U.S. Army Corps and made journeys to Oregon in 1842 and California in 1843–44, before his 1846 sojourn in Alta California. Frémont appeared at Sutter's Fort in the winter of 1845 and then, claiming to be short of supplies, at Monterey in January 1846. He was active in the conquest and accepted the surrender of Andrés Pico at Cahuenga. He served in the U.S. Senate from California and was the first Republican candidate for president, in 1856. After serving in the Civil War, he spent the rest of his life as a territorial governor and as a promoter of various western development projects. See Hart, *Companion*, 172–73.

William A. Gale was a Boston trader. He first visited California in 1810 as a clerk on board the *Albatross* and returned in 1822 on board the *Sachem* to initiate the hide and tallow trade on behalf of the Boston firm of Bryant and Sturgis. He visited California a number of times, eventually marrying María Francisca Marcelina Estudillo at San Diego on May 21, 1827. He died in Massachusetts in 1841. Because of his spectacles, he was popularly known as *cuatro ojos* (four eyes). See Bancroft, *History of California* 3: 750–51; and Rhoades, "Foreigners," 87–88.

Francisco García Diego y Moreno was born in Jalisco in 1785. He joined the Franciscans at Our Lady of Guadalupe College near Zacatecas and was ordained a priest in 1808. He became vicar of the college in 1832. When the missions in Alta California were handed over to the Zacatecans, he headed north, arriving in Monterey in 1833. He became the first Catholic bishop of California in 1840 and established his residence in Santa Bárbara. His tenure as a bishop was difficult, and he died in 1846. See Geiger, *Franciscan Missionaries*, 98–103.

William Garner was born in 1803 in England and arrived in California in 1826, when he deserted from an English whaling ship in Santa Bárbara. From 1832 he was associated with Isaac Graham's group near Monterey and also worked as a lumberman there. He was naturalized in 1839 and revealed the existence of the 1840 foreigners' plot to the authorities. He operated a boardinghouse in Monterey from 1844 to 1848 and was killed in an expedition against the indigenous people in 1849. See Bancroft, *History of California* 3: 754.

Archibald Gillespie was born in Pennsylvania in 1812 and was a lieutenant in the marines in 1846. He arrived at Monterey in April of that year on a mission to assist Larkin in persuading the *californios* to join the United States. He also delivered a secret message to Frémont, which appears to have encouraged him to become more belligerent. He served in the military during the conquest. His arbitrary behavior while he was in charge of the Los Angeles garrison sparked a *californio* revolt. He was wounded at San Pascual. He spent most of the rest of his life in California and died in 1873. See Hart, *Companion*, 186.

José Joaquín Gómez was a trader from Mexico who arrived in Alta California in 1830. He was appointed *sub-comisario* at Monterey in 1831. He served on the Monterey *ayuntamiento* and the *diputación* in the 1830s, and he was granted a *rancho*, Verjeles, between Monterey and San José. See Bancroft, *History of California* 3: 758–59.

Manuel Gómez was an artillery soldier who came to Alta California in 1816 and served at San Francisco and Monterey. He was promoted to lieutenant for his part in trying to defend Monterey from Bouchard. He returned to Mexico in 1822. See Bancroft, *History of California* 2: 470.

Rafael Gómez was born around 1800. He was a Mexican lawyer who came to California as *asesor* in 1830. He served on the Monterey *ayuntamiento* in 1835 and on the *diputación* the following year. At the end of the 1830s he was killed by a horse on his *rancho*, Tularcitos, near Santa Clara. See Bancroft, *History of California* 3: 759.

Vicente Gómez was a Mexican ruffian who had acquired the nickname The Castrator for the ferocity with which he was alleged to have treated anyone of Spanish blood who came under his power. He was exiled to California in 1825.

He then found his way to Sonora and was killed in Baja California in 1827. See Bancroft, *History of California* 3: 16.

Macedonio González was a Mexican soldier who participated in a number of campaigns against the indigenous peoples on the Baja California frontier. He took part in the movements against Alvarado in 1837 and was imprisoned for a time at Sonoma. He eventually settled in Alta California, and Bancroft reports that he was living in San Diego in 1864. See Bancroft *History of California* 3: 760.

Rafael González was born around 1786 and came to Alta California in 1833 with José Figueroa, as customs administrator and *sub-comisario* at Monterey. He served as *alcalde* at Monterey in 1835 and worked at the Customs House from 1837 to 1846, He also served on the departmental *junta* from 1839 to 1843. He died in Monterey in 1868. See Bancroft, *History of California* 3: 761.

Teodoro González was born around 1806 in New Spain and came to Alta California as an otter hunter in 1825. He served on the Monterey *ayuntamiento* in 1836 and was appointed acting *alcalde* by Governor Chico. He served as *alcalde* in 1837 and in various offices in the early 1840s. He remained in California after the U.S. conquest and died in the early 1880s. See Bancroft, *History of California* 3: 761.

Isaac Graham was born in Kentucky and moved west as a fur trapper in the 1820s. He entered Alta California from New Mexico in 1833 and settled at Natividad, outside of Monterey. He seems to have operated a distillery there which catered to hunters and deserting sailors. He supported Alvarado in 1836. Accused of leading a rebellion against the Alta California government in 1840, he was sent to Mexico City for punishment. Upon his return, he settled near Santa Cruz, where he operated a sawmill. He supported Micheltorena in 1844 and 1845 and continued to live at Santa Cruz until his death in 1863. See Bancroft, *History of California* 3: 762–63.

José Antonio de la Guerra was the son of José de la Guerra y Noriega. Born in 1805, he was a cadet in the Santa Bárbara military from 1818 to 1828. He married María Concepción Ortega. He was a *síndico* and *alcalde* in Santa Bárbara in the 1830s and a member of the *diputación* in 1835 and 1836. He served as captain of the port at Santa Bárbara from 1837 to 1840 and as administrator at Mission La Purísima in 1841 and 1842. After the conquest he continued to live in the Santa Bárbara area and served as sheriff of San Luis Obispo. See Bancroft, *History of California* 3: 768–69.

José de la Guerra y Noriega was born in Spain in 1779. He came to Mexico in the 1790s to work in his uncle's store, and soon after that he entered the military. He arrived in Alta California in 1801, where he served until 1806 in

Monterey. In that year he was made lieutenant at Santa Bárbara, and soon afterward he moved to San Diego, where he remained until 1809. By acting as his uncle's commercial agent in Alta California, he was able to improve his financial condition greatly. He was promoted to commander of the Santa Bárbara presidio in 1815, and in that position he basically remained until 1842, when he retired from the military. He died in 1858. See Thompson, *El Gran Capitán*.

Nicolás Gutiérrez came to Alta California as a captain in 1833 with Governor Figueroa. He was promoted to lieutenant colonel in that same year and acted as *comisionado* for the secularization of Mission San Gabriel from 1834 to 1836. He served as acting governor from January to May 1836 and again after the expulsion of Chico the next year. He himself was expelled by Alvarado at the end of 1836. Little is known of his later career. See Bancroft, *History of California* 3: 772.

William Edward Petty Hartnell was born in Lanchashire, England, in 1798. In 1819 he went to South America to clerk for the firm of Begg and Company, and he arrived in California in 1822. In partnership with a fellow Begg clerk, Hugh McCullough of Scotland, he formed McCullough, Hartnell, and Company and did a large business with the missions in the 1820s. On April 30, 1825, he married María Teresa de la Guerra. Business reverses in the late 1820s forced the dissolution of his partnership with McCullough, and Hartnell supported himself with a variety of enterprises. He received a grant for Alisal *rancho*, outside of Monterey. In the mid-1830s he opened a short-lived school in Monterey. In 1839 Alvarado appointed him *visitador general* of the missions. He worked at the Customs House in the 1840s and made a brief trip to Hawaii, most likely with Osio, shortly after the U.S. invasion. Employed by the U.S. military as an interpreter and translator in the late 1840s and early 1850s, he died in 1854. See Dakin, *Lives of William Hartnell*.

José María Herrera came to Alta California with Echeandía in 1825 as *comisario*. He later became involved in controversies with Echeandía and was exiled for alleged involvement in the Solís revolt. He returned to Alta California in 1834 with the Híjar-Padrés party as secretary of Bandini's Cosmopolitan Company. He himself stayed out of controversy, although his wife, Ildefonsa González, became romantically involved with José María Castañares. Herrera left Alta California in 1836 and may have been *contador* of the Customs House at Guaymas in 1839. See Bancroft, *History of California* 3: 466; and Hutchinson, *Frontier Settlement*, 203.

José María Híjar was born around 1793 in Guadalajara and served for many years in the Jalisco state congress, where he most likely became acquainted with Valentín Gómez Farías. When Gómez Farías got a bill authorizing a colonization effort for Alta California passed by the Mexican congress, Híjar was appointed director of the colony and *jefe político* of Alta California. Political change in Mexico prevented his assuming the political office, and the colony ran afoul of Governor Figueroa and the *californios*. He was sent back to Mexico in 1835. Ironically, he returned to Alta California in 1845 as a member of a Mexican commission and died that year in Los Angeles. See Hutchinson, *Frontier Settlement*, 184–85, 374–75.

Gil Ibarra was born in San Diego in 1784. He served as *síndico* of Los Angeles in 1831 and as *alcalde* there from 1836 to 1837, when he opposed Alvarado. Like many of Alvarado's erstwhile opponents, he was granted a *rancho* in 1841. See Bancroft, *History of California* 4: 688.

Juan María Ibarra, a lieutenant in the army, came to Alta California with the Mazatlán squadron in 1819. He was stationed at San Diego from 1821 to 1830. He supported Zamorano in 1832 and was commander at Santa Bárbara from 1833 to 1836. He left Alta California in 1836. See Bancroft, *History of California* 4: 688.

William Brown Ide was born in 1896 in Massachusetts and came overland to California in 1845. He settled near Sonoma and was a leader of the Bear Flag Revolt. He became bitter when Frémont took control of the movement in the summer, but he served as a private in the California battalion during the war. He returned to Sonoma and served as a surveyor there and as a public official in Colusa. He died in 1852. See Hart, *Companion*, 235; and Bancroft, *History of California* 4: 688–89.

Manuel Jimeno Casarín was born in New Spain. He came to Alta California in 1828 as *sub-comisario* and *contador* at the Customs House. Two of his brothers, José Joaquín and Antonio, were Franciscan missionaries in Alta California. Manuel held a large number of public offices; he was *síndico* and *alcalde* at Monterey, as well as a member of the *diputación*. He was Governor Alvarado's secretary and filled the same office for Governor Micheltorena. In the early 1830s he married Angustias de la Guerra. He returned to Mexico in 1853 and died that same year. See Bancroft, *History of California* 4: 692.

Thomas ap Catesby Jones was born in Virginia in 1790 and was commander of the U.S. Navy Pacific Squadron in 1842. He took Monterey in that year, thinking that perhaps war had broken out between the United States and Mexico. The United States apologized for the incident and briefly relieved him of command, but restored it to him quickly. He died in 1859. See Hart, *Companion*, 250.

Stephen Watts Kearny was born in New Jersey in 1794. A career soldier, he served in the army in the War of 1812 and later commanded the Army of the West in 1846. He also served as military governor at Santa Fe. After crossing overland to California, he was defeated at the battle of San Pascual on

December 6, 1846. He died two years later in St. Louis, after having served in Mexico as governor in Veracruz and Mexico City. See Clarke, *Stephen Watts Kearny*.

Kiril Khlebnikov was the agent for the Russian-American Company. This business was founded in 1799 as a trading concern along the shores of Alaska and the Pacific Northwest. From 1812 to 1841 the company had a trading post at Fort Ross on the coast of Alta California, north of San Francisco. Between 1817 and 1832 Khlebnikov served as manager of the company's office at New Archangel (Sitka), and he made at least twelve trips to Alta California. He died in 1838. See Shur, *Khlebnikov Archive*.

Thomas Oliver Larkin was born in Massachusetts in 1802 and came to Alta California in 1832. He lived in Monterey as a trader. He supported Alvarado in 1836 and was appointed U.S. consul eight years later. In 1845 President Polk and Secretary of State Buchanan made him a confidential agent to try to bring Alta California peacefully into the United States. He died in San Francisco in 1858. See Hague and Langum, *Thomas O. Larkin*.

Jacob Primer Leese was born in 1809 in Ohio. He traded along the Santa Fe Trail in the early 1830s and moved into Alta California in 1834. He lived at Yerba Buena (San Francisco) from 1836 to 1841, when he moved to Sonoma. He married Rosalía Vallejo, the sister of Mariano Guadalupe Vallejo. In 1846 he was captured by the Bear Flaggers. He was vice-president of the Society of California Pioneers in 1855. In 1864 he was granted almost two-thirds of Baja California as part of a colonization enterprise. After the failure of this project, he left California in 1865 and did not return until his old age. He died in 1892. See Hart, *Companion*, 274; and Martínez, *History of Lower California*, 406–12.

William Alexander Leidesdorff was born in 1810 in the Virgin Islands. He moved to the United States as a youth and worked in New Orleans as a cotton broker. He came to Alta California in 1841 as manager of the *Julia Ann* and engaged in trade at San Francisco. Appointed vice-consul at San Francisco by Larkin in 1845, he invested heavily in San Francisco real estate. He died in 1848. See Bancroft, *History of California* 4: 711; and Hart, *Companion*, 275.

Antonio María Lugo was the son of Francisco Lugo, a native of Sinaloa who arrived in Alta California soon after 1769. Antonio María was born in 1775 and joined the military at an early age. He married María Dolores Ruiz. He remained in the army until at least 1809 and was granted a *rancho*, San Antonio, in 1810. He served as *alcalde* at Los Angeles in 1816 and 1818, as *juez de campo* in 1833 and 1834, and on the *ayuntamiento* in 1837 and 1838. He died in 1860. See Bancroft, *History of California* 2: 719.

Bonifacio Madariaga was born about 1809 in New Spain. He was a clerk at Monterey from 1830 and served on the *ayuntamiento* in 1836. In the same year he married twice-widowed María Josefa Vallejo de Estrada, the mother of Juan Bautista Alvarado. He left Alta California in 1842. See Bancroft, *History of California* 4: 727.

Juan Malarín, a Peruvian of Italian extraction, first arrived in Alta California in 1820 as master of the vessel *Señoriana*. He returned in 1824 as master of the *Apolonia*. As a result of his returning the *Asia* to Mexico for Argüello, he was made a lieutenant in the Mexican navy. He married Josefa Estrada and made his home in Monterey, where he served on the *tribunal superior* in the 1840s. He died in 1849. See Bancroft, *History of California* 4: 728.

Marín was the leader of the Coast Miwok north of San Francisco. While resisting a Spanish expedition in 1815 or 1816, he was captured and brought to San Francisco. He escaped and carried on hostilities against the soldiers from a base near San Rafael. He was captured again in 1824 and spent his last years at Mission San Rafael. See Bancroft, *History of California* 4: 729.

Ignacio Martínez was born in Mexico City in 1774 and came to Alta California around 1800. He served at Santa Bárbara and San Diego before being sent to San Francisco as a lieutenant in 1817. He succeeded Luis Argüello as commander in 1822 and acted in that capacity until 1827. From 1828 to 1831 he had various stints as acting commander and commander. He retired from the military in 1831 and then held a number of public offices, such as *alcalde* of San Francisco, member of the *diputación*, and *regidor* at San José. He owned a large ranch, Pinole, in Contra Costa, across the bay from San Francisco. He died at some point before 1852. See Bancroft, *History of California* 4: 733.

Henry Mellus was born in Massachusetts in 1816. He arrived in California aboard the *Pilgrim* in 1835. He settled in California in 1839 as a trader for Appleton and Company. Together with his partner, W. D. M. Howard, he purchased much property after 1845 in San Francisco, Los Angeles, and Sacramento. He fell ill in 1850 and returned east, where he remained until 1859, when he came back to Los Angeles. He was elected mayor there in 1860, but he died shortly thereafter. See Bancroft, *History of California* 4: 737.

William Mervine was born in 1791 and served as captain of the U.S.S. *Cyane* in 1846. He occupied Monterey in July and was sent south to relieve Gillespie in Los Angeles in October. He was defeated by the *californios* in this attempt. He served as commander of the U.S. Pacific Fleet in 1855–57 and as a captain in the Civil War. He died in 1868. See Hart, *Companion*, 314; and Bancroft, *History of California* 4: 739.

Manuel Micheltorena was a native of Oaxaca, New Spain. Little is known of his career before 1840, when he was involved in suppressing a revolt in Mexico City. Appointed governor of Alta California in 1842, he arrived with some three hundred soldiers, many reported as being ex-convicts and all thoroughly disliked by the *californios*. He attempted to restore undistributed mission lands and property to the church but was generally unsuccessful. He was expelled in 1845, fought against the U.S. forces in 1846, and served as a member of the Mexican congress in 1847. In 1850 he was *comandante general* of Yucatán. He died in 1853. See Bancroft, *History of California* 4: 740.

John S. Misroon, a lieutenant on the *Portsmouth* in 1846, was sent by Montgomery to Sonoma and New Helvetia to check on the condition of those held prisoner by the Bear Flaggers. He invested in a San Francisco lot while he was in the area. See Bancroft, *History of California* 4: 742.

Eugenio Montenegro served under Alvarado in 1837 and was a corporal in the Monterey Customs House guard. He was *sub-comisario* from 1838 to 1840 and worked for the *tribunal superior* in 1842. He owned a lot in San Francisco in the early 1840s and served as a captain of the auxiliary cavalry in 1845–46. In 1850 he reportedly lived in San Luis Obispo. See Bancroft, *History of California* 4: 743.

John Berrien Montgomery was commander of the U.S. vessel *Portsmouth*, which was stationed at San Francisco during the Bear Flag Revolt. Later in life he commanded the Charlestown, Massachusetts, and Washington, D.C., navy yards. He died in 1873. See Hart, *Companion*, 330.

Bernardo Navarrete was a lieutenant in the Mexican army who came to Alta California with Governor Figueroa in 1833. He served at Monterey and left Alta California with Gutiérrez in 1836. See Bancroft, *History of California* 4: 752.

Manuel del Castillo Negrete was the *comandante general* in Jalisco in 1840 and the brother of Luis del Castillo Negrete, who had served in Alta California as an adviser to Governor Gutiérrez. See Bancroft, *History of California* 3: 466; 4: 30.

Blas Ordaz was from the area near Burgos, Spain, and came to Mexico in 1819. He worked at Mission San Francisco in 1820-21 and accompanied Luis Argüello on his 1821 journey to northern Alta California. He worked at a number of missions, chiefly Santa Ynés (1824–33) and San Fernando (1837–47). He remained in Alta California through the U.S. invasion and died at Mission San Gabriel in 1850. See Geiger, *Franciscan Missionaries*, 208–10, 170–74.

José Joaquín Ortega was the son of José María Ortega and María Francisca López. A member of the *diputación* in the early 1830s, he married María Pico, the sister of Pío and Andrés Pico. He served as administrator of Mission San Diego from 1835 to 1840 and as *mayordomo* of Mission San Luis Rey from 1843 to 1845. See Bancroft, *History of California* 4: 760.

José Francisco Ortega, a native of Guanajuato, New Spain, entered the military in 1755 and came to Alta California in 1769 with Gaspar de Portolá and

Junípero Serra. He commanded the garrison at San Diego for eight years and was one of the founders of Santa Bárbara, where he also served as commander. He was married to María Francisca López. He died in 1798. See Bancroft, *History of California* 1: 663, 670–71.

Romualdo Pacheco was born in Guanajuato, New Spain, and joined the army. Like Echeandía, he was in the engineering corps. He accompanied Echeandía to California when the latter was appointed governor in 1825. From 1827 to 1828 he served as aide-de-camp and acting commander at Monterey. He also served as acting commander at Santa Bárbara from 1828 to 1829. He was killed while fighting in support of Governor Victoria at the battle of Cahuenga in 1831. His son, also named Romualdo, became acting governor of California in 1875. See Bancroft, *History of California* 4: 764; and Genini and Hitchman, *Romualdo Pacheco*, 3–13.

José María Padrés was a native of Puebla and a member of the engineering corps in the military. He accompanied Echeandía in 1825 but was posted to Baja California. In 1827 he served in the Mexican congress and came to Alta California in 1830 as *ayudante inspector*. An ardent proponent of the secularization of the missions, he was sent back to Mexico by Governor Victoria in 1831. He returned to Alta California in 1834 with the colonizing effort started by Valentín Gómez Farías. He became embroiled in a bitter controversy with Governor Figueroa and the *californio* elite and was sent back to Mexico in 1835. Nothing is known of his later life. See Hutchinson, *Frontier Settlement*, 182–84, 370–79.

Ignacio Palomares served in a number of posts in the Los Angeles area: he was *juez de campo* in 1834 and 1840, a member of the *ayuntamiento* in 1835, *juez de paz* in 1841, and *alcalde* in 1846. He opposed Alvarado in 1837. He died at Pomona in 1882. See Bancroft, *History of California* 4: 766.

Roberto Pardo was a sergeant in the Mazatlán squadron at Monterey by 1820. In 1824 he served at La Purísima, and he was commander at Santa Bárbara from 1842 to 1845. See Bancroft, *History of California* 4: 767.

Cosme Peña was a lawyer who came to Alta California with the colonization party in 1834, with an appointment as *asesor* to succeed Rafael Gómez. He joined Alvarado's side in 1836 and was made his secretary. He later affiliated with Ángel Ramírez and was imprisoned at Sonoma. He left Alta California in 1839. See Bancroft, *History of California* 3: 594; 4: 771.

Antonio Peyri was born in 1769 in Catalonia, Spain. He was ordained a priest in 1793. He arrived at San Francisco in 1796 and was the founder of Mission San Luis Rey in 1798. Under his leadership the mission was said to produce the best grape wine in Alta California. He remained there until he left Alta California in 1832. He took two Indians boys, Pablo Tac and Agapito Amamix, with him, and intended to have them study for the priesthood. Both, however, died during their studies. Peyri himself, regretting that he had left California, died in Spain. See Geiger, *Franciscan Missionaries*, 192–96.

Andrés Pico, the son of José María Pico of Sinaloa and María Eustaquia Gutiérrez of Sonora, was born in San Diego in 1810. In the late 1830s he was active in the southern opposition to Alvarado and was arrested and sent to Sonoma. From 1839 to 1842 he served as *alférez* at San Diego. He undertook a mission to Mexico for Governor Micheltorena in 1844. On his return he continued to serve in the military, mainly in the Los Angeles area. He commanded the *californios* in their victory over the U.S. forces at San Pascual and later negotiated the Treaty of Cahuenga with Frémont. He was elected to the state assembly in 1851 and served in the state senate from 1860 to 1861. He died in 1876. See Bancroft, *History of California* 4: 776–77; and Meier, *Mexican American Biographies,* 176–77.

José de Jesús Pico, the son of José Dolores Pico and Isabel Cota, was born at Monterey in 1807. He sided with Solís from 1828 to 1829 and with Alvarado from 1836 to 1838. He was one of the instigators of the revolt against Micheltorena in 1844, fought with Flores in 1846, and later served in the California assembly in 1853. See Bancroft, *History of California* 4: 777–78.

Pío Pico, older brother of Andrés, was born at San Gabriel in 1801. He served in the *diputación* in 1828, and as a *vocal*, he was one of the leaders of the opposition to Victoria in 1831. He served as one of the acting governors in 1832. He was a leader in the 1836–37 opposition to Alvarado. He served as the administrator of Mission San Luis Rey from 1834 to 1840. After the expulsion of Micheltorena, he became *jefe político,* and in that capacity he frequently quarreled with José Castro, the *jefe militar.* He fled to Mexico in 1845 but returned in 1848 and lived in southern California until his death in Los Angeles in 1894. See Pico, *Historical Narrative;* Bancroft, *History of California* 4: 778-79; and Meier, *Mexican American Biographies,* 177–78.

Pablo de la Portilla came to Alta California in 1819 with the Mazatlán troops and was stationed at San Diego from then until 1838. He was made commander of the garrison in 1831 and in that year opposed Victoria. He was commissioned, charged with secularizing Mission San Luis Rey from 1833 to 1835. In 1836 he backed Chico and opposed Alvarado. In 1838 he enlisted under the banner of Carlos Carrillo and left Alta California after Carrillo's defeat. He was stationed in Guaymas in 1846. See Bancroft, *History of California* 4: 782.

Víctor Prudón was born in France around 1809 and came to Mexico in 1827. He arrived in California as a teacher with the Gómez Farías colonization group in 1834. He married Teodosia Bojorques. He served as president of the Los Angeles vigilantes in 1836 and as Governor Alvarado's secretary from 1837 to

1838. He worked in the same capacity for Mariano Guadalupe Vallejo in 1841 and served as Vallejo's emissary to Mexico in 1842. He was arrested with Vallejo by the Bear Flag soldiers in 1846. His whereabouts after 1853 are unknown. See Bancroft, *History of California* 4: 784–85; and Rhoades, "Foreigners," 70–71.

Ángel Ramírez was a former friar who had left his order around 1820 and had participated in the Wars of Independence. Apparently a friend of Gómez Farías, he arrived in Alta California in 1834 as administrator of the Customs House. He served in that capacity until 1836, when Alvarado removed him. He was arrested in July 1837 and died at Mission San Luis Obispo in 1840. See Bancroft, *History of California* 3: 587–88.

José Ramírez, an artillery lieutenant, came to California in 1820 and served in Monterey. He married María de Jesús Salvadora Ortega, daughter of José María Ortega of the Refugio *rancho*. She was born in 1800 and was the younger woman to whom Osio refers in chapter 4. Ramírez returned to Mexico in 1826. See Bancroft, *History of California* 5: 688.

José María Ramírez came to Alta California in 1825 with Governor Echeandía as an *alférez* in the military. He served at San Diego, where he married Dolores Palomares. He was administrator at three missions and took part in the revolts against Victoria in 1831 and Alvarado in 1838. See Bancroft, *History of California* 5: 687–88.

Manuel Requena was a trader from Yucatán, Mexico, who arrived in Alta California in 1834. He married Gertrudis Guirado. He served as *alcalde* of Los Angeles in 1836 and was active in the opposition to Alvarado from 1836 to 1838. He served in the departmental *junta* from 1839 to 1841 and again as *alcalde* in 1844. In the first two decades of U.S. rule, he often was a member of the Los Angeles city council. He died in 1876. See Bancroft, *History of California* 5: 691–92; and Meier, *Mexican American Biographies,* 189.

William A. Richardson was born in England in 1795. He arrived in Alta California aboard the whaling ship *Orion* in 1822 and was allowed to stay. He married María Antonia Martínez, daughter of Ignacio Martínez. He traded and acted as a pilot in northern California until 1829. He then lived at San Gabriel until 1835, after which he returned to the north. He lived at Sausalito from 1841 and also served as captain of the port at San Francisco. He managed Angel Island for Osio in the 1840s. He died in 1856. See Hart, *Companion,* 413; and Bancroft, *History of California* 5: 694.

Robert Ridley was a native of England who arrived in Alta California in 1840. He worked as a clerk and married Juana Briones. He was captain of the port at San Francisco in 1846 and, as a Mexican official, was arrested by the Bear Flaggers. He died in 1851. See Bancroft, *History of California* 5: 695.

Antonio Ripoll was born at Palma, Mallorca, in 1785. After being ordained a priest, he reached New Spain in 1810 and San Diego in 1812. He worked at Missions La Purísima, Santa Ynés, and San Miguel. He trained a company of local indigenous people to fight Bouchard in 1818 and was at Santa Bárbara when the 1824 Chumash revolt broke out. He accompanied Father Vicente Sarría on the Portilla expedition to bring the Chumash fugitives back to the missions. He secretly left Alta California with Father José Altimira in 1828. He was last reported as being on Mallorca in 1832. See Geiger, *Franciscan Missionaries*, 207–8.

Alfred Robinson was born in Massachusetts in 1806 and came to California in 1829 as a clerk for Bryant and Sturgis Company, the same enterprise for which William Gale worked. He engaged in the hide and tallow trade for a number of years and in 1836 married Ana María de la Guerra, daughter of José de la Guerra y Noriega of Santa Bárbara. He returned to the East in 1842 and four years later anonymously published *Life in California*, which became a standard U.S. account of Mexican Alta California. Robinson returned to California in 1849 as an agent for the Pacific Mail Steamship Company. He lived in Santa Bárbara and San Francisco for the remainder of his life. He died in 1895. See Bancroft, *History of California* 5: 698; and Rhoades, "Foreigners," 72–74.

Juan José Rocha came to Alta California with Governor Echeandía in 1825. He was posted to Monterey, serving as *alférez* there. He was acting commander during the Solís revolt and was jailed by the rebels. He served as administrator of Missions San Juan Capistrano and San Gabriel in the 1830s and was active in the movement against Alvarado in 1837. The date of his death is uncertain. See Bancroft, *History of California* 5: 699.

Antonio Catarino Rodríguez was a native of San Luis Potosí in Mexico and came to Alta California in 1809. He worked for nine years at Mission San Luis Obispo, then went to La Purísima. He died at San Luis Obispo in 1824. See Geiger, *Franciscan Missionaries*, 208–10.

José Antonio Rodríguez was a soldier in Alta California from the 1790s. He died in 1837. See Bancroft, *History of California* 5: 701.

José Mariano Romero came to Alta California with the Híjar-Padrés colonization expedition in 1834. He was a schoolteacher in Monterey from 1834 to 1836 but left Alta California with Gutiérrez in 1836. See Bancroft, *History of California* 5: 703; and Hutchinson, *Frontier Settlement*, 323.

Juan María Salvatierra was born in Milan, Italy, in 1648. After entering the Society of Jesus in Genoa, he went to Mexico for the study of theology. After teaching at the seminary at Puebla, he was assigned to the missions and worked in Chínipas for ten years. After a stint as rector of the Jesuit college at Guadalajara, he established the first permanent Jesuit mission of Loreto in Baja

California in 1697. Except for a brief term as Jesuit provincial of New Spain (1704–6), he served there until his death at Guadalajara in 1717. See Crosby, *Antigua California*, 409.

Francisco Sánchez was the son of José Antonio Sánchez. He was a soldier of the San Francisco company from 1824 and continued to serve in military and civilian offices in the San Francisco area. In 1846 he was acting commander there and commanded the Mexican troops at Santa Clara the following January. He lived in San Francisco and San Mateo after the conquest, serving on the San Francisco Board of Supervisors in 1850. He died in 1862. See Regnery, *Battle of Santa Clara*, 141–42; and Bancroft, *History of California* 5: 710.

José Antonio Sánchez, a native of Sinaloa, Mexico, was a member of the military company at San Francisco in the 1790s; he received various promotions until he rose to command the San Francisco garrison from 1829 to 1833. He had a reputation as a skilled fighter against the indigenous peoples and participated in more than twenty campaigns against them. He retired in 1836 and died seven years later. See Bancroft, *History of California* 5: 710.

Vicente Sánchez held a variety of public offices in Los Angeles during the Mexican period. He was present in Los Angeles as early as 1814 and was *alcalde* in 1826 and 1831. He also served in the *diputación* in 1828. In 1831 Victoria backed him against the *ayuntamiento*, which wanted to depose him, and Sánchez managed to send José Antonio Carrillo into exile. He served as *alcalde* again in 1845. See Bancroft, *History of California* 5: 711.

Vicente Francisco de Sarría was a native of Spain and had taught at the Franciscan establishment in Bilbao before arriving in Mexico in 1804 and in Alta California in 1809. He worked at Mission San Carlos in Carmel until 1828. He served as prefect of the missions from 1812 to 1818 and from 1824 to 1830. He became embroiled in a dispute with the government for refusing to take the oath supporting the constitution of 1824, and in that same year he was involved with the expedition to the interior against the Chumash Indians. In 1828 he was moved to Mission Soledad, where he stayed until his death in 1835. See Bancroft *History of California* 2: 396–97; Engelhardt, *Missions and Missionaries* 2: 3–4; 4: 815; and Geiger, *Franciscan Missionaries*, 228–35, 297.

Francisco Sepúlveda was born around 1790 and settled in Los Angeles in 1815. He served on the *ayuntamiento* and as acting *alcalde* in 1825. He was commissioner for Mission San Juan Capistrano from 1836 to 1837 and was granted a *rancho* in 1839. See Bancroft, *History of California* 5: 716.

José Sepúlveda was born in 1803. He married María Francisca de Paula Ávila. He served on the Los Angeles *ayuntamiento* in 1833, as *alcalde* in 1837, and on the *ayuntamiento* again in 1839. From Alvarado he received two land grants,

Ciénega de las Ranas and Rancho San Joaquín. He served as subprefect in 1845 and died in 1875. See Bancroft, *History of California* 5: 716; and Wittenburg, "Three Generations," 220–43.

Florencio Serrano arrived in Alta California with the Híjar-Padrés party in 1834. He served in a variety of public offices in Monterey. In the late 1830s he was clerk to various officials in Monterey and secretary to the *alcalde*. In the 1840s he himself served as both first and second *alcalde* and also as *síndico* of Monterey. He died in 1877. See Bancroft, *History of California* 5: 716–17.

George Seymour was the admiral in charge of the British Pacific Fleet in 1846. See Bancroft, *History of California* 5: 717.

Mariano Silva was an artillery captain at Monterey from 1840 to 1846. He surrendered the city to Sloat in July 1846. In 1847 or 1848 he went to Mazatlán. See Bancroft, *History of California* 5: 720.

John Drake Sloat was born in New York in 1781. He joined the navy in 1800 and by 1844 had risen to commander of the U.S. Pacific Fleet. He took possession of Monterey on July 7, 1846, but left the command in California to Stockton at the end of July and returned east. He commanded the Norfolk navy yard from 1848 to 1850. He retired in 1855 and died in 1867. See Hart, *Companion*, 478–79.

William Smith was born in Virginia and first came to Alta California around 1800 on board the ship *Hazard*. In 1811 he was chief mate of the *Albatross*, one of William Heath Davis' vessels, and he was commanding it in 1816 when he was arrested for smuggling at Santa Bárbara. He was in Alta California continuously after 1836, mainly aboard various trading vessels and, for a time, in Santa Bárbara. He died in Sonoma in 1846. See Bancroft, *History of California* 5: 723; and Phelps, *Alta California*, 74-76.

Pablo Vicente de Solá was born in Vizcaya, Spain. The date of his arrival in the New World is unknown, but he was sufficiently well established by 1805 as a captain in the military that he was appointed temporary *habilitado general* of the Californias. He served in that office until 1807. He rose to the rank of lieutenant colonel by the time he was appointed governor in 1814. A brother of his, Faustino de Solá, was a Franciscan and had served in the Alta California missions—at San Luis Obispo and at San Francisco—from 1786 to 1790. The governor's appearance was reported as "normal height, heavy build, short neck, large and somewhat long head, wide face, very few teeth, hair almost white, with a deep and calm voice." He served as governor until 1822. After his return to Mexico he served on the Commission for the Development of the Californias. See Bancroft, *History of California* 2: 470–73; 5: 727; Geiger, *Franciscan Missionaries*, 274; Hutchinson, *Frontier Settlement*, 117; and Torre, "Reminiscencias," 3.

Joaquín Solís was a leader in the 1829 revolt in which a number of soldiers rose up to protest their lack of pay. Little is known about him. He had apparently fought in the Wars of Independence, had then turned to crime, and was sentenced to California in 1825. He was living outside of Monterey at the time of the revolt. In 1830 he was sent back to Mexico. See Bancroft, *History of California* 3: 68–69.

Antonio Soto was born at Santa Clara in 1797. His father, Francisco José Dolores Soto, was the first child to be baptized at Mission San Francisco, on August 10, 1776. Antonio's grandfather, Ignacio, had been born in Sinaloa in 1748 or 1749. All three generations of Soto men—Ignacio, Francisco, and Antonio—served as soldiers at the San Francisco presidio. Antonio was killed in 1829, in the expedition against Estanislao. In 1817 Antonio Soto married María Encarnación Pacheco y Sánchez. Her own roots were also deep in Alta California and its military. She had been born at Santa Clara in 1800. Her father, Miguel Pacheco, was a San Francisco soldier. Her mother, Juana María Lorenza Sánchez, was the second child (after Francisco José Dolores Soto), and the first girl, to be baptized at Mission San Francisco, on August 25, 1776. On October 26, 1819, María Encarnación gave birth to her second daughter, Narcisa Florencia. On February 15, 1838, at Mission Santa Clara, Narcisa Florencia married the widower Antonio María Osio. See Bancroft, *History of California* 1: 291, 716; 5: 728; and Mutnick, *Some Alta California Pioneers* 1: 3, 1082–85.

David Spence was born in Scotland around 1798. He came to Alta California in September 1824 to manage a meat packing plant in Monterey for Begg and Company. He went into business for himself in 1827, and in 1829 he married Adelaida Estrada, daughter of José Mariano Estrada. He served as *alcalde* of Monterey in 1835 and was on the *diputación* in the following year. He was *juez de paz* in 1839. He also served in some public offices after Alta California became part of the United States. He died in 1875. See Bancroft, *History of California* 5: 730–31.

Abel Stearns was born in Massachusetts in 1798 and moved to Mexico in 1826. After becoming a naturalized Mexican citizen, he moved to Alta California in 1829. Unsuccessful in his attempt to obtain a land grant, he was active against Governor Victoria in 1831 and settled in Los Angeles as a trader in 1833. There he married Arcadia Bandini, daughter of Juan Bandini. He served as *síndico* in the first half of 1836 and supported Alvarado over the next few years. He was also active against Governor Micheltorena and worked with Larkin for the joining of Alta California to the United States. He became a large landowner and participated in the constitutional convention of 1849 and held various offices thereafter. He died in San Francisco in 1871. See Bancroft, *History of California* 5: 732–33.

Robert Field Stockton was born in New Jersey in 1795. He joined the navy as a young man and served in the War of 1812. He arrived in Monterey in July 1846 and soon after was appointed as commander to succeed Sloat. He resigned in 1847 and returned east. He served as a U.S. senator from New Jersey from 1851 to 1853 and died in 1866. See Hart, *Companion*, 503; and Bancroft, *History of California* 5: 735.

José María del Refugio Suárez del Real was born in New Spain about 1804. Ordained in 1831, he was a member of the first group of Zacatecan Franciscans to enter Alta California with Governor Figueroa in 1833. He served at Mission San Carlos from that date until 1843; during that time he had additional responsibilities in the city of Monterey, where he bought a house in 1837. In 1844 he moved to Mission Santa Clara, at which he served until he left for Mexico in 1851. He had a reputation for sexual peccadilloes in both Monterey and Santa Clara. He left the Franciscans upon his return to Mexico and served as a parish priest at San José del Cabo in 1853. The date of his death is unknown. See Geiger, *Franciscan Missionaries*, 249–51.

John Sutter was born in Germany in 1803 and, after failing in business in Switzerland and traveling in northern Mexico as well as Alaska and Hawaii, settled in Alta California. He received a huge grant in the Sacramento Valley from Alvarado, in an attempt to check the influence of Vallejo. Using indigenous laborers practically as serfs, he turned New Helvetia into an almost feudal estate. In 1845 he assisted Micheltorena against the rebels and later supported the U.S. invasion. He was a member of the constitutional convention in 1849, the year after gold had been discovered on his ranch. By the mid-1850s squatters had taken most of his land, and he was able to survive because the California legislature awarded him a pension. When that was not renewed in 1878, he moved to Lititz, Pennsylvania, where he died in 1880. See Hart, *Companion*, 508.

Tomás Talamantes was born around 1792 and lived in Los Angeles. He participated in the battle of Cahuenga in 1831 and served as *juez de campo* in Los Angeles in 1844. See Bancroft, *History of California* 5: 742.

Tiburcio Tapia was born in San Luis Obispo in 1798. Attached to the Santa Bárbara presidio, he was head of the guard at Mission La Purísima when the Chumash revolt broke out. He served in the *diputación* in 1827 and 1833 and as *alcalde* of Los Angeles in 1830 and 1836. He also held a series of offices in connection with the Cucamonga *rancho*, which he was granted in 1839. He continued to hold office into the 1840s. See Bancroft, *History of California* 3: 636.

Rafael Téllez came to Alta California as a lieutenant colonel with Micheltorena in 1842 and left in 1844. He later became acting commander at Mazatlán and was in that position when the U.S. forces captured the city in 1848. He died later in 1848. See Bancroft, *History of California* 5: 744.

Joaquín de la Torre was the son of José Joaquín de la Torre and María de los Angeles Cota. He was a member of the Monterey military company and in 1840 was one of the guard who accompanied the Graham exiles to Mexico. In 1846 he fought at Olompali. He was killed by a bandit he was trying to arrest near Santa Bárbara in 1855. See Bancroft, *History of California* 5: 750.

Francisco Torres was born around 1806 in Guadalajara. He was a physician and was the secretary and a teacher at the Institute of Public Instruction in his home city. In June 1833 he wrote a long letter to the official government paper in Mexico City about the precautions that might be employed against the Asiatic cholera that had recently broken out there. He accompanied the Gómez Farías colony to California and was accused of directing an insurrection against the government in Los Angeles. He was exiled in 1835. See Hutchinson, *Frontier Settlement*, 353–54.

Francisco Xavier de la Concepción Uría was born near Pamplona, Spain, in 1770. He arrived in Mexico in 1795 and was sent to Alta California at the end of the following year. He worked at Missions Santa Bárbara, La Purísima, and San Fernando until 1805, when he returned to the Colegio de San Fernando. He came back to Alta California in 1808 and, after a short time at Mission Santa Cruz, worked for many years among the Chumash at Mission Santa Ynés. After the 1824 revolt he worked at Santa Bárbara, Soledad, and San Buenaventura. He died at Santa Bárbara in 1834. See Geiger, *Franciscan Missionaries*, 257–59.

Félix Valdés was a battalion commander of Micheltorena's *cholos*. See Bancroft, *History of California* 5: 754.

Antonio del Valle, a lieutenant in the army, arrived in Alta California in 1819 and served at San Francisco in the early 1820s. He was jailed for a time in the mid-1820s, apparently as a result of a quarrel with Luis Argüello. In 1832 he supported Zamorano and in 1834 was commissioner at San Fernando. He opposed Alvarado in 1836 and supported Carlos Carrillo two years later. He was granted a *rancho*, San Francisco, about thirty miles west of Mission San Buenaventura in 1839. He died in 1841. See Bancroft, *History of California* 5: 755.

Ignacio del Valle was the son of Antonio del Valle. He came to California in 1825 with Echeandía and served at Santa Bárbara and San Diego in the late 1820s. In 1831 and 1832 he opposed both Victoria and Zamorano. In 1836 he supported Gutiérrez against Alvarado, and two years later he supported Carlos Carrillo. He had to go into brief exile as a result. After his father's death he lived on the family *rancho* and continued to fill various Mexican public offices in the 1840s and Los Angeles municipal offices in the early 1850s. He died in 1880. See Bancroft, *History of California* 5: 755–56.

Ignacio Vallejo, founder of the Vallejo dynasty in Alta California, was born in Jalisco, New Spain, in 1748. He entered the army at an early age and arrived in San Diego in 1774. He worked at Missions San Luis Obispo and San Carlos in the 1780s. After reenlisting in the army in 1787, he was promoted to corporal in 1789 and to sergeant in 1805. He died in Monterey in 1831. He and his wife, María Antonia Lugo, had thirteen children. See Bancroft, *History of California* 5: 756.

José de Jesús Vallejo, a son of Ignacio Vallejo and María Antonia Lugo and the older brother of Mariano Guadalupe Vallejo, was born in San José in 1798. He was an active participant in the defense of Monterey against Bouchard. He later held various military and civilian offices in Alta California, including the position of administrator of Mission San José after 1836. After the U.S. conquest he remained at Mission San José, serving for a time as postmaster there. He died in 1882. See Bancroft, *History of California* 5: 757.

Mariano Guadalupe Vallejo was born in Monterey in 1808. He entered the military in 1824 and was promoted to *alférez* in 1827. He was involved in a number of expeditions against the indigenous peoples, notably against Estanislao in 1829, when his victory was marred by summary executions and a brutal massacre. He served in the *diputación* in the early 1830s and as commander of San Francisco from 1831 to 1834. In 1832 he married Francisca Benicia Carrillo. He founded Sonoma in 1835 and from that time generally remained in the northern part of Alta California. Alvarado appointed him military commander in 1836, and he held that position until the arrival of Micheltorena in 1842. Even though he was not unfriendly to the notion of a U.S. takeover of Alta California, he was arrested by the Bear Flaggers in 1846. After his release he became one of the leading proponents of cooperation with the new authorities. He served in the constitutional convention in 1849 and the state senate the following year. As the California resident best known to both the *californios* and the U.S. settlers, he was instrumental in persuading a number of his fellows to cooperate with the researches of Bancroft and his staff, although he was not always pleased with the portrayal of his people in the pages of the seven-volume *History of California*. He lived at Sonoma until his death in 1890. See McKittrick, *Vallejo*; Bancroft, *History of California* 5: 757–59; Meier, *Mexican American Biographies*, 232–33; and Sánchez, "Mariano Guadalupe Vallejo," in Sánchez, Pita, and Reyes, *Crítica*, 138.

Salvador Vallejo, a son of Ignacio Vallejo and María Antonia Lugo, and the younger brother of Mariano Guadalupe Vallejo, was born in Monterey in 1814. In 1836 his brother made him captain of the militia at Sonoma, and he engaged in many campaigns against the indigenous peoples in the area. He was married to María de la Luz Carrillo. He served as *juez de paz* and as administrator of San Francisco Solano. He was held prisoner by the Bear Flaggers in 1846. During the

Civil War he served in Arizona, and later he lived with his brother at Sonoma until his death in 1876. See Bancroft, *History of California* 5: 759; McKittrick, "Salvador Vallejo"; and Sánchez, "Salvador Vallejo," in Sánchez, Pita, and Reyes, *Crítica*, 92.

José Viader was from Catalonia, Spain. He arrived in Mexico in 1795 and went to Alta California in 1796. He was assigned to Mission Santa Clara in that year and remained there until he left for his native Spain in 1833. He and Magín Catalá worked together for three decades. During that time Viader was generally in charge of the temporal concerns of the mission. See Geiger, *Franciscan Missionaries*, 263–65.

Manuel Victoria was an infantry officer born in Tecpan, New Spain. In 1829 he requested an appointment in Baja California for reasons of health, and he was appointed governor there. In 1830 Alta California was added to his responsibilities. He assumed office on January 31, 1831, less than a month after Echeandía's secularization decree. He became involved in a series of disputes with the *californios*, and the *diputación* organized a movement against him within a few months of his arrival. He defeated a rebel army in December 1831 at Cahuenga, near Los Angeles, but he was so badly wounded that he had to leave for Mexico. Little is known of his later career. See Hutchinson, *Frontier Settlement*, 142–50.

María del Rosario Villa was married to Domingo Félix. She was executed by the Los Angeles vigilantes in 1836 for helping her lover, Gervasio Alipás, kill Félix. See Bancroft, *History of California* 3: 416–20.

Tomás Antonio Yorba, son of Antonio Yorba, who had come to Alta California in 1769, and María Josefa Grijalva, was born in 1787. He served in the *diputación* in 1830 and 1832, and in 1831 he was auxiliary *alcalde* at Santa Ana, where his family had a *rancho*. He was involved, with José Sepúlveda, in political controversies in Los Angeles in the late 1830s. He died in 1845. See Bancroft, *History of California* 5: 782; and Hart, *Companion*, 571.

Agustín Vicente Zamorano was born in San Agustín, Florida, in 1798. His father was a soldier who was assigned in 1809 to New Spain, where Agustín entered the military in 1821. He joined the engineering corps in 1824 and accompanied Echeandía to Alta California in the following year. He served as the governor's secretary for five years and was made commander at Monterey in 1831. After Victoria left Alta California, Zamorano was one of three de facto *jefes* who ruled until the arrival of José Figueroa in 1833. He was Figueroa's secretary for two years and operated the first printing press in Alta California. In 1835 he was made commander of San Diego. He became involved in the movement against Alvarado from 1836 to 1837, and when that failed, he left for Mexico. He returned to Alta California with Micheltorena in 1842 but died shortly after arriving in San Diego. See Harding, *Zamorano*.

Glossary

Abajeño   Mexican inhabitant of the southern area of Alta California, south of San Luis Obispo.

Administrador   The person in charge of a mission after secularization.

Alcalde   A local magistrate, usually a member of the municipal council; the chief executive officer of a pueblo. He possessed a combination of executive and judicial authority.

Alcalde (Indian)   The highest-ranking neophyte in the mission hierarchy. He was supposed to be elected by the neophytes, and he possessed a real, if limited, authority in supervising the mission Indians and in maintaining order.

Alcalde mayor   A chief magistrate in charge of a district; a regional governmental post combining judicial, administrative, and tax-collecting duties; subordinate to the *gobernador* of the region.

Alcaldesa   The wife of the alcalde.

Alférez   An ensign; the lowest-ranked military officer, approximately equal to a modern army second lieutenant.

Andalusian   A native of Andalucía, a southern province of Spain.

Angelinos   The inhabitants of Los Angeles.

Arribeño   A Mexican inhabitant of the northern area of Alta California, from San Luis Obispo north.

Arroba   A bulk measurement equal to 25.36 pounds.

Asamblea   The name of the Alta California legislature in 1843.

Asesor   A legal adviser to the government; a lawyer appointed to advise the judge in the conduct of law proceedings.

Atole   A cooked mixture of water and ground, dried grains; a staple mission food.

Auxiliares   Indian auxiliaries recruited from the ranks of reliable neophytes in older, established missions to assist in explorations or in the establishment or defense of new missions.

Ayudante de plaza   An officer at a specific locale who received his orders directly from the general or another superior. Other titles included *ayudante general*, *ayudante inspector*, and *ayudante de campo*.

Ayuntamiento   A town council.

Californio   Regional name for a non-Indian inhabitant of Alta California. Any *gente de razón* reared or, later, born and reared in California was a *californio*. The term had been used in Antigua California since 1700 and came into popular use in Alta California by the 1820s, with the growth of the first generation of California-born Mexicans.

Capilla   A chapel; also any room in a jail designated as a holding area for a prisoner awaiting execution.

Carajo   Derogatory term equivalent to "prick." Also used as an exclamation of extreme surprise (a play on the word *caramba*), like "Hell!" or "I'll be damned!"

Carlistas   The supporters of Carlos Carrillo.

Castillo   A fortress or coastal defense battery.

Catalán   A native of Catalonia, Spain.

Cédula real   A royal decree issued by a council over the king's signature.

Chalupa   A narrow canoe or small boat that has a cover and two masts for sails.

Cholo   A derogatory term for a *mestizo* or person of mixed European and Indian heritage.

Comandante   Commandant or commander.

Comisaría   Commissariat or branch of the army in charge of providing food and other supplies for the troops.

Comisario   The officer in charge of the warehouse.

Comisión   A special appointment, one that carried unusual or additional duties.

Comisionado   Noncommissioned soldier (usually a sergeant or corporal) appointed by the commander of the presidio to serve as a liaison between the presidio and the towns or missions. Duties included supervising the *alcalde* and exercising military and judicial authority. Also, with secularization the *comisionado* was the temporary supervisor of the former mission.

Compadre   The term by which the godfather and godmother address the father of their godson or goddaughter and by which the father and mother address the godfather. Also means "protector," "benefactor," or, popularly, "very close friend."

Considerando   The word with which each item in a legal document begins: "Whereas."

Contador   An accountant.

Cuartel   Barracks or garrison.

Cuera   From the word *cuero*, which means "hide" or "leather." A heavy, knee-length, usually sleeveless jacket made of up to seven layers of buckskin or cowhide and bound at the edges with a strong seam. This distinctive armor garment gave the presidio soldier the name by which he was known for more than two centuries: *soldado de cuera*.

Curandero   A practitioner of folk medicine.

Departamento   Department; governmental unit corresponding to a state or territory. Under the centralist Mexican government after 1836, Alta California, formerly a territory, became a department.

Diegueños   The inhabitants of the *pueblo* of San Diego; the Indians of the area.

Diputación territorial   The elected assembly which usually met at Monterey during the Mexican period in California. A consultative body to the governor of the territory.

Diputado   A delegate or member of the *diputación territorial*; also the territorial/departmental delegate to the lower chamber of the Mexican national congress.

Don/Doña   A title of respect. In California it was accorded to any Spaniard, officer, or person from an important, respected family. Used before the first name. Can also be used to express extreme respect or extreme disdain.

Embarcadero   Wharf.

Escolta   The escort or squad of soldiers assigned to protect a missionary at a mission.

Excelentísimo Señor   A term of respect and courtesy which a person uses when addressing someone of high rank or social stature.

Fanega   A dry measure of weight, the equivalent of about 1.6 bushels. Also a land measurement, *fanega de sembradura*, equivalent to 8.8 acres.

Frontera   The frontier between settled and unsettled areas. The northern region of Baja California.

Fusil   A flint-lock musket: gun, rifle of infantry.

Gabrieleño   Name given to the Indians of the Los Angeles area, derived from Mission San Gabriel Arcángel.

Gente de razón   Literally, "people with the capacity to reason," meaning any non-Indian.

Gentile   A non-Christian Indian.

Gobernador   Governor of a region or province.

Gutierreños   Belonging to, supporters of, or associated with someone by the name of Gutiérrez.

Habilitado general   An officer in a Spanish regiment charged with its supplies or money; a quartermaster or paymaster.

Hacienda   As a unit of measurement, it was equivalent to five square leagues or 21,690 acres. Also, very large estates were generally called *haciendas*. Variable factors defining *haciendas* included capital, labor, land, markets, technology, and social recognition. The most developed missions and *ranchos* in Alta California approximated the small-scale *haciendas* of northern Mexico.

Hechicero   A wizard or sorcerer; the pejorative name given to Native American shamans by Jesuit and other missionaries.

Hijo del país   Native son.

Idem   Latin term which means "the same."

Jefe   Leader, head, or superior. Followed by adjectives such as *militar, político, principal,* and *superior*.

Juez de campo   Judge of the countryside. Official in charge of roundups and disputes involving cattle or grazing.

Juez de paz   Judge or justice of the peace; replaced the office of *alcalde* in some areas after 1836. Combined municipal and judicial powers within the *pueblo*.

Junta   A congress, an assembly, a council. Any meeting of persons to speak about business. A group used to administer or govern, usually ad interim.

Lancha A barge, small yacht, or a sailing launch; the smallest boat used regularly to cross the Gulf of California.

League A standard Spanish measure of distance, approximately 2.6 miles.

Licenciado A university degree usually held by priests and lawyers in canon or civil-criminal law.

Maromero Acrobat or rope dancer.

Mayordomo A foreman or supervisor of a mission under the priest, or of a ranch under the owner.

Mazateco A person from Mazatlán, Mexico.

El Mentidero A place where people gather to gossip. Derived from the Spanish verb *mentir*, which means "to lie."

Mestizo A person of mixed European and Indian heritage.

Navío A ship that is larger than a frigate (*fragata*).

Neophyte Term used to describe the Christian mission Indians.

Padre comisario An office created for the administration of the Indies by the commissary general in Madrid, which eventually operated in California in 1812. This official relieved the president of the missions of some of his offices and duties. He was generally in charge of finance and supplies at the missions and at the home *colegio*. The office had general supervision over the missionaries of the mission district and dealt with the territorial government on mission matters.

Paje A neophyte youth selected by a missionary to serve as his page or assistant.

Pendolista A penman or calligrapher, or someone who spends all of his time keeping records, for example, an accountant.

Peón A worker or unskilled laborer.

Peso The monetary unit of Spanish America; eight *reales* equaled one *peso*. In the first half of the nineteenth century, a *peso* was roughly equivalent to one U.S. dollar and two Russian rubles.

Plana mayor General staff.

Plaza Town square, fortified town, or military base.

Pozole A thick soup of cornmeal, beans, hominy, marrow bones, and scraps of meat.

Presidio A frontier military garrison; the fortified location and community of such a garrison.

Pronunciados Rebels or insurgents.

Pronunciamiento Insurrection, uprising.

Pueblo The populace; a village or town. The smallest municipal entity, possessing an *ayuntamiento* or town council.

Ranchería An Indian village or settlement, usually referring to the non-Christian Indians.

Ranchero A rancher.

Rancho   An estate granted, under a variety of laws, to an individual. In common usage, a *rancho* was usually an estate devoted generally to the raising of cattle. A *rancho* usually covered approximately four square miles, but some covered up to thirty square miles. A *rancho* could also be one of the units of a *hacienda*, in which case it would be run by a *mayordomo* responsible to the *hacienda administrador* or *hacendado*. The size and specific characteristics of *ranchos* varied according to the region in which they were located. Variables included labor, land, production for market or subsistence, availability of water, and climate.

Rancho del Rey   A *rancho* operated by the local presidio for the support of the soldiers and their families.

Rancho Nacional   The name given to the *ranchos del Rey* after Mexican independence.

Real   A monetary unit. Eight *reales* equaled one *peso*.

Receptor   Receiver, treasurer.

Reduction   A mission or the process of missionization. The state of affairs resulting from the indigenous peoples' being grouped together closely at and around the missions. The word pointed to its Latin root, *reducere*, "to lead back," in this case meaning to lead the indigenous peoples back into the faith.

Regidor   A member of the *ayuntamiento*.

Sarape   A narrow blanket that can be worn or thrown over a saddle.

Sargento   A sergeant.

Síndico   A public attorney or advocate/representative of a mission.

S.Q.B.S.M.   Abbreviation for "Servidor que besa su mano," or "Servant who kisses your hand."

Teniente   A lieutenant, or the officer who was second in command of a military unit.

Tlaco/claco   A copper coin widely available in mining areas from 1849 on.

Tribunal superior   The highest judicial body in Alta California.

Tule   Any of several grassy or reedlike plants growing in the marshy lowlands of the southwestern United States. Spanish word derived from Náhuatl *tullin*.

Vaquero   A cowboy. In Mexican California they were generally indigenous people and frequently from Baja California. They tended the large stock herds under the direction of a *mayordomo*.

Vara   A measure of length, equivalent to 32.99 inches.

Vizcayan   A person from the Biscay (Vizcaya) region in northern Spain.

Virrey   A viceroy; the chief royal administrator of a *virreinato*, or viceroyalty. New Spain was one of two viceroyalties in the New World.

Visitador general   A friar appointed by the general of the order to conduct a formal visitation or inspection of a province or apostolic college and its personnel and to hold a canonical chapter.

Vocal   Member of the assembly.

Bibliography

Primary Sources

Archivo General de la Nación, Mexico City

Osio, Antonio María. "Minutes of the 1832 Meetings of the *diputación territorial* of Alta California." Gobernación, Legajo 120, Expedientes 15, 18.

Sarría, Vicente Francisco de. "Carta al Obispo de Sonora." Undated letter (probably late summer 1824), Justicia Eclesiástica, Legajo 31, Expedientes 54–56.

The Bancroft Library, University of California, Berkeley

Abrego, José. "Relación." 1877. MS. C-E 65.9.

Alvarado, Juan Bautista. "History of California." 5 vols. Translated by Earl R. Hewitt. 1876. MS. C-D 1–5.

Amador, José María. "Memorias sobre la historia de California." 1877. MS. C-D 28.

Arce, Francisco. "Carta a Antonio María Osio." 1846. C-D 30.7.

Arce, Francisco. "Memorias históricas de Don Francisco Arce." 1877. MS. C-D 30.

Bandini, Juan. "Apuntes para la historia de la Alta California desde el año de su fundación en 1769 hasta el año de 1845." N.d. MS. C-D 6–7.

Bandini, Juan. Documentos para la historia de California, 1776–1850. C-B 68.

Bernal, Juan. "Memorias de un californio." 1877. MS. C-D 43.

Berreyesa, Antonio. "Relación." 1877. MS. C-D 44.

Bojorques, Juan. "Recuerdos sobre la historia de California." 1877. MS. C-D 46.

Boronda, José Canuto. "Notas históricas sobre California." 1878. MS. C-D 47.

Bowman, Jacob N. "Index of the Spanish-Mexican Private Land Grant Records and Cases of California." 1958. MS.

Carrillo, Julio. "Statement of Julio Carrillo." 1875. MS. C-E 66–67.

César, Julio. "Cosas de indios de California." 1878. MS. C-D 109.

Coronel, Antonio Franco. "Cosas de California." 1877. MS. C-D 61.

Espinosa, Clemente. "Breves notas históricas." 1877. MS. C-D 74.

Estudillo, José María. "Datos históricos sobre la Alta California." 1878. MS. C-D 76.

Ezquer, Ignacio. "Memorias de cosas pasadas en California." 1878. MS. C-D 77.

Fernández, José. "Cosas de California." 1874. MS. C-D 10.

Flores, Miguel. "Recuerdos históricos de la Alta California." 1877. MS. C-D 80.

Galindo, Eusebio. "Recuerdos de Eusebio Galindo." 1877. MS. C-D 172.

Gantner, John Oscar. "Notes on the Life of My Father." 1947–48. MS. C-D 5034.

García, Inocente. "Hechos históricos de California." 1878. MS. C-D 84.

García, Marcelino. "Apuntes sobre el General Micheltorena." 1877. MS. C-D 86.

Garnica del Castillo, Nicanor. "Recuerdos sobre California desde el año de 1842." 1877. MS. C-D 88.

Germán, José de los Santos, and Luis Germán. "Sucesos en California." 1878. MS. C-D 89.

Gómez, Juan. Documentos para la historia de California, 1785–1850. C-B 78.

Gómez, Vicente. "Lo que sabe sobre cosas de California." 1876. MS. C-D 90.

González, Mauricio. "Memorias de la historia de California." 1877. MS. C-D 91.

González, Rafael. "Experiencias de un soldado de California." 1878. MS. C-D 92.

Guerra Hartnell, María Teresa de la. "Narrativa de la distinguida matrona californiana." 1875. MS. C-E 67.2.

Guerra Ord, María de las Angustias de la. "Ocurrencias en California." 1878. MS. C-D 134.

Guerra y Noriega, José de la. Documentos para la historia de California. 7 vols. 1878. C-B 59–65.

Hussey, John A. "Fort McDowell, Angel Island, Marin and San Francisco Counties." GSA registry no. W-Cal-191. U.S. Department of the Interior, War Assets General Services Administration, Sept. 1949.

Juárez, Cayetano. "Notas sobre Cayetano Juárez, capitán de la milicia de California en 1841." 1875. MS. C-E 67.1.

Larios, Justo. "Convulsiones de California." 1878. MS. C-D 114.

Lorenzana, Apolinaria. "Memorias de la beata." 1878. MS. C-D 116.

Lugo, José del Carmen. "Vida de un ranchero." 1877. MS. C-D 118.

Machado Alipás de Ridington, Juana de Dios. "Los tiempos pasados de la Alta California." 1878. MS. C-D 119.

Osio, Antonio María. Antonio María Osio Papers, 1823-1853. C-B 833.

Osuña de Marrón, Felipa. "Felipa Osuña de Marrón: Recuerdos y papeles." 1878. MS. CD-120.

Palomares, José Francisco. José Francisco Palomares Papers, 1839-1847.

Palomares, José Francisco. "Memorias de José Francisco Palomares." 1877. MS. C-D 135.

Pérez, Eulalia. "Una vieja y sus recuerdos." 1877. MS. C-D 139.

Pérez, Juan. "Recuerdos históricos de California." 1877. MS. C-D 140.

Pico, José Dolores. "Diario de la expedición al lago de los tulares." 1826. MS. C-C 233.

Pico, Pío. Documentos para la historia de California: Archivo de la familia Pico. 1877. C-B 88.

Bibliography

Pico, Pío. "Narración histórica." 1877. MS. C-D 13.

Pico de Avila, María Inocente. "Cosas de California." 1878. MS. C-D 34.

Pinto, Rafael. "Apuntaciones para la historia de California." 1878. MS. C-D 142.

Pinto, Rafael. Documentos para la historia de California. N.d. C-B 90.

Rodríguez, Jacinto. "Narración." 1874. MS. C-E 65.4.

Rodríguez, José Brígido. "Recuerdos históricos sobre California." 1877. MS. C-D 149.

Romero, José María. "Memorias." 1877. MS. C-D 150.

Sánchez, José Ramón. "Notas dictadas por José Ramón Sánchez." 1875. MS. C-E 66–67.

Savage, Thomas. "Reports of Labors in Archives and Procuring Material for History of California, 1876–79." 1879. MS. C-E 191.

Serrano, Florencio. "Apuntes para la historia de California." 1877. MS. C-D 156.

Torre, Esteban de la. "Reminiscencias." 1878. MS. C-D 163.

U.S. Commission for Ascertaining and Settling Private Land Claims in California. Papers. 70/66 C.

Valdez, Dorotea. "Reminiscencias." 1874. MS. C-D 65.8.

Vallejo, José de Jesús. "Historical Reminiscences of California." Translated by Brother Henry De Groote. Edited by Elinor Butler. 1875. MS. C-D 16.

Vallejo, Mariano Guadalupe. "Historical and Personal Memoirs Relating to California." 5 vols. Translated by Earl R. Hewitt. 1875. MS. C-D 17–21.

Vallejo, Mariano Guadalupe. Vallejo Family Papers, 1832–1889. 76/79 C.

Véjar, Pablo. "Recuerdos de un viejo." 1877. MS. C-D 169.

Vischer, Edward. Edward Vischer Papers, 1853–1878. 77/37 C.

Published Accounts

Alvarado, Juan Bautista. *Vignettes of Early California: Childhood Reminiscences of Juan Bautista Alvarado.* Translated by John H. R. Polt with an introduction and notes by W. Michael Mathes. San Francisco: Book Club of California, 1982.

Argüello, Luis Antonio. *The Diary of Captain Luis Antonio Argüello, October 17–November 17, 1821: The Last Spanish Expedition in California.* Translated by Vivian C. Fisher with an introduction by Arthur Quinn. Berkeley: Friends of The Bancroft Library, University of California, 1992.

Arrillaga, José Joaquín de. *Diary of His Surveys of the Frontier, 1796.* Translated by Froylan Tiscareño. Edited and annotated by John W. Robinson. Los Angeles: Dawson's Book Shop, 1969.

Atondo y Antillón, Isidro. *First from the Gulf to the Pacific: The Diary of the Kino-Atondo Peninsular Expedition, December 14, 1684–January 13, 1685.* Transcribed, translated, and edited by W. Michael Mathes. Los Angeles: Dawson's Book Shop, 1969.

Bibliography

Beeler, Madison S., ed. *The Ventureño Confesionario of José Señán, O.F.M.* Berkeley: University of California Press, 1967.

Biggs, Beatrice. "The Diary of Rafael Gómez: Monterey in 1836." *Southern California Quarterly* 45.3 (1963): 265–69.

Blackburn, Thomas. "The Chumash Revolt of 1824: A Native Account." *Journal of California Anthropology* 2.2 (1975): 223–24.

Bowman, Alan P. *Index to the 1850 Census of the State of California.* Baltimore: Genealogical Publishing Co., 1972.

Brandes, Raymond. "Times Gone by in Alta California: The Recollections of Sra. Doña Juana Machado Alipás de Wrightington." *The Californians* 8.4 (1990–91): 43–51.

Browne, J. Ross. *Muleback to the Convention: Letters of J. Ross Browne, Reporter to the Constitutional Convention, Monterey, September–October, 1849.* San Francisco: Book Club of California, 1950.

Corney, Peter. *Early Voyages in the North Pacific, 1813–1818.* Fairfield, Wash.: Ye Galleon Press, 1965.

Cutter, Donald C. *California in 1792: A Spanish Naval Visit.* Norman: University of Oklahoma Press, 1990.

Cutter, Donald C. "A Franciscan Visit to the Russians: Father Payeras at Fort Ross." *Archivum Franciscanum Historicum* 85 (1992): 653–70.

Dana, Napoleon Jackson Tecumseh. *Monterrey is Ours! The Mexican War Letters of Lieutenant Dana, 1845-1847.* Edited by Robert H. Ferrell. Lexington: University Press of Kentucky, 1990.

Dundonald, Thomas Cochrane, Earl of. *Narrative of Services in the Liberation of Chile, Perú, and Brazil from Spanish and Portuguese Domination.* London: J. Ridgeway, 1859.

Farnham, Thomas Jefferson. *Travels in California.* Foreword by Joseph A. Sullivan. Oakland, Calif.: Biobooks, 1947.

Farris, Glenn, trans. and ed. "Visit of the Russian Warship *Apollo* to California in 1822–1823." *Southern California Quarterly* 75 (1993): 1–13.

Figueroa, José. *Manifesto to the Mexican Republic.* Translated and edited by C. Alan Hutchinson. Berkeley: University of California Press, 1978.

Flores, José María. "La carta de Flores." Translated by Thomas Workman Temple II. Introduction by Douglas S. Watson. *California Historical Society Quarterly* 12 (1933): 147–54.

Forbes, Alexander. *California: A History of Upper and Lower California from Their First Discovery to the Present Time.* London: Smith and Elder Co., 1839.

Galvin, John. *The Coming of Justice to California: Three Documents Translated from Spanish by Adelaide Smithers.* San Francisco: J. Howell Books, 1963.

Geiger, Maynard, O.F.M. "Fray Antonio Ripoll's Description of the Chumash Revolt of 1824 at Santa Barbara." *Southern California Quarterly* 52.4 (1970): 345–64.

Bibliography

Geiger, Maynard, O.F.M. "Six Census Records of Los Angeles and Its Immediate Area between 1804 and 1823." *Southern California Quarterly* 54.4 (1972): 313–42.

Gibson, George Rutledge. *Journal of a Soldier under Kearny and Doniphan, 1846–1847.* Edited by Ralph P. Bieber. Glendale, Calif.: Arthur H. Clark Co., 1935.

Gómez, Rafael. "The Diary of Rafael Gómez: Monterey in 1836." Translated by Beatrice Biggs. *Historical Society of Southern California Quarterly* 45 (1963): 265–69.

González, Rafael. *A Spanish Soldier in the Royal Presidio of Santa Bárbara,* Translated by Jarrell C. Jackman. Edited by Richard S. Whitehead. Santa Barbara, Calif.: Bellerophon Books, 1987.

Hammond, George P., ed. *The Larkin Papers: Personal, Business, and Official Correspondence of Thomas Oliver Larkin, Merchant and U.S. Consul in California.* 10 vols. Berkeley: University of California Press, 1951–68.

Hewes, Gordon, and Minna Hewes. "Indian Life and Customs at Mission San Luis Rey." Translation of the Pablo Tac MS. *The Americas* 9.1 (1952–53): 87–106.

Hudson, Travis. "The Chumash Revolt of 1824: Another Account from the Notes of John P. Harrington." *Journal of California and Great Basin Anthropology* 2.1 (1980): 123–26.

Janssens, Victor Eugene August. *The Life and Adventures in California of Don Agustín Janssens, 1834–1856.* Translated by Francis Price. Edited by William H. Ellison and Francis Price. San Marino, Calif: Huntington Library, 1953.

Jimeno Casarín, Manuel. *Indexes of Land Concessions from 1830–1846.* San Francisco: Kenny and Alexander, 1861.

Kelsey, Harry, ed. *The Doctrina and Confesionario of Juan Cortés.* Altadena, Calif.: Howling Coyote Press, 1979.

Lugo, José del Carmen. "Life of a Rancher." *Historical Society of Southern California Quarterly* 32.3 (1950): 185–236.

Machado Alipás de Ridington, Juana de Dios. "Times Gone by in Alta California: Recollections of Señora Doña Juana Machado Alipás de Ridington." Introduction and translation by Raymond S. Brandes. *Historical Society of Southern California Quarterly* 41.3 (1959): 195–240.

Mathes, W. Michael. *Documentos para la historia de la transformación colonizadora de California, 1679–1686.* 3 vols. Madrid: J. Porrúa Turanzas, 1964.

Mathes, W. Michael. *La frontera ruso-mexicana: Documentos mexicanos para la historia del establecimiento ruso en California, 1808–1842.* Mexico City: Secretaría de Relaciones Exteriores, 1990.

Mathes, W. Michael, ed. "El comisionado del imperio mexicano visita la frontera ruso-mexicana." *Calafia* 6.6 (Jan. 1989): 7–11.

Mollins, Margaret, and Virginia E. Thickens, eds. *Ramblings in California: The Adventures of Henry Cerruti.* Berkeley: Friends of The Bancroft Library, University of California, 1954.

Bibliography

Northrup, Marie E. "The Los Angeles *Padrón* of 1844." *Historical Society of Southern California Quarterly* 42.4 (1960): 360–417.

Nunis, Doyce B., Jr. "Six New Larkin Letters." *Southern California Quarterly* 49.1 (1967): 65–103.

Nunis, Doyce B., Jr., ed. *The California Diary of Faxon Dean Atherton, 1836–1839.* San Francisco: California Historical Society, 1964.

Onís, José de. *Las misiones españolas en los Estados Unidos.* Bilingual edition of Pablo Tac's "Memories of Mission San Luis Rey." New York: Neff Lithographing Co., 1959.

Palóu, Francisco. *Palóu's Life of Fray Junípero Serra.* Translated and annotated by Maynard Geiger, O.F.M. Washington, D.C.: Academy of American Franciscan History, 1955.

Perkins, William. *Three Years in California: William Perkins' Journal of Life at Sonora, 1849–1852.* Edited by Dale L. Morgan and James R. Scobie. Berkeley: University of California Press, 1964.

Pérouse, Jean François de la. *Monterey in 1786: The Journals of Jean François de la Pérouse.* Edited by Malcolm Margolin. Berkeley, Calif.: Heyday Books, 1989.

Phelps, William Dane. *Alta California, 1840–1842. The Journal and Observations of William Dane Phelps.* Introduced and edited by Briton Cooper Busch. Glendale, Calif.: Arthur H. Clark Co., 1983.

Pico, Pío. *Don Pío Pico's Historical Narrative.* Translated by Arthur P. Botello. Edited with introduction by Martin Cole and Henry Welcome. Glendale, Calif.: Arthur H. Clark Co., 1970.

Robinson, Alfred. *Life in California during a Residence of Several Years in That Territory.* New York: Wiley and Putnam, 1846.

Sánchez, Rosaura, Beatrice Pita, and Bárbara Reyes. *Crítica Monograph Series.* No. 68. San Diego: University of California, San Diego, 1994.

Señán, José Francisco de Paula. *The Letters of José Señán, O.F.M., Mission San Buenaventura, 1796–1823.* Translated by Paul D. Nathan. Edited by Lesley Byrd Simpson. San Francisco: J. Howell Books, 1962.

Shur, Leonid Avelevich. *The Khlebnikov Archive.* Fairbanks: University of Alaska Press, 1990.

Turner, Henry Smith. *The Original Journals of Henry Smith Turner.* Edited by Dwight L. Clarke. Norman: University of Oklahoma Press, 1966.

Venegas, Miguel. *Juan María de Salvatierra of the Company of Jesus.* Translated, edited, and annotated by Marguerite Eyer Wilbur. Cleveland: Arthur H. Clark Co., 1929.

Vowell, Richard Longeville. "Memorias de un oficial de marina inglés al servicio de Chile durante los años de 1821–1829." Translated by J. T. Medina. Santiago de Chile, *Imprenta Universitaria* (1923): 16–31.

Weber, Francis J. *Holy Cross Mission: A Documentary History of Santa Cruz.* Hong Kong: Libra Press, 1984.

Weber, Francis J. *Mission of the Passes: A Documentary History of Santa Inés.* Hong Kong: Libra Press, 1981.

Secondary Sources

Books, Dissertations, and Theses

Alekseev, A. I. *The Odyssey of a Russian Scientist: I. G. Voznesenskii in Alaska, California, and Siberia, 1831–1849.* Translated by Wilma C. Follette. Edited by Richard A. Pierce, Kingston, Ont.: Limestone Press, 1987.

Altman, Janet Gurkin. *Epistolarity: Approaches to a Form.* Columbus: Ohio State University Press, 1982.

Alvarez, Robert R., Jr. *Familia: Migration and Adaptation in Baja and Alta California, 1800–1975.* Berkeley: University of California Press, 1987.

Bancroft, Hubert Howe. *California Pastoral.* San Francisco: The History Company, 1888.

Bancroft, Hubert Howe. *History of California.* 7 vols. San Francisco: The History Company, 1884–90.

Bancroft, Hubert Howe. *Literary Industries.* San Francisco: The History Company, 1890.

Bancroft, Hubert Howe. *Popular Tribunals.* 2 vols. San Francisco: The History Company, 1887.

Bannon, John Francis. *The Spanish Borderlands Frontier, 1513–1821.* New York: Holt, Rinehart and Winston, 1970.

Bauer, K. Jack. *The Mexican War.* New York: Macmillan, 1974.

Bealer, Lewis. "The Privateers of Buenos Aires, 1815–1821: Their Activities in the Hispanic American Wars of Independence." Ph.D. diss., University of California, Berkeley, 1935.

Beck, Warren A., and Ynez D. Haase. *Historical Atlas of California.* Norman: University of Oklahoma Press, 1974.

Becker, Robert H. *Designs on the Land: Diseños of California Ranchos and Their Makers.* San Francisco: Book Club of California, 1969.

Becker, Robert H. *Diseños of California Ranchos: Maps of Thirty-seven Land Grants, 1822–1846.* San Francisco: Book Club of California, 1964.

Blanco, Antonio. *La lengua española en la historia de California.* Madrid: Cultura Hispánica, 1971.

Blasing, Mutlu Konuk. *The Art of Life: Studies in American Autobiographical Literature.* Austin: University of Texas Press, 1977.

Brack, Gene M. *Mexico Views Manifest Destiny, 1821–1846: An Essay on the Origins of the Mexican War.* Albuquerque: University of New Mexico Press, 1975.

Briggs, Donald, and Marvin Alisky. *The Historical Dictionary of Mexico.* Metuchen, N. J.: Scarecrow Press, 1981.

Browne, J. Ross. *Resources of the Pacific Slope.* New York: D. Appleton and Co., 1869.

Caillet-Bois, Teodoro. *Historia naval argentina.* Buenos Aires: Emece Editores, 1944.

Caillet-Bois, Teodoro. *El proceso de Bouchard.* Buenos Aires: Publicaciones del Instituto de Investigaciones Históricas, 1936.

Carosso, Vincent P. *The California Wine Industry: A Study of the Formative Years.* Berkeley: University of California Press, 1951.

Carranza, Angel J. *Campañas navales de la República Argentina.* 4 vols. Buenos Aires: N.p., n.d.

Castañeda, Antonia I. "Presidarias y Pobladores: Spanish-Mexican Women in Frontier Monterey, Alta California, 1770–1821." Ph.D. diss., Stanford University, 1990.

Churchill, Charles Bradford. "Adventurers and Prophets: American Autobiographers in Mexican California, 1828–1847." Ph.D. diss., University of California, Santa Barbara, 1988.

Clar, C. Raymond. *Quarterdecks and Spanish Grants.* Felton, Calif.: Glenwood Publishers, 1971.

Clark, Donald Thomas. *Monterey County Place Names: A Geographical Dictionary.* Carmel Valley, Calif.: Kestrel Press, 1991.

Clark, Harry. *A Venture in History: The Production, Publication, and Sale of the Works of Hubert Howe Bancroft.* Berkeley: University of California Press, 1973.

Clarke, Dwight L. *Stephen Watts Kearny: Soldier of the West.* Norman: University of Oklahoma Press, 1961.

Clauss, Francis J. *Angel Island: Jewel of San Francisco Bay.* Menlo Park, Calif.: Briarcliff Press, 1982.

Clavigero, Francisco Javier. *The History of [Lower] California.* Translated from Italian and edited by Sara E. Lake and A. A. Gray. Stanford, Calif.: Stanford University Press, 1937.

Cleland, Robert Glass. *The Cattle on a Thousand Hills: Southern California, 1850–1880.* San Marino, Calif.: Huntington Library, 1941.

Cook, Sherburne F. *The Conflict between the California Indians and White Civilization.* Berkeley: University of California Press, 1976.

Cook, Sherburne F. *The Epidemic of 1830–1833 in California and Oregon.* University of California Publications in American Archeology and Ethnology, vol. 43, no. 3, 303–25. Berkeley: University of California Press, 1955.

Cook, Sherburne F. *Expeditions to the Interior of California: Central Valley, 1820–1840.* Berkeley: University of California Press, 1961.

Cook, Sherburne F., and Woodrow Borah. *Essays in Population History: Mexico and California*. Vol. 3. Berkeley: University of California Press, 1979.

Couser, G. Thomas. *Altered Egos: Authority in American Autobiography*. New York: Oxford University Press, 1989.

Cowan, Robert G. *Ranchos of California: A List of Spanish Concessions, 1775–1822, and Mexican Grants, 1822–1846*. Los Angeles: Historical Society of Southern California, 1977.

Crosby, Harry W. *Antigua California: Mission and Colony on the Peninsular Frontier, 1697–1768*. Albuquerque: University of New Mexico Press, 1994.

Crouch, Dora P., Daniel J. Garr, and Axel I. Mundigo. *Spanish City Planning in North America*. Cambridge, Mass.: Massachusetts Institute of Technology Press, 1982.

Dakin, Susanna Bryant. *The Lives of William Hartnell*. Stanford, Calif.: Stanford University Press, 1949.

Diccionario Porrúa de historia, biografía, y geografía de México. 5th ed. Mexico City: Editorial Porrúa, 1986.

Dobie, J. Frank. *The Mustangs*. Austin: University of Texas Press, 1984.

Eisenhower, John S. D. *So Far from God: The U.S. War with Mexico, 1846–1848*. New York: Random House, 1989.

Emparán, Madie Brown. *The Vallejos of California*. San Francisco: Gleeson Library Associates, University of San Francisco, 1968.

Engelhardt, Zephyrin, Fr. *The Holy Man of Santa Clara: On Life, Virtues, and Miracles of Fr. Magín Catalá O.F.M.* San Francisco: James H. Barry Co., 1909.

Engelhardt, Zephyrin, Fr. *Mission La Concepción Purísima de María Santísima*. Santa Barbara, Calif.: Mission Santa Bárbara, 1932.

Engelhardt, Zephyrin, Fr. *Mission San Carlos Borromeo (Carmelo)*. Edited by Fr. Felix Pudlowski. Santa Barbara, Calif.: Mission Santa Bárbara, 1934.

Engelhardt, Zephyrin, Fr. *The Missions and Missionaries of California*. 4 vols. San Francisco: James H. Barry Co., 1908–15.

Engelhardt, Zephyrin, Fr. *Mission San Juan Bautista, a School of Church Music*. Santa Barbara, Calif.: Mission Santa Bárbara, 1931.

Engelhardt, Zephyrin, Fr. *Mission San Luis Obispo in the Valley of the Bears*. Santa Barbara, Calif.: Mission Santa Bárbara, 1933.

Engelhardt, Zephyrin, Fr. *Mission Santa Inés, Virgen y Mártir, and Its Ecclesiastical Seminary*. Santa Barbara, Calif.: Mission Santa Bárbara, 1932.

Engelhardt, Zephyrin, Fr. *San Diego Mission*. San Francisco: James H. Barry Co., 1920.

Engelhardt, Zephyrin, Fr. *San Fernando Rey, the Mission of the Valley*. Chicago: Franciscan Herald Press, 1927.

Engelhardt, Zephyrin, Fr. *San Francisco or Mission Dolores*. Chicago: Franciscan Herald Press, 1924.

Bibliography

Engelhardt, Zephyrin, Fr. *San Gabriel Mission and the Beginnings of Los Angeles.* San Gabriel, Calif.: Mission San Gabriel, 1927.

Engelhardt, Zephyrin, Fr. *San Juan Capistrano Mission.* Los Angeles: Standard Printing Co., 1922.

Engelhardt, Zephyrin, Fr. *San Luis Rey Mission.* San Francisco: James H. Barry Co., 1921.

Engelhardt, Zephyrin, Fr. *San Miguel, Arcángel: The Mission on the Highway.* Santa Barbara, Calif.: Mission Santa Bárbara, 1931.

Engelhardt, Zephyrin, Fr. *Santa Barbara Mission.* San Francisco: James H. Barry Co., 1923.

Eversole, Robert Wayne. "Towns in Mexican Alta California: A Social History of Monterey, San José, Santa Bárbara, and Los Angeles, 1822–1846." Ph.D. diss., University of California, San Diego, 1986.

Fabre, Genevieve, ed. *European Perspectives on Hispanic Literature of the United States.* Houston: Arte Público Press, 1988.

Folkman, David Izatt. *The Nicaragua Route.* Salt Lake City: University of Utah Press, 1972.

Fontana, Bernard L. *Entrada: The Legacy of Spain and Mexico in the United States.* Tucson, Ariz.: Southwest Parks and Monuments Association, 1994.

Forbes, J. Alexander. *Mexican Titles in the States and Territories of the United States.* San Francisco: W. A. Woodward and Co., 1891.

Francis, Jessie Davies. *An Economic and Social History of Mexican California, 1822–1846.* New York: Arno Press, 1976.

Gates, Paul W. *Land and Law in California: Essays on Land Policies.* Ames: Iowa State University Press, 1991.

Geary, Gerald J. *The Secularization of the California Missions, 1810–1846.* Catholic University of America Studies in American Church History, vol. 17. Washington, D.C.: Catholic University of America, 1934.

Geiger, Maynard, O. F. M. *Franciscan Missionaries in Hispanic California, 1769–1848: A Biographical Dictionary.* San Marino, Calif.: Huntington Library, 1969.

Genini, Ronald, and Richard Hitchman. *Romualdo Pacheco: A Californio in Two Eras.* San Francisco: Book Club of California, 1985.

Gerhard, Peter. *A Guide to the Historical Geography of New Spain.* Cambridge: Cambridge University Press, 1972.

Gerhard, Peter. *The North Frontier of New Spain.* Princeton, N.J.: Princeton University Press, 1982.

Gibson, James R. *Imperial Russia in Frontier America: The Changing Geography of Supply of Russian America, 1784–1867.* New York: Oxford University Press, 1976.

Gibson, James R. *Otter Skins, Boston Ships, and China Goods: The Maritime Fur Trade of the Northwest Coast, 1785–1841.* Seattle: University of Washington Press, 1992.

Bibliography

Gómez-Quiñones, Juan. *Roots of Chicano Politics, 1600–1940*. Albuquerque: University of New Mexico Press, 1994.

Grimal, Pierre. *The Dictionary of Classical Mythology*. New York: Blackwell, 1985.

Griswold del Castillo, Richard. *The Treaty of Guadalupe Hidalgo: A Legacy of Conflict*. Norman: University of Oklahoma Press, 1990.

Gudde, Erwin G. *California Place Names*. Revised and enlarged edition. Berkeley: University of California Press, 1969.

Gutiérrez, Ramón A. *When Jesus Came, the Corn Mothers Went Away: Marriage, Sexuality, and Power in New Mexico, 1500–1846*. Stanford, Calif.: Stanford University Press, 1991.

Gutiérrez, Ramón A., and Genaro Padilla, eds. *Recovering the U.S. Hispanic Literary Heritage*. Houston: Arte Público Press, 1993.

Haas, Lisbeth. *Conquests and Historical Identities in California, 1769–1936*. Berkeley: University of California Press, 1995.

Hageman, Fred C., and Russell C. Ewing. *An Archaeological and Restoration Study of Mission La Purísima Concepción*. Santa Barbara, Calif.: Santa Barbara Trust for Historic Preservation, 1980.

Hague, Harlan, and David J. Langum. *Thomas O. Larkin: A Life of Patriotism and Profit in Old California*. Norman: University of Oklahoma Press, 1990.

Hale, Charles A. *Mexican Liberalism in the Age of Mora, 1821–1853*. New Haven: Yale University Press, 1968.

Hansen, Woodrow James. *The Search for Authority in California*. Oakland, Calif.: Biobooks, 1960.

Harding, George L. *Don Agustín Zamorano*. New York: Arno Press, 1976.

Harlow, Neal. *California Conquered: War and Peace on the Pacific, 1846–1850*. Berkeley: University of California Press, 1982.

Hart, James D. *A Companion to California*. New edition, revised and expanded. Berkeley: University of California Press, 1987.

Hawgood, John A. *First and Last Consul: Thomas Oliver Larkin and the Americanization of California*. San Marino, Calif.: Huntington Library, 1962.

Heizer, Robert F., ed. *California*. Vol. 8 of *Handbook of North American Indians*, edited by William C. Sturtevant. Washington, D.C.: Smithsonian Institution, 1978.

Hittell, John S. *A History of the City of San Francisco and Incidentally of the State of California*. San Francisco: A. L. Bancroft and Co., 1878.

Hittell, Theodore H. *History of California*. 4 vols. San Francisco: Pacific Press Publishing House, 1885–97.

Hoffman, Ogden. *Report of Land Cases Determined in the United States District Court for the Northern District of California*. San Francisco: Numa Hubert, 1862.

Hoover, Mildred Brooke. *Historic Spots in California*. 4th ed. Revised by Douglas E. Kyle. Stanford, Calif.: Stanford University Press, 1990.

Bibliography

Hurtado, Albert L. *Indian Survival on the California Frontier*. New Haven, Conn.: Yale University Press, 1988.

Hutchinson, C. Alan. *Frontier Settlement in Mexican California: The Híjar-Padrés Colony and Its Origins*. New Haven, Conn.: Yale University Press, 1969.

Jackson, Robert H. *Indian Population Decline: The Missions of Northwestern New Spain, 1687–1840*. Albuquerque: University of New Mexico Press, 1994.

Jackson, Robert H., and Edward Castillo. *Indians, Franciscans, and Spanish Colonization: The Impact of the Mission System on California Indians*. Albuquerque: University of New Mexico Press, 1995.

Jackson, Sheldon G. *A British Ranchero in Old California: The Life and Times of Henry Dalton and the Rancho Azusa*. Glendale, Calif.: Arthur H. Clark., 1977.

Johnson, David Alan. *Founding the Far West: California, Oregon, and Nevada, 1840–1890*. Berkeley: University of California Press, 1992.

Jones, Frances Carey. "California in the Spanish American Wars of Independence: The Bouchard Invasion." M.A. thesis. University of California, Berkeley, 1921.

La Fontaine, Jean. *Fables, contes et nouvelles*. Paris: Bibliothèque de la Pléiade, 1954.

Langellier, John Phillip, and Daniel Bernard Rosen. *El Presidio de San Francisco: A History under Spain and Mexico, 1776–1846*. Denver: National Park Service, 1992.

Langum, David J. *Law and Community on the Mexican California Frontier: Anglo-American Expatriates and the Clash of Legal Traditions, 1821–1846*. Norman: University of Oklahoma Press, 1987.

Lefevere, André. *Translating Literature: Practice and Theory in a Comparative Literature Context*. New York: Modern Language Association of America, 1992.

Lesage, Alain René. *La historia de Gil Blas de Santillana*. Translated into Spanish by Fr. José Francisco Isla and annotated by Evaristo Peña y Marín. New York: D. Appleton and Co., 1865.

Livingston, Dewey. *Ranching on the Point Reyes Peninsula: A History of the Dairy and Beef Ranches within Point Reyes National Seashore, 1834–1992*. Point Reyes Station, Calif.: National Park Service, 1993.

Lockhart, Katharine Meyer. "A Demographic Profile of an Alta California Pueblo: San José de Guadalupe, 1777–1850." Ph.D. diss., University of Colorado, 1986.

Lope de Vega y Carpio, Félix. *La gatomaquia*. In *Biblioteca de Autores Españoles* 38: 435–52. Madrid: Rivadeneyra, 1856.

Lopéz Urrutia, Carlos. *La escuadra chilena en México (1822): Los corsarios chilenos y argentinos en los mares del norte*. Buenos Aires: Editorial F. de Aguirre, 1971.

Martínez, Pablo L. *Guía familiar de Baja California, 1700–1900*. Mexico City: Editorial Baja California, 1965.

Bibliography

Martínez, Pablo L. *A History of Lower California*. Mexico: Editorial Baja California, 1960.

Mathes, W. Michael. *Las misiones de Baja California, 1683–1849*. La Paz: Editorial Aristos, 1977.

McKevitt, Gerald, S.J. *The University of Santa Clara: A History, 1851–1977*. Stanford, Calif.: Stanford University Press, 1979.

McKittrick, Myrtle M. *Vallejo: Son of California*. Portland, Oreg.: Binford and Mort, 1944.

Meier, Matt S. *Mexican American Biographies: A Historical Dictionary, 1836–1987*. Westport, Conn.: Greenwood Press, 1988.

Meldrum, George Weston. "The History of the Treatment of Foreign and Minority Groups in California, 1830–1860." Ph.D. diss., Stanford University, 1948.

Meyer, Michael C., and William L. Sherman. *The Course of Mexican History*. 4th ed. New York: Oxford University Press, 1991.

Monroy, Douglas. *Thrown among Strangers: The Making of Mexican Culture in Frontier California*. Berkeley: University of California Press, 1990.

Moorhead, Max. *The Presidio: Bastion of the Spanish Borderlands*. Norman: University of Oklahoma Press, 1975.

Mutnick, Dorothy Gittinger. *Some Alta California Pioneers and Descendants*. 2 vols. Lafayette, Calif.: Past Time Publications, 1982.

Northrop, Marie E. *Spanish-Mexican Families of Early California, 1769–1850*. 2 vols. Burbank, Calif.: Southern California Genealogical Society, 1987.

Ogden, Adele. *The California Sea Otter Trade, 1784–1848*. Berkeley: University of California Press, 1941.

Ong, Walter J. *Orality and Literacy: The Technologizing of the Word*. London: Methuen, 1982.

Padilla, Genaro. *My History, Not Yours: The Formation of Mexican American Autobiography*. Madison: University of Wisconsin Press, 1993.

Palmer, Alan, ed. *An Encyclopedia of Napoleon's Europe*. New York: St. Martin's Press, 1984.

Phillips, George Harwood. *Chiefs and Challengers: Indian Resistance and Cooperation in Southern California*. Berkeley: University of California Press, 1975.

Phillips, George Harwood. *Indians and Intruders in Central California, 1796–1849*. Norman: University of Oklahoma Press, 1983.

Pitt, Leonard. *The Decline of the Californios: A Social History of Spanish-Speaking Californians, 1846–1890*. Berkeley: University of California Press, 1966.

Prendergast, Thomas F. *Forgotten Pioneers: Irish Leaders in Early California*. San Francisco: Trade Pressroom, 1942.

Preston, R. N., comp. *Early California Atlas: Northern Edition*. 2d ed. Portland, Oreg.: Binford and Mort. 1983.

Bibliography

Quinn, Arthur, *Broken Shore: The Marin Peninsula, a Perspective on History.* Salt Lake City: Peregrine Smith, 1981.

Ratto, Hector R. *Capitán de navío Hipólito Bouchard.* Buenos Aires: Secretaría de Estado de Marina, 1961.

Rawls, James J. *Indians of California: The Changing Image.* Norman: University of Oklahoma Press, 1984.

Regnery, Dorothy F. *The Battle of Santa Clara, January 2, 1847.* San José: Smith and McKay Printing Co., 1978.

Rhoades, Elizabeth R. "Foreigners in Southern California during the Mexican Period." M.A. thesis, University of California, Berkeley, 1924.

Rice, Richard B., William A. Bullough, and Richard J. Orsi. *The Elusive Eden: A New History of California.* New York: Alfred A. Knopf, 1988.

Ríos-Bustamante, Antonio J. "Los Angeles, Pueblo and Region, 1781–1850: Continuity and Adaptation on the North Mexican Periphery." Ph.D. diss., University of California, Los Angeles, 1985.

Ríos-Bustamante, Antonio J. *Mexican Los Angeles: A Narrative and Pictorial History.* Encino, Calif.: Floricanto Press, 1992.

Ríos-Bustamante, Antonio J., ed. *Regions of La Raza: Changing Interpretations of Mexican American Regional History and Culture.* Encino, Calif.: Floricanto Press, 1993.

Ríos-Bustamante, Antonio J., and Pedro Castillo. *An Illustrated History of Mexican Los Angeles, 1781–1985.* Chicano Studies Research Center Publications, University of California Monograph no. 12. Berkeley: University of California Press, 1986.

Robinson, W. W. *Land in California.* Berkeley: University of California Press, 1948.

Rojas, A. R. *The Vaquero.* Charlotte, N. C.: McNally and Loftin, 1964.

Ruiz, Ramón Eduardo. *Triumphs and Tragedy: A History of the Mexican People.* New York: W. W. Norton and Co., 1992.

Samaniego, Félix María. *Fábulas.* Madrid: Clásicos Castalia, 1969.

Schuetz-Miller, Mardith K. *Building and Builders in Hispanic California, 1769–1850.* Tucson, Ariz.: Southwestern Mission Research Center, 1995.

Senkewicz, Robert M. *Vigilantes in Gold Rush San Francisco.* Stanford, Calif.: Stanford University Press, 1985.

Shumway, Burgess. *California Ranchos: Patented Private Land Grants.* San Bernardino, Calif.: Borgo Press, 1988.

Slatta, Richard W. *Cowboys of the Americas.* New Haven, Conn.: Yale University Press, 1990.

Smilie, Robert S. *The Sonoma Mission, San Francisco Solano de Sonoma.* Fresno, Calif.: Valley Publishers, 1975.

Tays, George. "Revolutionary California: The Political History of California during the Mexican Period, 1822–1846." Ph.D. diss., University of California, Berkeley, 1932.

Bibliography

Thompson, Joseph, O.F.M. *El Gran Capitán: José de la Guerra*. Los Angeles: Franciscan Fathers of California, 1961.

Tikhmenev, P. A. *A History of the Russian-American Company*. Translated and edited by Richard A. Pierce and Alton S. Donnelly. Seattle: University of Washington Press, 1978.

Tuthill, Franklin. *The History of California*. San Francisco: H. H. Bancroft and Co., 1866.

Weber, David J. *The Mexican Frontier, 1821–1846: The American Southwest under Mexico*. Albuquerque: University of New Mexico Press, 1982.

Weber, David. J. *The Spanish Frontier in North America*. New Haven, Conn.: Yale University Press, 1992.

Weber, Francis J. *The California Missions as Others Saw Them: 1786–1842*. Los Angeles: Dawson's Book Shop, 1972.

Whelan, Harold A., SS.CC. *The Picpus Story: The Sacred Heart Fathers' Missionary Activity in the Sandwich Islands and Early California, 1826–1856*. Pomona, Calif.: Apostolate of Christian Renewal, 1980.

Worcester, Donald E. *Sea Power and Chilean Independence*. University of Florida Monographs, Social Sciences, no. 15. Gainesville: University of Florida Press, 1962.

Wright, Doris Marion. *A Yankee in Mexican California: Abel Stearns, 1798–1848*. Santa Barbara, Calif.: Wallace Hebberd, 1977.

Articles

Álmaguer, Tomás. "Ideological Distortions in Recent Chicano Historiography: The Internal Model and Chicano Historical Interpretation." *Aztlán* 18.1 (1987): 7–28.

Ames, George Walcott, Jr. "Gillespie and the Conquest of California." *California Historical Society Quarterly* 17.2–4 (1938): 123–40, 271–84, 325–50.

Archibald, Robert R. "Indian Labor at the California Missions: Slavery or Salvation." *Journal of San Diego History* 24.2 (1978): 172–82.

Archibald, Robert R. "Price Regulation in Hispanic California." *The Americas* 33.4 (1976–77): 613–29.

Bakken, Gordon Morris. "Mexican and American Land Policy: A Conflict of Cultures." *Southern California Quarterly* 75.3–4 (1993) 237–62.

Barry, J. Neilson. "Peter Corney's Voyages, 1814–1817." *Oregon Historical Society Quarterly* 33.4 (1932): 355–68.

Bealer, Lewis. "Bouchard in the Islands of the Pacific." *Pacific Historical Review* 4.4 (1935): 328–42.

Beattie, George W. "Spanish Plans for an Inland Chain of Missions in California." *Historical Society of Southern California Annual Publications* 14.2 (1929): 243–64.

Bibliography

Berninger, Dieter. "Immigration and Religious Toleration: A Mexican Dilemma, 1821–1860." *The Americas* 32.4 (1974–75): 549–65.

Bowman, J. N. "The Birthdays of the California Missions." *The Americas* 20.3 (1963–64): 289–308.

Bowman, J. N. "California Indians Baptized during the Mission Period, 1770–1834." *Southern California Quarterly* 42.3 (1960): 273–77.

Bowman, J. N. "History of the Provincial Archives of California." *Southern California Quarterly* 64.1 (1982): 1–97.

Bowman, J. N. "The Names of the California Missions." *The Americas* 21.4 (1964–65): 363–74.

Bowman, J. N. "The Resident Neophytes of the California Missions, 1769–1834." *Historical Society of Southern California Quarterly* 40.2 (1958): 138–48.

Bowman, J. N. "Weights and Measures of Provincial California." *California Historical Society Quarterly* 30.4 (1951): 315–38.

Brack, Gene M. "Mexican Opinion, American Racism, and the War of 1846." *Western Historical Quarterly* 1.2 (1970): 161–74.

Broadbent, Sylvia. "Conflict at Monterey: Indian Horse Raiding, 1820–1850." *Journal of California Anthropology* 1.1 (1974): 86–101.

Brown, Madie M. "General M. G. Vallejo and H. H. Bancroft." *California Historical Society Quarterly* 29.2 (1950): 149–59.

Burgess, Sherwood. "Lumbering in Hispanic California." *California Historical Society Quarterly* 41.3 (1962): 237–48.

Burgess, Sherwood. "Pirate or Patriot? Hypolite Bouchard and the Invasion of California." *American West* 11.6 (1974): 40–47.

Burrus, Ernest J. "Francisco María Piccolo (1654–1729), Pioneer of Lower California, in the Light of Roman Archives." *Hispanic American Historical Review* 35.1 (1955): 61–76.

Carreño, Alberto María. "The Missionary Influence of the College of Zacatecas." *The Americas* 7.3 (1950–51): 297–320.

Castañeda, Antonia I. "Gender, Race, and Culture: Spanish-Mexican Women in the Historiography of Frontier California." *Frontiers: A Journal of Women's Studies* 11.1 (1990): 8–20.

Castañeda, Antonio I. "Memory, Language, and Voice of Mestiza Women on the Northern Frontier: Historical Documents as Literary Text." In *Recovering the U.S. Literary Heritage*, edited by Ramón A. Gutiérrez and Genaro Padilla, 265–77. Houston: Arte Público Press, 1993.

Castañeda, Antonia I. "The Political Economy of Nineteenth Century Stereotypes of Californians." In *Regions of La Raza: Changing Interpretations of Mexican American Regional History and Culture*, edited by Antonio Ríos-Bustamante, 189–211. Encino, Calif.: Floricanto Press, 1993.

Castillo, Edward D. "The Assassination of Padre Andrés Quintana by the

Indians of Mission Santa Cruz in 1812: The Narrative of Lorenzo Asisara."
California History 68.3 (1989–90): 116–25.

Castillo, Edward D. "An Indian Account of the Decline and Collapse of
Mexico's Hegemony over the Missionized Indians of California." *American
Indian Quarterly* 13.4 (1989): 391–408.

Caughey, John. "The Distant Dawn of Empire." *California History* 60.1 (1981):
6–27.

Champlin, Brad. "The Mission at Sonoma." *Pacific Historian* 22.4 (1978):
357–60.

Clark, Harry. "Their Pride, Their Manners, and Their Voices: Sources of the
Traditional Portrait of the Early Californians." *California Historical Quarterly*
53.1 (1974): 71–82.

Costeloe, Michael P. "Santa Anna and the Gómez Farías Administration in
Mexico, 1833–1834." *The Americas* 31.1 (1974–75): 18–50.

Coughlin, Magdalen, C.S.J. "Boston Smugglers on the Coast (1797–1821): An
Insight into the American Acquisition of California." *California Historical
Society Quarterly* 46.2 (1967): 99–120.

Driver, Les. "Carrillo's Flying Artillery: The Battle of San Pedro." *California
Historical Society Quarterly* 48.4 (1969): 335–49.

Egan, Ferol. "Twilight of the Californios." *American West* 6.2 (1969): 34–42.

Elías, Julio. "Cruceros de Brown, Bouchard, y Cochrane antes de la expedición
libertadora de San Martín." *Revista del Centro de Estudios Histórico-Militares del
Perú* 19 (1971): 30–40.

Engstrand, Iris H. W. "An Enduring Legacy: California Ranchos in Historical
Perspectives." *Journal of the West* 27.3 (1988): 36–47.

Engstrand, Iris H. W. "The Legal Heritage of Spanish California." *Southern
California Quarterly* 75.3–4 (1993): 205–36.

Evans, Eliot A. P., and David W. Heron. "Isla de los Angeles: Unique State Park
in San Francisco Bay." *California History* 66.1 (1987): 25–39.

Faulk, Odie B. "The Presidio: Fortress or Farce?" In *New Spain's Far Northern
Frontier,* edited by David J. Weber, 67–78. Albuquerque: University of New
Mexico Press, 1979.

Fernández, Ferdinand F. "Except a California Indian: A Study in Legal
Discrimination." *Southern California Quarterly* 50.2 (1968): 161–76.

Ferrer, José. "La bandera argentina en California, 1818." *Publicaciones de la
Universidad Nacional del Litoral, Sante Fe, Argentina* 78 (1969): 95–114.

Fritzsche, Bruno. "San Francisco, 1846–1848: The Coming of the Land
Speculator." *California Historical Quarterly* 51.1 (1971): 17–34.

García, Mario T. "The Californios of San Diego and the Politics of Accommodation, 1846–1860." *Aztlán* 6.1 (1975): 69–85.

Garr, Daniel J. "Los Angeles and the Challenge of Growth, 1835–1859."
Southern California Quarterly 61.2 (1979): 147–58.

Bibliography

Garr, Daniel J. "Planning, Politics, and Plunder: The Missions and Indian Pueblos of Hispanic California." *Southern California Quarterly* 54.4 (1972): 291–312.

Gates, Paul W. "The California Land Act of 1851." *California Historical Quarterly* 50.4 (1971): 395–430.

Gates, Paul W. "Carpetbaggers Join the Rush for California Land." *California Historical Quarterly* 56.2 (1977): 98–127.

Gates, Paul W. "The Frémont-Jones Scramble for California Land Claims." *Southern California Quarterly* 56.1 (1974): 13–44.

Geiger, Maynard, O.F.M. "Biographical Data on the California Missionaries (1769–1848)." *California Historical Society Quarterly* 44.1 (1965): 291–310.

Geiger, Maynard, O.F.M. "The Building of Mission San Gabiel: 1771–1828." *Southern California Quarterly* 50.1 (1968): 33–42.

Geiger, Maynard, O.F.M. "The Internal Organization and Activities of San Fernando College, México City (1734–1858)." *The Americas* 6.1 (1949–50): 3–31.

Geiger, Maynard, O.F.M. "The Story of California's First Libraries." *Southern California Quarterly* 46.2 (1964): 109–24.

Grenier, Judson A. "Addenda to J. N. Bowman's 'History of the Provincial Archives of California.'" *Southern California Quarterly* 66.3 (1984): 257–61.

Griswold del Castillo, Richard. "The Del Valle Family and the Fantasy Heritage." *California History* 59.1 (1980): 2–15.

Grivas, Theodore. "Alcalde Rule: The Nature of Local Government in Spanish and Mexican California." *California Historical Society Quarterly* 40.1 (1961): 11–32.

Guest, Florian. "Municipal Government in Spanish California." *California Historical Society Quarterly* 46.4 (1967): 307–35.

Guest, Francis F., O.F.M. "The California Missions Were Far From Faultless." *Southern California Quarterly* 76.3 (1994): 255–304.

Guest, Francis F., O.F.M. "Cultural Perspectives on California Mission Life." *Southern California Quarterly* 65.1 (1983): 1–65.

Guest, Francis F., O.F.M. "An Examination of the Thesis of S. F. Cook on the Forced Conversion of the Indians in the California Missions." *Southern California Quarterly* 61.1 (1979): 1–77.

Guest, Francis F., O.F.M. "The Indian Policy under Fermín Francisco de Lasuén, California's Second Father President." *California Historical Society Quarterly* 45.3 (1966): 195–224.

Guest, Francis F., O.F.M. "An Inquiry into the Role of the Discipline in California Mission Life." *Southern California Quarterly* 71.1 (1989): 1–68.

Guinn, J. M. "The Passing of the Rancho." *Historical Society of Southern California Publications* 10.1–2 (1915–17): 46–53.

Gutiérrez, David G. "Significant to Whom?: Mexican Americans and the History of the American West." *Western Historical Quarterly* 24.4 (1993): 519–40.

Haggland, Mary H. "Don José Antonio Aguirre: Spanish Merchant and Ranchero." *Journal of San Diego History* 29.1 (1983): 54–68.

Hague, Harlan. "The Reluctant Retirement of Thomas O. Larkin." *California History* 62.1 (1983): 60–66.

Hale, Charles A. "José María Luis Mora and the Structure of Mexican Liberalism." *Hispanic American Historical Review* 45.2 (1965): 196–227.

Hale, Charles A. "The War with the United States and the Crisis in Mexican Thought." *The Americas* 14.2 (1957–58): 153–73.

Hanks, Robert J. "Commodore Jones and his Private War with Mexico." *American West* 16.6 (1979): 30–33, 60–63.

Hargis, Donald E. "Native Californians in the Constitutional Convention of 1849." *Historical Society of Southern California Quarterly* 36.1 (1954): 3–13.

Holterman, Jack. "The Revolt of Estanislao." *Indian Historian* 3.1 (1970): 43–54.

Holterman, Jack. "The Revolt of Yozcolo." *Indian Historian* 3.2 (1970): 19–23.

Hornbeck, David, and Marcy Tucey. "The Submergence of a People: Migration and Occupational Structure in California, 1850." *Pacific Historical Review* 46.3 (1977): 471–84.

Hudson, Dee Travis. "Chumash Canoes of Mission Santa Bárbara: The Revolt of 1824." *Journal of California Archeology* 3.2 (1976): 5–15.

Huggins, Dorothy. "The Pursuit of an Indian Chief." *California Folklore Quarterly* 4 (1945): 158–67.

Hughes, Charles. "The Decline of the Californios: The Case of San Diego, 1846–1856." *Journal of San Diego History* 21.3 (1975): 1–31.

Hutchinson, C. Alan. "The Mexican Government and the Mission Indians of Upper California, 1821–1835." *The Americas* 21.4 (1964–65): 335–62.

Hutchinson, C. Alan. "An Official List of the Members of the Híjar-Padrés Colony for Mexican California, 1834." *Pacific Historical Review* 42.3 (1973): 407–18.

Jackson, Robert H. "Demographic Change in Northwestern New Spain." *The Americas* 41.4 (1984–85): 462–79.

Jackson, Robert H. "Gentile Recruitment and Population Movements in the San Francisco Bay Area Missions." *Journal of California and Great Basin Anthropology* 6.2 (1984): 225–39.

Jackson, Sheldon G. "The British and the California Dream: Rumors, Myths, and Legends." *Southern California Quarterly* 57.3 (1975): 251–70.

Jensen, James M. "John Forster: A California Ranchero." *California Historical Society Quarterly* 48.1 (1969): 37–44.

Johns, Sally Cavell. "Viva Los Californios: The Battle of San Pascual." *Journal of San Diego History* 19.4 (1973): 1–13.

Johnson, John R. "The Chumash and the Missions." In *Archaeological and Historical Perspectives on the Spanish Borderlands West*, vol. 1 of *Columbian Consequences*, edited by David Hurst Thomas, 365–75. Washington, D.C.: Smithsonian Institution Press, 1989.

Bibliography

Johnson, Kenneth M. "The Battle of San Pasqual." *Pacific Historian* 21.4 (1977): 368–73.

Jore, Leonce. "The Fathers of the Congregation of the Sacred Hearts (called Picpus) in California." Translated by L. Jay Oliva. *Southern California Quarterly* 46.4 (1964): 293–313.

Kells, Robert E., Jr. "The Spanish Inheritance: The Mexican Forces of Alta California, 1822–1846." *Journal of the West* 20.4 (1981): 12–19.

Kells, Robert E., Jr. "The Spanish Legacy: A Chaotic Military in a Semi-Feudal Province." *Californians* 7.3 (1989–90): 50–56.

Kelsey, Harry. "European Impact on the California Indians." *The Americas* 41.4 (1984–85): 494–511.

Killea, Lucy Lytle. "The Political History of a Mexican Pueblo: San Diego from 1825 to 1845." *Journal of San Diego History* 12.3–4 (1966): 3–35, 17–42.

Kindall, Cleve E. "Southern Vineyards: The Economic Significance of the Wine Industry in the Development of Los Angeles, 1831–1870." *Historical Society of Southern California Quarterly* 41.1 (1959): 26–37.

Lamar, Howard. "From Bondage to Contract: Ethnic Labor in the American West, 1600–1890." In *The Countryside in the Age of Capitalist Transformation: Essays in the Social History of Rural America*, edited by Steven Hahn and Jonathan Prude, 293–324. Chapel Hill: University of North Carolina Press, 1985.

Langellier, John Phillip, and Katherine Meyers Peterson. "Lances and Leather Jackets: Presidial Forces in Spanish Alta California, 1769–1821." *Journal of the West* 20.4 (1981): 3–11.

Langum, David J. "Californios and the Image of Indolence." *Western Historical Quarterly* 9.2 (April 1978): 181–96.

Langum, David J. "*Californio* Women and the Image of Virtue." *Southern California Quarterly* 59.3 (1977): 245–50.

Langum, David J. "Sin, Sex, and Separation in Mexican California: Her Domestic Relations Law." *Californians* 5.3 (1987): 44–50.

Larson, Daniel O., John R. Johnson, and Joel C. Michaelsen. "Missionization among the Coastal Chumash of Central California: A Study of Risk Minimization Strategies." *American Anthropologist* 96.2 (1994): 263–99.

Lawrence, Eleanor. "Mexican Trade between Santa Fé and Los Angeles, 1830–1848." *California Historical Society Quarterly* 10.1 (1931): 27–39.

Layne, J. Gregg. "The First Census of the Los Angeles District." *Historical Society of Southern California Quarterly* 18.3 (1936): 81–99.

Layne, J. Gregg. "José María Flores: California's Great Mexican Patriot." *Historical Society of Southern California Quarterly* 17.1 (1935): 23–27.

Levy, Jo Ann. "Under Siege at Mission Santa Clara." *Californians* 7.4 (1989–90): 30–34.

Lothrop, Gloria Ricci. "Rancheras and the Land: Women and Property Rights in Hispanic California." *Southern California Quarterly* 76.1 (1994): 59–84.

Bibliography

Mason, William M. "Alta California's Colonial and Early Mexican Era Population, 1769–1846." In *Regions of La Raza: Changing Interpretations of Mexican American Regional History and Culture,* edited by Antonio Ríos–Bustamante, 169–87. Encino, Calif.: Floricanto Press, 1993.

Mason, William M. "Indian–Mexican Cultural Exchange in the Los Angeles Area, 1781–1834." *Aztlán* 15.1 (1984): 123–44.

Mathes, W. Michael. "A Biographical Note on Isidro de Atondo y Antillón, Admiral of the Californias." *California Historical Society Quarterly* 48.3 (1969): 211–18.

Mathes, W. Michael. "Some Reflections on California, 1776." *Journal of San Diego History* 22.4 (1976): 48–53.

Mathes, W. Michael. "Sources in Mexico for the History of Spanish California." *California History* 61.3 (1982): 223–26.

Mawn, Geoffrey P. "*Agrimensor y Arquitecto:* Jasper O'Farrell's Surveying in Mexican California." *Southern California Quarterly* 56.1 (1974): 1–12.

McCorkle, Thomas. "Intergroup Conflict." In *Handbook of North American Indians,* edited by William C. Sturtevant, vol. 8, *California,* edited by Robert F. Heizer, 694–700. Washington, D.C.: Smithsonian Institution, 1978.

McGloin, John Bernard, S.J. "William Richardson, Founder and First Resident of Yerba Buena." *Journal of the West* 5.4 (1966): 493–503.

McKee, Irving. "The Beginnings of California Winegrowing." *Historical Society of Southern California Quarterly* 29.1 (1947): 59–71.

McKittrick, Myrtle M. "Salvador Vallejo." *California Historical Society Quarterly* 29.4 (1950): 309–31.

Meighan, Clement W. "Indians and the California Missions." *Southern California Quarterly* 69.3 (Fall 1987): 183–201.

Miranda, Gloria. "*Gente de Razón* Marriage Patterns in Spanish and Mexican California: A Case Study of Santa Bárbara and Los Angeles." *Southern California Quarterly* 63.1 (1981): 1–21.

Miranda, Gloria. "Hispano-Mexican Childrearing Practices in Pre–American Santa Barbara." *Southern California Quarterly* 65.4 (1983): 307–20.

Miranda, Gloria. "Racial and Cultural Dimensions in *Gente de Razón* Status in Spanish and Mexican California." *Southern California Quarterly* 70.3 (1988): 265–78.

Moriarity, James Robert, II. "Accommodation and Conflict Resolution Techniques among Southern California Indian Groups." *Southern California Quarterly* 56.2 (1974): 109–22.

Mullen, Kevin. "Crime, Politics, and Punishment in Mexican San Francisco." *Californians* 7.5 (1989–90): 46–55.

Nelson, Howard J. "The Two Pueblos of Los Angeles: Agricultural Village and Embryo Town." *Southern California Quarterly* 59.1 (1977): 1–11.

Neri, Michael C. "Gonzales Rubio and California Catholicism, 1846–1850." *Southern California Quarterly* 58.4 (1976): 441–57.

Bibliography

Neri, Michael C. "Narciso Durán and the Secularization of the California Missions." *The Americas* 33.3 (1976–77): 411–29.

Newmark, Marco R. "Antonio Francisco Coronel." *Historical Society of Southern California Quarterly* 36.2 (1954): 161–62.

Nunis, Doyce B., Jr. "Medicine in Spanish California." *Southern California Quarterly* 76.1 (1994): 31–57.

Ogden, Adele. "Hides and Tallow: McCulloch, Hartnell, and Co., 1822–1828." *California Historical Society Quarterly* 6.3 (1927): 254–64.

Padilla, Genaro. "Recovering Mexican-American Autobiography." In *Recovering the U.S. Hispanic Literary Heritage*, edited by Ramón A. Gutiérrez and Genaro Padilla, 153–78. Houston: Arte Público Press, 1993.

Peterson, Charles S. "Hubert Howe Bancroft: First Western Regionalist." In *Writing Western History: Essays on Major Western Historians*, edited by Richard W. Etulain, 43–70. Albuquerque: University of New Mexico Press, 1991.

Peterson, Richard H. "Anti-Mexican Nativism in California, 1848–1853: A Study of Cultural Conflict." *Southern California Quarterly* 62.4 (1980): 309–27.

Peterson, Richard H. "The Foreign Miner's Tax of 1850 and Mexicans in California: Exploitation or Expulsion." *Pacific Historian* 20.3 (Fall 1976): 265–72.

Pisani, Donald J. "Squatter Law in California, 1850–1858." *Western Historical Quarterly* 25.3 (1994): 277–310.

Ríos-Bustamante, Antonio. "Nineteenth Century Mexican Californians: A Conquered Race." In *Regions of La Raza: Changing Interpretations of Mexican American Regional History and Culture*, edited by Antonio Ríos-Bustamante, 237–69. Encino, Calif.: Floricanto Press, 1993.

Rojas, Lauro de. "California in 1844 as Hartnell Saw It." *California Historical Society Quarterly* 17.1 (1938): 21–27.

Samponaro, Frank N. "Santa Anna and the Abortive Anti-Federalist Revolt of 1833 in Mexico." *The Americas* 40.1 (1983–84): 95–107.

Sánchez, Federico. "Rancho Life in Alta California." In *Regions of La Raza: Changing Interpretations of Mexican American Regional History and Culture*, edited by Antonio Ríos-Bustamante, 213–35. Encino, Calif: Floricanto Press, 1993.

Sánchez, Rosaura. "Nineteenth-Century Californio Narratives: The Hubert H. Bancroft Collection." In *Recovering the U.S. Hispanic Literary Heritage*, edited by Ramón A. Gutiérrez and Genaro Padilla, 279–92. Houston: Arte Público Press, 1993.

Sandos, James. "Christianization among the Chumash: An Ethnohistoric Perspective." *American Indian Quarterly* 15.1 (1991): 65–89.

Sandos, James. "From 'Boltonlands' to 'Weberlands.' " *American Quarterly* 46.4 (1994): 595–604.

Sandos, James. "Levantamiento! The 1824 Chumash Uprising." *Californians* 5.1 (1987): 8–20.

Sandos, James. "Levantamiento! The 1824 Chumash Uprising Reconsidered." *Southern California Quarterly* 67.2 (1985): 109–33.

Schwaller, Robert F. "The Episcopal Succession in Spanish America, 1800–1850." *The Americas* 24.3 (1967–68): 207–71.

Scott, Paul T. "Why Joseph Chapman Adopted California and Why California Adopted Him." *Historical Society of Southern California Quarterly* 38.3 (1956): 239–46.

Servín, Manuel P. "The Beginnings of California's Anti-Mexican Prejudice." In *An Awakened Minority: The Mexican-Americans,* edited by Manuel P. Servín, 2–17. Beverly Hills, Calif.: Glencoe Press, 1974.

Servín, Manuel P. "California's Hispanic Heritage: A View into the Spanish Myth." In *New Spain's Far Northern Frontier,* edited by David J. Weber, 117–33. Albuquerque: University of New Mexico Press, 1979.

Servín, Manuel P. "The Secularization of the California Missions: A Reappraisal." *Historical Society of Southern California Quarterly* 47.2 (1965): 133–49.

Shipek, Florence C. "California Indian Reaction to the Franciscans." *The Americas* 41.4 (1984–85): 480–93.

Sizelove, Linda. "Indian Adaptation to the Spanish Missions." *Pacific Historian* 22.4 (1978): 393–402.

Smith, Gene A. "Thomas ap Catesby Jones and the First Implementation of the Monroe Doctrine." *Southern California Quarterly* 76.2 (1994): 139–52.

Smith, Gene A. "The War That Wasn't: Thomas ap Catesby Jones' Seizure of Monterey." *California History* 66.2 (1987): 104–13.

Spencer-Hancock, Diane, and William E. Pritchard. "El Castillo de Monterey: Frontline of Defense." *California History* 67.3 (1984): 230–41.

Stephenson, Terry E. "Tomás Yorba, His Wife Vicenta, and His Account Book." *Historical Society of Southern California Quarterly* 23.3–4 (1941): 127–56.

Tanner, John D., Jr. "Campaign for Los Angeles—December 29, 1846, to January 10, 1847." *California Historical Society Quarterly* 48.3 (1969): 219–41.

Tays, George. "Captain Andrés Castillero, Diplomat." *California Historical Society Quarterly* 14.3 (1935): 230–68.

Tays, George. "Mariano Guadalupe Vallejo and Sonoma." *California Historical Society Quarterly* 16.2–4 (1937): 99–121, 216–54, 348–72; and 17.1–3 (1938): 50–73, 141–67, 219–42.

Tays, George. "The Surrender of Monterey by Governor Nicolás Gutiérrez, November 5, 1836." *California Historical Society Quarterly* 15.4 (1936): 338–63.

Temple, Thomas Workman II. "Some Notes on the 1844 *Padrón de Los Angeles.*" *Historical Society of Southern California Quarterly* 42.2 (1960): 418–22.

Tyler, Helen. "The Family of Pico." *Historical Society of Southern California Quarterly* 35.3 (1953): 221–38.

Vigil, Ralph H. "The Hispanic Heritage and the Borderlands." *Journal of San Diego History* 19.3 (Summer 1973): 32–39.

Bibliography

Vigil, Ralph H. "The New Borderlands History: A Critique." *New Mexico Historical Review* 48.3 (1973): 189–208.

Warren, Viola Lockhardt. "Medical Quacks and Heroes of Early California." *Historical Society of Southern California Quarterly* 41.2 (1959): 101–16.

Weber, David J. "American Westward Expansion and the Breakdown of Relations between Pobladores and 'Indios Bárbaros' on Mexico's Northern Frontier, 1821–1846." *New Mexico Historical Review* 56.3 (1981): 221–38.

Weber, David J. "Failure of a Frontier Institution: The Secular Church in the Borderlands under Independent Mexico, 1821–1846." *Western Historical Quarterly* 12.2 (1981): 25–43.

Weber, David J. "Here Rests Juan Espinosa: Toward a Look at the Image of the 'Indolent Californios.' " *Western Historical Quarterly* 10.1 (Jan. 1979): 61–69.

Weber, David J. "Mexico's Far Northern Frontier, 1821–1845: A Critical Bibliography." *Arizona and the West* 19.3 (1977): 225–66.

Weber David J. "Mexico's Far Northern Frontier, 1821–1854: Historiography Askew." *Western Historical Quarterly* 7.3 (1976): 279–93.

Weber, David J. "Stereotyping of Mexico's Far Northern Frontier." In *An Awakened Minority: The Mexican-Americans,* edited by Manuel P. Servín, 18–26. Beverly Hills, Calif.: Glencoe Press, 1974.

Weber, Francis J. "California's Gold Discovery: The Record Set Straight." *Pacific Historian* 18.3 (1974): 16–19.

Weber, Francis J. "John Thomas Doyle, Pious Fund Historiographer." *Southern California Quarterly* 49.3 (1967): 297–303.

Weber, Francis J. "The Los Angeles Chancery Archives." *The Americas* 21.4 (1964–65): 410–20.

Weber, Francis J. "The Pious Fund of the Californias." *Hispanic American Historical Review* 43.1 (1963): 78–94.

Whitehead, Richard S. "Alta California's Four Fortresses." *Southern California Quarterly* 65.1 (1983): 67–94.

Winther, Oscar Osburn. "The Story of San José, 1777–1869, California's First Pueblo." *California Historical Society Quarterly* 14.1–2 (1935): 3–27, 147–74.

Wittenburg, Mary Joseph, S.N.D. "Three Generations of the Sepúlveda Family in Southern California." *Southern California Quarterly* 73.3 (1991): 197–250.

The Family of Antonio María Osio

Antonio María Osio y Higuera

b. 1800, in Baja California
d. November 5, 1878, in Rancho La Palma, Baja California

m. Dolores Argüello, November 28, 1822,
in San José del Cabo, Baja California

Number of children: 4

m. Narcisa Florencia Soto, February 15, 1838,
in Santa Clara, Alta California

Number of children: 13

The Ancestors of Antonio María Osio

Parents

Juan de la Cruz Osio y Castro
  b. Unknown, in Baja California
  d. Unknown

Juana Higuera y Heredia
  b. Unknown, in Baja California
  d. Unknown

Paternal Grandparents

Antonio Ocio y Rodríguez
  b. ca. 1738, in Baja California
  d. Unknown

María Jesús de Castro
  b. Unknown, in Baja California
  d. Unknown, in Baja California

m. After 1777, in Baja California

Paternal Great-Grandparents

Manuel de Ocio
  b. 1700, in Andalucía, Spain
  d. June 17, 1771, in Baja California

Rosalía Rodríguez y Larrea
  b. 1717, in Loreto, Baja California
  d. 1752, in Baja California

m. 1736, in Baja California

The Family of Antonio María Osio and Dolores Argüello

María de los Dolores Guadalupe Argüello y Moraga

b. June 30, 1801, in San Francisco, Alta California
d. December 1827, in Monterey, Alta California

m. Antonio María Osio, November 28, 1822,
in San José del Cabo, Baja California

Number of children: 4

Children

José Salvador Osio y Argüello
b. March 4, 1824, in San José del Cabo, Baja California
d. March 26, 1862, in Monterey, Alta California

Luisa Antonia de Altagracia Osio y Argüello
b. April 9, 1826, in Monterey, Alta California
d. April 22, 1826, in Monterey, Alta California

Antonio María Osio y Argüello
b. April 9, 1826, in Monterey, California
d. April 9, 1826, in Monterey, California

María de la Paz Maximiana Osio y Argüello
b. May 29, 1827, in Monterey, Alta California
d. November 7, 1827, in Monterey, Alta California

The Family of Antonio María Osio and Narcisa Florencia Soto

Narcisa Florencia Soto y Pacheco
b. October 26, 1819, in San Francisco, Alta California
d. Unknown

m. Antonio María Osio, February 15, 1838,
in Santa Clara, Alta California

Number of children: 13

Children

José Antonio Osio y Soto
  b. June 1839, in Monterey, Alta California
  d. December 8, 1840, in Monterey, Alta California

Juan de la Cruz Osio y Soto
  b. November 22, 1840, in Monterey, Alta California
  d. October 30, 1898, in Ensenada de Todos los Santos, Baja California

Antonio Osio y Soto
  b. April 7, 1842, in Monterey, Alta California
  d. February 1848, in Monterey, Alta California

Beatriz Osio y Soto
  b. November 3, 1843, in Monterey, Alta California
  d. Unknown

José Manuel Osio y Soto
  b. August 14, 1845, in Monterey, Alta California
  d. April 4, 1851, in Monterey, Alta California

María Lucrecia Osio y Soto
  b. 1846, in Hawaiian Islands (Islas Canacas)
  d. January 22, 1905, in Rancho La Palma, Baja California

Antonia Osio y Soto
  b. 1850, in Monterey, Alta California
  d. April 10, 1872, in San José del Cabo, Baja California

Leonor Victoria Osio y Soto
  b. December 23, 1850, in Monterey, Alta California
  d. October 7, 1878, in San José del Cabo, Baja California

Manuel Osio y Soto
  b. 1852, in San José del Cabo, Baja California
  d. Unknown

María Plácida Osio y Soto
  b. February 7, 1853, in San José del Cabo, Baja California
  d. Unknown

Family of Antonio María Osio

Juan Manuel Osio y Soto
  b. April 13, 1855, in San José del Cabo, Baja California
  d. Unknown

María Josefa de Jesús Osio y Soto
  b. March 19, 1859, in San José del Cabo, Baja California
  d. Unknown

Josefa Antonia Nemesia Osio y Soto
  b. October 31, 1860, in San José del Cabo, Baja California
  d. Unknown

Index

Index

Bancroft, Hubert Howe, 8–10, 12, 18–20; assessment of *californio* dictations, 252n12; denigration of Osio, 284n21

Bandini, Juan, 5, 18, 252n12, 281n32; biography, 318; Cosmopolitan Company, 291n28; Híjar-Padrés colony, 291n28; intrigue against Alvarado, 179, 303n3; struggle against Victoria, 283nn16, 17

Barron, Eustace: biography, 318; British consul, 200

Barroso, Leonardo, 114–16; biography, 318

Bartolo Crossing, 114–15, 284n32, 314n25

Bases de Tacubaya, 212, 309n25

Battle of Angostura, 313n21

Battle of Buena Vista, 313n21

Battle of Cahuenga (1831), 108–11, 284n22

Battle of Cahuenga (1845), 220–21, 311n43

Battle of Cerro Gordo, 313n21

Battle of Natividad, 313n22

Battle of San Buenaventura, 74, 305n22, 205n26

Battle of San Gabriel, 74, 236–38, 314nn25, 26, 27

Battle of San Pascual, 74, 239–41, 314n26

Battle of Santa Clara, 313n22

Bay of Biscay, 257n5

Beach of Doña Brígida, 263n10

Bear Flag rebellion, 74, 226–31, 312n7

Begg, John, 70, 274n30

Bering Strait, 70

Bodega Point, 54, 267n27

Bolton, Herbert Eugene, 248

Boronda, José Canuto, 257n3

Bouchard, Hipólito, 16, 18, 22, 27–28, 76; in Alta California, 44–53, 260nn1, 2, 262n7, 263nn8, 9, 265nn15, 16, 17, 266nn18, 19; biography, 318

Bradford, William, 16

Brown, William, 260n1

Buelna, Joaquín, 52, 298n52

Buena Vista Lake, 273n24

Bustamante, Anastasio, 306n29; appoints Victoria, 281n4

Caballero, Fr. Félix, 107, 283n15

Caballero, José, 303n3

Cabo San Lucas, 42

Cahan, Abraham, 16

Cahuenga, 17, 173, 220

Cahuillas: horsethieving, 291n33

Calderón, Josefa Sánchez, 13

California Land Act, 6

California legislature: land and mining issues, 307n11

Californio women: examples of bravery and zeal, 60–61, 162–63; reaction to decree of religious tolerance, 160, 172

Calleja del Rey, Félix María, 256n1, 262n7

Canton, 43

Cantúa, Manuel, 231; biography, 318

Carquínez Strait, 33, 153

Carrillo, Anastasio, 12, 19, 61; Alvarado loyalist, 159, 161; biography, 318–19; Chumash uprising, 58, 61, 265n16, 271n14; meeting with Sepúlveda, 166–68

Carrillo, Carlos, 12, 19, 74, 158, 271n14; agreement with Osio, 300n13; arrested by Alvarado, 305n28; biography, 319; as governor, 187–93, 305n17; meeting with Sepúlveda, 166–68; relations with Chico, 137; speech to Mexican congress, 296n24

Carrillo, José Antonio, 178, 271n4, 278n10; actions against Alvarado, 187, 192; battle of Cahuenga, 110–11; biography, 319; imprisoned by Alvarado, 189; Plan of San Diego, 106–08, 283nn16,17; Treaty of Cahuenga, 314n27

Castañares, José María: affair with Herrera's wife, 143, 295n15; biography, 319

Castañares, Manuel: Alvarado envoy to Mexico, 74, 203; appointed Customs administrator, 207, 309n17; biography, 319

Castañeda, Juan: biography, 319–20; commander of Carrillo forces, 305n22

Index